Dr. Mom's
Healthy Living

Sandra K. Livingston Ellis, M.H.

Dr. Mom's
Healthy Living

Sandra K. Livingston Ellis, M.H.

Published by Dr. Mom's Healthy Living, LC

Printed by
Hedgehog
Print & Media

801-765-9100
www.whyhedgehog.com

Cover design by Reid Johns, ZD Creative
rjohns@zdcreative.net
Cover Photography by Taunya Brown & Glen Ricks

Dedication

This book is dedicated to my family. To my husband and best friend, Steve: for his love, his encouragement, his belief in me, and his dedication to the pursuit of truth. To my incredible children, their spouses, and my perfect grandchildren who have given so much meaning to my life. They have been my guinea pigs, my cheerleaders, my assistants, and a constant source of joy. Many times it has been their faith and perseverance which has carried me through. To my parents, Perry and Juanita Livingston, who gave me life, and taught me to focus on those aspects of it which have eternal significance.

Acknowledgements

My deepest gratitude to all those who have helped to bring these incredible truths out of darkness and into the light in my life; my friends, my students, the parents who have allowed me to attend their births, and my teachers. You have helped my knowledge to grow and my understanding to increase. I cherish the time we have spent together.

The one person who has helped to make my acquaintances with so many of you possible is David Christopher. Thank you, David, for your friendship, your encouragement, and your trust. Your willingness to carry on and share your father's herbal legacy has not only had a profound impact on many of our lives, but will continue to have an impact for generations to come. My hope is that each of us who have had the privilege of sharing in this legacy will have the courage to continue to carry the torch and bring light to many who are looking for a better way.

A special "thank you" to Ron Bohannon, M.A., a fantastic writing instructor at Utah Valley State College, for taking the time to tutor me and for editing this work. In his words, "This is much more manageable."

I also want to express appreciation to my long time friend, Reid Johns, for his continued support with his incredible talents as a graphic design artist. Thanks for hanging in there with me, Reid!

Drs. Ellis and Clayton, thank you for supporting this book and for allowing me to include your wonderful "forwards." There have been many doctors along my path which have taught me valuable lessons about the human body, have encouraged me in the pursuit of truth, and have been there to help me when I felt overwhelmed. To all of you – you know who you are – thank you for your open-mindedness, your help and your compassion.

Some of the hardest lessons I had to learn came through watching the deaths of two awesome women in the same year, Jill Inkley (1965 – 2000) and Kris Gammon (1955 -2000). Both of these women taught me valuable lessons which I will never forget. Probably, one of the lessons which has had the greatest impact on my life is: Knowing is not enough. All of the knowledge on health which the world has to offer will not save us if we don't live it. We have to walk the walk, not just talk the talk. Until we become living examples of these truths, we are not safe from disease, degeneration or aging. I am so grateful that our paths in life crossed!

Forward

Charles T. Ellis, M.D.

I first became interested in "Alternative" medicine in medical school out of pure intellectual curiosity. As I progressed in my medical studies, I started using "Alternative" treatments on myself for various ailments for which "Modern Medicine" (I prefer the term "Industrial Medicine") had no treatments and really had no idea as to the pathophysiology of these ailments. After proving the efficacy of these alternative medical treatments on myself, I began recommending them to my patients, who likewise had many ailments that were a mystery to "Mainstream" medicine. But even more, I strongly urged my patients to take control of their own medical destiny, to educate themselves about the various alternative treatments, and become knowledgeable about the theories, techniques, and schools encompassed by alternative medicine.

That is why I am indebted to and thankful for the great pioneers and practitioners of alternative medicine, such as Sandra K. Livingston Ellis, M.H. Because of their selfless dedication to finding better ways to heal their patients, they have shown us all the path to better health and better, longer, more productive lives.

THOUGHTS ON HEALTH
BY A PRACTICING PEDIATRICIAN

Dr. Keith Clayton, Provo, Utah

After reviewing the wealth of materials found in *Dr. Mom's Healthy Living* by Sandra Livingston Ellis, I am more enthusiastic than ever in my own quest to help American families get away from the "pills and bills" form of medicine that is practiced by so many and return to solid principles of basic good health including:

- Natural, simple and healthful eating
- Exercise as intended by our Creator
- Family life as it should be

I was touched by the following quotation by Thomas Edison in *Dr. Mom:*

> The doctors of the future will give no medicine, but will interest his patients in the care of the human frame, in diet, and in the cause and prevention of disease.

We are the doctors of the future mentioned by Edison so many years ago but we have not made good on his prediction of intensive focus on healthful living, good diet and prevention of disease.

FIRST, HEALTHFUL EATING

Daily we read of scientific studies that suggest the unfortunate results of our national epidemic of poor eating: Published Research confirms:

- Dietary factors may play a significant role in the the reason so many children have ADHD, report Boris and Mandel, Annals of Allergy, May 1994.
- "...the suggestion that diet may contribute to behavior disorders in children must be taken seriously." Egger, et al, Lancet, March 9, 1985.
- "These results suggest that pediatricians and other practitioners might consider dietary modification worth trying, particularly in younger children." Kaplan et al, Journal of Pediatrics, 83 (January 1989), pp. 7-17.
- "This study demonstrated a functional relation between the ingestion of a synthetic food color (tartrazine) and behavioral change..." Rowe and Rowe, Journal of Pediatrics, 125 (November 1994) pp. 691-8.

As mentioned in *Dr. Mom* we, as a nation have a tremendous national health emergency, poor diet. If this seems overstated I challenge you to park in front of WalMart for a few minutes and watch the families as they walk in and out of the store . . . so many are grossly obese. And, nearly always, the entire family is overweight. Why? I share Sandy Ellis' viewpoint that these families "in health crisis" are struggling because they have poor family habits of nutrition, exercise and family life.

If you are concerned about your child's weight, you are in good company. According to Samuel S. Gidding, M.D., pediatric cardiologist at Virtua-duPont:

> Childhood obesity is a serious problem. Over the past 20 years, the number of children who are overweight has increased by more than 50 percent and the number of

extremely overweight children has nearly doubled. About 25 to 30 percent of school-age children in the United States are overweight or obese, which puts them at a high risk for heart disease, diabetes, high cholesterol, sleep apnea, asthma, orthopedic problems, hypertension and other health problems.

> THE WHOLE FAMILY NEEDS THE ADVICE ON NUTRITION FOUND IN *DR. MOM.*

Parental eating habits are the key to those of their children. A nationally recognized authority on nutrition, Dr. Gidding, reminds parents to take a look at their own eating habits to see if they are setting a good example:

Family involvement is encouraged in identifying eating habits, exercise and lifestyle patterns that can be modified through nutrition counseling and behavior techniques. Eliminate unhealthy foods from your household rather than singling out your child and prohibiting her from eating them; keep healthy snacks in a place where your child can easily get to them; limit television and computer time and make time to exercise with your child. Exercise is the simple thing that you can do to lower your cholesterol and blood pressure and make you feel better.

I'm sure you will share my revulsion of our national eating habits as you read *Dr. Mom.* We must get back to the basics as suggested by Mrs. Ellis in her exhaustive study of natural health through nutrition and active lifestyle.

As to the amount of food we consume, we need to get away from "Supersize" fast foods and feed our families good, natural, fresh food. When our child says, "I'm hungry," feed him or her, and when a child says, "I'm full," stop feeding.

Does the child know he needs some peas? No. Does a child know how much he wants to eat? Yes. Thus, the responsibility of parents is to provide the variety of foods children need and then allow them to obey their internal cues and eat as much or as little as they want. What a wealth of nutritional information is now available to you as you leaf through *Dr. Mom.*

SECOND, GET PHYSICAL

Show kids how much fun it is to be physically active. Exercise is extremely important in maintaining one's health, and active parents inspire active kids. In fact, one of the best predictors of whether a child will be active is the activity level of the parents. Dads seem to have particularly strong influence when it comes to an active lifestyle, perhaps because they're often not around as much and therefore what they do is more noticeable.

Eating, exercise and healthful living are all interconnected in their ability to help us find a joyful and healthy life. Consider these recently published facts about healthful living:

1. Breast-feeding is associated with a decreased rate of obesity in childhood.
2. Exercise is important to keep weight off and to avoid complications for obese children.
3. Exercise must be associated with decreased calorie intake to be effective in weight loss.
4. The more television a child watches the more obese they are . . . there is a sliding scale correlation between the two.
5. Television correlates with obesity for three reasons:
   a. Increased snacking while watching TV
   b. Increased viewing of advertisements for foods and junk foods increase eating.
   c. Decreased exercise while watching TV
6. Increased water consumption during meals helps fill children up with fewer calories:
   a. Serve soups
   b. Drink a lot of water with meals
   c. Eat foods high in water content . . . salads, fruits, and vegetables
7. Parents lay off . . . "the more parents try to control how much their children are eating, the less capable children are of controlling their won food intake; the satiety gets externalized."
8. Offer good foods to children but let them decide what to eat and when.
9. Soda is consumed at a rate of at least double ten years ago. Soda is a drink of water and seven teaspoons of sugar.

THIRD, LET'S GET BACK TO REAL FAMILY LIFE

The fact that mental health is problematic in our schools should come as no surprise from a nation where at a high school graduation, only 50% of homes even have a father present. How many of our children come home from school to a home with no parent present at all? How many of our "two-income" families would be better off with less income for unneeded trivia and toys and more attention to healthful family life as suggested in *Dr. Mom* by Sandra Ellis?

Recent surveys find anxiety and depression are "most problematic" among high school and middle school students. Is there a connection between the deterioration of the American family and the emergence of "epidemic" depression, ADHD, and sexually transmitted disease? I say, "Yes."

As a pediatrician, I can assure you that about 80% of the "medical problems" experienced by American youth today are the result of poor lifestyle choices, especially sexual, drug abuse and dietary behavior.

A recent publication headline screamed, "Scourge and Plague of HIV Marches on in Youth of our Nation." The statistics on U.S. youth and HIV infection remain alarming: 50% of the 40,000 new HIV infections annually occur among youth (ages 13 – 24). At least 67% of HIV positive young people have contracted the disease sexually. A study of gay young men found that 80% of those who were positive for HIV had no idea they were infected. In our country today, 70% of teens have had sex by the time they are in 12th grade.

I have been led to believe that if the rate of HIV infection and AIDS continues at the present rate in our country, by the year 2020 it will take our entire gross national product just to care for the infected people in the USA. The best protection, a moral lifestyle taught by parents who are home with their children, feeding nutritious natural foods and exercising and working along side each other.

Let us all study through the pages of priceless information that "Dr. Mom" puts within our reach. Let us resolve to start today to feed our family better, teach them a moral lifestyle and play and exercise with them. No. We cannot fix all the problems in our families today, but we can take the advice of a great man, Spencer W. Kimball; "Do it. Do it right. Do it now. Do it right now."

Table of Contents

Preface

"Life is a journey – not a destination!" As you read and ponder the information contained in this book, you will be sharing in part of my journey and the journey of my family. I hope by making my life "an open book" and sharing these experiences, you will gain more insight into some of the simple truths which are all around us, yet go unnoticed by most of us due to our conventional programming.

Starting out life as a very typical, conventional, middle-class American baby-boomer, born in a hospital, living in a suburb of California, going to a public school, and standing in line for one of the first polio immunizations administered by eating a sugar cube. When those were found to be ineffective, I stood in line for the inoculations. When the "hippie era" came to San Francisco, my father moved us to a small farm in northern California near Mt. Shasta to spend the second half of my childhood helping raise beef, pork, chicken, milk and a large garden.

At the ripe old age of 18, in my first semester of college, I married a blue-collar worker and began a family. In the beginning, most of my children were born in the hospital, all attended public schools, were immunized, were taken to the doctor when they got sick, each of them had a mouth full of fillings, and each of them attended Sunday school on Sunday mornings. I went through a divorce when I was 28-years-old and six months later married a white-collar worker who was 11 years older than I. Sound pretty typical so far?

In 1983, when Steve and I married I had five young children; he had four. We put them together, which gave us nine children; seven were eight and younger. We went on to have four more children together. Steve adopted my five giving us a grand total of thirteen children. O.K., maybe this isn't exactly typical, but we were still very conventional in the way we cared for them.

In 1994, Steve was diagnosed with diabetes and told that he would be insulin-dependent. Unfortunately, as an airline pilot, if he were to start using insulin, he would be grounded. I still had 12 unmarried children and could not afford to have him grounded, so I went on a search to find an alternate way to control his blood sugar levels. That search led me into an incredible world of self-reliance and independence that I could only have imagined before this time. However, once we chose to become more and more responsible for our own health and the health of our family, we became not so conventional any more.

When you pick up a book like this, I suspect you may be questioning some of the "conventional" wisdom we all take so much for granted. That is one of the most exciting aspects of our journey! The ability to question, to explore, to wonder; and, if we are actually brave enough to look beyond our "comfort zone" to discover there is a whole incredible world of truth and beauty out there, kept from us because it doesn't fit in the neat little package of insurance policies, government funding, and conventional wisdom.

From the time we are born, most of us go through life accepting the "fact" that we are randomly at the mercy of whatever disease attacks us – that growing old means we lose our health, our strength, our mobility and possibly our minds. What if I were to tell you this is not necessarily the truth? We have choices – more than most of us are aware. We have responsibility for our own health, but go through life unaware of it.

This is the part of my journey I wish to share with you. If you are open-minded enough to listen and to learn – I think you will find much of this information as amazing and as exciting as I have. You've already taken the first step by opening the cover of this book. Keep going --learn how to enjoy life to its fullest, step out of your "comfort zone" and enjoy the journey!

This book is entitled "Dr. Mom" because my children and their friends have always affectionately referred to me with this title. Having a regular column in the *Health Source* newspaper entitled "Ask Dr. Mom," a reader once E-mailed me and asked why I assumed the right to call myself a doctor. I would like to answer that question now. Quoting Patch Adams as he stood in front of a medical review board, "Is not a doctor someone who helps someone else? . . . When did the name doctor get treated with such reverence? . . . At what point in history did a doctor become more than a trusted and learned friend who visited and treated the ill?" I am extremely grateful to the many doctors who have been there to assist me in the emergencies of my life, but I hope through this book, we can look at a broader picture of what it means to serve one another, starting with our own families.

This book is divided into five sections. The first section is entitled: "A Year of Discovery." It is written much like a journal telling how I began to step out of my "comfort zone" and begin taking greater responsibility for the health of my family. I have included this section because I hope it will be reassuring to those who are just beginning. It is normal to be naïve, it is normal to be frightened, it is normal to be confused and it is normal to feel guilty when you step away from your programming. That first year was enlightening, awe-inspiring, frightening, challenging, confusing, and down-right scary. Since I will never see things again the way I did that first year, I have not tried to explain it or change it; I have just left it the way it was. Hopefully, this will help you follow me in my learning curve.

The second section is "Cleanse and Nourish." This is by far the most important section to the whole book. Everything else discussed will be based on the principles in this section, which hold the key to changing your entire life. Here is where you will find the ancient secrets of health, longevity, and joy emphasizing that everything is based on the principles of "cleansing and nourishing" the body.

The third section is dedicated to women and their specific health concerns, including pregnancy, labor and delivery.

The fourth section is a "Reference Guide," listing different conditions and ailments, along with products that I have seen help many people. It also contains many of my own personal experiences.

The fifth section is a "Practical Applications / How to" section. Hopefully, this will help in explaining how to use certain herbs and/or how to apply them.

As each of us begin our journey into this phenomenal world of health, self-control, self-discovery, and self-responsibility – we tend to stay within our conventional thinking in the way we use this knowledge. For example, when I began to understand that there is an alternative to prescription drug use; I substituted herbs for prescriptions. In other words, I was still treating symptoms with medicine. I just went from chemical drugs to natural substances. This is a huge improvement and a much safer alternative, but my thinking was still the same – treat the disease. As I have traveled down this path – my thinking has come around 180 degrees. I now realize that true health is not about treating disease. It is about being disease-free. It's about being completely healthy and not worrying about disease. Isn't that an amazing concept!

As we begin to realize that the system we have trusted for so long is not perfect, many people tend to become resentful and bitter. It is not necessary to "hate" the system to start adding truth to your life. I am extremely thankful to live in a land where we are blessed with technology that can save a life in an emergency. I am also grateful for the many men and women who have dedicated their lives to helping the sick and disabled. Many of them have sacrificed much to ease the suffering of others.

It is just time to realize that our health is our own responsibility. It is not something we should shift to someone else. We make choices everyday which will determine how we live our lives – whether we will spend it sick and tired all the time or whether we will live life to its fullest because we are full of vibrant health and energy. The point is, begin where you are comfortable when you are ready. Take this information one step at a time and incorporate it into your life where it feels right and appropriate.

I encourage all who read this book to follow up with the materials offered on the "works cited" page. The information contained in this book is just the beginning of an awesome journey. Continue to study, to learn and to educate yourselves on all of the fascinating truths of life.

Section I

A Year of Discovery

Section I
A Year of Discovery Overview

When I was a teenager, my father bought *Back to Eden* by Jethro Kloss, a juicer, and began experimenting with vegetable juices. He believed the body was capable of healing itself if it had the right nutrients. He had found a principle he knew would work, but like most of us, he got caught up in everyday living and was over whelmed by how much there was to learn about the human body, the right foods and food combinations, the correct herbs to use for different problems, and all of the other facets of holistic health and healing.

My father passed away with a brain tumor when I was 22-years-old. I truly believe if we had understood and used the principles contained in that book, my father would still be with us today. Being exposed to this concept early in my life helped me to recognize truth as I came to different crossroads in my life, but like him, I had always gotten side-tracked with everyday living and had been too inclined to fall back on the medical system.

In 1994, life took a turn – Steve's diabetes began the quest to find alternate ways to care for this problem. Not only did I find ways to deal with diabetes, I found a whole new way of life.

Discovering the School of Natural Healing, I began to study to become a Master Herbalist. In the process of gaining knowledge, and then applying what we had learned, we began to have some experiences which were absolutely amazing. In 1995, David Christopher, the director of the school, asked me to write some of these experiences down so he could use them as testimonials. There were so many of them, he published them in a little 100 page book, which became the first *Dr. Mom*. The experiences from that first book are contained in this section. David wrote the forward for the first book. I was very touched and surprised by what he wrote. It read:

> We, as a nation, are far too dependent on others for our most basic need – good health. Most have the mistaken notions that they need and can afford to see a doctor for every little thing that goes wrong with their health. Naturally, our money would be well spent if it could buy good health, but it can't!
>
> Proportionally we, as a nation, spend more on health care than any other nation. Logically this should equate to

superior health as a populace. Yet it does not. There are over forty other countries that rate better than the U.S.A. in freedom from disease.

We propose that the quickest and easiest solution to this ineffective medical system is to have an herbalist in every home. Herbs are time-tested, safe and effective, and through their application 97% of health care needs can be provided within the family. This would free doctors to provide emergency medicine which constitutes about 3% of health care.

In *Dr. Mom,* Sandra Ellis pushes this new boundary between home and emergency care, showing us that herbs and natural healing techniques are not only superior in health care, but also in different aspects of emergency medicine. Sandra found tremendous success in prayerfully applying the teachings of the school in crisis situations.

During classroom time she would often relate these many experiences and I couldn't help thinking, "There is some kind of black cloud hovering over this lady's family."

Although the circumstances related in this book were very serious, even dark and foreboding, Sandra found the silver lining in her family's adversities. She gained more confidence and experience in this miracle year than most herbalists find in a lifetime.

Read, ponder and pray about this book. It could save your life.

As I look back, through a decade of experience to that first year, I realize that I see a lot of things differently now. However, I also realize for those who are just beginning, this process can seem overwhelming and frightening. Sometimes, as teachers, we don't do a very good job of putting all of the directions on the road map – we just assume that some things are understood because we have been doing them for so long. That is one of the reasons I have decided to leave these experiences in this book – I want you to understand that you do not have to be a Master Herbalist, or have a Ph.D. to be healthy. The herbs and herbal combinations referred to in this book are safe. They are easy experimentally and are phenomenal in that they can help you accomplish nature's balance very quickly. Keep it simple, remembering the foundational principles of "cleansing and nourishing." Have faith in yourself and faith in your body's ability to heal and rebuild itself. You just need the willingness and determination to learn and then try. As you read through this section, I hope you will come to understand that if I can be successful – anyone can be successful.

Written from a journal to preserve what really happened, even though some of it is very personal and down-right embarrassing. See how inexperienced, how unsure, and how frightened I sometimes was, and understand that even though many of the things I did would not be considered "correct" as far as measurements, ratios and procedures are concerned – they still worked.

For ease of reading, I would like you to meet my immediate family members, so you will know who I am referring to as I share these journal entries: Stephen, Paul, Wesley, Juanita, Jennifer, Myrna, Kelly, Nathan, Taunya, Aaron, Amanda, Joseph, & Megan.

The meaning of life, and the unique nature of life,
is in its diversity. The philosophy of survival is based on the
philosophy of diversity.
--Mikhail Gorbachev

Beware of little expenses; a small leak will sink a great ship.
-- Benjamin Franklin

At thirty-five I couldn't get an insurance policy for even the smallest amount that could be written, because – and you name it – I had it. I was sickly all my life, and I never knew a well day before I was thirty-five. I had rheumatoid arthritis in my youth, so I missed much school. It was disgraceful. I was on crutches so many times with this rheumatoid arthritis, and I had heart trouble, high blood pressure, and much more. At thirty-five, I repeat, I couldn't get any insurance policy – they all turned me down. But twenty years later the company I was working with insisted, because there were certain things that I knew that nobody else in the company knew, and they wanted to insure me for $100,000.00. Well, two doctors made the examination, and I passed with a clean bill of health. One doctor said (after he looked at my age and the remaining personal data), "May I take your blood pressure a couple of more times?" He had already taken it five times before, and I had a perfect systolic and diastolic. Both doctors were amazed, and one said, "You have the venous structure of a seventeen year old boy." This was accomplished through proper diet and herbs.
-- John R. Christopher, M.H., N.D.

Chapter One
A Medical Crisis

My mother, age 76, had recently moved in with me because she had several compression fractures of the spine due to osteoporosis. She had been on Prednisone, which contributes to osteoporosis, for several years to help her arthritis and was bedridden. There wasn't much I could do to relieve her suffering.

One morning, I checked on Mom at about 5:00 to make sure she was O.K. – she seemed to be resting peacefully. At 7:00 when I checked on her again, she was running a fever. This had happened before, but this time I was really concerned about her. I found a doctor who was an internal specialist who was willing to see her. When I took her to the doctor, she said that mom had pneumonia in both lungs, her oxygen saturation was low, and she had a temperature of 102 degrees. The doctor sent me home with antibiotics and said she would send someone over with oxygen.

When I got mom back home and into bed, I noticed her coloring had changed – around her mouth and arms, she looked extremely pale, almost grey. I called the doctor's office, the nurse said, "She only looks that way to you because she is flushed with fever. Alternate Tylenol with Advil and call back in the morning." As I was getting off of the phone, the man with the oxygen arrived.

He had to turn the tank up much higher than the doctor had recommended in order to get her to a normal saturation level. She looked so bad he stayed with me for an hour. When he left, Mom said she needed to go to the bathroom. She had uncontrollable diarrhea. I had already changed her sheets twice because as the fever breaks, she soaks the bed with perspiration. I had attempted to give her an Advil, but she immediately threw it up.

I called the doctor's office back and told the nurse to listen to me very carefully. I said, "My mother is losing fluids faster than I can replace them. She is sweating profusely, throwing up and has uncontrollable diarrhea. She needs intravenous fluids to replace what she is losing." The doctor said to bring her to the hospital.

When I arrived at the hospital, my mother's bowels and bladder were emptying on their own. She was mortified! I by-passed admitting and took her directly to her room. As the nurses helped her into the shower, I went to admit her. When I returned to the room, the end of her bed was cranked up, putting her in a head-down position. I asked them what they were doing – they told me they had to push the blood back to her heart. Her blood pressure was 55 over 30, her body temperature was 85 degrees. They took some chest X-rays, then told me her left lung was full of infection. When I asked the doctor if the infection was a separate thing from the pneumonia, he said it was a very serious pneumonia. I asked, "How serious?" He replied, "If you have any brothers or sisters, you need to call them."

After notifying my brothers and sisters that our mother was not expected to live through the night, I called one of my neighbors, who was a doctor to get a second opinion. He came to the hospital to see me. When I explained to him what happened, he said, "Your mom has gone into shock and was only minutes away from cardiac arrest. If you had waited any longer before bringing her in, it would have been too late."

Mom was put on several antibiotics intravenously to fight the infection. At about 2:00 in the morning, she woke up and wanted to know what was going on. She didn't remember much of what had happened and was not happy that I had brought her into the hospital, but I explained there was no choice.

Later, when the doctor came in, he asked me if mom was diabetic. I said, "No, why do you ask?" He said her blood sugar was high. I said, "Well, that's probably from the glucose they had in her IV last night." He explained to me that she had not been given any glucose, just a saline solution. I told him if he didn't believe me, he could look in the trash can where they had put it. He did, and sure enough, there was the empty bag of glucose!

After this crisis, we took Mom home and began to learn how to prevent an emergency like this from happening. Mom's immune system was extremely weak. Whenever she gets a cold, it turns into pneumonia. As we began to start using herbs, she learned how to use cayenne and echinacea. When she felt like she was coming down with something she would take some cayenne and soak in a hot tub or get into a hot shower, so she could sweat out the toxins. Then she would use cayenne ointment on her throat and chest to help her breathe and control whatever cough she might have. She also took echinacea to boost her immune system. Just by using these simple herbs, she has been able to keep herself from suffering with anything as serious as that pneumonia for ten years.

The secret of caring for a patient is caring for a patient.
-- Sir William Osler

Q: Why are 30 percent of Americans overweight?
A: Because of a most basic confusion! They don't know when they are thirsty;
they also don't know the difference between "fluids" and "water."
-- F. Batmanghelidj, M.D.

Physicians think they are doing something for you by labeling
what you have as disease.
-- Immanuel Kant

The worst sin toward our fellow creatures is not to hate them,
but to be indifferent to them: that's the essence of inhumanity.
-- George Bernard Shaw, 1897

Chapter Two
My Herbal Initiation

When I first began to study alternative health, I attempted to do it on my own, through reading and studying whatever I could find. For anyone who has ever attempted this, you know how confusing it can be. There are thousands of plants in the world. There are hundreds of books about them – many of which contradict each other. So, how do you decide who to believe?

In the midst of my confusion, a neighbor told me about a home study course she was taking to learn about herbs. I was excited about having some type of structured course to take, so I enrolled in the same course. As I began to study, I realized this course was based on Chinese medicine, so I started learning about the "yin and yang," along with the elements – wind, fire, water, & wood. Herbs were divided into categories which fell under these elements. We were taught you had to be careful how you used them because "fire" herbs will burn the "wood" herbs and "water" herbs douse "fire" herbs. It was all very confusing.

About this same time, my teenage daughter, Myrna had a friend, Dana, who had been in a horrible construction accident. He was working to save up enough money to serve as a missionary for two years. Three days before his nineteenth birthday, his arm was pulled into a cement mixer and badly mangled. He was rushed to a hospital where all of the broken pieces were pinned to a metal plate.

Three months later, he went back to the doctor to get his medical clearance to serve as a missionary. When the doctor looked at his x-rays he was extremely concerned, he told Dana there was not one sign of healing taking place in these bones. He told Dana he would give him 30 more days, but, if there was still no sign of healing after that time, they would have to start doing something more drastic, such as: bone grafts, treatment for infection of the inner bone, and, as a last resort, amputation. Naturally, Dana was frightened, but Myrna said, "Don't worry. Let's go talk to my parents."

She brought him home and asked her dad if he had any suggestions on what Dana could do. At the time, I was a brand new student, and didn't have a clue what to do, In fact, I was more confused now than I ever had been. Steve told me I needed to teach him about herbs. It was obvious that something needed to be done, so I went to the phone book and started calling health food stores. When I called the first two stores, I asked, "What do you recommend for broken bones?" The answer, "Comfrey." Well, at least, I had the same answer twice in a row – comfrey must be good for broken bones.

The third store I called happened to be Dr. Christopher's Herb Shop. When I asked them what they recommended for broken bones, they said, "BF&C". Well, two out of three wasn't bad. I asked the young man on the phone why he didn't recommend comfrey. He explained that BF&C was an herbal combination with comfrey in it. He said by combining it with other herbs, it works even better than alone. When asked what BF&C stood for, he replied, "Bone, Flesh & Cartilage." This young man seemed to know what he was talking about so I went to Dr. Christopher's Herb Shop.

In the store, I bought a large bag of cut comfrey (just to be on the safe side), a bottle of BF&C capsules, and two books about Dr. Christopher. I began to read and could not put these books down. For the first time, since I had begun this journey, someone made sense. Christopher, obviously an educated man; kept things simple. They made sense, and the information rang true to me.

As I read, I began to understand the principle of "cleanse and nourish", so we put Dana on the extended herbal cleanse with LB, LG, JuniPars, and Red Clover Combination (for instructions on this cleanse, see section V). We also worked out a daily routine of soaking his arm morning and night in the comfrey, taking five BF&C capsules three times per day, and keeping BF&C ointment on his arm at night.

Now, let me share my ignorance. Having never grown up with tea in the house, I didn't even know enough to strain it. When we figured out that soaking would help the arm – I put a large canning pot on the stove, dumped in about ¼ of a pound of cut comfrey and heated up the water. I knew absolutely nothing about making a tea or a decoction. I just knew it should be warm and strong – i.e. the ¼ pound of comfrey – I poured it in until the water looked dark. After it was nice and hot, I picked that pot up, carried it to Dana, put it on the floor, and said, "Put your arm in this". He was a brave young man because it looked like old swamp water.

Before I discovered that BF&C comes in an ointment, I attempted my first poultice. I knew we only had 30 days to fix this arm, so I wanted to be sure the bones were being fed 24 hours a day. I took some BF&C powder and mixed it with wheat germ oil until it looked like a paste. We spread this on Dana's arm. Within two hours, you could literally blow the powder off his arm because the body had soaked in all of the oil. This is when I began to understand what an incredible medium the skin is for getting nutrients into the body.

Skin is so amazing! If you put the world's deadliest virus on the skin, it can not get into the body unless the skin is broken. However, if you put something on the skin that the body needs, it is like every pore becomes a straw, sucking the nutrients into the body. The skin is an incredible medium for getting nutrients, medicinal properties and moisture into the body. When you are working with infants, the aged or infirmed, this is an important thing to remember.

At the end of thirty days, Dana went back to see the doctor. He was so excited about the results, he brought the x-rays home for me to see. The doctor said he had never seen anything like it before. His body built a new bone! This bone came from the good bone above the break, bridged across the broken pieces and tied into the good bone below the break. Starting with this new bone, you could see the healing taking place all down through the shattered pieces. The doctor had given him medical clearance to serve as a missionary.

Later, he did have to go into surgery because of a problem with the metal plate. After the surgery, he had a cast on and his arm became extremely swollen. We put ice on it, and elevated it, but could not bring down the swelling. It was swollen up over the top and bottom of the cast causing discomfort. We remembered the JuniPars formula has herbs in it that act as diuretics, causing the body to flush excess fluid, so we gave him four capsules. Within a short time, the swelling was down.

After this experience, I enrolled in the School of Natural Healing, which was founded by Dr. John R. Christopher and began my studies in earnest.

After seeing how successful this treatment had been on Dana, I began to wonder about my mother. If Dana could build a brand new bone in thirty days that had never existed before, then why couldn't my mother rebuild the bones she already had?

I started trying to figure out a way to soak all of my mother's bones the way we soaked Dana's arm. We finally figured out that we could turn the bathtub into a big "pot" of tea, just by putting the herbs into a cloth which could be rubber banded at the top to hold the herbs. We had a bathtub Jacuzzi so we put the ball of herbs in the water and turned on the jets. It steeped a wonderful tea, so at least once per day, we soaked Mom in the tub. We changed her diet to include lots of distilled water, fruits, vegetables, grains, nuts and seeds. Within a couple of weeks, she was out of the bed and within a month she was able to go up and down the stairs on her own.

Several years after this experiment, Mom fell and broke her arm. When I took her to the emergency room to have the arm x-rayed I was totally amazed at what I saw. The bones looked normal. Formerly, when she had been x-rayed for the compression fractures, her bones looked like Swiss cheese because the osteoporosis was so bad. Now she has normal bone structure. I told the doctor about the difference. He said, "Whatever you are doing, you should bottle it, you'd make a fortune." How do you bottle "a life style" change? It had only been three years since I had seen the x-rays of Mom's osteoporosis, my testimony of how fast the body can heal itself was growing by leaps and bounds. Steve told me I was like the bumble bee. Aerodynamically, it cannot fly, but it doesn't know that, so it flies anyway. This is the way I was with the body – I didn't know osteoporosis was incurable; we just fixed it anyway.

There were many times in that first year we had a chance to keep experimenting with this procedure.

In late August, a neighbor of ours was in a bad car accident. He was thrown through the windshield going 65 miles per hour. He had several fractures of the spine and some head injuries. When he was released from the hospital, there were several places on his upper back where there was no feeling due to nerve damage; I could tell he was extremely concerned over the lack of feeling, so I rubbed some cayenne ointment onto his back. Within seconds, he could feel it burning. We told his parents about soaking in comfrey, using the cayenne ointment and taking BF&C orally. They followed through and were amazed at how fast he began to recover and move around.

That winter, we received three calls in one week for different injuries. They all used the same treatment. The first one was an injured disk in the spine. The man had a lot of inflammation and pain. He didn't like the muscle relaxants and pain killers the doctor prescribed, so he wanted to know if we could help. We told him that 5 BF&C capsules three times per day, soaking in the comfrey, and applying a fomentation of BF&C directly to the spine had worked well before. We also suggested he alternate moist heat, then cold on his back to help reduce the inflammation during the day. Then at night, apply the BF&C ointment along with the Professor Cayenne ointment directly on the spine. He repeated this cycle as often as he could through the weekend and got the relief he was looking for.

A couple of nights later, we were asked to help someone who could not sleep due to a broken rib. He used the same procedures, along with some Lobelia tincture applied to the rib to help with pain relief.

The third call came from another neighbor whose husband had injured his hand and could not pick anything up. Again, we referred him to comfrey, BF&C, and cayenne.

During this same year, Jennifer, who was 18, was in a car accident and broke her back. The x-rays showed she had severe whip lash and a compression fracture of the seventh vertebrae. We took her home, used the same procedure as we had used before and she recovered completely.

It had been a year since I began studying with the school. One day, in my course material, I was listening to a video tape of one of Dr. Christopher's lectures. Talking about broken bones, he said if

BF&C were used correctly, even shattered bones would come back together like a jigsaw puzzle. At first, I had a hard time believing what I was hearing. One of the things I knew I still needed doctors for was setting broken bones. Now, Dr. Christopher is saying the body would bring them back together on its own – that was an incredible concept.

Not too long after hearing this, Wesley, who was 21, accidentally backed over one of our eight-week old puppies. The puppy survived, but could not put any weight on one of her legs. When I picked her up to see how badly she was injured, I could feel and hear the bones gritting back and forth in her leg. It was obviously shattered. The puppy was shaking, crying and in a great deal of pain. Steve said, "We just need to put her out of her misery."

I thought back to that tape of Dr. Christopher's, realizing I held in my hands the answer to whether or not his theory was true. In those years my family used to conspire against me. If anyone coughed, I was excited because now I had someone to experiment on, so my children got together and said, "If anyone gets sick, do not tell Mom." Well, I said something to Steve that my family hated to hear. I responded with, "Dr. Christopher says . . . . . " Steve kind of rolled his eyes back and said, "O.K., if you want to experiment on this poor puppy; I can always put it down tomorrow."

I thought that was a rude thing to say, so I used his razor to shave the puppy's leg. After shaving all of the fur off of it, we wrapped it in a BF&C fomentation, using a hot "corn bag" to keep it warm. (See section V for instructions on fomentations & corn bags.) I had to hold the leg constantly in my hand so the bones would not move. Every time she would try to change position, sneeze or move in any way she would cry out because of the pain. We alternated hot and cold, being careful not to put any weight on the leg.

It became apparent we were going to have to invent a way for her to relieve herself, so Steve went to the medical supply store, bought some plaster tape and an Ace bandage. We coated the leg with BF&C ointment, wrapped it with gauze, then molded the tape to her leg and let it dry, creating a half cast (somewhat like a plaster splint). Then, using the Ace bandage, we wrapped it around her leg, around her neck, and around her leg until we had her leg anchored to her neck, so when she went outside, she couldn't put any weight on the leg. Whenever she got thirsty, we gave her comfrey tea to drink, when she got hungry, we put a tablespoon of BF&C powder in her food.

The first three or four days, she didn't want to move around much, but as the leg began to heal, she wanted to get back to her normal activities. After a week, she refused to sit still for the treatment any more, so I put a full cast on the leg and turned her loose. It took her about two hours to chew the cast off. For the first few days she limped on it, by the end of two weeks, she was starting to walk on it, by the end of three weeks, she was running on it. The whole experience was really amazing! After a month had passed, we gave her to a new home; there was no sign that she had ever been injured; no limp, no deformity.

Several months later, when Nathan broke his foot, he was complaining of a lot of pain. Our chiropractor x-rayed it. Wade told him he had a spiral break of the 5th metatarsal and the bone had rotated. He said, "I know your mother and I know she won't do this, but I am legally obligated to tell you that you need to see an orthopedic surgeon to get the bone pinned back into place." Nathan thanked him, came home, where we did the same thing with him that we had done with the puppy. (I didn't tie his foot to his neck). By the end of two weeks, he was off of the crutches, by the end of four weeks, he was back playing basketball.

These are the experiences which began to teach me how incredible the human body is at repairing itself when it has the proper tools (nutrients) to work with. No matter how bad the injury was – the body always knew what to do to bring itself back into balance once it had the correct building blocks. With injuries of this nature, doctors usually have three choices: they can set it, drug it or cut it. Then the body must do the best it can to repair itself and we have to find a way to live with it while it heals. By giving the body what it needs to rebuild itself, the healing process becomes faster and easier.

The light of the world will illuminate within you when you
fast and purify yourself.
-- Ghandi

A fool thinks he needs no advice, but a wise man listens to others.
-- Proverbs 12:15

God gave us memories,
That we might have June roses in the December of our lives.
-- James Barrie

You don't get harmony when everybody sings the same note.
-- Doug Floyd

Chapter Three
Common Emergencies

So many examples of everyday emergencies most people would go to a doctor with can be avoided without a lot of medical expense and trauma.

One afternoon, Myrna was home working on a quilt at the sewing machine. She accidentally slid her finger under the needle and it went through her finger, entwining the thread through the tissue. My daughter, Kelly, was brave enough to get the pliers and pull the needle out, but they couldn't figure out how to get the thread unwoven from her finger, so they called Cherie, a neighbor of ours who took care of her family naturally.

When Cherie arrived at the house, she went to work on Myrna's feet using reflexology. She worked on the corresponding toe until Myrna's finger was numb enough to pull out the thread. By the time I got home from grocery shopping, the crisis was over.

A few weeks later, my daughter Amanda, who was seven, came to me, pulled up her shirt and wanted to know what was on her stomach and back. Some areas had a type of red rash – in other areas distinct red spots. I knew it wasn't chicken pox, so I looked it up in a medical encyclopedia. It turned out to be measles.

In *Herbal Home Health Care,* Dr. Christopher recommends chickweed, so we put Amanda in a warm bath with it in the water. After the bath, we put plantain ointment on the spots and gave her echinacea to boost her immune system. Other than the fact that she had spots, you would never have known she was sick; unlike when I was a child, having measles was miserable.

One night at 2:00 A.M., Taunya came to my room complaining of a pain in her side. I had no idea what to do for her, but I remembered reading that lobelia is sometimes used as a painkiller, so I told her to get the lobelia tincture and rub it into the painful area. In about 20 minutes she was back to sleep. What a wonderful discovery this turned out to be.

Some of my daughters also tend to have severe cramps with their monthly periods, especially if the don't drink their red raspberry and blessed thistle tea. One night one of them was really miserable with them and I was really tired, so I got the Lobelia tincture and figured that I didn't have anything to lose by trying it. I gave her about ¾ of a dropper full orally and we both slept the rest of the night.

Another afternoon, I heard Megan, age two, screaming like she was really hurt. She was stung by a bee. Out of habit, I pulled out the baking soda and made a paste to put on it. She kept crying. Her foot was getting larger; it was hot and hard. I pulled out my herb books – Dr. Christopher recommends plantain ointment, so I washed off the baking soda and put on plantain. As her system absorbed it, I applied more. Within a couple of hours it went back down and she was fine.

Weeks later, Megan looked like she was coming down with pink-eye. Steve had been using the Herbal Eyebright Formula to help his eyes due to the diabetes, so I mixed some up for Megan and used a dropper to put it in her eyes. She cried because of the cayenne in the formula and I felt bad about it, so I went to the herb shop and bought some plain eyebright herb to make into a mild tea. I didn't have to use it, however, because the first treatment cleared up the problem.

When my sister came out for a visit, she had some prescription medication for pink eye for her children. She told me that when she uses it, she has to hold them down because it burns so bad and she has to use it consistently for five to seven days or the pink eye will flair up again. I don't think I'll worry about a little cayenne any more.

During the fall, Nathan, age seventeen, worked for his uncle on a pipeline, coming home every couple of weeks for the weekend. During one of his weekend visits, I felt strongly impressed to put together a first aid kit for him, so I gathered together several different ointments and told him what and how to use each one. That week at work he got a deep gash on his arm, and needed stitches. They were working out in the middle of nowhere, so he packed it with BF&C ointment and taped it together. It healed without any infection or problem.

One Sunday afternoon, everyone was in the kitchen, helping to prepare Sunday dinner. Nathan was slicing peeled potatoes on a cheap potato slicer where you pull the potato across a sharp, razor-like metal strip. Nathan's hand slipped off of the potato and his finger went through the slicer, cutting off the ball of his finger.

He was squeezing it so tight the end of his finger was white. I told him to let it go so I could look at it. He said he couldn't because he could see the bone in the end of his finger and if he let go, it would bleed too heavily. I told him to go ahead and let go of the pressure so I could see what would happen. He was right, within seconds the blood was running down his finger, covering his hand and going down to his elbow. The only place it was still connected was behind the finger nail. He applied pressure again. Then, we gave him some cayenne, waited a couple of minutes and told him to release the pressure again. This time it just did a little bit of seeping. If I took him to the emergency room it would probably take about 6 – 8 stitches to close it and then he would always have an irritating scar on the end of his finger. The ball of the finger seemed to be in place, so I told him to pack it with BF&C, tape it in place and let it heal.

Before he went to bed he took four echinacea capsules to boost his immune system and a dropper full of lobelia tincture to help him relax. I worked on his feet to help with the pain until he was comfortable. About five in the morning, Nathan woke up in a lot of pain. During the night his finger had become entangled in his blankets, pulling the gauze wrap off of the finger. The ball of his finger had become twisted and was on top of the finger. I told him it was too late now to get stitches and that we were going to have to get the finger back down where it belonged. We packed it with BF&C again, used a butterfly strip to tape the finger back down, then wrapped it with gauze and tape. We repeated the echinacea, lobelia, and reflexology.

At one point, Nathan became frustrated with the whole thing and wanted me to cut the flesh off. He said it was dead and would not heal, so I picked up a sewing needle, poked the severed part of his finger, watched him jump and told him, "It is not dead yet – you just need to give it a chance." We found when it was kept wrapped, it became white and not very healthy looking, so he developed a routine of taking the bandaging off every two days to soak it in a BF&C decoction. Then he would leave it exposed to the air for an hour or two. Then we would pack it in BF&C ointment, tape it down and wrap it.

In three weeks, the finger was completely healed without any sign of scarring. I was totally amazed because there was not so much as even a line where the finger had been cut.

Months later, while I was working on a crisis with Megan, Joey, age six, came into my room in the middle of the night saying his ear hurt. I was so tired from being up with Megan that I just wanted to help him get back to sleep, so I put a couple of drops of Lobelia in his ear to help the pain and a couple of drops of Mullein oil to break up the congestion. He went back to sleep and so did I. The next night, he came in with the same complaint and I used the same treatment. He went back to sleep. The third night he was really in a lot of pain and the same treatment did not work. I knew it was my fault because each night I had just treated the pain (the symptom) and not the infection (the cause). This time I got up and took care of it the way I should have in the first place. I held the bottle of mullein oil under hot water until it was body temperature and put 3 or 4 drops in his ear. Then I got out the garlic oil and did the same thing with it (garlic oil kills infection). Normally, this takes care of most ear aches, but I had let it get bad. After soaking a cotton diaper in the hot decoction of three parts mullein to one part lobelia, I wrapped it around his head so that it covered the glands in his neck and covered his ears. I held him the rest of the night with the fomentation on while he slept. The next night we used the mullein oil and garlic oil again. This treatment totally solved the problem.

One afternoon Aaron was hanging over the sink with blood running out of his nose. He said he didn't know what had happened, it just started bleeding. There was a bottle of cayenne tincture sitting next to the sink so I gave him some in water. I told him to count to 10 and the bleeding would be stopped. He did and it was.

Recently, I renewed my CPR and First Aid certification. In the class we were told that if someone is bleeding from the nose, to lean them forward between their knees and just let it bleed until it stops. I don't know how long a nose might bleed with this method or how much blood could be lost, but I do know if you will keep some cayenne on hand, within 10 - 30 seconds, the problem is solved.

Whenever we go out into the woods as a family, Amanda always seems to find the stinging nettle. I'm not sure if she is allergic to it or not, but she immediately breaks out in large uncomfortable welts. In our herbal classes, David Christopher told us that wherever you find poison oak, poison ivy or stinging nettle, within ten to twenty feet you will find one of God's erasers – mullein, plantain or hounds tongue. Mandy has learned to recognize mullein, so when she needs help, she picks a couple of leaves, crumples them up in her hand and lays them on the welts. Within about five minutes the Mullein clears up the problem.

Just by learning how to use the few simple herbs in this chapter, we have saved ourselves many sleepless nights and several trips to an emergency room.

Never eat anything whose listed ingredients cover more
than one-third of the package.
-- Joseph Leonard

Medications are palliatives.
They are not designed to cure the degenerative diseases of the human body.
-- F. Batmanghelidj, M.D.

The reasonable man adapts himself to the world;
The unreasonable one persists in trying to adapt the world to himself.
Therefore all progress depends on the the unreasonable man.
-- George Bernard Shaw

Chapter Four
A Miscarriage

Five and a half months into her pregnancy, Cherie, having had contractions all day and spotting, called early in the evening to ask if I had any lobelia tincture. She had been using false unicorn and lobelia to stop the early labor. Dr. Christopher often refers to lobelia as the "thinking" herb; it assesses what the body needs and guides the other herbs to do what needs to be done. If the pregnancy is healthy, false unicorn and lobelia will stop the early labor. If there is a problem it will help the body to abort the fetus, usually eliminating the need for a D&C.

We called a friend of ours who had recently been successful in stopping an early labor, and asked her what she had done. She told me she had used the following herbs: red raspberry leaf, false unicorn, vitamin E, cramp bark, wild yam, and lobelia.

Hearing her story, we decided to pick up what we didn't already have and take them to Cherie, who we found lying on the couch in labor. She wanted to try the herbs we had brought over, so I gave them to her. The contractions started to slow down, so we thought we might be on the right track. She had a Doppler, so we checked for the baby's heartbeat, but could not find one.

I started to give her some more cramp bark, but felt prompted to give her some cayenne. This startled me because I didn't see any need for it. As I was pondering what to do, Cherie asked for some cayenne.

Little did I know the placenta was detaching and she needed the cayenne to prevent bleeding. Cherie got up and went to the bathroom. When she came back to the couch, the contractions started up in earnest.

Cherie was getting extremely uncomfortable, but I didn't want her to get up again, so her husband, Chad, grated up some ginger root which we put on her stomach, then laid a warm, wet towel over it. Ginger root is very relaxing in a tub of water during labor. She began to gush some blood and to be more uncomfortable. She had fought so hard to hang on to this baby, but had not felt it move in two weeks. Now she told Chad, "Let the Lord's will be done." She became extremely restless and uncomfortable, so we used some olive oil on her lower back along with pressure to relieve some of the discomfort. A few minutes later, she said she could feel the baby coming. She asked Chad to pick it up. I lifted her top leg, as she was lying on her side, and there was the baby, still completely contained in the amniotic sack with the placenta attached to it. Chad was visibly shaken by what he saw, so I reached down, picked up the baby, and handed him to Cherie.

I watched for any sign of life; movement, pulsation, anything, but there was nothing. Cherie held him and talked to him for some time. It was difficult to see him inside of the amniotic sac because the amniotic fluid was a dark, red, brown color.

She sent for Micka, her oldest daughter, to come and see him. Micka was brokenhearted over the loss, but was a great strength to her mother. Eventually, Cherie wanted me to break the sac so she could see the baby. Chad had thought it would be a girl, Cherie thought it was a boy. It turned out to be a boy, they named Benjamin. He was about 11 inches long and seemed to be completely formed except for the cartilage on the end of his nose. Cherie wrapped him up and cradled him next to her breast. I was kneeling above her head massaging her neck while Chad and Micka massaged her ankles and feet. As she cradled him, she sang a song entitled: I Am A Child of God.

It was the most angelic rendition I have ever heard. While she was singing, Chad, Micka and I were biting our lips, to not sob out loud as the tears flowed freely. How grateful I was to share in this sacred experience. What an example of strength and humility. When she was finished singing, she said, "You were all supposed to join in." We couldn't even answer her. A short time later I heard her say under her breath, "Be still, and know that I am God."

Steve, uncomfortable intruding on their privacy had gone to sleep in an easy chair. Myrna and Taunya came by to see the baby at about 1:00 AM, so he went home with them. Later, Cherie told me it had meant a great deal to Chad to have Steve there. Apparently, he knows what it is like to be condemned for staying home and not going to a hospital, so he really appreciated the support.

I stayed until about 5:00 to make sure Cherie would be all right. It is quite common to have a lot of heavy bleeding with a miscarriage. Fortunately, she did not have this problem. When we examined the baby closely, we saw that the placenta was too small for the size of the baby, the cord had problems in a couple of places and the baby's chest was blue.

A few hours later, Steve and I had an appointment with some family members. During the course of the conversation, we shared with them what had happened the night before. They were extremely upset. They told me Cherie should have been in a hospital – that I was not trained to deal with life and death situations such as this one. We tried to explain to them that there was nothing which could have been done to save this baby, but they informed me it was not up to me to make that kind of judgment call. When I told them it was Cherie's choice to stay home, they said, "Yes, and now she doesn't have her baby, does she?"

Being upset when we left their home, I decided to get a second opinion, so I went to see a family practitioner, whom I had assisted in labor and delivery several times. I told him what had happened the night before. He said,

> If there has been no movement for two weeks, the baby was already gone. You cannot have a healthy baby without a healthy placenta. If it was too small, it detached some time ago, causing it to shrink up, which would account for the color of the amniotic fluid because it would have bled into the amniotic fluid. The color you describe is that of old blood. There would have been nothing I could have done even if I had seen her from the day she conceived. With your training and experience she was where she needed to be and I have no doubt you did all that could have been done in much better surroundings than in a hospital.

After being attacked for what I had done, it was reassuring to talk to someone with more experience and be told I had done the right thing. I have discovered this year when you break with convention, there will be opposition. All I can say is that the inner peace which is gained will far outweigh the negative influences. You just have to learn to be cautious about who you share your new discoveries with.

My life is my MESSAGE.
-- Mahatma Gandhi

Your circulation it corrects, without unpleasant side effects.
It is, I think, the perfect drug; may I prescribe, my friends –
The Hug!
-- Henry Matthew Ward

Our greatest weakness lies in giving up.
The most certain way to succeed is always to try one more time.
-- Thomas Edison

The pessimist complains about the wind;
The optimist expects it to change;
The realist adjusts the sails.
-- William Arthur Ward

Chapter Five
Free Agency

Kelly was working at McDonald's where she was able to help some of her co-workers herbally, including her night manager, Lisa.

Lisa's father was in a V.A. Hospital in Oregon, scheduled for a heart transplant. Unfortunately, her father's health was deteriorating so fast that they didn't think he would live through the transplant. Lisa asked Kelly to have us talk to her.

Lisa's dad was only in his forties and the doctors could not figure out what was wrong with his heart. He had been healthy and strong until he had gone to Panama with his military unit, where he became extremely ill, so they brought him back to the states. They ran all the tests on him that they knew, but could not figure out why his heart was so weak.

When Lisa told us about him, Steve turned to me and said he thought it was parasites. (Steve is a retired Lt. Col. with the Air Force; so he is familiar with some of the problems they have in Central America). We had just finished reading *A Cure for all Cancer* by Hulda Clark, so we told Lisa about Clark's parasite cleanse. She uses black walnut hull tincture in its green state, wormwood, and cloves. We gave her a copy of the program and wished her luck with her father.

A couple of months later, we took our little ones in to McDonald's to play on the new playground. Lisa saw us there and came over to tell us how grateful she was for our help. We hadn't done anything except tell her about that one program, but, apparently, it had been enough to save her father's life. The doctors had given up hope for her father and had told the family to just make him as comfortable as possible. When they received the program for the parasites they immediately went to work on it and were able to stop the deterioration. Lisa said he was up and getting around like the father she had remembered. She said the doctors were pleased because now he was strong enough for a transplant.

I was in total shock when she told me this – it seemed to me if he could pull up from certain death, then why couldn't he just continue to rebuild his own heart. It would be a lot less complicated than going through with a transplant. She wanted to know if that was possible. We assured her it was. We told her about Dr. Christopher's extended herbal cleanse, cayenne, garlic, and hawthorne berry syrup.

Three months later, Lisa called to let us know her father had implemented the herbs. His heart had completely rebuilt itself. He was able to go back to work and continue on with his life. It is amazing someone on the brink of death can completely turn it around with the use of a few simple herbs, even when all of our technology has failed. I never cease to be amazed at what the human body is capable of doing. The doctors never knew what the problem was or why it reversed itself.

Another of Kelly's co-workers came to work one afternoon really sick with a bad cold. She was so miserable Kelly called me up and asked if I would bring some cayenne down to work, so I brought down four capsules. The co-worker decided to go home, take two capsules, a hot shower, two more capsules, and then go to bed. She asked everyone at work to cover for her and went home to try this treatment. After a couple hours of sleep, she felt so much better, she came back to work to finish her shift. Unfortunately, when she came back, the supervisor was there. She explained what happened, but the supervisor was still unhappy with her because she didn't believe she could have been that sick at the beginning of her shift and then well enough to finish it.

We have discovered this year that if people want help and ask for it, they will usually follow the program and get results. However, if they do not ask for help themselves, it usually will not work. You cannot and should not try to push natural healing on other people. If you do, you will discover what Dr. Christopher meant by "incurable people." They are not willing to do what needs to be done to cure themselves.

I really discovered this when a friend of ours had a severe staph infection in his leg. I had heard that they were planning to amputate the leg, so I called and offered to research staphylococcus and let them know what to use to get rid of it. They thanked me for the offer and the concern, but said they would follow the doctor's advice. His leg was amputated at the hip at the age of sixteen.

A few years after this experience, a dear friend of mine was diagnosed with breast cancer. She underwent two radical mastectomies, removal of part of her liver, chemotherapy, radiation and was, eventually sent home to die. She had twelve children. One evening she was talking to me about her daughter's wedding which was coming up in a month. She told me that she just couldn't believe it was time for her to go – she had so much left here to do.

I explained to her that it might not be time, but she was the only one who could do anything about it. She had been trained as a nurse and would not listen. Three months later she was gone. Her grandchildren will never know that fantastic woman in this life.

Another lesson was learned. In spite of how excited we get as we realize how incredible the body is at healing itself, we cannot save the world. We use our herbal knowledge within our own families and, where possible, with those who come to us for education. Wherever we can help, when asked, we try to do as much as we can. Unfortunately, we have learned over the years that even when people ask, many times they are looking for a magic pill to cure them – most are not willing to make the life style changes necessary to truly be healthy. This is something we must graciously accept, even when you know their choices may kill them. Everyone is entitled to choose their own path.

The price of freedom is eternal vigilance.
-- Thomas Jefferson

Choose what is best, habit will soon render it agreeable and easy.
-- Pythagoras (582-500 B.C.)

There is no biological reason
why human beings should not reach the age of 150.
-- Dr. Alexis Carrel, Rockefeller Institute

It was a thousand and one times more healthy in the past.
I've been to America, and your life didn't seem very healthy.
You spray the food with artificial chemicals. The fruits in your country are big
and they look good, but they have no taste.
-- Mir Ghazanfar Ali Khan

Chapter Six
The Challenge of Appendicitis

Late Sunday evening, I find myself overwhelmed and awe-struck at the events which have taken place this weekend. As we have traveled this path of self-reliance, there are some hidden fears I have continued to carry with me. In spite of the many ways I have watched the body heal itself, there are a few conditions I have been afraid to face because of my programming which tells me that if I do not turn to a hospital, it could prove fatal. Appendicitis is one of those conditions. A couple of weeks ago, at the herbal classes I am taking, we were told that one whole class would be dedicated to appendicitis. At the time, my stomach tied in a knot and I thought, "I sure hope I get to take this class before I have to deal with it." I have not had the class yet. This weekend Jennifer has had acute appendicitis.

As I sit here and ponder what has taken place, I wonder why so many situations have required me to "act" before I've had a chance to study. I feel as though the path I am traveling has thrown me into some type of "apprenticeship" with a power greater than my own. For instance: with Dana's crushed arm I learned as we went. Those valuable lessons have since been used to help my mother and many other people with similar problems. With Cherie, I was prompted to do things I had never done before. Later, I studied the principles I had applied and found them all documented and explained. I was able to use what I had learned to help others in labor. Taunya came to me in the middle of the night, crying with a side ache. I used Lobelia tincture and discovered that it helped with the pain. We have used cayenne to stop cold after cold in a matter of hours, even with Mom, who usually ends up with pneumonia.

It seems as though Providence purposefully has me deal with these things before I know what to do. It's as though He wants me to know He is the teacher, not man, not the books. He is the source all truth comes from. Each time I have one of these experiences, when it's over, I research it. Each time I verify what I have done and learn more, but during the crisis I have to rely on the Spirit and/or intuition because I don't know what to do. This weekend my head and my heart have really battled with each other. My heart tells me I am doing the right thing, but my head is full of all of the things I have been taught concerning conventional medicine.

I am so thankful for the chain of events which was put into motion to help me. All of the other experiences I have had to deal with – broken bones, cuts, childbirth, colds, coughs, etc. – have all had a certain familiarity because I've dealt with them before, but this weekend I was out of my element.

Friday, when I came in from getting groceries, I went up to check on Mom and found her in bad shape. For some reason her arthritis had flared up. Her joints were not only extremely stiff and sore, but they had hard knots on them that looked like bone spurs. I rubbed Professor Cayenne Ointment into her knees, down her legs, and all around her ankles.

Then Jenny came up to tell me she had gotten sick at work and her stomach hurt. I wasn't really surprised because she has been working in a sub shop, living on a lot of "meat-ball" subs. However, watching her, it soon became apparent this was not a normal stomach ache.

In *Back to Eden,* Kloss describes appendicitis:

> The appendix becomes inflamed when its opening into the intestine is blocked, and it cannot empty its contents properly. If the swelling and inflammation continue without proper treatment, the appendix may rupture, producing a very severe infection in the abdomen that may under certain conditions prove fatal.
>
> Symptoms: Nausea and vomiting, pain and distress around the navel and in the right lower abdomen, constipation or loose stools, rapid pulse and usually a rise in temperature to 100 to 102 degrees. The pain is made worse by pressing on the abdomen or by movement. Drawing the knee up may ease the pain. (267)

Herbal Home Health Care verified Kloss's description and added:

> Constipation is one of the causes of appendicitis to an extent, and of course, wrong diet, which diet would include the use of devitamized foods such as white flour products, cane sugar products (all refined sugars), greasy and fried foods, tea, coffee, chocolate, and wrong combinations of foods. These must be strictly avoided in appendicitis, as

must alcoholic drinks, tobacco, and all stimulating food and drink.

. . . Cleanse the colon thoroughly with an enema, preferably herb, taking as much water as possible, as hot as possible. The treatment is of great value and will often relieve the pain immediately. If using a herb enema, use either spearmint, catnip, white oak bark, bayberry or wild alum root. When herbs are not available, use plain water. If the pain continues after the colon has been cleansed, then use a very warm enema of catnip alone. Then apply hot and cold fomentations to the region of the appendix and the full length of the spine. This will aid in the cleaning process and relieve pain.

. . . When suffering an attack of appendicitis, go on a liquid diet, drinking alkaline broths, fruit juices, and drink several glasses of slippery elm (or comfrey) every day. Alternating hot and cold castor oil fomentations brings tremendous relief. (Christopher 35-36)

Jenn could not stand up straight, so I had her lay down on the couch and checked her abdomen. She was tender all over, the worse pain being to the right of her naval, watching how her right leg was drawn up to ease the pain and then, seeing her become nauseated; it was pretty obvious she fit the description. Somehow I knew we were dealing with appendicits.

Christopher said to use a poultice made of powdered Lobelia, Ginger root, Slippery Elm, and crushed Mullein leaves. I had everything except the Mullein, so I called Cherie, my neighbor. She didn't have any, but she knew where some was growing, so she picked it and brought it over. We made the poultice.

Christopher also suggested Comfrey tea and herbal enemas to clean out the colon. The only type of enema I was aware of were commercial "fleet" enemas which come from the pharmacy, so she gave herself an enema using the commercial brand. Following the enema, we gave her some comfrey tea to drink, applied lobelia tincture to her abdomen, followed by the poultice and a hot wet towel. We alternated the heat with a zip-lock bag full of ice. Cherie asked for my reflexology chart and started working on

Jenn's feet, rubbing the appendix and bowel areas. On the bottom of the feet are areas which represent every part of the body – a "blueprint" which reflects what is going on in different areas of the body. If there is a problem area, it will reflect in the feet as pain, crystals (small granules), or tightness. When you stimulate the nerve endings in the feet, a signal is sent to the central nervous system where it is analyzed. It then sends a message to the particular organ and stimulates it. Several times when we have worked the feet, Jenny will tell us that she can feel things bubbling around inside or that her stomach is cramping.

Around 11 P.M. a strange thing happened. A friend was spending the night with Taunya. Some of Cherie's boys were over, so there was a lot of energy in the room. The friend brought in a jar of jelly beans and started passing them around to everyone. I had a horrible feeling come over me. It's hard to explain, but I felt as though I had to protect Jenny from something harmful. I tried to ignore it at first, but it just got stronger, so I took Taunya by the arm and said, "I know this sounds ridiculous, but you have got to get that sugar out of the room. I just have a horrible feeling about it." I know those teenagers and Steve, for that matter, thought I was absolutely crazy. I can't explain it myself, but it was very real. I felt a great need to be in tune and I couldn't allow that kind of distracting energy in the room.

Jenn was in a lot of pain, so I got some warm water and added a few drops of Catnip and Fennel tincture to it. I only had an enema bulb for infants, so I told Jenny to do another enema using three or four bulbs of herb water. She was extremely repulsed by the enemas and the poultices, but she was willing to cooperate. Around 2:00 A.M., she seemed to relax a little bit, so I suggested she get some rest. Cherie went home and I slept on the couch next to Jenny for a couple of hours.

Saturday morning the pain was worse. I had her use a "fleet" enema, then I gently rubbed on lobelia tincture and put some fresh poultice on, alternating cold and hot compresses. I went to work on her feet using reflexology. About 10:00 Cherie called to see how she was doing. She asked if I still felt good about taking care of this at home. I told her I felt like I needed to do more. I was frightened, but still didn't feel good about taking her to the hospital. She asked, "Would you like me to call my midwife, who is also a home health nurse and an herbalist? She might be able to help." At this point, I welcomed all the help I could get.

She put me on a conference call with Donna, who said, "My son had an acute appendicitis attack at home. I followed the same program you are doing, but when his appendix ruptured, he insisted on going to the hospital because the pain was so bad. At the hospital he was taken into surgery where they removed the appendix. When the doctor finished operating on him, he told me that there had been absolutely no sign of any infection. He had never seen anything like it. I think if he had stayed home, the appendix would have healed just like any other injury in the body."

While I was on the phone with them, Jenny doubled up in such pain that I thought she was going to pass out. She looked clammy and pale. I handed the phone to Steve and had him tell them that I couldn't talk any more. I put ice on her stomach and worked on her feet as much as I could. When she calmed down, I called them back. I told Cherie I was extremely worried about Jenny and was considering taking her in. I kept thinking, "She could die and it will be my fault for not getting her in sooner." Donna volunteered to come over to check her vital signs.

When Donna arrived, she took Jenny's blood pressure, pulse and temperature. When she saw that it was 97.5, her whole countenance lit up. She showed it to me and said, "You're on top of it. There is no fever, which means there is no infection. You're doing the right things to keep it cleaned out and she's going to be fine." I asked her, "Do you think the appendix has ruptured?" She said, "It probably has because the pain was so intense and now is under control. There really is no way we can tell for sure, but at least you are on top of the situation. What kind of enema are you using?" I told her, she said I needed to get an enema bucket from a medical supply store, so Steve left to get one.

Jenny was complaining of a bad headache – Donna said it was the body's signal to cleanse some more, so she did another "fleet" enema. After the enema, Jenny said she was passing mucus from the bowel. Donna said, "You see, the body is cleaning itself out."

When I began to work on her feet again, it seemed to verify this fact. Instead of hurting in her appendix reflex spot, the extremely tender areas were in the pancreas and the adrenal glands. It appeared the lymph system had taken over to clean every thing out. How grateful I was for Donna's help and encouragement.

Jenny dozed off, so I went up to my room, closed the door, took a shower and then knelt by my bed and tried to express my gratitude to God for all of the help I had received this weekend. When Jenny woke up, she used the enema bucket to give herself a catnip enema. She was still passing mucus from the bowel and was starting to get hungry, but I would only let her have herbal teas (comfrey or chamomile), distilled water, or pure apple juice.

Saturday night was pretty rough for Jenn, but the pain was never as bad as it had been that morning. I continued with the same treatment; Lobelia, poultice, hot and cold packs, foot reflexology, and herbal enemas. About two or three o'clock in the morning we both fell asleep on the couch again.

Sunday, Jenny was still sore and hurting, but she was doing much better. She was really hungry, so I let her have some watermelon. That night she was cramping again, so we spent our third night on the couch together.

Monday morning, a friend of Jenn's came by to see her. He told her that her appendix couldn't have ruptured because his mother said if it had, she would have died. I'm not sure anyone will ever believe what happened here this weekend.

Monday, Jenny was up moving around and doing great. She was still sore, but doing well otherwise. She took a bath and when she got out, she asked, "Do you think if my appendix ruptured it would cause a bruise?" I said, "It might, if there was any internal bleeding involved." She showed me on her abdomen where a slight bruise was coming to the surface.

I called Donna to tell her Jenny was doing much better. She said, "You need to know that a friend of mine had a son die from a ruptured appendix because they didn't know what to do and they didn't get help fast enough. Appendicitis is not anything to play around with. You have to know how to cleanse the body or get to a hospital for help because if you don't do something it can be fatal." I asked, "Why didn't you tell me this on Saturday?" Her reply, "I knew you had the situation under control and that everything would be O.K."

It is truly amazing to me that whenever I am in over my head, either I am impressed to do what needs to be done or the right person shows up at the right time to help me through the crisis.

This country, with its institutions, belongs to the people who inhabit it.
Whenever they shall grow weary of the existing government, they can exercise
their constitutional right to dismember or overthrow it.
-- Abraham Lincoln
Inaugural Address, 1861

No more than one or a few decades remain
before the chance to avert the threats we now confront will be lost and the
prospects for humanity immeasurably diminished.
-- Union of Concerned Scientists
World Scientists' Warning to Humanity
December 1992

Fluoride is an industrial waste product generated during the production of
aluminum, phosphate, pesticides, coal-burning power,
gasoline, fertilizer, steel, copper and glass.
--U.S. EPA Report PB85-199321, April 1985

Chapter Seven
The Harvest

Following a dinner we had just attended, we ended up at the Nichols' for a short program. While everyone was standing around visiting, Steve called me off to the side of the yard to point out some Mullein which was growing there. Mr. Nichols has a beautifully manicured yard, so Steve knew it was not growing there by mistake. While he was pointing it out to me, Mr. Nichols happened to see us, so he asked us if we were interested in herbs. I said, "Yes, very much."

He wanted us to see what else he had planted. All around the outside border of his yard, he had planted all kinds of herbs. I asked him if he ever harvested them to use them and he said he really didn't know what to do with them, he had just felt impressed to grow them. He had several that he had brought in from other areas which were not native to Utah. Equipped with a book on herbs, he had tried to focus on the medicinal ones. They were wonderful! It was exciting for me because I had never seen most of them in their natural state.

A couple of months later when the first snow came, Mr. Nichols called Cherie and told her if we wanted to harvest the plants, we were welcome to do so. Gathering up some of our children to help, we went right over. Mr. Nichols showed us which ones could be cut close to the ground, which ones to only take the leaves, and which ones to take some of the root. After working for a couple of hours, we had a dozen garbage sacks full of herbs.

Again, this was something I had never done before. When I got home, we laid out sheets and blankets to lay the herbs on. There wasn't much floor space left to walk on! I looked through my books to figure out what to do with them from this point and discovered that I could gather them together by the stems in groups of 4 or 5 with a rubber band and hang them on lines, like clothes lines.

They needed to be out of direct sun so when they were completely dried, they would still be just as green as when we picked them. We went into the basement and stretched out several lines. We had them hung across the stairs going to the basement and everywhere else we could find to stretch a line. The leaves that were loose, such as comfrey, we laid out on the sheets.

When the plants were completely dried, we crushed them into amber glass bottles, labeled them with the name of the herb, the date, and where we had gotten them. Then, stored them in a cabinet where the light could not reach them.

Along with drying the herbs, we began to experiment with making our own herbal combinations, tinctures and ointments. What a feeling of independence! I was beginning to understand that just about everything I needed grew somewhere close by. It could be harvested and then made into my own medicines. Not only was it less expensive than buying them, but, usually, they were stronger and, of course, fresher than what you can buy in the store. It also gave me the added freedom of being able to customize them according to the needs of my family.

All of us, at one time or another, wonder what we would do in an emergency, such as a natural disaster, if we could not run to the grocery store or pharmacy to get what we need. It was a wonderful feeling to know I was not dependent on the "system" any more to take care of my family's medicinal needs. It was truly liberating!

I was extremely grateful to Mr. Nichols for his generosity, but even more than that, I was amazed at the grand design of things. It seems that my path continues to cross the paths of others who are like-minded, but with different talents. I sit in awe of all there is to learn and do in this amazing world. Forty years of my life have come and gone without noticing too many people in the "herbal" world. Now, all of a sudden, it seems they are everywhere.

For example: Cherie sets a quiet and powerful example by the way she takes care of her family which leads many to ask questions and to ponder a different way from the one they are conditioned to. Daryl, another friend, has groups of people come to her home periodically where she teaches classes on the things she has researched and she does a lot of experimenting with herbal combinations and preservation. Mr. Nichols tenderly plants and grows the herbs. Then, generously shares their harvest. I have been blessed with a lot of hands-on experience to teach me how to use them and to benefit from their wonderful healing properties.

I am truly amazed at how our lives have touched one another and strengthened one another. It is comforting to know we are not alone on this planet.

Behold the turtle:
He only makes progress when he sticks his neck out.
-- James Conant

Our massive tampering with the world's interdependent web of life . . .
could trigger widespread adverse effects, including unpredictable collapses of
critical biological systems whose interactions and dynamics we only imperfectly
understand . . . We the undersigned, senior members of the world's scientific
community, hereby warn all humanity of what lies ahead.
-- Union of concerned Scientists, including 102 Nobel laureates
World scientists' warning to humanity
December 1992

Come, my friends, Tis not too late to seek a newer world.
-- Alfred Tennyson

Chapter Eight
The Cold Sheet Treatment & Cayenne

My friend's daughter, Micka, was sick with pneumonia, causing a horrible cough. Cheri asked if I had any herbs to help her daughter. This was a Thursday and they were planning to have a lot of family coming in on Sunday for their son's missionary farewell. Cheri told me Micka had been born prematurely, that she had had a hole in her heart which required two surgeries as a baby, and she had been left with a lot of scar tissue. I told her I had just finished reading about a procedure used to treat pneumonia which is called the "cold sheet treatment." Having never attempted it before, I was pretty apprehensive, but knew this was suppose to be a specific treatment for pneumonia, so we gathered up the supplies we would need and went to their home.

In *The Cold Sheet Treatment* pamphlet, Dr. Christopher states:

> When your cold has advanced into a severe, chronic condition, or when you have no success with the first simple remedies, the Cold Sheet Treatment program is the next step you want to take. It successfully blends hydrotherapy with herbal therapy to clean out the body of its poisons and toxins. It works to break up systematic congestion, such as viral infections and pneumonias that prevents normal bodily functions through the use of hot water and diaphoretic herbs. It is a very safe healing modality because it works with the body instead of against it.
>
> Hydrotherapy has been used for centuries to heal the sick. It was once a common practice of doctors. The Romans built their famous baths in England not for pleasure bathing, but for health and treating illness. Hydrotherapy works well because the body is made up of over eighty percent liquid. Much of the fluids in the body are toxic, loaded with cholesterol, mucus, etc. When they are replaced in a natural way through hydrotherapy, with good liquid, we gain a healthy body (9).

When I arrived with Taunya and a laundry basket full of supplies, they too, looked a little apprehensive. I showed them the book I had been reading and explained to Cherie how it worked. The whole purpose of the treatment is to build an artificial fever which will cause the body to sweat out the toxins. I'm sure this is the same concept which was used by the Indians when they would sit in a sweat lodge and then jump in a cold river.

When Micka found out the whole procedure began with an enema, she was not impressed. However, they understood the concept of creating a "healing crisis," so she agreed to give it a try.

As it turned out, Cherie was almost as sick as Micka, so we used the treatment on both of them. We made up some Catnip tea to use for the enema and some hot yarrow tea to drink. After completing the enema, which they were to retain as long as possible, we put them in a hot tub of water with cayenne, ginger and dry mustard. They were to soak as long as possible, drinking at least three glasses of the hot yarrow while in the tub.

When Micka got out of the tub, we wrapped her in a cold, wet cotton sheet. The sheet had gone through a cold rinse cycle in the washer, which wrung it out so that it was not dripping. We then put her to bed, still wrapped in the wet sheet and piled on quilts. We chopped up some garlic, mixed it into some petroleum jelly and put it on the bottom of her feet, after massaging them with olive oil. The body will not pull in the petroleum jelly, but it is a way to suspend the garlic, so the body can draw on it.

Micka did not care for this procedure. She was pretty miserable and kept asking me when she could get up. I told her when the sun came up would be a good time. After she had been wrapped up for about 30 minutes, I slid my hand under the sheet to see if she had worked up a sweat. She was hot and sweating profusely. I said, "This is great! It's working! You have a wonderful cleanse going." She just looked at me like I was crazy.

On Sunday, Micka and Cherie spoke at the farewell and you never would have known they were recovering from pneumonia.

While Nathan was working for his uncle in Nevada, he bought an energetic, playful baby ferret and brought her home for a pet. I warned him that he needed to keep her contained because we have a two-story entry with an open balcony on the second floor. I was afraid if she started playing on the balcony, she could be killed by falling to the tile floor below. Of course, everyone assured me they would watch her.

On a Monday night we invited the Wrights over for dinner. After dinner, the adults were sitting in the living room, which is next to the entry. All of a sudden, we heard a sickening thud. I jumped up and saw the ferret laying on the tile, bleeding from her mouth and nose. Growing up on a farm, I know what an animal looks like when it is dying, so I scooped her up, handed her to Steve and told him he needed to take her out back to end her suffering.

In the meantime, word reached Nathan, who was playing basketball outside. He came running in, took the ferret from his father and turned to me, saying, "Mom, isn't there anything you can do?" By now, there was blood coming out from behind her eyes. Obviously, there was nothing I could do, but I wasn't about to tell my sixteen-year-old son that. I remembered David Christopher, in one of our herbal lectures; say that if you administer cayenne for bleeding, just count to ten and the bleeding will stop.

I told Myrna to get my cayenne tincture. I put some in a dropper and then shot it directly into that ferret's mouth. When the cayenne hit her tongue, she started flinging her head back and forth, with saliva flying everywhere. We couldn't hold on to her any more, so we put her on the floor where she began to run, making about six laps around the living room. When we picked her up again, there was no sign of hemorrhaging. She wouldn't let me get near her with the cayenne tincture again, so I put some cayenne ointment behind her ears and on the bottom of her feet. We watched her closely for a couple of hours and then let her sleep. She slept for about 12 hours, but when she woke up, she was fine. The next morning she was running and playing as though nothing had ever happened. However, we don't have to worry about the balcony anymore, because she would not even risk jumping off of the bed.

CIRCUMSTANCES?
I make circumstances!
-- Napoleon Bonaparte

The trouble with being punctual is that nobody's there to appreciate it.
-- Franklin P. Jones

Don't Bunt. Aim out of the ball park. Aim for the company of immortals.
-- David Ogilvy

Millions of Americans are hopelessly hooked on potato chips, hamburgers,
candy bars and cola. Their lives are spent in a miserable limbo between
sickness and health. They're slowly killing themselves, gorging their way into
obesity, hypoglycemia, diabetes and heart disease.
-- Paul A. Stitt, Biochemist

Chapter Nine
Chronic Conditions

Up to this point, all of the experiences I have shared with you have had rapid and obvious results. It has been easy to see the beneficial action of the herbs. However, the reason is because each of these cases has been an acute condition. The person was in a healthy state and then for some reason, due to accident or illness, there was an immediate challenge which could have been a potentially dangerous situation.

When you are dealing with a chronic illness, the results may not be as obvious. Chronic illnesses have been going on for a long time and may take a long time to clear up. I have had the opportunity to work with three situations this year that I would have to put into this category. Two of them were existing problems and one started out acute and became chronic. This is what I have learned thus far, though I am still researching and learning what to do in chronic cases.

The first was Steve's diabetes. As I mentioned earlier, Steve was diagnosed with diabetes a couple of years ago. Because there are several cases of diabetes in his family, we knew what a serious disease we were dealing with. Steve's case is more serious than most adult onset diabetes due to the fact that he is not over weight. In most cases, if you change your diet, exercise and lose the excess weight, you can get it under control. Steve didn't have any excess weight to lose. This disease has a lot of undesirable side effects such as loss of vision, tingling in the extremities, nerve damage, impotency, internal organ damage (heart, kidneys, liver, etc.) and many others. It affects the whole body. Steve began to experience several of these symptoms.

During the first year, we began changing our diet and Steve tried to get as much exercise as possible. Most of the time this meant going for walks in whatever city he was in or just walking up and down the stairs in the hotel he was in for the night. He was adamant about not using insulin – if an airline pilot has to go on insulin, he is automatically grounded. He also knew that once he started using insulin, his body would not need to make it anymore and would stop production. We both felt there must be a way to restore his body to its natural function.

Cutting back on sweets and getting a little more exercise helped, but it did not stop the disease, so the doctor put him on oral medication and he began keeping track of his blood sugar levels at home. Eventually, he was grounded due to high blood sugar levels. In the meantime, we began our study of herbs and diabetes.

Steve took the oral medications the doctor gave him and we went to work on the problem with herbs. During this past year, we have tried many different things, monitoring his blood to see which ones were working. The prescription medications have never kept it under control, and the herbs have never kept it under control, but the combination has had wonderful results.

As Steve's eyesight was going downhill fast, he started wearing bifocals and was still losing a lot of his long distance vision, so he began using Dr. Christopher's Eyebright formula. He faithfully washed his eyes in the formula morning and night. His vision became more and more clear and is now much better than mine.

We were concerned about the damage to his internal organs, especially the kidneys, so he started taking the JuniPars formula three times per day. He takes five of the PancTea formula three times per day to rebuild and strengthen the pancreas, along with five of the Adrenetone formula three times per day to rebuild and strengthen the adrenal glands. He uses chlorophyll to counteract impotency and for the last three months, he has been taking pancreas and adrenal glandulars.

We are experimenting with the glandulars right now because some people believe that when an organ, such as the pancreas, becomes extremely weak and damaged it may not have enough strength to take in the nutrition it needs. The glandular which is made up of like tissue, taken from an animal, has the same vibrational level, so the theory is it will help target the sick organ, taking the herbs directly where they are needed. The program he is using takes four months, so I am not sure what the outcome will be.

Since we have not been able to control the diabetes solely with the herbs yet, it would seem it is not possible. However, I know that is not true. When Steve was unable to pass his flight physical due to high blood sugar levels, he was sent in for a battery of tests to see what kind of damage had been done to his system. When the first doctor finished, he told him if it were not for his blood sugar levels, he would not know he had diabetes because there was no sign of the normal damage which this disease causes. I have not been able to get to the source of what is causing, Steve's diabetes yet, but I know that so far the herbs have been able to feed his system in such a manner that we have been able to protect him from the serious consequences of diabetes.

I think the answer to overcoming this disease entirely lies in changing the stress levels we have lived under for many years, increasing his amount of exercise and getting closer to the ideal in the way we eat. I am a novice. I still have many things to learn, but I know I will find a way to control this disease. This experience, however, shows you that you will not always have immediate and miraculous results, especially when you are dealing with a chronic, ongoing disease like this one. As you can see, we can work with the medical profession hand in hand with the natural methods until we get serious conditions under control.

POSTSCRIPT: O.K., I told you I would present my original year just the way it happened so you can follow my "learning curve." However, I do not want anyone coming to this chapter to figure out how to take care of diabetes. Please go to Section II and look it up in the "reference guide" to learn how to cure this disease. It is curable, but it takes a complete lifestyle change. It is not going to be done just by taking herbs or any other type of magic pill.

There are several challenges in this chapter which took time for me to overcome. The first one has to do with the oral medications. When Steve got everything under control enough to retake his flight physical, he had to list all of the medications he was on along with the dosage. One of the medications he was on was Glucotrol. He was told that it helps the pancreas to produce insulin. When the nurse saw he was taking eight of these per day, she told him he should never take more than four because tests have shown that more than four are ineffective and it will kill the pancreas faster. Steve said, "What do you mean Faster?" She told him this medication forces the pancreas to make insulin and to work much harder than normal. This is why the oral medication is only good for a couple of years because it will eventually burn out the pancreas and then you will have to go on insulin. Doctors know this when they prescribe the medicine, but it is used as an effective way to stall off taking insulin for a couple of years.

Steve was furious when he left that lab. All of those months he had been trying so hard to rebuild his pancreas, only to find out he had been unknowingly killing it. He walked out of the lab and threw all of the prescription drugs away. He has not taken them since.

The glandulars are also something I would never recommend to anyone. The fact is the tissue in these glandulars is dead – there is no vibration to them and, if there was, it certainly would not match the tissue of a live person. Not to mention the fact, I would be real concerned about what animal it is being taken out of and what condition the animal was in when it was taken. The third is diet. I used to believe a vegetarian lifestyle would take care of this problem; I was wrong. This condition literally takes a lifestyle change! The system has to be alkalized and rebuilt with live food. Again, depending on what type of diabetes you have and how far it has progressed – you must be as aggressive as what you are dealing with or it will win.

The second experience involves my mother, when she came to stay with us a year and a half ago; we did not expect her to live very long. She was a walking drug store, in very poor health, on high blood pressure medication, high doses of Prednisone for arthritis, stool softeners, Advil, Extra-strength Tylenol, thyroid medication, high cholesterol medication and whatever else would help with bad headaches. Mother was seventy-six-years-old and on her way out. As mentioned earlier, she had severe osteoporosis, a weakened immune system and severe arthritis, along with the problems she was on medication for.

In the first chapter, I related our first big emergency after she had sustained three compression fractures to the spine. Since that time, the biggest changes she has made is that she mainly drinks distilled water instead of tap water or carbonated drinks. Her diet has changed in the same ways that ours has and when she starts to come down with something, we get on top of it immediately. She takes a bath in the comfrey at least three times per week and when she needs help, we use the same herbal remedies with her as we use with the rest of the family. If she needs a stool softener, she reaches for the Fen LB which heals and builds as much as it cleans out. If she feels a cold coming on, she reaches for the cayenne, and, if her joints are swollen or sore, she reaches for the BF&C ointment and the Professor Cayenne ointment. Because Mom is not strict about her dietary habits, when we are able to go out to eat as a family, she still orders red meat, desserts and soda. However, she is a new person, she goes up and down the stairs several times per day and has not been seriously ill in a year. The only prescription medication she is still on is her thyroid medicine. She sometimes uses Alleve for her arthritis, and the rest is done herbally. As she learns and uses the herbs more, her health will only improve. Isn't that a wonderful thing to look forward to at seventy-seven!

The third and last example was probably the hardest one that I have dealt with this year because it was so intense for so long. In late August, Steve, Megan and I took my mother out to Arkansas to visit her mother who is ninety-eight-years-old. We flew into Tulsa, borrowed a car from my sister, drove to northeast Arkansas, and stayed two days with another sister. We had a pretty uneventful trip and returned home safely. Shortly after we returned, Jenny's appendicitis hit. As she was recovering, Megan, age two, seemed to be coming down with a cold. I did all of the normal herbal things, such as giving her echinacea, Children's Composition formula, and hot steam baths. The Children's Composition formula is made up equal parts of yarrow, elder flower and peppermint, but, for the first time, it didn't seem to be helping.

Megan began to cough up mucus. I thought, since my sister smokes, maybe Megan's lungs were just cleaning out the foreign matter she had taken in during our visit. She seemed to do pretty well during the day, but at night she would wake up choking on the mucus. I put her into bed with me so that I could help her through the coughing spells. They were terrible. She had a hard time getting her breath and I had never seen anyone cough up so much mucus! There would literally be a half cup or more.

In reading *The ABC Herbal,* Steven Horne quotes Dr. Shook:

> . . . in his *Advanced Treatise in Herbology,* he says: For the treatment of colds, influenza, and fevers of all kinds, there is no remedy knwn to man that is so safe, sure and speedy as elder flowers, an all-around alterative, blood purifier, and general systemic cleanser. They are without a superior.
>
> Because elder flowers are emetic and womewhat nauseating to some people, the ideal synergist to blend with them in the treatment of colds, fevers, and so forth is peppermint. Peppermint is a stimulant, nervine, calmative, and antiemetic, and the combination is world-famed as the greatest fever remedy ever known to man.
>
> Considering that right after the last world war, upwards of six million people died of influenza and that millions have died since, is it not a very great privilege and blessing to be in possession of the knowledge of such a remedy?
>
> The great herbalist, Henry Box of Plymouth, England says, 'For colds, influenza, fevers, inflammation of the brain, pneumonia (inflammation of the lungs), stomach, bowels or any part, this is a certain cure, I have never known it to fail, even when given up and at the point of death. It will not only save at the eleventh hour, but at the last minute of that hour. It is so harmless that you cannot

use it amiss, and so effectual that you cannot give it in vain.' (16)

Bronchitis was the only thing I could associate this with, so I researched whatever I could find on the topic. I tried soaking a piece of wool in castor oil, applied it to her chest, covered with a piece of plastic and then a heating pad to draw out whatever was causing this horrible cough. We built a tent in the family room, so she and I could sit in it with a steaming pan of comfrey and peppermint. The only problem with this method is that you have to keep reheating the water. We tried baking an onion at low temperatures and putting the slices on her chest. It seemed that no matter what I tried, I could not get this cough to stop. During the days, she did pretty well, but the nights were terrible. I told everyone to keep her away from all dairy, which is mucus-forming, and not to let her have any sugar. There didn't seem to be any fever, so I knew we were keeping the secondary infections at bay. I just couldn't stop that cough or figure out what was causing it. This went on for about six weeks before I discovered what I was dealing with.

Reading *Herbal Home Health Care* by Dr. Christopher I finally discovered this was not bronchitis, it was whooping cough. His description is:

> Symptoms are violent convulsive coughs (paroxysms), consisting of several expirations followed by a loud, sonorous whooping inspiration. This is generally a children's disease and begins with spasmodic coughing spells. The face reddens and the eyes bulge. Sore throat and often vomiting may occur. . . Whooping cough is a rapid accumulation of mucus in the throat, which causes choking and will cause death if not cleared. Eliminate the mucus as fast as possible. (116)

I had no idea where she had come in contact with this disease, but now I knew what I was dealing with. I looked through all of my books to research whooping cough. I learned that it usually lasts about three months and goes through varying stages. After the first week of incubation, there is nothing that can be done medically, it just has to run its course.

We have a four-poster bed, so we used sheets and rubber bands to completely enclose it. We set up a hot water vaporizer with eucalyptus oil inside our tent. *Herbal Home Health Care* referred to a recipe from Dr. Shook for whooping cough, so I made some of the syrup. The recipe for this syrup is:

> Two ounces marshmallow root, two ounces garden thyme, one quart distilled water. Slowly simmer the herbs in the distilled water until reduced to one pint, strain, press, return liquor to saucepan and add two pounds brown sugar (substitute honey if desired), simmer 5 minutes. Skim off scum as it rises, cool, bottle and keep in a cool place. For children use 1 tsp for cough. (118)

After researching everything possible, this is what we distilled it down to: we used the vaporizer in an enclosed area to open her breathing passages; we used Dr. Shook's formula for the cough and each night, I rubbed her chest and back down with lobelia, mullein oil, and the Anti-spasmodic tincture to help relax the spasms. At last, we were both able to get some sleep. She would have one or two spells per night and the rest of the time we could sleep.

In the last stages of the disease, she threw up whatever she had eaten at dinner. After a couple of weeks of this, I was really getting concerned because she did not have much of an appetite and she was so little she was beginning to look like one of the starving children on infomercials. David Christopher gave me some recommendations on what I could do to get her built back up. With toddlers it is especially hard, because they will not always drink the teas and thing that would do them the most good. He gave me several great suggestions, but the two that became the turning point for us was rubbing her down with olive oil two or three times per day and giving her raw goat's milk to drink. There have been cases where people have literally been kept alive just by rubbing them down with olive oil to feed their systems. The raw goat's milk has live enzymes in it which helped stimulate her digestive system, so she could hold her food down. I watched it turn her around. She started regaining more energy, she looked healthier and started regaining her appetite.

This experience shows that, again, we did not have an immediate, miraculous cure, but we were able to bring our daughter safely through a dangerous disease with no side-effects, no trauma from needles or strangers, and no secondary infections that would commonly occur in situations like this. The herbal treatments and hydrotherapy worked with her body to do what needed to be done to bring her body back into a healthy balance.

In June, Juanita visited some friends out of state. They told her that their two-year-old granddaughter had come down with whooping cough at the same time Megan had. They told her that she had been in the hospital for a while with whooping cough and had to return later with pneumonia. In June, ten months after getting the disease, she was still on antibiotics for all of the secondary infections and she would be on them for three to six months more. As hard as this disease was to take care of at home, I am so thankful that is what we were able to do and that the body was able to overcome it in four months instead of taking a year or more.

By being able to break our old emotional bonds and negative thought processes
-- which is what I believe is meant in the *Bible* by the phrase
"breaking the lineage of iniquity"
– we will be able to go forward in our lives and achieve our full potential.
-- D. Gary Young, N.D.

Diet-related diseases account for 68% of all deaths.
-- Dr. C. Everett Koop

When it comes to health, nine men in ten are suicides.
-- Benjamin Franklin

The cure of the part should not be attempted without treatment of the whole, and
also no attempt should be made to cure the body without the soul, and therefore
if the head and body are to be well you must begin by curing the mind:
That is the first thing . . . For this is the great error of our day in the treatment of
the human body; that physicians separate the soul from the body.
-- Plato, Chronicles 156 e

Chapter Ten
Not-So-Common Emergencies

Megan was still recovering from when she was sick with whooping cough. It was mild now and she coughs only once or so during the night, but it bothers me she had not fully shaken it yet.

One Saturday in January, she seemed to be coming down with a cold, so that evening I did a modified cold sheet treatment on her to try to stop it. I put her in a hot tub with cayenne and ginger, then wrapped her in a cold, wet sheet, bundled her up in a quilt and sat in the recliner with her.

On the ten o'clock news, they had a clip showing Primary Children's Hospital in Salt Lake City, they were talking about how the hospitals were all overflowing with young children who had a viral pneumonia they were calling RSV. They said that because it was viral there was nothing they could do for it except to let it run its course. However, they warned if the child's breathing becomes fast and labored or if the fever gets to high, bring them into the hospital. They could help with intravenous fluids and by giving oxygen. I recalled the statement that Dr. Christopher made when he said, "In the last days, the doctors will throw up their hands and say that there is nothing more that we can do."

At about 3:00 am, Megan's breathing became extremely rapid and labored. I didn't know how her little lungs and heart could keep up this pace for very long. The realization hit me that she was in critical condition and that she could die. I thought about a book I had been reading where we are admonished many times not to rely on the arm of flesh. I also thought about holding my grandson in the hospital two years before with his nose bleeding from the oxygen tube that had been put up his nose, and the four or five times he had been stuck trying to get the IV into his dehydrated veins. I thought about how the pioneers had lost their children to croup until the Indians had shown them how to place wild onions on their chests to open up their breathing.

I crossed a bridge that night and decided if Megan was going to die, she would do it peacefully in my arms and not in the ER. I pleaded with the Lord to show me what to do because I knew I was losing her. Up to this point, I have always felt very strong promptings on what to do and what to use. This time, as I pleaded for answers, the thought came into my mind, "You already know what to do. Be aggressive and fight back!"

Steve started boiling water for some catnip tea and chopping up some garlic. I took Megan back to the bathtub and put her in a hot tub of water with cayenne, ginger, and yarrow. As the yarrow would swirl around, I said, "Look, Meggie, the pretty flowers are coming to help you." When I took her out of the tub, while the pores were still open, I rubbed X-Ceptic tincture into her chest and back for the antibiotic properties, rubbed mullein oil into her chest and back to break up the congestion. We gave her the catnip enema to clean out the bowel, and then sliced up a warm onion to lay on her chest. Orally, I gave her Kid-e-mune (Echinacea), to boost her immune system and the Children's Composition formula. I also gave her a dropper full of lobelia to relax the bronchial tubes. We put the chopped garlic into Vaseline and packed it on the bottom of her feet, so that her body could draw on the antibiotic properties of the garlic. The last thing we did was start up the hot water vaporizer with eucalyptus oil in it to help her breathe.

Throughout the next 24 hours I repeated the hot tub, X-Ceptic, mullein oil, Kid-e-mune, Children's Composition formula, and onions five or six times. By sun-up she was breathing much better and by evening she was back to normal. For the next couple of days, I used the X-Ceptic and mullein oil externally, the Kid-e-mune and Children's Composition internally.

Daryl, a friend of mine, made some of Dr. Shook's garlic syrup and brought that to me. It was so potent I could only get Megan to take a little bit in a glass of grape juice twice a day. After three days, not only had we licked the virus, but the cough which had been lingering since September was gone! It was great to see her healthy again.

Dr. Shook's recipe for garlic syrup is:

Peel 1 pound garlic cloves; run them through a meat mincer and put into a large jar. Mix equal parts of pure vinegar and distilled water (sufficient to cover the minced garlic). Shake well and let stand for 4 hours. Strain and add an equal part of hot syrup of brown sugar. Stir and shake together. Seal and keep in a cool place. Note: Do not boil garlic.

As a student, Juanita was working in her schools custodial department. One Saturday morning I got a phone call asking if I could bring something to put on her hand because she had burned it.

Juanita said they were supposed to clear the walkways of snow that morning. She was the supervisor on the job and had three other people working with her which she was responsible for. When they went to get the shovels and chemicals, there were only three and a half pairs of gloves, so she gave the three pairs to her co-workers along with the shovels. She followed them, with one glove on to hold the bucket and used her bare hand to scatter the chemicals which melt the ice. When it didn't bother her hand for the first hour, she thought it would be okay. She didn't realize it takes time before you know the extent of a chemical burn.

Dr. Christopher's burn paste called for comfrey, wheat germ oil and raw honey. I couldn't find any wheat germ oil, so had to stop at the store to get some. One of the lessons I am learning this year is that if you want to be self-sufficient, there are certain supplies you need to keep on hand because emergencies never happen when it's convenient.

When we met Juanita at the college, one of her co-workers was with her, trying to help her. She had been burying her hand in the snow to get some relief from the pain. They had tried to get her to go to see a doctor at the clinic on campus, but she had refused, saying her parents were on the way. I had grabbed my aloe vera plant as I went out of the door, so I began by cutting open one of the leaves and coating her hand and fingers in the aloe vera gel from inside the leaf. We mixed up the burn paste and put a thick coating all over her hand and fingers. I had a cotton diaper with me which we tore into strips and wrapped her fingers individually, so they would not stick together. Then we made larger strips to wrap her whole hand with. We finished by wrapping the whole hand up with an Ace bandage. Her friend was fascinated by the whole procedure and was impressed by how much better Juanita was feeling when we finished. She had been extremely pale and shaky when we arrived from shock and pain.

We repeated the burn paste three more times during the weekend and by Tuesday, she was able to remove the wrappings and start using her hand again. There was no permanent damage or scars. Comfrey definitely is one of my favorite herbs, having a number of different uses, the one I love is its miraculous action as a "cell proliferate."

A month later, I was racing the clock, as usual, trying to make sure my family had dinner and that I was ready for class, having enrolled in massage therapy on Tuesday, Wednesday, & Thursday evenings. One of my children told me that a friend of theirs was in the bathroom and was in bad shape. They said the week before when they had all been sledding, Sean had wrecked on a three-ski and had come down hard on his scrotum. They said he had tried to suffer with it in silence for the past week, but now it was so swollen and sore, he had to tell. He had been to a doctor earlier in the day for a physical in order to turn his papers in to serve as a missionary. The doctor told him he may have split the testee and arranged for him to see another doctor later in the day. This was between visits.

When Sean came out of the bathroom, he looked terrible. His face was drawn with pain and he was having a hard time moving around. I quickly wrote out some instructions and gave them to Nathan. The instructions told him to use ¾ cup mullein and ¼ cup lobelia in a half gallon of water, simmer it down to half its original volume, strain it and soak a cotton diaper in it. Place on the swollen area for 20 minutes. Then use an ice pack. I told him to repeat the hot fomentations and ice pack as often as possible through the evening. Then I took off for class.

When I got home at midnight, Jenny was waiting up to inform me that we had saved Sean from surgery! Naturally, I was taken aback because I hadn't given it much thought after I told Nathan what to do.

Here is what happened. After I left, Sean's mother took him to the second doctor. The doctor told him he had to get his bladder empty by nine o'clock that evening or he would have to go to the hospital and be catherized. If they could not empty it that way, then he would have to go to surgery and have the urethra opened. Due to the tremendous pain, he had not completely emptied his bladder for a week. When Nathan went to his house to help with the fomentation, he remembered how we had used JuniPars to take the swelling out of Dana's arm, so he gave six of them to Sean. Then he made up the fomentation and had him apply it. After taking the six JuniPars and one round of the hot fomentation and ice pack, he was able to completely empty his bladder. It was about 8:40 pm.

Sean kept the fomentation on all night while he slept. The next day he was able to go to work and felt great. When he went back to the doctor for a checkup, the doctor said it was a miracle he had been healed so much in 24 hours. Then he gave him a shot of pain-killers. When he got back home, he walked in the front door and passed out from the narcotics.

    The last experience I would like to share was definitely a life-threatening situation. Again, I feel the need to emphasize that each person must decide for themselves what they are and are not comfortable taking care of at home. I want people to understand that there are alternatives to the system we have all come to rely on, but each person must decide what they are comfortable with and not feel trapped into doing things a certain way because of the people around them. One of the things I have come to a deep understanding of this year as I have studied herbology, midwifery, massage therapy, acupressure, and different forms of Chinese medicine is that truth is found in many different areas. Each of us need to seek out and adapt those pieces of truth into our life. Then set aside the pieces that do not fit. I have shared these thoughts with you because this next experience was a very special one to me and again, I felt directed to do what we did. I have a deep amount of respect and trust in the parents which were involved, but each individual is different and what worked for them may need to be adapted in a different way for someone else. Therefore, I would caution you to proceed carefully before attempting this yourself.

    We have had a long, cool, wet spring this year. All of a sudden, in June, summer hit with a vengeance. Tuesday morning Cherie called to say that Joe, her 18-year-old son, was in shock, that his arms were purple and she was afraid they were going to lose him. She said he had worked all day in the sun on Friday and Saturday. Sunday morning he slept in until noon, something he never does. He was quiet and reserved at church. That afternoon he played a little bit of basketball outside in the sun. By Monday, he couldn't hold anything down. At first they thought he had the flu and treated it accordingly. Unfortunately, one of the things they used was the "cold sheet treatment." Remember, we use this to create a fever and raise the heat in the body to sweat out toxins.

Cherie mentioned to the next-door neighbor that Joe was extremely sick. The neighbor said he had had too much sun. Cherie then realized she was dealing with a heat stroke. Monday night Cherie and Micka took turns keeping a cool cloth on Joe's head to cool him down, rubbing his temples to help with the severe headache, giving him some watermelon and any other fluids that might stay down to rehydrate him. Joe was extremely thirsty so he tended to gulp the fluids, then they would come back up. Tuesday morning his extremities had turned purple and cold, his face was flushed and hot. He told his mom he didn't hurt anymore.

When Cherie called, I told her I would be right over. As I had Myrna and Taunya put some things together, I called her back and suggested she start giving him some cayenne to help with his circulation.

I picked up the *School of Natural Healing* text and looked up "shock." It said:

> A state of profound depression of the vital processes due to various causes from emotional trauma to injury which reduces the blood pressure and venous return, thus impairing circulation which may cause irreversible circulatory failure and eventually death. (47)

Under the heading of Herbal Aids, it said:

> When a person goes into shock, the administration of medicinal aids orally will often be difficult or impossible. In this case an anus injection (or enema) which will cause relaxation is applicable. Use one cup (to a pint maximum) of catnip, peppermint, skullcap, spearmint, or valerian. Massage the abdomen and parts of the spine with lobelia

externally and make sure that the patient gets undisturbed rest. Cayenne should be taken internally to equalize the blood pressure and insure that the internal functions will remain stabilized during the intense systemic distress. (47)

We gathered up lobelia tincture, cayenne, catnip and the enema bucket. As I was leaving, Nathan reminded me that when a person has heat stroke, they lose a lot of the salts and minerals from their body. Driving to their home, I remembered that celery is full of organic salts and that alfalfa contains every mineral known to man.

When we arrived, Joe's extremities were grey-white to purple and cold to the touch. His face was extremely flushed and hot. He seemed to be very tired and not real coherent. Rolling him on to his stomach, we rubbed lobelia tincture into his spine. In shock, the central nervous system is in overload and lobelia will help it to relax. It is also a "thinking" herb so it can help to orchestrate the other herbs. Cherie had been giving him some "shock tea," which had helped to get some cayenne into his system. I suggested using some celery and alfalfa juice. In the mean time, we gave him two more cayenne capsules and started massaging him. Each of us took an arm or leg and started massaging to get the circulation back. As soon as it was ready, he was given the alfalfa and celery juice.

Myrna had brought along her massage table, so we put Joe on the table, applied more lobelia to his spine and then used olive oil to massage him. Gratefully, Myrna and Taunya had come with me. With Cherie and Micka, that made five of us to work on him. I applied a cold, damp cloth to the back of his neck, then massaged his back while the other four worked on each of his arms and legs. When the catnip tea was cooled down to room temperature, we had Joe give himself an enema, holding it in as long as possible to give his body a chance to absorb some of the fluid.

When he was finished, we gave him two more cayenne capsules and put him back on the table. We continued to work his neck, back, arms, legs, and feet trying to get the circulation back in them. His head began to throb again and his hands began to tingle. We told him this was a good sign because it meant we were making progress. I'm not sure he agreed. After we had massaged him for a couple of hours, his arms and legs were getting warmer, but his hands and feet were still dry and cold to the touch. I knew that Cherie was concerned about how purple they were and I felt like we needed to do more, but I wasn't sure what else to do. I tried to block out the talking and joking searching for inspiration. I knew the heat we needed in his hands and feet had to come from the inside out, but so far it wasn't going far enough to reach the feet and hands. We had brought it down his arms and legs, but it wasn't enough. Dr. Thompson taught that cold is death and heat is life. We needed a healthy, moist heat.

The feeling came to me that we needed to put him in a hot yarrow bath. I told Cherie what I wanted to do. She had the same concern I had, what would happen if we got him too hot again? She said she trusted my feelings, so we had his dad put him in a hot bath with yarrow. We told him to soak for as long as he was comfortable and to keep a cool wet cloth on his face, so his head would not start throbbing again.

Nervous about what we were doing, I looked in the *School of Natural Healing* again, looking up "circulation." It said,

> You should think of diaphoresis in any case where general circulation is involved such as inflammation of the lungs, pleurisy, peritonitis, inflammation of the stomach, spleen, bowels, kidneys, bladder, uterus or brain. It makes little difference where the trouble may be, diaphoresis is practically essential when you need to equalize the circulation. Maintain a frequent outward flow of blood, and you will have your patient on the highway to recovery. (233)

Yarrow is a diaphoretic herb; it draws out and induces perspiration. I was also concerned about kidney failure because his lower back was hurting, so I looked up "kidneys." It said,

> The nervous system is also influenced, and ultimately the whole circulation is affected as a result of an increased blood flow. Accompany internal diaphoretics by stimulating baths and friction with a coarse towel or massage." (234)

It then went on to describe the specific benefits of yarrow. How often I have seen this pattern repeated. We rely on a power greater than our own and then gain an understanding of the mechanics. Joe was in the tub for some time (his dad kept a close eye on him) and when he came out, his hands and feet were warm and pink. When I pressed in on his fingernails and let go; they went right back to their normal pink color. We had the circulation back! Now it was time for him to sleep and regain his strength.

As I was leaving, Cherie and Chad both thanked me for helping, I told them they were welcome, but I felt a deep sense of gratitude for being allowed to help. I am always in awe of the things we are being taught. As I drove home and thought back over the day, it became even more clear what the body had done. We put the salts and minerals back in his body with the celery and alfalfa, stabilized the circulation with the cayenne, relaxed the trauma to the central nervous system with the lobelia, introduced fluids with the catnip enema, stimulated the system with the massage along with feeding the body with the olive oil, and when the time was right, the yarrow and moist heat from the bath were able to draw everything out where it needed to be.

Later, my sister, Sue called from Tulsa and I told her what we had done. She works for an R.N. making reservations for an HMO. Sue told her boss what we had done and was surprised at how strong her reaction was to the situation. She told Sue we could not possibly have known how close to death he was. She said we should have had Joe in the emergency room. Sue asked what they would have done for him and she said they would have put him on intravenous fluids and electrolytes. Sue asked if that would have saved him. Her boss said they would have hoped so, but as far gone as his limbs were, it might have been too late. Sue was a little confused and asked why we should have taken him to the emergency room if they couldn't save him. Her boss informed her they were trained to deal with life and death situations.

Return with honor.
-- Mothers Everywhere

Be different. Then you can make a contribution.
Otherwise, you just echo something;
You're just a reflection.
-- Hugh Nibley

Conscience is that still small voice that is sometimes too loud for comfort.
-- Bert Murray

To live only for some future goal is shallow.
It's the sides of the mountain that sustain life, not the top.
-- Robert Pirsig

Chapter Eleven
Summary

As you can see, we have had an eventful year at our house. Some of these experiences have been funny, some have been frightening, but each one has turned out to be a wonderful learning experience. As I have tried to point out, I had some very strong feelings and convictions about what I was doing. I never advise anyone else to deal with potentially dangerous situations unless they have the same feelings and convictions. These decisions are something each family must decide on their own.

Herbal medicine is not a new fad. It has existed since the time of Adam. An advertisement in a magazine said:

> More than 50% of America's farm products today consists of plants used by the Indians before Columbus planted his flag. They include beans, chocolate, corn, cotton, peanuts, potatoes, pumpkins, tobacco and tomatoes. To combat illness, the Indian has given us arnica, cascara, cocaine, ipecac, oil of wintergreen, petroleum jelly, quinine and witch hazel. Botanists have yet to discover, in 400 years, any medicinal herb which was not used by the Indians.

In *Spirit Herbs,* Mary Atwood tells us:

> In his book, *American Indian Medicine,* Virgil Vogel points out that there is no question that the American Indians independently discovered the enema tube and bulb syringe and that their use was widespread. Animal or fish bladders were used in conjunction with inserts made from small hollow bones or reeds. Vogel quotes early reports of Indian medical practice.
>
> 'Pierre Charlevoix was certain that the Indians were 'in possession of secrets and remedies which are admirable'. . . 'A broken bone was immediately set and was perfectly solid in eight days time.' Of especial importance is his observation in 1721 of the use of enema syringes: 'In the northern parts they made much use of glisters, a bladder was their instrument for this purpose. They have a remedy for the bloody-flux which seldom or never fails; this is a juice expressed from the extremities of cedar branches after they have been well boiled.'

Native Americans believed that purging the body was a necessary precursor to religious rites (for the shaman) and healing rites (for the patient), regardless of the suspected reason for the illness. Sweat lodges, fasting, syringes and strong herbal mixtures promoted excretion of unwanted substances through perspiration (diaphoretic), vomiting (emetic) or ejection through the bowels (cathartic).

These cleansing practices, except for vomiting, continue to grow in popularity with certain health-oriented advocates. Enthusiasts attest to the benefits. If Native Americans used inner-body cleansing techniques, how badly do you think overfed, under exercised, overmedicated and chemically overloaded Americans need such methods! Yet they are generally avoided or considered unmentionable by the medical profession, including gastroenterologists, and the general public. (122 - 123)

We are told in the scriptures, " . . . if ye are prepared ye shall not fear." How many of us are prepared to take care of our own families in case of some disaster or ourselves, for that matter? Somehow in the last 100 years we have become programmed to believe that we need to shift the responsibility for our health to other people. We listen to the ads on television to tell us what is healthy to eat and then, the minute anything goes wrong we run to a doctor.

Admirably, many friends and family are in the various medical fields, and are people who have devoted their lives to the service of others. However, we should not be naïve enough to shift the responsibility of our own health and well-being to other people. The medical people of today are trained to work on serious problems, but not necessarily on how to prevent those problems from occurring. They are also greatly hindered by the medical system itself.

My son, Stephen called me one afternoon from Texas, wanting to know what to do with his two-month-old daughter, Elizabeth. They had taken her to the doctor with a mild fever and cold. The doctor wanted to do a spinal tap on her to check for spinal meningitis. I asked Stephen if anyone else had been sick in the family and he said that they had all been passing around a cold. I told him that it stood to reason that Elizabeth had the same thing they had all had and to get her out of there, explaining that the doctor was obligated to run these tests because if he doesn't and Elizabeth gets worse, he could be sued. Unfortunately, this kind of nonsense dictates a lot of the procedures that doctors have to follow in order to protect themselves. I told him, again, to get her out of there and take her home where she belongs.

I hope some of the experiences I have shared with you will help you to see that we all can take better control of our lives and our health. Our families are our stewardship and the way will be made open for each of us to be more prepared to take care of that stewardship if we will seek for the knowledge to do it and then have the faith and the strength to practice it. In 2 Timothy 1:7 we are told, "God hath not given us the spirit of fear; but of power, and of love, and of a sound mind."

Section II

Cleanse and Nourish

"Cleanse & Nourish" Overview

When I was 39-years-old, I began to have the experiences described in Section I, *A Year of Discovery*. Next month, I will be 50-years-old. In this incredible decade of experience and learning, my brother-in-law, graduated from medical school once told me, "Sandy, when I started medical school, one of the professors stood up and said, 'What you will learn today is "absolute truth" and you will accept it as "absolute truth", knowing that five years from now, there will probably be another "absolute truth." Ironically, science sees truth as hypothetical and evolving.

In some ways, this is how I feel about the last ten years. Before I began my study of herbs, I "knew" that we desperately needed doctors in our everyday lives for immunizations, disease, emergencies, healthy children, etc.. I "knew" that in order to raise healthy children, we had to feed them from the four basic food groups. As I began my study of herbs and nutrition, I came to understand that the things I had always known to be "truth" were not necessarily true any more. There were many things which could be taken care of better at home in a much more natural way. As I learned more, I came to take greater responsibility for my own health and the health of my family.

In the process, I attempted to convince many of my family members that they didn't need to run to the doctor all the time. I tried to convince them of many things that had taken me a life-time of experience to understand. As many of them became resentful and distant, I realized that each of us is at a different place on our journey; each of us is at a different level of understanding. Probably, one of the greatest things I came to understand is that each person has the right to make this journey at their own pace. If we try to force our ways of doing things on to someone else as the only way that is right, we have stepped over into the category of a "fanatic" and will alienate ourselves from those we love the most. When this happens we have lost the spirit of the very "truth" we are trying to embrace.

True optimal health is not about treating disease, naturally or unnaturally – it is about being disease-free, full of energy, physically active, mentally sharp, lean & strong, emotionally and spiritually at peace with yourself and the world around you. It is about literally finding health within yourself. There really are no "magic pills." You will never find it in a bottle of any kind. It is a choice you have to make. How badly do you want to achieve it? Are you willing to make the lifestyle changes necessary to tap into nature's vitality?

In the process of getting from where you are now to where you ultimately can be, there are many whole foods, juices, herbs, oils and supplements that can help to undo past damage, cleanse the system of toxins, and nourish the cells so that you can get where you want to be, but they are only aids – a means to an end – not the ultimate goal.

This section is designed to help you find a map that works for you; understanding that your path may not be exactly like someone else's. For example, if I were to ask each of my daughters to bring a fruit salad to dinner, each salad would be different and would probably contain different types of fruit, but the end result would be the same. Each would bring a delicious, healthy fruit salad to dinner. Each of us is different, part of a wonderful universe of different colors and personalities.

Absolute truth is eternal. It never changes. It will be the same yesterday, today and tomorrow. As we journey through life, we are presented with many pieces of truth, along with social conventions. Our goal, therefore, is to incorporate whatever truth we can into our present circumstances. For some, money is no object. For others, it is a constant struggle. For some, climate lends itself to plenty of fresh produce. For others, produce is rare. For some, life is relatively peaceful and uneventful. For others, life is a constant challenge. We have to find our own path to optimal health which will fit into the circumstances of our own lives – our own reality.

This section is about obtaining optimal health. Everything else we do is based on the foundation of "cleansing and nourishing." If you incorporate this foundation into your life – "you shall run and not be weary, and shall walk, and not faint . . . and shall find wisdom and great treasures of knowledge, even hidden treasures." (Smith)

To lengthen thy life, lessen thy meals.
-- Benjamin Franklin

Open your mind for the doors of wisdom are never shut.
-- Benjamin Franklin

The body heals itself:
The physician is only nature's assistant.
-- Hippocrates, the father of medicine

The doctor of the future will give no medicine,
but will interest his patients in the care of the human frame,
in diet, and in the cause and prevention of disease.
-- Thomas Edison

Chapter One
Health in America

Let's take a look at health in America at the beginning of the new millennium. How are we doing as a nation? Does education or wealth provide us with good health? If not, why?

The United Press released an article stating our money is not buying good health. Another article ranked the U.S. 24th for long, healthy life expectancy, which means there are 23 other countries in the world where people stand a better chance of living a long, healthy life without average American habits. This is ridiculous!! We live in the most affluent, industrialized country in the world with the most comfortable living conditions and it is killing us.

U.S. News and World Report, May 10, 1999, reports on the "killer" bacteria we are dealing with now. According to the article, we have caused this problem by the abuse and overuse of antibiotics. You see, bacteria are actually living organisms which are fighting for their life. When we constantly throw antibiotics at them, they are forced to mutate in order to live. Then we are forced to find a new antibiotic or immunization to combat them perpetuating a vicious circle. The article points out this is one of the reasons pneumonia has become such a dangerous condition. Mutant strains of bacteria have literally become immune to the antibiotics traditionally used to combat them.

In the July 26, 2000 issue of the Journal of the American Medical Association (JAMA, Vol. 284, No. 4) Barbara Starfield, MD, MPH of the Department of Health Policy and Management, John Hopkins School of Hygiene and Public Health, talks about the deficiencies of U.S. medical care.

- Evidence from a few studies indicate that 20 percent to 30 percent of patients receive contraindicated care
- An estimated 44,000 to 98,000 die each year as a result of medical errors
- The U.S. population does not have anywhere near the best health in the world. Of 13 countries in a recent comparison, the United States ranks an average of 12th (second from the bottom for 16 available health indicators)

- The U.S. ranks behind Japan, Sweden, Canada, France, Australia, Spain, Finland, the Netherlands, the United Kingdom, Denmark, and Belgium.
- The poor performance of the United States was recently confirmed by the World Health Organization, which used different indicators, and ranked the United States as 15th among 25 industrialized countries.
- 'The health care system also may contribute to poor health through its adverse effects.' For example:
    12,000 deaths/year from unnecessary surgery
    7,000 deaths/year from medication errors in hospitals
    20,000 deaths/year from other errors in hospitals
    80,000 deaths/year from nosocomial infections in hospitals (nosocomial infections are the kind of infections you get in a hospital such as staph)
    106,000 deaths/year from non-error, adverse effects of medications

'These total 225,000 deaths per year from iatrogenic causes'(iatrogenic means it was "doctor" induced).

- 'These estimates are for deaths only and do not include adverse effects that are associated with disability or discomfort.'
- If other estimates are used, the deaths due to iatrogenic causes would range from 230,000 to 284,000.
- 'In any case, 225,000 deaths per year constitutes the third leading cause of death in the United States, after deaths from heart disease and cancer.'
- An estimate of adverse effects in outpatient care and including adverse effects other than death concluded that between 4 percent and 18 percent of consecutive patients experience adverse effects in outpatient settings, resulting in 116 million extra physician visits, 77 million extra prescriptions, 17 million emergency department visits, 8 million hospitalizations, 3 million

long-term admissions, 199,000 additional deaths, and $77 billion in extra costs.

Starfield notes that there is a 'relationship between iatrogenic effects (including both error and non-error adverse events) and type of care received.' Specifically, there is a high availability of medical technology in the United States; i.e., the availability of MRI and CT in the U.S. is second only to Japan. However, Japan, ranks highest on health, whereas the United States ranks among the lowest. Starfield explains this by noting that the results of such diagnostic procedures often result in the patient being hospitalized, causing a 'cascade effect' that leads to an adverse iatrogenic event, while in Japan, such diagnostic procedures result in "the common practice of having family members rather than hospital staff provide the amenities of hospital care.'

- 'Recognition of the harmful effects of health care interventions, and the likely possibility that they account for a substantial proportion of the excess deaths in the United States compared with other comparably industrialized nations, sheds new light on imperatives for research and health policy.'

According to the American Medical Association's own journal, we learn the three leading causes of death in America are: Heart disease, cancer, and iatrogenic causes (mainly from prescription drugs).

According to Dr. Robert S. Mendelsohn, the statistics may look a little different:

Conservative estimates – such as that made by a congressional committee – say that about 2.4 million operations performed every year are unnecessary, and that these operations cost $4 billion and 12,000 lives, or five percent of the quarter million deaths following or during surgery each year. The independent Health Research Group says the number of unnecessary operations is more than 3 million. And various studies have put the number of useless operations between eleven and thirty percent. My feeling is that somewhere around ninety percent of surgery is a waste of time, energy, money and life.

One study, for example, closely reviewed people who were recommended for surgery. Not only did they find that most of them needed no surgery, but fully half of them needed no medical treatment at all. The formation of committees to review tissue removed in operations has resulted in some telling statistics. In one case, 262 appendectomies were performed the year before a tissue committee began overseeing surgery. During the first year of the committee's review, the number dropped to 178. Within a few years, the number dropped to 62. The percentage of normal appendices removed fell fifty-five percent. In another hospital, the number of appendectomies was slashed by two-thirds after a tissue committee went to work.

. . There are dozens of common operations they would no doubt see as useful most of the time, such as cancer surgery, coronary bypass surgery, and hysterectomies. Yet, as far as I am concerned, ninety percent of the most common operations, including these, are at best of little value and, at worst, quite harmful. (49-50)

Statistics like these suggest iatrogenic errors are actually a leading cause of death in America. Whatever the case, with few exceptions, iatrogenic causes, heart disease, and cancer are self-inflicted and entirely avoidable. It is time to wake up, as individuals and as a nation. If we want to live a long, healthy, productive life, we need to start making wiser choices when it comes to taking responsibility for our own health. This is not a responsibility we should shift to someone else.

In the field of mental health, we turn to *Toxic Psychiatry,* where Dr. Peter Breggin tells us:

Many people continue to think of the psychiatrist as the wise, warm, and caring person who will help them tackle their problems. But the modern psychiatrist may have no interest in 'talking therapy.' His or her entire training and commitment is more likely devoted to 'medical diagnosis' and 'physical treatment.' He or she may look at you with all the empathy and understanding of a pathologist staring through a microscope at germs, and then offer you a drug.

. . . Because this may be hard for you to believe, let me put it another way. The next time you go to a psychiatrist, you may find yourself in the office of someone who has never been taught how to talk with you about your problems or those of your family. Nor has he or she been trained to understand personal and family conflicts. Instead the doctor will listen, make some observations, jot down some notes, make a medicalized diagnosis, and prescribe a physical treatment. He or she may even draw blood and listen to your heart. Not your metaphorical heart; your flesh and blood heart. But as we'll see, attempts to substitute physical interventions for human services often are doomed to cause more harm than good. (11)

Statistics prove that health in America is not good. So, how have we done this to ourselves? There are many factors involved in this problem, some of which we have control over and some which we don't. Let's get started by looking at something we do have control over - our diet.

"You, the individual can do more for your health and well being
than any doctor, any hospital, any drug, any exotic medical device."
-- Surgeon General's Report

There is no safe drug. Eli Lilly himself once said that a drug without toxic
effects is no drug at all. Every drug has to be approached with suspicion.
--Robert S. Mendelsohn, M.D.

. . re-examine all you have been told at school or church or in any book, dismiss
what insults your soul, and your very flesh shall be great poem.
-- Walt Whitman
-- Leaves of Grass preface, 1855

Chapter Two
We Are What We Eat

At a health expo a few years ago in Southern California, I was in a booth next to a chiropractor who had written a book entitled, *Long Life Now.* I asked him what had inspired him to write this book. He said it originally began in Washington D.C. when he was 19-years-old, while he was serving there with the army. He and two of his comrades went to see the Washington monument for the first time. Being young and full of energy, they ran up the steps to the monument. Years later at the age of 36, he went back to climb those 898 steps again, only to find that the stairway was closed and had been closed for some time! It seems there were too many 30 and 40-year-old men having heart attacks attempting to climb the stairs. He said the monument was not only a powerful symbol of our nation, but, now, it had become a powerful symbol of our nation's ill-health.

He decided to research what makes us so different from people who have been discovered in remote areas of the world who live long, healthy lives, relatively disease free, mentally alert, physically active, living past the age of 100 and dying with all of their teeth and hair. One of the areas Dr. Lee Hitchcox looked at was diet. The pyramid he created from the Hunza diet, a people known for their longevity, looked like this:

Long Life Now Diet Pyramid

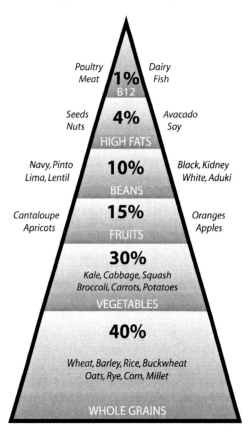

As you can see, 40% of their diet came from whole grains, things such as; wheat, barley, oats, etc.. Then, 30% from vegetables; notice that we are not talking about iceberg lettuce here. We are talking about dark green and yellow vegetables like broccoli, cabbage, kale, and things that will stay fresh through the winter such as potatoes and squash. Then, 15% of the diet is from fresh fruit, 10% from legumes, and 4% of the diet comes from foods high in fats, such as avocados, nuts and seeds. These are the types of fats that the body needs, can easily digest and readily use. This is a completely different type of fat than what you would find in modern day shortenings and processed cooking oils. Only 1%

of the diet comes from animal products such as meat and dairy! The type of dairy that is used sparingly in this example is fresh goat's milk, not homogenized, pasteurized cow's milk.

Now let's compare this pyramid to the average American diet:

Average American Diet Pyramid

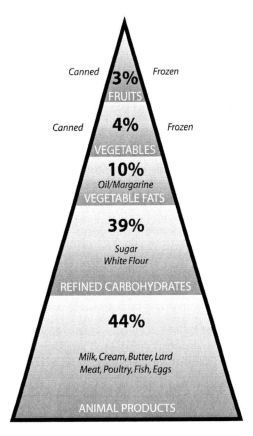

In the average American diet, 44% of our consumption is from animal products! The most detrimental part of this is not the fact that almost half of our diet is coming from dead animals, but the contaminants in those animals and their by-products, such as eggs and milk. If you are buying meat and animal products from a grocery store, you need to understand that most of those animals have been pumped full of steroids, hormones, immunizations, antibiotics, and pesticides. There are a lot of chemicals used on these animals to get them to grow fast and live long enough to make it to the slaughter house. When you ingest any of these products into your body, you are also taking in all of these chemicals. In *Mad Cowboy* by Howard F. Lyman he states,

> Nearly all meat in America is contaminated with such man-made carcinogens as dioxins, a family of chemicals related to Agent Orange, and DDT, the notorious chemical that was banned domestically over twenty-five years ago but that remains in the ground (and will remain there, unfortunately, for thousands of years to come) and therefore in the crops fed to animals. Crops grown for cattle feed are permitted to, and almost always do, contain far higher levels of pesticides than crops grown for human consumption. About 80 percent of pesticides used in America are targeted on four specific crops – corn, soybeans, cotton, and wheat – that are the major constituents of livestock feed. Since animals store pesticides and other toxic substances in their fat, they get their most concentrated doses of these carcinogens when they eat other animals. And we in turn get even more concentrated doses of carcinogens when we eat them.
>
> According to a 1975 study by the Council on Environmental Quality, 95 percent of the human intake of DDT came from dairy and meat products (21).

After reading these statistics, one of our first questions should be, "aren't cows herbivores? How could they possibly consume another animal?" Taken from the same book, we read,

> When a cow is slaughtered, about half of it by weight is not eaten by humans: the intestines and their contents, the head, hooves, and horns, as well as bones and blood. These are dumped into giant grinders at rendering plants, as are the entire bodies of cows and other farm animals known to be diseased. Rendering is a $2.4 billion-a-year industry, processing forty billion pounds of dead animals a year. There is simply no such thing in America as an animal too ravaged by disease, too cancerous, or too putrid to be

welcomed by the all-embracing arms of the renderer. Another staple of the renderer's diet, in addition to farm animals, is euthanized pets - the six or seven million dogs and cats that are killed in animal shelters every year. The city of Los Angeles alone, for example, sends some two hundred tons of euthanized cats and dogs to a rendering plant every month. Added to the blend are the euthanized catch of animal control agencies, and roadkill. (Roadkill is not collected daily, and in the summer, the better roadkill collection crews can generally smell it before they can see it.) When this gruesome mix is ground and steam-cooked, the lighter, fatty material floating to the top gets refined for use in such products as cosmetics, lubricants, soaps, candles, and waxes. The heavier protein material is dried and pulverized into a brown powder - about a quarter of which consists of fecal material. The powder is used as an additive to almost all pet food as well as to livestock feed. Farmers call it 'protein concentrates.' In 1995, five million tons of processed slaughterhouse leftovers were sold for animal feed in the United States. I used to feed tons of the stuff to my own livestock. It never concerned me that I was feeding cattle to cattle.

In August 1997, in response to growing concern about the spread of bovine spongiform encephalopathy (or Mad Cow disease), the FDA issued a new regulation that bans the feeding of ruminant protein (protein from cud-chewing animals) to ruminants; therefore, to the extent that the regulation is actually enforced, cattle are no longer quite the cannibals that we had made them into. They are no longer eating solid parts of other cattle, or sheep, or goats. They still munch, however, on ground up dead horses, dogs, cats, pigs, chickens, and turkeys, as well as blood and fecal material of their own species and that of chickens. About 75 percent of the ninety million beef cattle in America are routinely given feed that has been 'enriched' with rendered animal parts. The use of animal excrement in feed is common as well, as livestock operators have

found it to be an efficient way of disposing of a portion of
the 1.6 million tons of livestock wastes generated annually
by their industry. In Arkansas, for example, the average
farm feeds over fifty tons of chicken litter to cattle every
year. One Arkansas cattle farmer was quoted in U.S. News
& World Report as having recently purchased 745 tons of
litter collected from the floors of local chicken-raising
operations. After mixing it with small amounts of soybean
bran, he then feeds it to his eight hundred head of cattle,
making them, in his words, "fat as butterballs." He
explained, 'If I didn't have chicken litter, I'd have to sell
half my herd. Other feeds are too expensive.' If you are a
meat-eater, understand that this is the food of your food.
(12-13)

O.K., so much for some of the chemicals and other
contaminants that are in animal products. Let's take a minute to
just consider dairy products. If we were to look at this from a
logical standpoint; how many other mammals drink milk after they
have been weaned? Humans are the only mammals on the face of
the planet who drink milk after they have been weaned, except for
our domestic pets which we have corrupted. Cow's milk is the
"perfect" food – for a calf that needs to go from 60 pounds to 300
pounds in one year.

The fact is: the drinking of cow milk has been linked to
iron-deficiency anemia in infants and children; it has been
named as the cause of cramps and diarrhea in much of the
world's population, and the cause of multiple forms of
allergy as well; and the possibility has been raised that it
may play a central role in the origins of atherosclerosis and
heart attacks. . . Most lay persons are not aware that the
milk of mammalian species varies considerably in its
composition. For example, the milk of goats, elephants,
cows, camels, yaks, wolves, and walruses show marked
differences, one from the other, in their content of fats,
protein, sugar, and minerals. Each was designed to
provide optimum nutrition to the young of the respective
species. Each is different from human milk. . . The

Federal Trade Commission in April, 1974, issued a 'proposed complaint' against the California Milk Producers Advisory Board and their advertising agency. In this complaint they cited the slogan 'Everybody Needs Milk' as representing false, misleading, and deceptive advertising. The Federal Trade Commission judged that enthusiastic testimonials by celebrities such as Olympic swimmer Mark Spitz, baseball pitcher Vida Blue, dancer Ray Bolger, columnist Abigail Van Buren, and singer Florence Henderson conveyed an inaccurate picture of the value of milk as a food. Quickly the dairymen changed their approach and came up with a new slogan: 'Milk Has Something for Everybody.' This is certainly technically correct. The question you must ask yourself before you drink that next glass of milk, however, is: do you really want that 'something?'(Oski 3-5)

People often include milk in their diet in order to get enough calcium. Women, who are concerned about osteoporosis often include dairy products in their diet, and in the diets of their children, to build strong bones. However, when we look at the following study, we realize this may not be the best source of calcium to use.

A 12-year Harvard study of 78,000 women demonstrated that those who drink cow's milk are more likely to have osteoporosis and brittle bones. . . The countries that consume the most cow's milk have the highest rates of osteoporosis. . . most people do not have the enzymes necessary to digest dairy products from cows. Cow's milk and cow cheeses are gluey, mucus-forming, and sticky – especially when pasteurized. Pasteurization destroys beneficial probiotic cultures (good bacteria) in the milk. (Wolfe 50-51 Beauty)

Dr. Christopher also warns against the use of dairy products.

Eliminate all dairy products - which include butter, cheese, cottage cheese, milk, yogurt, etc. These are all mucus-forming substances and, in most cases, are extremely high in cholesterol (especially butter). (Christopher 7 Diet)

In *The Miracle of Fasting,* Paul Bragg points out that not only are dairy products unhealthy, extremely mucus-forming, but are also totally indigestible.

All dairy products are especially mucus-forming. No animal in the world except man drinks milk after being weaned. The modern diet includes butter and butter substitutes, margarines, processed shortenings and hydrogenated oils and fats which are the plugging saturated fats. These are unhealthy for the body. Our bodies have a normal temperature of 98.6 degrees. To digest and assimilate these solid, hardened, saturated fats, we would have to have a heat of 300 degrees in our bodies. (106)

Let's continue to take a look at the pyramid. Refined white sugar and flour make up 39% of the American diet. When Dr. Christopher (founder of the School of Natural Healing) was alive, he would not even let his staff refer to these products as food. He said the only thing it was good for was wall paper paste, which is exactly how it acts in our intestines. Paul A. Stitt, a former corporate biochemist said,

Wheat flour is one food which is especially ravaged by processing. In the refining process, more than half of each of the most essential nutrients is sold for making pet food. The milling process destroys 40% of the chromium present in the whole grain, as well as 86% of the manganese, 89% of the cobolt, 68% of the copper, 78% of the zinc, and 48% of molybdenum. By the time it is completely refined, it has lost most of its phosphorus, iron, and thiamine, and a good deal of its niacin and riboflavin. Its crude fiber content has been cut down considerably as well. White flour is wheat flour that has been plundered of most of its vitamin E, important oils and amino acids. Yet all of these nutrients are needed for a satisfied, healthy body. While whole-wheat flour is one of the most nutritious foods, processing sees to it that the white flour found in most products is nutritionally worthless. (127-128)

Dr. Christopher adds a second witness to the detrimental nature of processed flour.

Flour, when heated and baked at high temperatures, changes to a mucus-forming substance. This is no longer a food, which means it has no life remaining therein. All wholesome food is organic, where unwholesome food or dead food is inorganic. (7 Diet)

Many books have been written on the damaging and addictive properties of sugar. In *Sugar Blues,* William Dufty gives us a short description of what sugar does in our system;

Refined sugar is lethal when ingested by humans because it provides only that which nutritionists describe as empty or naked calories. In addition, sugar is worse than nothing because it drains and leeches the body of precious vitamins and minerals through the demand of its digestion, detoxification, and elimination made upon one's entire system.

So essential is balance to our bodies, that we have many ways to provide against the sudden shock of a heavy intake of sugar. Minerals such as sodium (from salt), potassium and magnesium (from vegetables), and calcium (from bones) are mobilized and used in chemical transmutation; neutral acids are produced which attempt to return the acid-alkaline balance factor of the blood to a more normal state.

Sugar taken every day produces a continuously over-acid condition, and more and more minerals are required from deep in the body in the attempt to rectify the imbalance. Finally, in order to protect the blood, so much calcium is taken from the bones and teeth that decay and general weakening begin.

Excess sugar eventually affects every organ in the body. Initially, it is stored in the liver in the form of glucose (glycogen). Since the liver's capacity is limited, a daily intake of refined sugar (above the required amount of natural sugar) soon makes the liver expand like a balloon. When the liver is filled to its maximum capacity, the excess glycogen is returned to the blood in the form of fatty acids.

These are taken to every part of the body and stored in the most inactive areas: the belly, the buttocks, the breasts, and the thighs.

When these comparatively harmless places are completely filled, fatty acids are then distributed among active organs, such as the heart and kidneys. These begin to slow down; finally their tissues degenerate and turn to fat. The whole body is affected by their reduced ability and abnormal blood pressure is created. Refined sugar lacks natural minerals (which are, however, in the sugar beat or cane). Our parasympathetic nervous system is affected; and organs governed by it, such as the small brain, become inactive or paralyzed. (Normal brain function is rarely thought of as being as biologic as digestion.) The circulatory and lymphatic systems are invaded, and the quality of the red corpuscles starts to change. An overabundance of white cells occurs, and the creation of tissue becomes slower.

Our body's tolerance and immunizing power becomes more limited, so we cannot respond properly to extreme attacks, whether they be cold, heat, mosquitoes, or microbes. Excessive sugar has a strong mal-effect on the functioning of the brain; the key to orderly brain function is glutamic acid, a vital compound found in many vegetables. The B vitamins play a major role in dividing glutamic acid into antagonistic-complementary compounds which produce a 'proceed' or 'control' response in the brain. B vitamins are also manufactured by symbiotic bacteria which live in our intestines. When refined sugar is taken daily, these bacteria wither and die, and our stock of B vitamins gets very low. Too much sugar makes one sleepy; our ability to calculate and remember is lost. (137-138)

In the average American diet, 10% is coming from vegetable fats; products such as margarine.

Margarine contains trans fats (hydrogenated fats) which elevate cholesterol more than other types of fat. Cancer and heart disease deaths are highest among users of trans fats. (Hitchcox 165)

Vegetables make up 4% of the diet, look at the side notes: canned or frozen. It's the same story with the 3% of fruits we consume. Instead of eating them fresh, we wait until they have been embalmed and then we eat them!

As you can see by looking at this pyramid, there is nothing on it that is still alive! We build life with life! The body is amazing. It will do everything it can to sustain life, struggle, adapt and endure as long as possible no matter how badly we abuse it, but sooner or later the degeneration begins to show.

A few generations ago, people maintained fairly good health until they were about 40 or 50-years-old. Then the arthritis, bursitis and high blood pressure began to set in and everyone would comment by saying, "Welcome to middle age." Each of us just accepted these symptoms as signs of growing older.

"In 1977, the United States had the dubious distinction of becoming the first nation in history whose people consumed more than 50 percent of their diet as processed items" (Wigmore 12). Since that time the consumption of processed food has grown by leaps and bounds. There are children in this generation who eat all of their food processed and the health of our nation is telling the story. Not only are we seeing obesity and heart disease in young children, but symptoms that we used to consider signs of middle age are now showing up in teenagers and young adults. Not to mention all of the new diseases that scientists and doctors are constantly trying to put new names to such as chronic fatigue syndrome, fibromyalgia, and others that our great grandparents had never heard of.

We are destroying ourselves by our lifestyles. Our poor bodies just cannot keep up with the abuse that is being heaped upon them from generation to generation. People who lived in Old Testament times had amazing health, strength and longevity. What has changed? Are we so different anatomically from what they were? In *Fast Food Nation,* Eric Schlosser tells us:

> What we eat has changed more in the last forty years than in the previous forty thousand. . . . The fast food chains

now stand atop a huge food-industrial complex that has
gained control of American agriculture. . . .Hundreds of
millions of people buy fast food every day without giving it
much thought, unaware of the subtle and not so subtle
ramifications of their purchases. They rarely consider
where this food came from, how it was made, what it is
doing to the community around them. They just grab their
tray off the counter, find a table, take a seat, unwrap the
paper, and dig in . . . .(Schlosser 10)
When food is processed, there is no way for us to know all of
the ingredients that have gone into the processing because the food
companies are not required to put all of the ingredients on the
labels. For instance, taken from the same book, we read:

The Food and Drug Administration does not require
flavor companies to disclose the ingredients of their
additives, so long as all the chemicals are considered by the
agency to be GRAS (Generally Regarded as Safe). This
lack of public disclosure enables the companies to maintain
the secrecy of their formulas. It also hides the fact that
flavor compounds sometimes contain more ingredients than
the foods being given their taste. The ubiquitous phrase
"artificial strawberry flavor" gives little hint of the
chemical wizardry and manufacturing skill that can make a
highly processed food taste like a strawberry.

A typical artificial strawberry flavor, like the kind found
in a Burger King strawberry milk shake, contains the
following ingredients: amyl acetate, amyl butyrate, amyl
valerate, anethol, anisyl formate, benzyl acetate, benzyl
isobutyrate, butyric acid, cinnamyl isobutyrate, cinnamyl
valerate, cognac essential oil, diacetyl, dipropyl ketone,
ethyl acetate, ethyl amylketone, ethyl butyrate, ethyl
cinnamate, ethyl heptanoate, ethyl heptylate, ethyl lactate,
ethyl methylphenylglycidate, ethyl nitrate, ethyl propionate,
ethyl valerate, heliotropin, hydroxyphenyl-2-butanone (10
percent solution in alcohol), aionone, isobutyl anthranilate,
isobutyl butyrate, lemon essential oil, maltol, 4-
methylacetophenone, methyl anthranilate, methyl benzoate,

methyl cinnamate, methyl heptine carbonate, methyl naphthyl ketone, methyl salicylate, mint essential oil, neroli essential oil, nerolin, neryl isobutyrate, orris butter, phenethyl alcohol, rose, rum ether, y-undecalactone, vanillin, and solvent. (Schlosser125-126)

The really disparaging thing is; how many people really know what all of these fancy words mean? Unless you are a chemist, how do you know what you are eating? For example, in many foods there is an ingredient referred to as carmine. Few know where this ingredient comes from.

One of the most widely used color additives – whose presence is often hidden by the phrase "color added" – violates a number of religious dietary restrictions, may cause allergic reactions in susceptible people, and comes from an unusual source. Cochineal extract (also known as carmine or carminic acid) is made from the desiccated bodies of female Dactlyopius coccus Costa, a small insect harvested mainly in Peru and the Canary Islands. The bug feeds on red cactus berries and color from the berries accumulates in the females and their unhatched larvae. The insects are collected, dried, and ground into pigment. It takes about 70,000 of them to produce one pound of carmine, which is used to make processed foods look pink, red, or purple. Dannon strawberry yogurt gets its color from carmine, as do many frozen fruit bars, candies, fruit fillings and Ocean Spray pink-grapefruit juice drink." (Schlosser 128-129)

This drives home the point that none of these things contain "live" enzymes. They are all processed, dead, chemically treated matter. This type of diet not only introduces a tremendous amount of toxic matter into the system, but it also causes a lot of mucus. Along with poisoning ourselves with chemicals, all of these processed products create a very acidic environment in the body which is a prime environment for disease to take hold. Our systems are over-loaded trying to process and eliminate all of the toxins, while, at the same time it is not being given anything alive to rebuild itself. To build life with life, we have to begin to turn this problem around.

In the scriptures we are told, ". . . from dust thou art, and unto dust shalt thou return" (Genesis 3:19). Ironically, as adults, our mortal bodies are made up from the same composition as mother earth. That is, 70% water (alkaline) and 30% matter (acid). In order to maintain this delicate balance we should be eating 70 – 80% alkaline producing foods and 20 – 30% acid producing foods. Basically speaking, alkaline producing foods come from fresh, raw fruits, vegetables, and sprouts. Acidic foods would be nuts, seeds, legumes, grains and anything that is processed. If we were to use this basic analogy, then every time we sit down to eat, we would need to have some form of salad covering about 70% of our plate, with 30% going to the acidic foods. Are you beginning to see how far we have deviated from the needs of our body in the name of convenience, conformity, and satisfying our addictions?

Dr. Robert Young suggests that in order to return our bodies to a more alkaline state, our food pyramid should look more like this:

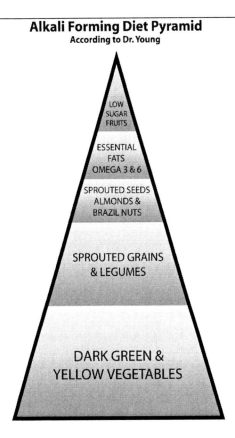

Alkali Forming Diet Pyramid
According to Dr. Young

LOW
SUGAR
FRUITS

ESSENTIAL
FATS
OMEGA 3 & 6

SPROUTED SEEDS
ALMONDS &
BRAZIL NUTS

SPROUTED GRAINS
& LEGUMES

DARK GREEN &
YELLOW VEGETABLES

As you can see, most of the diet would consist of dark green & yellow vegetables, eating as many raw as possible, followed by sprouted grains & legumes. The essential fats would come from eating foods high in the omega 3 & 6 fatty acids such as nuts, avocados, olive oil, flax oil, etc. Young believes:

> . . . there is only one physiological disease – the over-acidification of the body, due primarily to an inverted way of eating and living. This over-acidification leads to the one sickness, or primary symptom – the overgrowth in the body of microorganisms, whose poisons produce the symptoms we call "diseases." (title page)

Louis Pasteur is credited with introducing the "germ theory" which teaches us that disease comes from the outside in. In other words, if we come in contact with a bacteria, virus, toxin or other disease-causing organism, we will become sick. Based on his theories, immunizations were introduced as a way to protect against these "infectious" organisms. This is the foundation that our American Medical Association and pharmaceuticals are built on.

At the same time that Pasteur was working on his theory, another scientist by the name of Antoine Bechamp believed that disease comes from the inside-out, not the outside-in. He believed that the environment was everything. For example, if someone were to walk into a room full of people and sneeze, exposing everyone to the same bacteria, why would half of the people get sick and the other half wouldn't? According to Bechamp's theory, it would be because half of the people in the room had a "welcome mat" out; meaning that the environment was right for the bacteria to thrive (acidic), whereas half of the room may have had a stronger immune system and cleaner environment (more alkaline), so no self-respecting bacteria would stick around.

We now have the technology to show that Bechamp was right. The environment within our body really is everything. Young also brings up another interesting idea – it is not just what we eat which can cause us to be overly acidic – it is also the way we live. Lifestyles of extreme stress, feelings of hatred, bitterness, anger and other negative emotions can weaken the immune system, cause over-acidification in the body and many symtomologies of disease.

So far we have looked at the diet of the Hunza, the typical American diet, and an alkaline producing diet. To build life with life, it just makes sense that the more raw, live food we can introduce into our diet the better off we will be.

In David Wolfe's book, *The Sunfood Diet,* he recommends a little different twist to the typical food pyramid. He states, ". . . raw plant food – is the key to unlocking humanity's dormant powers" (13).

The *Sunfood Diet* is a 100% raw food diet. Everything that is eaten is full of life. This may be the ultimate way for anyone to eat who wants to experience healthy living. However, as stated, depending on your living conditions, work environment, climate, economic circumstances – your reality – this type of a diet is not always possible or practical. It is, however, a goal worth moving toward when it comes to bringing more fresh, live food into our diets.

In *The Sunfood Diet,* Wolfe states:

> I discovered there are three essentials to The Raw-Food Diet (actually to any diet) or imbalances will occur. One can eat other foods, but these three elements must be there to achieve harmony. In every single long-term 100% raw-foodist I have encountered, I discovered the following dietary pattern:
> 1. Green-leafy vegetables
> 2. Sweet fruits
> 3. Fatty foods
> If one of these food classes is missing in the diet for a significant period of time (ranging from a few weeks to several months), imbalances will occur. (158)

The balance Wolfe he is referring to would look like this:

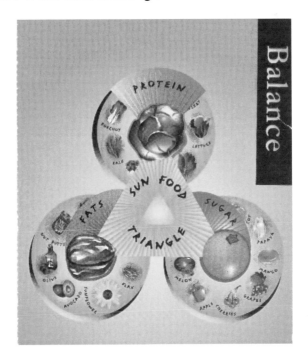

In the protein circle are mainly green-leafed foods.
     Green-leafed vegetables are the true body builders. They
     are our true 'protein food'. They contain all the amino
     acids we require. Real strength and building material
     comes from green-leafed vegetables where the amino acids
     are found. If we look at the gorilla, zebra, giraffe, hippo,
     rhino, or elephant we find they build their enormous
     musculature on green-leafy vegetation . . . protein can be
     adequately supplied by raw plant foods. Animal protein is
     not necessary. The consumption of cooked animal protein
     has been statistically correlated with all the major diseases
     of civilization. As the cooked animal protein increases in
     the diet, the rate of disease increases in a one-to-one
     correlation (for more on this see John Robbin's book *Diet
     For a New America*) Most of the diseases of civilization are
     actually caused by animal-protein poisoning because
     protein-dominant animal foods are acid-forming and not
     natural foods for humans to consume. Fat-dominant plant
     foods are far more important. (187)
In the sugar circle are the fresh fruits.
     Eat natural sugar foods for intelligence. Cognition is
     dependent on blood sugar. Our brains run exclusively on
     oxygen and glucose (fruit sugar). That ought to give us a
     clue as to what our natural fuel is. Glucose is the fuel of
     our being. . . but it must be taken in the correct form. Sugar
     in the diet should come from one primary source: sweet
     fruits with seeds. (169)
In the fats circle we find the nuts, seeds, avocados, and olives.
     Eat fatty raw plant foods for longevity. Living a long and
     vibrant life is a matter of minimizing free radical damage to
     the body through a diet rich in antioxidants. A free radical
     is an electron-deficient molecule produced from oxygen
     and cooked fat in the body. In seeking to acquire another
     electron, a free radical is capable of combining with and
     destroying enzymes, amino acids, and other cellular
     elements. Whole plant foods rich in polyunsaturated fat
     (walnuts, sunflower seeds, flax seeds, hemp seeds) always

contain antioxidants, such as Vitamins E, C, carotene, and selenium. Other raw plant foods, such as citrus fruits, contain the antioxidant bioflavonoids. Deep green leaves contain the antioxidant beta-carotene. (181)

What are the benefits of living on a diet such as the one we have just discussed. Again, turning to *Sunfood Diet,* we read the testimony of David Wolfe:

> Words alone cannot describe the level of health I have been privileged to attain eating a 100% raw plant-food diet. All that comes to mind is that I feel an immense gratitude. . . When I went raw, I began to study the simple things, like my fingers and toes. I marveled at their dexterity and the functions they served. I became very aware of all my bodily systems: respiratory, circulatory, cardiac, glandular, and digestive. I was awestruck at the efficiency of our human organs. How could I ever have taken my body for granted? How could anyone? It was like being a billionaire and not realizing that you are rich. I thought about the less tangible things like sleep cycles, dreams, and the true nature of Life. I was filled with a new-found reverence for all living things. (277)

We have looked at several different diets in this chapter and discussed the pros and cons of many different foods. Begin to set goals and improve where you are. If you are living on a diet of processed foods, then begin now to add more fresh fruits and vegetables. If you are a junk-food junkie, begin now to start snacking on things like fresh fruit smoothies, raw nuts, raisins, fruit – things that will satisfy your craving for sweets and fats.

Do not begin your journey with a guilt trip. Begin with a determination to make today better than yesterday – to move in a positive direction. Life is a challenge. Decide now that you are equal to the challenge. The point is, begin where you are comfortable. Take this information one step at a time and incorporate it into your life where it feels right and appropriate.

A wise man should consider health is the greatest of human blessings.
-- Hippocrates, the father of medicine

Eat to live, not live to eat.
-- Benjamin Franklin

Let food be your medicine and medicine be your food.
-- Hippocrates

Chapter Three
Channels of Elimination

In the early 1800's there was an herbalist by the name of Samuel Thompson. Quite often his teachings are referred to as "Thompsonian medicine." He had an enlightening analogy on how the human body works. He would compare the body to a wood stove. If you put clean burning fuel into a wood stove, you will get a lot of abundant heat with very little waste. The human body works in the same way – if you put the right kind of fuel into the body – you will have boundless energy with very little waste. If, however, you put in the wrong type of fuel – you will have very little heat (or energy) and a lot of waste.

To extend this metaphor, the wood stove has four chimneys on it representing the main four channels of elimination in the human body:

1. respiratory
2. digestive
3. urinary
4. skin

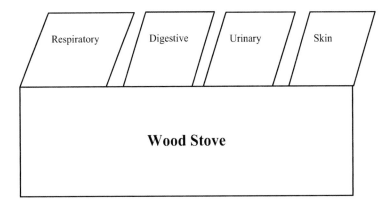

Now, if each of us can agree that the "Creator" knew what He was doing when He created us, that we are not some type of experimental model, then we can all agree that this body was designed to work properly. If this is the case, then we need to understand that when the body takes in something that does not belong in it – such as bacteria, a virus or any other type of toxin, the body attempts to eliminate it.

If the body uses the respiratory system to eliminate the problem, we will see symptoms such as; a runny nose, runny eyes, sneezing, cold-like symptoms. This is why modern medicine will never find a cure for the "common cold." The cold is the cure! The body is trying to eliminate something that does not belong there. Most of us since childhood have been taught that a runny nose is not socially acceptable, so we reach for a decongestant or anti-histamine to stop the body from doing what it was designed to do. When we do this, we drive the problem deeper, which is why a cold will last for 10 to 14 days and then, quite often, go into a secondary infection of some kind; such as an ear infection or bronchitis. In our house, a cold lasts no more than 24 – 48 hours because we have learned to help the body eliminate whatever is causing the problem.

If the body chooses the digestive system to eliminate through, we will see symptoms such as diarrhea, nausea or other flu-like symptoms. If the body chooses the urinary system, we might see a bladder infection or kidney stones. If the body chooses the skin, we might see things such as acne, eczema, moles, warts, any thing out of the ordinary that appears on the skin. All of these are signs that the body is trying to eliminate something. Therefore, if we run to the store and buy some cortisone cream to put on the skin for a problem area, have we fixed the problem? No! We may relieve some of the symptoms, such as burning or itching, but we have not fixed what is causing the problem.

When I first began to study alternative methods of healing, I used to consider some of the early herbalists, such as: Samuel Thompson, Jethro Kloss, John Christopher, to be extremely "sadistic." When looking up a child's upper respiratory infection, for example, the first thing many of them would recommend was an enema. In the early days, I would think, "What is the matter with them? The problem is not even on that end!" I have now come to understand that those early herbalists had a good understanding of how the body works.

You see, if the body chooses one of those four chimneys to eliminate waste and it is plugged up – it has to choose a different chimney for elimination. Usually, the body will the digestive system to eliminate. If, however, it is plugged up, the body will quite often use the respiratory system. The early herbalists understood this, so they would recommend using an enema. Knowing that if this channel was open – the body would eliminate where it wanted to in the first place and the cold symptoms would disappear.

Can you begin to see how holistic this health paradigm is from the one we have been traditionally taught? The body knows what it is doing! We need to learn how to work with it and provide it with what it needs to succeed instead of always trying to treat symptoms.

This is the foundational law of "cleanse and nourish." If we understand that the body is a "whole" entity that is all connected, then we will come to understand that we have to treat the "whole" body, not just the area where we are seeing symptoms. When we "cleanse and nourish," we eliminate the body's toxins and then we give it the tools (nourishment) it needs to rebuild itself.

Consider another analogy to help bring this into perspective. If you had a fish tank which was filthy and the fish were sick, would you treat the fish or clean up the tank. Anyone who has ever even owned a gold fish knows that you have to clean up the tank or the fish will never get better. It is the same with the human body. Every cell is bathed in fluid. If we do not clean up the environment, we can not expect the body to heal itself. We may be able to clear up a few symptoms temporarily, but if we have not cleaned out what is causing the problem, we will see the symptoms resurface again and again – not only in the same way, but also in other parts of the body.

In the last chapter, we compared Pasteur's and Bechamp's theories of disease and environment. Let me take this one step further and show you what the blood stream looks like with different environments. This first illustration shows what a drop of live blood should look like under a microscope.

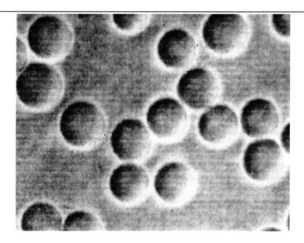

Red blood cells are round, vibrant, separated and illuminating light around each one. The fluid that surrounds them is clear. This is your river of life!

Scientists have now come to understand that there is something in the red blood cells which they call the microzyma.

Thirty years prior to the rise of monomorphism, Bechamp brought his attention to tiny "molecular granulations" found in body cells, which other observers had noted before him. They had been scantily defined, and no one had identified their status or function. After 10 years of careful experimentation, Bechamp brought to the world in 1866 the profound revelation that the granules were living elements. He renamed them microzymas, meaning 'small ferments.' During the following 13 years, Bechamp, with his devoted co-worker, Professor Estor, developed and refined the Theory of Microzymas. The essence of this theory is that the microzyma, an independently living element, exists within all living things, and is both the builder and recycler of organisms. It inhabits cells, the fluid between cells, the blood and the lymph. (Young 26)

The significant thing about this element is that it cannot be created nor destroyed. It can only organize and disorganize itself, which means it will mutate to fit whatever environment we give it to live in. For example, let's take a look at a couple more blood samples I took when I was practicing as a microscopist.

In this graphic we can see the red blood cells are misshapen and the fluid surrounding them is filthy.

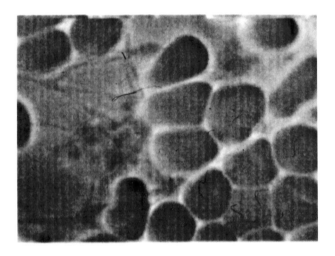

In this example we see the red blood cells are all stuck together.

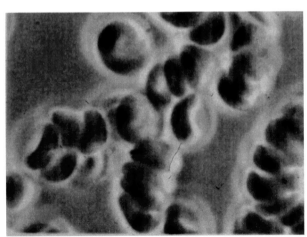

In this next illustration we note that the red blood cells are white in the center. If you were able to see this sample alive under the microscope, you would also notice that the cells are literally quivering. If you were to watch the sample for any length of time, you would eventually see the cell poop out the white center, leaving a yeast ball to float freely in the blood stream.

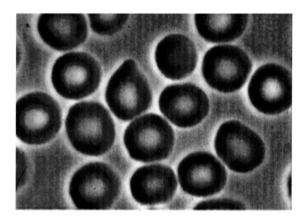

As a practicing microscopist, taking hundreds of live blood samples, I only saw one that looked as clear as our first example. This particular person had been on a vegan diet for years. Everyone else had mutated blood such as the later examples.

Do you see how we literally can control the condition under which our "river of life" has to function? Eventually, the environment we create for ourselves will catch up to us and we will have to suffer the consequences. If you are genetically prone to a weak pancreas, your consequences might be diabetes. If you are genetically prone to a weak heart, then your consequences might be heart disease. Our bad habits affect each one of us differently depending upon what our genetic make-up is and what our environment is.

The truly incredible thing about our body is that it is constantly building new cells which replace the old. That means if we are diligent about removing the toxins and giving the body the right building blocks, we can literally recreate ourselves with a healthier body each time our cells are replaced. It is truly an amazing process. We just have to take responsibility for what we want to replace them with.

So, getting back to the analogy of the wood stove, if we understand there are important eliminative channels the body uses, then it would be prudent for us to keep these channels in good working order. How do we do this?

After many years of study and experience, the following list contains a few simple suggestions of things you can do to get started. Let's begin with different factors to help keep the respiratory system healthy:

a) Breathe deeply – we need to remind ourselves several times per day to inhale and fill our lungs up. Most of us live fairly stressful lives where we are always in a hurry. We run here and there always racing the clock. The opposite of this would be a sedentary life style where we spend most of our time behind a desk or in front of the television or computer. In either instance, chances are you have become a shallow breather. We need to remind ourselves periodically to take big, deep breaths that will fill up and expand our lungs with oxygen.

b) EXERCISE – it is extremely important to do some form of exercise every day of your life. Along with helping us take in oxygen, this will move the lymph (another source for elimination) and get our blood flowing, which is how the oxygen reaches every cell in our body.

c) Drink lots of pure water. We need to keep all of the cells in the body hydrated. When the respiratory system becomes dried out, it is much more prone to bacteria and infections. "Chronic cellular dehydration painfully and prematurely kills. Its initial outward manifestations have until now been labeled as diseases of unknown origin" (Batmanghelidj X).

d) Keep lots of fresh, live plants around. We have this wonderful partnership with the plant kingdom – they put off fresh oxygen which we desperately need and we exhale carbon dioxide which is what the plants need to live. When we have live plants in our homes and offices, they are constantly putting oxygen back into the air for us to breathe, along with helping the air to stay moist.

e) In the winter, if you are running any type of heating system, it will help to put some type of humidity back in to the air, so that our respiratory system does not become dried out. This can be done just by putting a pot of water on the stove to simmer. There are also professional humidifiers on the market which can be installed into your home.

f) Do not smoke and try to avoid as much second-hand smoke as possible.

g) Stay away from dairy products which produce a lot of mucus in the respiratory system. You would be surprised at how many chronic colds and ear infections can be cleared up just by getting a child off of dairy.

h) Fresh air – try to get fresh air everyday – even if it's just by opening up some windows. It is not healthy to constantly be breathing recycled air.

Over the years, I have discovered there are some simple things we can do to help keep the digestive system healthy:

a) Eating fresh food with lots of fiber. Fiber is the Drano of digestion.

Lack of fiber leads to constipation, chronic pancreatitis, colitis, Crohn's disease, cancer and straining. Straining leads to varicose veins, hemorrhoids, diverticulosis and hiatal hernias. The same pattern repeats in countries throughout the world: big stools, little hospitals – little stools, big hospitals (Hitchcox 107).

Another benefit of eating fresh food is that it comes with it's own enzymes to help break it down. There are many people with digestive problems due to a lack of enzymes.

b) Fasting – we will cover fasting in greater detail in the next chapter, but suffice it to say, it is a wonderful way to cleanse the colon and keep it healthy. It is also an easy way to give the digestive system a rest.

c) Drink lots of water – this is extremely important to digestion and elimination.

Food can't be digested without water. There is an actual chemical process that goes on in your body that's known as "hydrolysis." It involves changing proteins, starches and fats into foods that various cells require in order to work properly. But water is also necessary to stimulate gastric glands in the stomach. In the intestines it helps facilitate the absorption of solids and the most important excretion of wastes. (Bragg 156)

d) EXERCISE – again, exercise is crucial to the health of the whole body. It brings blood and oxygen into the area and keeps everything moving. Our muscles were meant to be moved and worked hard. If they are not moved on a regular basis, they will begin to degenerate and atrophy.

e) Cleansing – consciously keep the colon cleaned out – most people who have studied health will tell you that all disease begins in the colon – we will discuss ways of doing this in the next chapter – just remember that it is crucial to vibrant health.

The type of fluid we put in our mouth is extremely important to the health of the urinary system. When you start to drink anything, remember the analogy of the "fish tank," then make wise choices.

a) Drink lots of water!! The kidneys and bladder both depend heavily on water to rid themselves of any body poisons and excretions on a regular basis.

Kidneys never stop working and constantly demand water, even when none is available. The body is then forced to supply it through dehydration to live" (Bragg 157).

b) Stay away from carbonated drinks, coffee, alcohol and other caustic substances. The urinary system is made up of very delicate tubing. When we drink substances such as these it is extremely hard on this tissue.

To help keep the skin healthy and maintain it's ability to eliminate toxins, we need to:

a) Drink lots of water – are you tired of hearing this yet? I can not begin to stress how important it is for us to get plenty of fresh, pure water to drink every day. Most people walk around dehydrated all the time. Generally speaking, men should be drinking 1 gallon of water per day and women should be drinking 2 – 3 quarts per day. The only exception to this would be if you were on a 100% raw diet and were getting a lot of water from the foods you are eating.

b) Get enough of the right kind of oils in your diet to keep the skin soft and supple. Most people have a hard time doing this, so I usually recommend taking a good oil supplement, such as wheat germ oil, flax oil, evening primrose oil or a good quality combination.

c) EXERCISE – this is extremely important when it comes to healthy skin. We need to work up a sweat and allow the impurities in the skin to be flushed out.

d) Get as much fresh air as possible – enjoy the sun! Like so many other myths of our day – it is not the sun that causes skin cancer – it is the toxins in our body. The sun merely helps draw them to the surface where they may take on the form of skin cancer. The sun is actually very healing. In *The Sunfood Diet,* Wolfe explains,

> A good sunbath is an incredible waste eliminator, as it draws toxins out of the skin. The skin is the body's largest eliminative organ." (303)

Dr. Christopher was a great believer in the suns ability to aid in health and healing.

> The sun is the world's greatest doctor but must be used by building up the exposed time in the sun gradually so as to not burn. Do not be alarmed by articles in national publications each spring, warning people to avoid sunbathing, saying it is cancer-forming. The sun cannot cause cancer. If you do not gradually increase the use of it, but lie in the sun for long lengths of time and burn, certainly it is dangerous for it will cause a severe toxic burn, but is not cancer-forming. If cancer is already in the bloodstream and the body, the sun can ripen it and bring it to the surface, but that is the only way skin cancer can result from the sun. . . ask any aborigine, Indian or member from any tribal area where only a loin cloth, if anything, is worn. There

is no cancer, although their bare skin is exposed constantly to the sun the year around. If any of them develop skin cancer, he would have been eating the civilized (?) man's food for a sufficient period of time to get the body into a toxic condition." (84-85 Home)

If we understand how the body works, then we will look at "diseased" conditions in a completely different way. Instead of trying to drug it, cut it, or burn it, we will look at the symptoms of the body and realize that the body is in a toxic state and is trying to eliminate a problem. Then we can work with the body to aid in elimination and healing. According to Dr. Christopher there are NO incurable diseases. People are only incurable when they are not willing to do what they need to do in order to fix the problem. We literally become slaves to our addictions, habits, and conventional lifestyles.

In this chapter we have discussed how the body eliminates to maintain health. It is important to note here that we can also be in a toxic state mentally, emotionally or spiritually. The body literally is a "whole" entity. True health comes when we bring ourselves into balance physically, emotionally, mentally and spiritually.

In the beginning God created the heavens and the earth. And the earth was without form, and void, and darkness was upon the face of the deep. And Satan said, "It doesn't get any better than this."

And God said, "Let there be light" and there was light. And God said, "Let the earth bring forth grass, the herb yielding seed, and the fruit tree yielding fruit," and God saw that it was good.

And Satan said, "There goes the neighborhood."

And God said, "Let us make humans in our image, after out likeness, and let them have dominion over the fish of the sea, and over the fowl of the air and over the cattle, and over all the earth, and over every creeping thing that creepeth upon the earth."

And so God created human in God's own image, male and female created he them. And God looked upon man and woman and saw that they were lean and fit.

And Satan said, "I know how I can get back in this game."

And God populated the earth with broccoli and cauliflower and spinach, green and yellow vegetables of all kinds, so man and woman would live long, healthy lives.

And Satan created McDonald's. And McDonald's brought forth the 99-cent double cheeseburger. And Satan said to human, "You want fries with that?" And humans said, "Supersize them." And humans gained 5 pounds. And Satan brought forth chocolate. And woman gained another 5 pounds.

And God said, "Try my crispy fresh salad."

And Satan brought forth Ben and Jerry's. And woman gained 10 pounds.

And God said, "I have sent thee heart-healthy vegetables and olive oil with which to cook them."

And Satan brought forth chicken-fried steak so big it needed it's own platter. And man gained 10 pounds and his bad cholesterol went through the roof.

And God brought forth running shoes and man resolved to lose those extra pounds.

And Satan brought forth cable TV with remote control so man would not have to toil to change channels between ESPN and ESPN 2. And man gained another 20 pounds.

And God said, "You're running up the score, Devil." And God brought forth the potato, a vegetable naturally low in fat and brimming with nutrition.

And Satan peeled off the healthful skin and sliced the starchy center into chips and deep-fat fried them. He created sour cream dip also. And man clutched his remote control and ate the potato chips swaddled in cholesterol. And Satan saw and said, "It is good." And man went into cardiac arrest.

And God sighed and created quadruple bypass surgery.

And Satan created HMOs.

-- Author Unknown

Chapter Four
Cleansing Programs

Beginning any type of cleansing program requires patience and perseverance, it is important to remember that you didn't get into the condition you are in over night and you will not be able to correct it overnight. Having said that, you will be amazed at how fast the body responds when it is given a chance to cleanse and heal itself. Our bodies tend to be very forgiving of the abuse we have heaped upon them once it realizes that we are trying to work with it.

If you are new to cleansing, you may find that on the good days you feel lighter and more energetic than you have in years; on the bad days, you could be tired, or emotionally and physically ill. Headaches and other cleansing symptoms are all a natural result of flushing toxins. These symptoms are referred to as a "healing crisis." In *The School of Natural Healing,* Christopher explains:

> As your body begins to cleanse, you will probably experience periodic aches and pains in the areas where the cleaning action is most acute and the wastage is loading the elimination system; there are times when you will feel very, very rough! Do not panic on the days after cleansing or during your periods of healing.
>
> In fact, the cleaning action may produce all symptoms and effects of severe illness, but don't blame the temporary problem onto the cleansing. Be comforted that the healing process is well underway, and the sooner such discomforts come, the better, for this means that the toxins and poisons are being eliminated – and the faster the cleansing, the quicker the healing. (570)

When trying to decide what type of cleansing program to use, you need to seriously evaluate your health. If you feel like you are in a fairly healthy state and would just like to increase your strength and vitality, then some type of on-going maintenance program will probably work well. However, if you are already in a critical or diseased state, then you need to seriously consider a much stronger approach to cleansing. The type of cleansing program you choose to do should equal whatever state of health you are in at this time. In other words, let the punishment fit the crime. In this book, as we begin to discuss different conditions, you will often see me repeat the phrase –"Be as aggressive as whatever it is you are fighting or it will win!" It is the same with cleansing – you have to be as aggressive as the toxic condition of your body or the toxins will win.

This chapter looks at several different cleansing programs and what is involved in doing them. One of my favorite programs and by far the least expensive is fasting. In *The Miracle of Fasting,* Paul Bragg states:

> Most people – because of their unwise habits in diet, drink and excesses – die prematurely, long before fulfilling their potential. Wild animals, undisturbed, live out their full term. Man's the only exception. Sadly, not more than one in a million lives out his natural life.
>
> Animals in their wild habitat know by instinct how to live, and what to eat and drink. They know how to fast by natural instinct when they get hurt or sick. Naturally, animals are led to eat what is good for them. But man eats and drinks anything and everything – consuming the most indigestible concoctions, washing it down with poisonous slops – and then wonders why he is sickly and does not live to be a centenarian!
>
> . . . The 'secret' of the glow of ageless health lies in maintaining internal cleanliness and regeneration. This requires eating natural, organically grown live foods, combined with other healthy practices such as fasting, drinking distilled water, exercising and deep breathing.
>
> When you purify your body with systematic fasting and live foods, you crave daily exercise. And by exercising you sculpt your body to become the person you want to be.(3-4)

An excellent way to use fasting as a cleansing program would be to set a side one day a week to do a water fast. On this day, drink only pure water, preferably distilled. The reason we recommend distilled water is because it is just pure H20. There is nothing else in it, so when it goes through your system it is hungry for inorganic minerals. As we go throughout our lives drinking tap water, well water and other sources of hard water, we take a lot of inorganic minerals (broken down rocks) into our body. We are not rock eaters and so the body cannot assimilate these types of minerals, and therefore, finds places to deposit them, such as our organs and joints. When we drink lots of pure distilled water it gathers up this inorganic material and helps to flush it out of our systems.

When you are comfortable with fasting one day a week, then add a three day water fast once a month. During these three days, you will, again, drink only pure water. Then as you cleanse and get stronger, you might want to add a seven day water fast, two to four times per year. For example, each time the seasons change which is approximately every three months, you could do a seven day water fast. Are you beginning to see that the things we are talking about in this book require commitment and lifestyle changes? If we want to be healthy and strong, then we need to make it a way of life, not just a temporary trial.

A word of caution – I am a great believer in fasting, but you need to work up to the longer fasts. In *The School of Natural Healing,* we are given this advice:

> Periodic fasting is good to cleanse the body, but a bodily famine is not required for cleansing. A cross-country runner would be committing suicide to make a grueling competitive twenty or thirty mile run without preparation and so it is with the fast; a person must work up gradually to the longer fasts. (Christopher 601)

Another thing to consider when attempting longer fasts is to remember that fasting can dump a lot of toxins in a relatively short period of time. If you have never done any cleansing before or you have not done any fasting before – you may start dumping more toxins than you can physically handle. So, start with one day fasts, begin changing your diet, and then work up to the longer fasts.

To give you an example of how efficient water fasting can be let me share what happened the first time I did a seven day fast. Many times I have been told by iridologists, reflexologists, and others that I have a lot of metal toxicity in my body. Metals can be pretty tough to clean out. It usually takes time to get to substances that can be buried as deep as metals. On the 5th day of my first seven day water fast, I woke up feeling like I had a piece of sheet metal in my mouth. My mouth literally tasted like metal. I went to the bathroom to look in the mirror and discovered that my tongue was coated in a thick white paste that smelled and tasted like metal. I could scrub it off with a toothbrush, but in a short time it would appear again. In the *Miracle of Fasting,* Bragg describes this phenomenon:

> Your tongue – your inside magic mirror – reveals how much toxic material is stored in the cells and vital organs of your body. . . A few days of fasting will coat the tongue with a thick, white, toxic material that has a strong odor. In fact, you can scrape the tongue clean but, in a few hours, the toxic coating usually returns. This is an indication of the amount of putrefying toxic filth, mucus, and other poisons that are accumulated in the body's cells that are now being eliminated from the inside surface of the stomach, intestines, organs and from all parts of the body. . . . Mother Nature shows the faster by coating the tongue that his body contains toxic poisons. (98-99)

Along with water fasts, another great way to cleanse is with juice. There are many who recommend juice fasts or juice cleanses. Dr. Christopher recommends that everyone do a three day juice cleanse once a month. Here is his recommendation:

> Step One: Prune Juice
> 16 oz. or more upon arising in the morning.
> Step Two: Olive Oil
> One or two tablespoons three times a day.
> Step Three: Cleansing Juice and Water
> 8 ounces of fluid every 30 minutes, alternating 8 ounces of juice with 8 ounces of distilled water throughout the day. (5 Three Day)

Over the years, I have discovered many tremendous benefits to fasting. Following is a list of just a few of them:

> 1. Fasting conserves energy – In *The Miracle of Fasting,* Bragg explains why this is so:

We eat food and as it passes through the body, it must be masticated, digested, assimilated and then the waste is eliminated. We have four great organs of elimination: the bowels, the kidneys, the lungs, and the skin. In order for these eliminative organs to work perfectly, the body must build a high Vital Force of body energy reserves.

It takes a tremendous amount of Vital Force to pass a large meal through the gastrointestinal tract and also eliminate the waste via the 30 foot tube that runs from the mouth to the rectum. It takes the great power of vital Force to pass liquids through the 2 million filters of the human kidneys. It takes Vital Force for the chemical power of the liver and the gallbladder to do their work in preparing food for the billions of body cells. It takes great Vital Force for the lungs to deeply inhale up to 2 quarts of oxygen with each breath, to purify the entire bloodstream in your body and expel the toxins and the carbon dioxide. It takes great Vital Force for the skin (often called your third kidney) with its 96 million pores, to throw off body toxins in the form of skin rashes, pimples, sweat and foul body odors. . . . By fasting we give our bodies a physiological rest. (6)

2. Fasting increases energy. After giving the body a rest by fasting, you will be amazed at how much stronger and energetic you will begin to feel.

3. Fasting sharpens the mind. "Fasting intensifies thoughts and wishes. After you fast on water for several days, your mind will become so clear it will astonish you" (Wolfe 247 Sunfood).

4. Fasting can help the healing process. "Alan Cott, M.D. noted in his book, *Fasting, the Ultimate Diet,* that 75% of those treated by fasting improved so remarkably that they were able to resume an active life!" (Bragg 202)

5. Another wonderful side effect of fasting is that it teaches us self-control which increases our self-esteem and our feelings of independence. We are no longer slaves to our addictions and habits, but we have control over our bodies and, as a result, our destinies.

Another cleansing program which is relatively simple and mild, is Dr. Christopher's extended herbal cleanse which includes Herbal LB, JuniPars, Barberry LG, and the Red Clover Combination. These are all herbal, trademarked formulas that have a tonic effect on the body. They help to cleanse and rebuild vital organs. Instructions for this cleanse are in Section V.

If your health concerns are more serious or you are just looking for a good detoxification program, then the Arise and Shine cleanse is quite often recommended. It is a complete 30 day program that comes with all of the herbs and instructions you need to do a fairly intensive cleanse. On this program you will have three meals a day for the first week (made of alkaline producing foods). The second week you have two meals a day, the third week, one meal per day and the last week there is no food – just the herbs contained in the program. Dr. Richard Anderson, N.D., N.M.D., creator of the Arise and Shine program, says in his book, *Cleanse and Purify Thyself:*

> The first step in overcoming dis-ease is to put a stop to its cause. This always begins by changing the habitual patterns of thoughts and feelings, which had been the invisible primal antecedent – the core cause. . . the second step toward perfect health of the body is to stop ingesting anything, including food, that does not contain enzymes, life-force and vital nutrients. In other words, avoid putting into your mouth anything other than fresh, raw foods, since cooked and frozen foods are lifeless or dead "foods" and they cause mucus, toxins, congestion, and excess acids. . . the third step toward overcoming dis-ease is to remove the congestion, toxins, acids, and everything else, from anywhere and everywhere within the body and mind, that contributes towards dis-ease. Some health professionals choose to address only the local area of obvious trouble

alone. But, as Dr. Bernard Jensen likes to say, "If you step on a cat's tail, it's the other end that yells!" Indeed, there is no single part of the body that is not affected by the whole, and visa versa. So, all congestion, toxins, and negativity must be removed, and it should begin with the removal of the mucoid plaque. . . The fourth step toward lasting health is to then supply the body with all the needed elements. This includes life-force, enzymes, essential nutrients, and positive thoughts. And most important of all is love – and lots of it. But it is extremely difficult to successfully complete this step until the third step has been accomplished, or is well on its way. (16)

If I had a life-threatening condition and wished to cleanse as intensely and quickly as possible, then I would probably start with the Arise and Shine Cleanse. Then move into something like Richard Shultz's "30 day Save Your Life Program," an extremely intense cleanse which was put together to help people who were terminally ill.

There are lots of different cleanses on the market. Do your research and make sure that the cleanse you choose is going to fit your situation and condition. Along with using these types of cleanses, if I were in a critical state, I would also find a good colon therapist and add some colonics to the regime, followed by wheat grass implants. This supplies important elements to your cleanse if you are dumping toxins faster than the body can naturally eliminate them. You need to provide a way for them to escape from the body so that they do not recycle back into the system. Suffice it to say, "You have to be as aggressive as whatever you are fighting or it wins."

One of the most important steps to making sure your cleanse is successful is preparation. When I plan on doing a cleanse, I always prepare myself mentally – knowing ahead of time there will be days when old emotions surface and make me crave comfort foods or cause me to need time alone to work through old sorrows and frustration, knowing there will be days when I am going to be tired, times when I will feel hungry or old cravings will surface which will cause me to start rationalizing a way to end my cleanse.

It is important to be already prepared for these events, to be mentally prepared to weather the storm and to have firmly planted in your mind why you are cleansing.

It is also important to have all of the supplies you are going to need, so that you do not allow yourself to become overly hungry, frustrated, or scrambling to find something at the last minute. Be sure to have some type of water bottle with you at all times. Quite often what we think of as hunger pains is the body's need for water. It is extremely important during a cleanse to drink plenty of water throughout the day. This works much better than trying to chug-a-lug two quarts before you go to bed. (especially if you don't want to be up all night in the bathroom)

Having said all of this, remember, life is never predictable, so if some crisis should come along which requires you to be up all night or to travel or which brings a lot of stress or physical exertion in to your life unexpectantly – know that you are in charge of your health – you can stop cleansing at any time and reschedule it for a later date.

Also remember, that because you are in charge, any of these cleanses can be adapted to fit your personal situation. The first time I did a seven day fast, I started with three days of apple juice and then finished with four days of water. This allowed me a transition time to go from food to water. Recently, during a two week fast I used two ounces of fresh wheat grass juice followed by fresh orange juice in the morning which contained Barleans Essentially for Women oils and Organa colloidal minerals. Then the rest of the day basically followed the Burroughs Master Cleanse (discussed in cancer section). Do what is going to work best for you and the situation you are living with – your reality.

If you are not in a position to do the type of cleansing you need to do at home, there are several retreats around the country where you can go to cleanse. In section V you will find a list of a few of them.

The principle of cleansing and nourishing works. I have seen it work miracles with people who were critically and sometimes terminally ill. Many people have been able to heal themselves of devastating conditions. Not only have I used it on myself many times, but my children have also used this principle, when traveling to third world countries, with remarkable results.

Consider when our son, Nathan, was 17-years-old he saw a poster in his favorite "climbing" store announcing an anthropologist looking for volunteers to go on a three-month expedition into an unexplored area of Africa. A group he put together, at the last minute could not go and, he had to put together a new group. Much to my dismay, he ended up choosing our son and a good friend of our family's, Wade, who is a chiropractor, to go with him.

Before going on the expedition, he spoke to Steve and I about the dangers that our son would encounter. For several hours he explained the great dangers: wild animals, natives, parasites and disease. He made it sound like another planet. It was very unnerving. However, he told me not to worry, because he had put many years of research into this and had a long list of immunizations and medications that would help to protect them. He also was having special long-sleeved shirts and long pants treated with insecticides so that they would not be bitten by mosquitoes or other insects.

As parents, we sometimes walk a thin line between encouraging our children to follow their dreams, be all that they can be and, at the same time, keep them from doing something stupid. Each of our children come to mortality with different personalities and different missions. Our job as parents is to help them discover and follow their paths in life. Well, in spite of the fears and reservations I had about this trip, I knew that it was part of Nathan's path, so I told the anthropologist he could go, but he was not going to have any of the immunizations or drugs. I told him that Nathan was only to take what I sent with him. He was very indignant and told me that I would have to sign release forms because he was not going to be responsible for my son's health. I assured him that he was right! He would not be responsible for my son's health.

Thirty days before Nate left, he went on Dr. Christopher's extended herbal cleanse to begin cleaning out his system. When he left I filled up a pill box with the cleansing herbs, along with some

Vitalerbs (these are comparable to a multi-vitamin, only they are made from whole plants). Along with cleansing, he needs nourishment, so I wanted to make sure no matter what he was forced to eat, he would have the vitamins and minerals he needed.

We made up a complete herbal first aid kit for Nathan with everything I could think of that he might need, along with a list of what to do in each instance.

We had three different paradigms which went into Africa. The anthropologist who believed in immunizations, drugs, and his own knowledge. Wade, the chiropractor, who didn't really believe in the drugs and didn't really believe in the herbs; just believed in a healthy life style. He started out taking the Malaria medication, but stopped a couple of weeks later due to hallucinations. The third was Nathan who used his herbs to cleanse and nourish.

When they arrived in Africa, Nathan noticed that none of the natives wore clothes; he thought that was cool, so he spent the next three months in a pair of shorts and sandals. No treated clothing. About two and a half weeks into the expedition, the anthropologist became extremely ill and was self-diagnosing himself with so many drugs that he became mentally unstable and was a threat to Nathan and Wade, so they took him to a village and left him there. The two of them decided to continue on with the expedition.

Shortly after arriving in Africa, the first aid list I had made fell into a river and was destroyed. This actually turned out to be a blessing because as they came into each village, they set up a first aid clinic. Wade did chiropractic adjustments and Nathan would try to help where he could with his herbal first aid kit. Without the instructions I had given him, he had to go off his own inspiration along with some trial and error. They had great success in helping the natives and so, word spread rapidly that two white doctors had come to help the people and they were welcomed into each village with open arms. About half way through the expedition, they came to a village where there were some missionaries with a radio and so Nathan was able to call home. He told me that he was still alive and that he was in a village that had been wiped out twice by E-boli. I was thrilled to know he was O.K. I was not thrilled to know where he was!

They brought home slides showing how they had lived by eating alligators, snakes, and other things to sustain life. They had pictures and video tape of dragging their kayaks through swamps, jungles, climbing trees and other situations that exposed them to all the parasites and disease we had been warned about.

Nathan returned home, after three months, like he had been on a week-end field trip. Other than the fact that he ate everything in sight, there were no side effects from his trip.

A year after the expedition we heard that the anthropologist was still in a hospital in Africa. I don't know if he ever came out alive or not.

Wade left Africa, with jungle ulcers and elephantitis, which is caused by parasites in the lymph system. On his way back to the states, he stopped over in France where he went mountain climbing with some inexperienced climbers. He got caught in a blizzard, and had to spend three days in a snow cave. When he came down off of the mountain, his big toes were black with frost bite. Arriving home, he had jungle ulcers, elephantitis, and frost bite. All of these he was able to cure naturally. (Look in the reference section to see how)

It was interesting to see the three viewpoints that went into Africa and the results that came out!

It would be easy to assume that Nathan was just young and had a strong immune system. However, we have used this same program many times with the same successful outcome.

When our two daughters, Juanita and Taunya, went to Honduras on a humanitarian trip for two weeks, we used these same combinations along with garlic, to keep the mosquitoes away, and chlorophyll, to build strong blood. Because Steve was a captain for the airlines, our two daughters, along with four other young people were able to travel on space-available passes. This means they were able to travel free, but only if there were empty seats on the airplanes. When they left Salt Lake City, everyone was able to get on the airplane. When they arrived in Houston on Wednesday, three seats were available on the plane to Honduras, so Juanita and Taunya were split up. Taunya got on the plane and Juanita had to wait for a flight the next day.

When Taunya arrived in Honduras, she had to move ahead with the main group, so it was Saturday before Juanita was able to catch up to her. Unfortunately, the cleansing herbs they had been taking were in Juanita's back pack. That meant she had gone at least four days without her herbs. The day after Juanita arrived, Taunya became very ill!

The doctor told Juanita they were not sure what Taunya had. It could be malaria or some type of jungle fever. He said they could try some different medications and an IV, but he couldn't guarantee that Taunya would live through the night. There was no way to life-flight her out of such a remote area, so Juanita told him there would be no experimenting. She knew that if they guessed wrong on which medication to use, the medication itself could become life-threatening. It took quite a bit of courage for her to stand up to the doctor and the nurses, but eventually they relented and left her alone. I have always considered it sad that this man's ego was so big; he wasn't willing to be open-minded enough to stay and work with Juanita. It was either his way or no way.

As night came on, Taunya developed a high fever, went into convulsions, lost the feeling in her hands, feet, and part of her face; then became delirious. Juanita said later, she had never been so frightened in her whole life. She was really afraid Taunya was not going to live through the night!

Juanita and the other four who had traveled with them worked with Taunya all through the night using reflexology, massage, herbs and prayer. They made sure she was kept hydrated by giving her Gatorade every 15 minutes. Before she became delirious, they gave her a dose of Dr. Christopher's Anti-plague orally; they used olive oil, lobelia tincture and cayenne oil on her spine during the convulsions to help her circulation and to relax the central nervous system, olive oil and garlic oil on her feet to fight infection, Dr. Christopher's X-ceptic on her stomach, again to fight whatever virus or bacteria attacking her, cool wet cloths wrapped around her head to keep the brain as cool as possible and lots of massage to bring circulation to her extremities. By about 6:00 a.m., the fever broke for the last time and the crisis was over.

It would appear from Taunya's experience that cleansing and nourishing does not always work. It is my belief, however, that her experience proves how much it does work. She was not able to stay with the program consistently and, so, paid a high price for it.

Thankfully, my daughter was with five other young people who had the faith, the knowledge and the strength to do what needed to be done! No one else in the group who stayed on their cleansing herbs had any problems. Each of the other 25 young people who used immunizations and medication had various symptomologies such as diarrhea, vomiting, headaches and chills.

It is important to choose a path, not just sit on the fence. Too many people make a decision that something is not good, i.e. immunizations, medications, processed foods, etc. . Unfortunately, they take the bad out of their life without replacing it with something good. We have to decide what path we are going to take to protect our health and then go for it. If you are going to let go of the "bad," then aggressively go after the "good." Make sure you are doing something to build the immune system, keeping the environment within the body clean and alkalized, along with giving the body the nutrients it needs to remain healthy and strong.

Then, when faced with some type of condition or disease – always turn to these principles first – cleanse and nourish. Get rid of the toxins, work with the body, give it the building blocks it needs to repair itself. Then let the body heal itself.

Sometimes it is easy to become overwhelmed – especially if you have already been to several specialists who have not been able to help you. In the early years, when people told me the name of their condition (which, quite often, I couldn't pronounce or spell), and then how many doctors they had already seen, I thought, "Why in the world are you calling me? I cannot possibly help you if all of these people have failed." After they explain how desperate they are, sometimes even concerned for their life, I take a deep breath and go back to the basics. Cleanse, nourish. Let the body heal itself. No matter what the health problem is, this is where we begin!

The secret of longevity is eating intelligently.
-- Gayelord Hauser

Breathing deeply, fully and completely energizes the body, it calms the nerves,
fills you with peace and helps keep you youthful.
-- Paul C. Bragg

Now I see the secret of the making of the best persons. It is to grow in the open
air and eat and sleep with Mother Earth.
-- Walt Whitman

Man does not die, he kills himself.
-- Seneca

Chapter Five
Build Life With Life

So, how do we get started? How do we transition from a life time of habits and addictions? Start by keeping it simple! Begin where you are comfortable. In order to obtain optimal health, we have to make significant lifestyle changes. If we have a family, this is not going to happen over night. It will take time and consistent effort, which eventually yields vital dividends.

The most important thing to recognize is where you are now and then where you want to be. Once you have established a starting point and have a goal in mind, then it is just a matter of mapping out a plan for getting there. Do not let yourself become discouraged and do not beat yourself up when you slip. Remember life is a journey, not a destination. We are going to make mistakes. We are going to stumble and fall. That is all a part of being alive and being human. The important thing is that we keep trying.

One of the biggest favors you can do for yourself is to start drinking lots of pure water. If you are in a position to do it; install some type of water purification system into your home. The best system is a distiller. There are many stores which carry counter-top distillers that are not very expensive. The next best system would be some type of "reverse osmosis" which can be installed under your kitchen sink.

Another simple, inexpensive addition you can start making in your life is to add wheat grass juice to your daily regime. Wheat grass is one of the purest forms of nutrition you can take. According to Ann Wigmore in *The Wheatgrass Book:*

Wheatgrass can help you restore a high energy level in two ways. First, by fulfilling nutritional deficiencies, and second, by removing wastes that clog your cells, blood, tissues, and organs.

Each of us is the keeper of over ten trillion little batteries called cells. Like flashlight batteries, our cells hold a charge of electricity. In order for this charge to be strong and steady we need to have a steady supply of the proper nutrients, especially the high-quality minerals, vitamins, enzymes, and amino acids contained in wheat grass juice. With the addition of wheatgrass and raw foods to your diet, your cells will store a maximum electrical charge, and you will have plenty of energy. At the same time, wheatgrass will help to release excess fats, mineral deposits, and proteins that are trapped in the organs of digestion and elimination, and in the blood, thus saving you energy that would otherwise be spent in your body's struggle to cleanse itself.

One thing you may notice right away after beginning the wheatgrass and raw (live) foods regimen is that you will need less sleep than you do now. Six hours of sleep – maybe even less – is adequate as long as it is deep and undisturbed sleep. Even though many people sleep in excess of eight hours a night, their sleep is chaotic and broken up by raids on the refrigerator and trips to the bathroom. These people often wake up feeling and looking exhausted.

During sleep, the body goes on "automatic" and balances and re-energizes its cells. Ideally, a night's sleep of four to six hours, and an optional afternoon nap of an hour, will give your body plenty of time to renew and refresh itself. But when your body is overloaded with food, more than half of it consumed at the evening meal, your sleep will be more restless and less restful. Whenever your cells are more out-of-balance, as often occurs during an illness, the more sleep you will need.

Wheatgrass and other raw foods are light, clean foods that nourish and cleanse the body, whereas red meats, cheeses, and sugared and processed foods are heavy and tend to congest and age our cells. After a few days of drinking and applying several ounces of wheatgrass juice, if you avoid heavy, clogging foods, your body's housecleaning burden will be reduced and one morning you will awaken from a short, deep, undisturbed sleep refreshed and renewed. As accumulated wastes and debris are removed, you will find that your energy and confidence will return. (2 & 4)

The biggest investment you will need to make in order to enjoy wheatgrass juice at home is a juicer. There are hand crank models that are much less expensive than the electric grass juicers. Once you have your juicer, you can begin to grow your own wheatgrass at home. Anyone interested in really doing something to improve health, should get *The Wheatgrass Book* by Ann Wigmore. It is written in a simple, easy to understand way which will teach you how to grow, harvest and use your own wheatgrass.

We have already discussed how important it is to start adding fresh, raw, live food to your diet. Sometimes seeing is believing. The difference between food that is alive and food that has no life in it is portrayed on one of the most amazing technologies that has recently been developed called Kirlian photography.

Kirlian photography does not just take a picture of the object it is looking at – it takes a picture of the energy field around the object. All living things run on energy (a type of electricity, if you will). Kirlian photography is designed to pick up the energy so that we can see how intense it is.

For instance, the following picture, taken from *Eating for Beauty* was made from a drop of stone-crushed olive oil. The energy field that it is emanating is amazing!

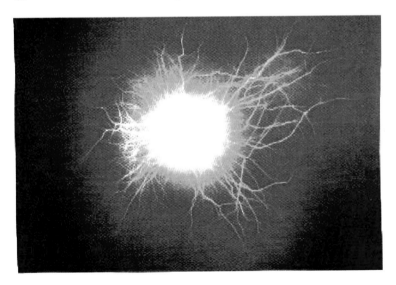

This next picture is a fig, cut in half. Can you see the brilliance in the light that is coming from it.

\

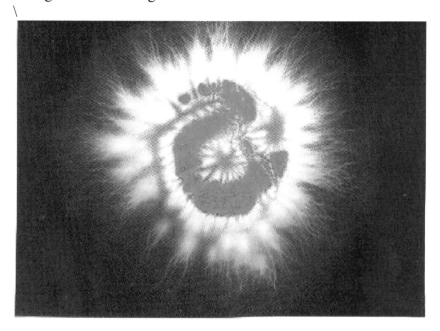

Light is energy. Look at the energy emanating from the food. Just imagine transferring that energy into every cell in your body. Imagine, if you will, that the fats, proteins, and sugars are feeding the matter in your body and the light or energy is feeding your spirit or life force.

Now, let's compare those pictures with a Kirlian picture of a Big Mac. As you can see, there is an amazing contrast. There is some light struggling to survive. The light you see is coming from the sesame seeds on top of the bun and from the lettuce sticking out on the sides.

Life builds life. Many books on the market will help you with recipes and suggestions. You might want to start with some vegetarian cook books and then move to some of the "raw" un-cook books. There are also some wonderful books on how to make your own fresh juices, or 101 ways to make a salad.

It's just a matter of getting started. If you are working with a family – begin with some subtle changes such as: adding a different salad to each meal. When it's time to replace the highly refined, processed cold cereal—invest in a good granola, making sure to get some soy, rice or nut milk to go on top of it instead of a dairy product. When fruit is in season, try as many different kinds as you possibly can so when your children want a snack they will have a variety to choose from – grapes, apples, oranges, bananas, apricots, peaches, etc. .

When you go to replace your cooking oil – instead of buying a processed vegetable oil – get virgin, cold pressed olive oil. Stop frying your food and begin baking, broiling or steaming it. If your family is used to white bread, start buying whole wheat bread and then move to a sprouted wheat bread. Instead of hamburger patties, try some of the different veggie burgers that are available. Instead of ice cream and milk shakes – start experimenting with fresh juices or fruit smoothies. When you prepare your meals, try having just one cooked food and have all of the other dishes fresh. This is what I mean about starting from where you are. Just start making wiser choices.

Some of these new choices will be more expensive, but if you stop buying the meat, dairy, and sugar you have traditionally purchased, it will free up some money to make healthier choices.

Another of the first investments, I recommend to people who are serious about obtaining optimal health is to invest in a juicer and a good quality blender. Juicing organic fruits, vegetables and wheat grass concentrates all of the incredible nutrients they contain.

As you know, my husband is a diabetic. I was told in the early stages of his disease that when a diabetic starts throwing ketones in their urine, it means the body is breaking itself down. Not knowing much about what that meant, I decided to buy some urine sticks to test my husband's urine just to see if he was throwing "ketones." Much to my surprise, he was! So, looking at the problem logically (which is not necessarily the same as looking at it medically), I decided that if his body felt the need to break itself down, he must not be getting enough concentrated nutrition to feed the cells. I immediately went out and bought vegetables to juice. Within 48 hours of putting him on fresh juices, he stopped throwing ketones. I have used this same method many times in my midwife practice and with people who are losing too much weight because their bodies are starving – in spite of the fact that they may be getting plenty to eat.

There are lots of juicers on the market. Some are extremely expensive, but it is not necessary to start with an expensive one. Some of the least expensive juicers are actually some of the most popular. For instance, The Juiceman is an inexpensive choice and it happens to be my husband's favorite because it is easy to clean. You need to make your choices as easy and convenient as you possibly can or you won't stick with it. If you become overwhelmed it will be too easy to slide back into old habits, so do yourself and your family a favor by keeping your goals realistic.

Another project you can start on to improve your health is to take inventory of the type of cookware you are using. If you are using aluminum or cast iron – you need to start changing over to glass or stainless steal. When you cook with aluminum, the aluminum can transfer into your food. According to Jethro Kloss in *Back to Eden:*

> Aluminum poisoning is so prevalent that I feel it is a part of my duty to give my experience and warn people against the use of aluminum.

> Some years ago we bought a nice supply of aluminum cooking utensils. Among them was a tea-kettle, which was constantly standing on the stove with some water in it. I would drink two or three cups of this water every morning and then some more about an hour before dinner. I developed terrible bowel trouble. I tried all kinds of remedies that ordinarily effected a cure, but neither herbs nor anything else did lasting good. I tried to find the cause, but everything failed. The doctors made all kinds of explanations of my condition, but they were all far from the cause.

> The condition grew worse until I said to my wife: 'Unless something helps me, I will surely die.' One day I described my condition to a person who told me that the description was similar to the distress aluminum poison would cause. I immediately began to search into the aluminum proposition. I read different books on aluminum poisoning. I also went to Washington to search for what the government had on the subject in the Food Department.

In those books I found reports of experiments that different doctors had made on who had died from supposed aluminum poisoning, and found that organs, such as the liver, spleen, and kidneys contained aluminum. They found that everyone who had had any practical experience with aluminum cooking utensils condemned them. For example, in Jefferson College at Philadelphia, many experiments have been made on aluminum, the findings of which are available in the Food Department at Washington.

I have boiled water in aluminum kettles and then some in granite ware. I poured some from each kettle into two different glasses. The particles of aluminum could easily be seen in the water boiled in the aluminum kettle. Many others have made the same experiment.

Everyone who knows anything about aluminum knows that it is poison. It flakes off very easily when food is cooked in it. I have seen heavy aluminum dishes that were all pitted on the bottom. Of course this aluminum had all gone into the food that was cooked in these utensils. (702-703)

Dr. Gary Young in *The Essential Oils* also warns against the use of aluminum:

Aluminum is a very toxic metal that can cause serious neurological damage in the human body – even in minute amounts. Aluminum has been implicated in Alzheimer's disease. (419)

At the back of this book you will find a page entitled, "Works Cited." This would be a great place to follow up to research other books which will help you on your road to getting the proper nutrition. Keep it simple and think "live." Also, remember the food pyramids. In order to stay balanced, we need to look at the foods contained in the last example of the three circles – fats, proteins, sugars. Typical super markets tend to have a limited amount of produce, but as you begin to explore the world of "fresh." You will be amazed at the infinite variety our generous Creator provides.

Another important point to emphasize about the principle we have been discussing in this section, "Cleanse & Nourish," is to make very clear that we have to keep these two elements balanced! It is just as important to give the body the building blocks it needs to repair and rebuild itself as it is to clean out the toxins. Let me give you an example of what I am talking about.

A mother shows up on my doorstep one day with a 4 ½ month old baby, she had adopted at birth from a mother who was on a lot of drugs. In other words, it was a "crack" baby. She had been to one of my lectures and decided that she needed to cleanse the drugs from this baby's system. She was exactly right.

To complicate the problem, this baby was very sick and only weighed about 6 pounds. She was doing a wonderful job with the cleansing. However, the thing to remember is that toxins are poisons. If we detoxify too fast, especially with the liver, it can cause a lot of problems. This baby could not handle the rate at which his liver was dumping the drugs. In a case like this, we have to back off of the cleansing and build strength with nourishment so that he can handle the next round of cleansing.

Balancing is an important thing to remember, even with adults. If you are cleansing and the symptoms just become too intense, then you probably need to slow the cleansing down a little bit. Build your strength back up and then hit it again. The only exception to this rule would be if you were dealing with an immediate life-threatening condition. In cases involving life and death, sometimes you have to "suck it up" a little more so that you accomplish what you are trying to do and be able to live!

Just remember! We cleanse and we nourish. Each is as important as the other. In order to achieve optimal health we must keep them in balance. The trick is: when we are doing the nourishing side of the equation – make sure that what you are consuming is truly nourishing, so that you are not trying to drive down the road with one foot on the brake and the other one on the gas!

Anything worth having is worth working for.
-- Andrew Carnegie

The significant problems we have cannot be solved at the same level of thinking with which we created them.
-- Albert Einstein

Since antiquity, the wisest and most successful doctors and healers, including Hippocrates himself, knew without doubt that the healing crisis marked an essential step upon the road to recovery of vibrant health. Passing through the healing crisis, and its less intense counterpart – the cleansing reaction – is an indicator that a significantly improved stage of health is being achieved.
-- Rich Anderson, N.D., N.M.D.

Chapter Six
The Need for Exercise

This section would not be complete if we did not include a chapter on exercise. I cannot over-emphasize how important regular exercise is to good health. If you are reading about these concepts for the first time, you may be too sick, too overweight, too tired, too out of shape to start with very much exercise right now, but you can do something! Start by getting out of bed. Walk, even if it's just to the corner and back. If you are bed-ridden, start stretching. Have someone help you move your muscles.

In one of Richard Shultz's *Save Your Life* tapes, he makes the statement, "Get them out of bed or they're dead." There is a lot of truth to this statement. We were meant to move! In the book, *Make the Connection* by Oprah and Bob Greene, they tell us:

> The number-one excuse people make about not exercising is that they don't have the time. If you find yourself making all sorts of excuses about time, then you're not ready to make the commitment to exercise. And you're not ready to change your life. (148)

Over the course of my life, through the ups and downs of exercise, I have had times when I have been suffering from physical, emotional and/or mental trauma. These can be extremely debilitating, sometimes to the point of not wanting to get out of bed or feeling like you can't function. Depending on the severity, you may have to give yourself time to mourn, heal, or recuperate, but as soon as it is possible, you have to find a way to start moving, again.

There are several positive side-effects to exercise that can be beneficial even when the rest of your life is out of control. The first one is that it causes the body to release endorphins which can help to give us a positive attitude in the face of tremendous challenge. Another benefit is that when everything in life seems to be going wrong, this is one place where we can feel like we still have some control. No matter what else is happening, we have the ability to commit one hour a day to working out! We just have to decide it is important enough to be on top of the priority list.

In *Body for Life,* Bill Phillips tells us:
> When you gain control of your body, you will gain control of your LIFE. . . . I firmly believe that a strong, healthy mind resides in a strong, healthy body. That, my friends, is a fact. When I see men and women who are out of shape, I see lives not fully lived. (1-2)

No matter where you are starting, I want you to know that I applaud you! There have been times when I was so out of shape it felt as though rigamortis was setting in. I know what it is like to climb a set of stairs and be out of breath at the top. I also know what it is like to feel the euphoria and triumph of finishing a 5-mile run. I know the excitement of being able to fit into a size 4 after having 5 children. I also know the horror of being 50+ pounds overweight and being so self-conscious that I didn't want to be seen in public. The point is: DO IT! Start now! Where ever you are; improve. Make the commitment and get started.

In *Body for Life,* Phillips shares the extraordinary story of a young man whose life was changed, simply because he decided to take charge of his life and incorporate an exercise program. His name is Lynn Lingenfelter:

> Lynn Lingenfelter's life changed forever on November 11, 1983. He was 16-years-old, a starting fullback, and captain of his Pennsylvania high school football team. Along with a friend, he headed into the woods that day near his family's home to hunt small game, something the two had done dozens of times before.

> They were climbing a steep mountain slope when Lynn's friend lost his footing. Even before Lynn heard the pop of his companion's .22-caliber rifle, he felt a thump in his back, "As if I'd been slugged with a baseball bat." As he was falling to the ground, Lynn glimpsed back at his friend, who was down on his knees, the weapon still clutched in his hand.

> 'His eyes were bigger than mine,' recalls Lynn.

> Lynn actually pulled himself up and tried to run for help. 'I went about 30 yards. Then I started to feel really sick. I could see only black and white, and I couldn't hear.

I stumbled and fell to the ground. I honestly thought I was going to die. I remember praying and saying, 'God, save me . . . I think I'm going.' Then I must have blacked out.'

Almost beside himself with panic and fear, Lynn's friend ran to get help. When he returned, it was with Lynn's younger brother, Mike.

'They found me lying on the ground, stone cold and blue. I wasn't breathing. By coincidence or fate, Mike had learned CPR in health-education class just a few days earlier. He got me breathing again and held me tight to keep me warm until the paramedics got there and took me to the hospital.'

The bullet had entered Lynn's lower back, ripped through his intestines, and come out through the front. He had lost a massive amount of blood while he was lying there on the hill. When he finally got to the hospital, the doctors told his family he had only a fifty-fifty chance of surviving. Lynn had to be given 38 pints of blood to replace what his body had lost.

'I don't remember all that much about the days that followed except I was in a lot of pain. I had one operation after another, one complication after another. I was in the hospital for the better part of five months.'

By the time Lynn was finally released, he had lost 50 pounds.

'I couldn't even bench press 100 pounds. But I set a goal of rebuilding my body by the time the next football season started. The doctors said that was impossible, which made me even more determined. I trained hard, and my mom fed me well.'

When the starting team ran onto the field the first Friday night of that next season, Lynn was among them, once again the starting fullback. The crowd stood and cheered.

'That was one of the most rewarding moments of my life. I remember thinking it was all over now – the tough times my family and I endured because of the hunting accident, those long, long months of not knowing if I'd ever recover.

I was ready now for that to become nothing more than a distant memory. Which, as time passed, it did,' explained Lynn.

If this were an after-school movie, that would be the end of the story. Music up. Fade out. But Lynn's saga, as he would soon learn, was not nearly over.

'I finished high school, got engaged to my sweetheart, Sara, and enrolled at Penn State University. This was in the fall of 1987. Doctors were being notified at that time of a newly discovered virus that seemed to lead to a fatal disease. One of the means of transmission was through tainted blood. They were told that anyone who received blood in recent years should be tested to see if they had the disease. I went in for my test, hardly giving it a second thought. To me, this was a formality, nothing more than that.'

Two weeks later, the telephone in Lynn's dorm room rang. (This disease was still new enough at that time that test results were given over the phone.) 'Lynn,' the doctor said, pausing for a moment, 'you have the HIV virus.'

Lynn didn't react. He didn't know how to react. A gunshot wound, although horrific, was something he could understand, something he could comprehend. But this . . . beyond what the doctors had told him, he didn't even know what HIV was – he only knew it was serious, extremely serious.

'My experience with the shooting had made me believe I could handle anything; I could get out of anything. But I remember all I could think when I got that phone call was, 'How do I get out of this?'

This was a death sentence, or so Lynn was told. The doctors said he had two years to live. Maybe three. Lynn's family was devastated. (5-7)

We all tend to make this same mistake – if a doctor tells us there is no hope – we believe them. We accept their professional opinion as ultimate truth. Then we wait and watch for each stage of the disease to progress to the next stage.

What do you think would happen if we listen to the diagnosis and then said to ourselves, "Oh, I guess I have allowed my body to become too toxic." Then do something about it! Cleanse out the toxicity, make the necessary life-style changes, and then get on with life. Wouldn't this be a much better way of looking at disease as compared to being programmed to accept the inevitable and then wait for it to happen? Back to Lynn's story:

Breaking the news to his fiancée, Sara, was one of the most difficult things he had ever done.

'Having to tell your fiancée you're dying – that you're HIV-positive – is something I wish no one in the world had to do. We met that evening at her dorm. I remember we were out back, and I said, 'Sara, you're not going to believe this. My test came back positive . . . I have the virus.' It hurt so bad.'

'We sat there for hours. She cried so hard she shook from head to toe. We were just kids. Sophomores in college. We had our whole lives ahead of us, so much to look forward to. And in just a few seconds . . . it all melted away.'

Sara tried for a time to stay with Lynn, but they believed there was no way it was going to work. Once she left, he dropped out of school.

'I basically dropped out of life. I was in denial, then I was angry, then I hit rock bottom. I was very depressed. I'd sleep 15 hours a day. Sometimes I wouldn't leave the house for a week. I drank beer and ate junk food and watched a lot of TV.'

In no time at all, Lynn ballooned to 230 pounds. He tried stemming the tide, but there was no stopping it.

'I'd go to a support group meeting every once in a while, but I wasn't really into it. I knew I needed help, but I didn't really want help. One of the things I've learned is that no one can help you until you've decided you're ready for it.'

He also learned that telling people he was HIV-positive meant facing almost certain dread and rejection.

'I remember when one of my friends found out, he asked me to meet him at a restaurant. We talked, and he said, 'My family comes first.' He repeated that phrase four or five times. I wasn't following what he meant. It turned out he didn't want me coming over to his house anymore because he was afraid I would infect his wife and children.'

Lynn's response, like so many people in such a situation, was to pull back.

'I learned to just keep my problems to myself. I didn't even admit to myself how miserable I was. I can look back now and see what a big mistake that was. One of the first steps in overcoming adversity is to honestly admit how you feel about it, to acknowledge that there is a problem. But I didn't know that then.'

And so his downward spiral continued.

'I was sick. I was dying. But I wasn't dying from HIV. I was dying from depression. In a way, I was killing myself. I'd built a prison for myself and filled it with misery. I was so consumed with negative images, I didn't care about myself or anyone around me. It just snowballed. It got out of control. I felt helpless, like I was stuck in the middle of a huge storm, and I couldn't move.'

'I knew deep down that I wasn't really a loser. Yet I was losing. I was waiting to die. The doctors told me that's all I had to look forward to. So that's what I was waiting for. I kept waiting. And waiting. Two years went past. Then three. Then nine. And I kept waiting.'

Lynn wasn't dead. But he wasn't alive either.

'That was a very strange place to be. I began to believe that maybe this HIV was not going to kill me. And that forced me to face myself and ask a very tough question: 'What is the purpose of my life?'

It was at this point Lynn began searching for answers. He started having vivid dreams of being a competitive athlete, of being strong and hopeful, with life stretching out in front of him like a bright sunlit path, rather than the dark, hollow tunnel he had been seeing.

'One morning – this was in early '97 – I awoke from one of these dreams, went in the bathroom, and looked at myself in the mirror. I looked like crap. I felt like crap. And I told myself I had to change. It was time to take the bull by the horns.'

He hauled himself to a local gym and began asking around for information on how to get in shape. One of the guys in the room handed him a copy of one of my publications.

'I had never been so fat. I didn't know what type of nutrition or exercise program I should be following. I looked at this magazine and really liked the way it was written. I felt like someone was talking to me and guiding me.'

'I didn't realize it at the time, but what I was finding was a lot more than fitness advice. I could relate to the tone, the language, the attitude of the articles. Beyond information, I was being taught a frame of mind, which inspired me more than all the preachers, teachers, doctors, and counselors who had tried to get through to me before.'

Lynn's timing couldn't have been better. One of the issues he picked up that spring included information about my contest. (Body for Life) Lynn's competitive fuse was relit.

'It was time for me to show I could be a winner again.'

Lynn took everything he had learned about himself, every emotion he had felt, and carried it all into the weight room.

'I couldn't fight the HIV virus physically. I mean, you can't punch it and beat it up. But every time I finished a hard workout, I felt like I had won a battle. Every day I stuck with my nutrition program, I felt I had taken one more step to climb out of the hole I had dug for myself.'

'At the end of the first week, I could actually feel a change. I literally felt better about myself. There wasn't much of a physical change at that point, but there was a big mental change. I felt good about myself: I'd forgotten what it was like.'

Lynn felt – finally – as if his life had direction again.

'Each day I got more and more confident because I was finally moving forward again. I was working toward a goal I could be proud of. Even if I didn't win the contest, I said to myself, 'Worst-case scenario, I'm gonna be in shape at the end of this.' I didn't know if I would win, but I knew I was gonna finish, and that, in itself, would be a victory.'

Not only did Lynn's s spirit revive, and not only did his body gain shape and strength, but his health – his body's response to the disease that lived within it – soared.

'I was – I am – HIV-positive. So it was especially important not to deprive my body of nutrients. I had to restrict calories to lose all the fat I put on over the years, so I ate a lot of low-fat, healthy foods like chicken, vegetables, fruit, potatoes, and nutrition shakes.'

'It's a bit awkward at first, but after a few weeks, I got used to it, and it wasn't hard to maintain. Today it's just a part of my life. I just wake up and do the right things and make the right decisions through out the day.'

And the rewards?

'When you get in great shape, you have so much more self-esteem. It enables you to handle things better. I'm positive that working out and rebuilding my body helped fight my depression.'

'Just knowing I was still capable of accomplishing something gave me confidence. I would come home from the gym each day and look in the mirror and say, 'At least one thing in my life is going right.' That was all I needed to keep going.'

'This may have saved my life. I've lived more in the past two years than I did in the entire decade before that – a lot more. And I've learned. Most of all, I've learned that time lost is lost forever. All those years – my twenties, essentially – they were wasted with frustration and anger, depression and shame.'

'For nine years I asked, 'Why me?' I replayed that hunting accident again and again in my mind. I obsessed about why my friend didn't have his safety lock on his gun. I wondered how things would have been different if the bullet hit me in the leg instead of going through my gut.'

'I was so angry this happened to me. I didn't do anything to anyone. I didn't deserve this. And then, after going through all that, to find out I was HIV-positive . . . it's impossible to understand. It's easy to feel sorry for yourself. It's very hard not to become angry and bitter.'

'But I learned that obsessing about it served no purpose other than to torture myself. I've had to forgive everyone and everything – my friend who accidentally shot me, the doctors, the system that let diseased blood be transfused into my body. I had to set myself free from all that and look forward, not back.'

It was literally taking his body into his own hands that started to set Lynn free, he told me. All he wanted in the beginning was to improve his body. He had no idea, he says today, that his entire existence would be raised to a greater level of fulfillment and freedom than he has ever known.

'Each day is a gift to me, and I do my best to enjoy it. I smile a lot, which is something I did very little of for nine years. I stay busy. When I was depressed, I used to watch a lot of TV. I think I watched enough TV for the rest of my life, so I try not to do that now. I go on walks with my fiancée, Evey. We go out to dinner. I like to be active. I like to be moving.'

'Each day, I try to do something new – to achieve a goal. I recently learned how to in-line skate and surf.'

Of all the people I've met in my life, the 'new Lynn' may be the most 'consistently upbeat' of them all. But why?

'Why am I happy? Because I decided to be happy. That's how simple it is. It's a choice I made. Then I acted on that choice. It took me 10 years to figure out that this was all up to me, and me alone.'

'It might sound strange to say that part of making that choice, of deciding to change, is learning how to surrender. I don't mean surrender as in giving up. I mean surrendering the negative emotions that hold so many of us back.'

Blame, shame, resentment. These are the feelings Lynn is talking about. The first step to taking your life into your own hands, he says, is to open those hands and empty them of the unhealthy, unproductive things they've been clinging to for so long.

'Complaining makes you more miserable and just makes problems worse. None of the problems I've faced ever went away by complaining. When you complain, you attract other people who complain. That's a dead-end street.'

'But it works the other way, too. When you decide to be happy, adventurous, and open-minded, you will find other people who have made the same decision.' (5-12)

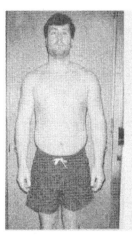

Lynn's story shows that the greatest obstacle to a good exercise program is attitude. It's in your mind. Working out is literally a mind over matter affair. So many people have let their bodies get so far out of shape that to do any movement at all hurts, so they just don't move. Please, do not make this mistake. If it hurts, start stretching it and restoring it to health. "When you nourish your body with pure energy, you transform from the inside out . . . No matter who you are, no matter what you do, you absolutely, positively do have the power to change" (Phillips XV & 81).

It is never too late to start. Dr. Willix, shares an example of how people in their 90's still benefit from exercise:

> In a study of 90-year-old men and women, researchers wanted to know if it was an inevitable fact of life that people deteriorate and get weaker as they age.
>
> These men and women lifted light weights for eight weeks. And guess what! After only two months, they nearly tripled the strength of their arms and legs. They were able to go from lifting about 15 pounds to lifting over 40 pounds.
>
> - Two of them were able to toss aside their canes, because they were now strong enough to walk on their own!
> - One was able to get up out of a chair without using his arms, something he'd not been able to do before lifting weights. (31)

Recently, a young couple asked me if I could help them. The husband was involved in a gun accident 10 months ago. He is now paralyzed from the waist down, has multiple pressure wounds, is extremely emaciated (underweight and weak), has constant infections, is depressed and has such a lack of circulation that the doctors have talked to him about amputating his legs at the hip.

First, we discussed getting the circulation going which involves exercise. Along with the herbs he is taking, his sunbathing, the cleansing, and the nourishing, he is installing a bar in his home to do pull-ups. He is also starting a work out program which involves resistance training (weight lifting) and cardio (going for runs in his wheel chair). Exercise is this important, even in (or maybe I should say especially in) cases of life and death.

This chapter is not about giving you a specific exercise program. There are many books, videos and DVDs on the market which can do that much better than I can. The best advice I can offer here is that for the best results, I recommend alternating resistance training with cardio work-outs. This way you can build lean muscle mass, strengthen muscles including your heart, and build up your endurance.

Another form of exercise which would use less impact would be yoga. In *Eating for Beauty,* David Wolfe suggests:

Considering there are close to 700 muscles in the human body, it would be nice to incorporate each muscle into our exercise program. This is accomplished most completely by practicing various forms of yoga.

Yoga moves energy throughout our body and releases memories, perceptions, and emotions. It also helps the body eliminate the residues of the cooked foods we have eaten over the years that are stored in our calves, thighs, torso, and buttocks, as well as, in our arms, back, shoulders, and neck.

Squeezing and twisting your muscles is similar to squeezing and twisting a soiled washcloth; it has a cleansing effect, yet at the same time, it opens the tissues to receiving more nourishing fluids. (218)

Along with whatever work-out program you choose to do, make sure you add some alternative activities for variety. If you constantly do the same work-out routine, your body will become accustomed to it and you will become bored. In *Make the Connection,* Greene recommends the following activities:

The best choice for your alternate activity would be one of four exercises – walking, jogging, aerobic dance, or stair stepping. But for more diversity, I have listed some others. I chose them based on their aerobic potential, ease of learning and performing, and convenience. I am not saying these are the only activities you should use, but I think they are the best. They are: Outdoor cycling, stationary cycling, rowing, cross-country skiing, swimming. (115)

In *The Sunfood Diet,* Wolfe issues a challenge:

If the success you seek is extraordinary, then you must begin immediately to set extraordinary goals. As long as you are going to dream, dream great dreams. As long as you are going for prosperity, go for it all! Spectacular success is always preceded by spectacular goal setting and mental preparation.

Release all limitations today! Set enormous goals! If your daily goal is just to make it home, eat unhealthy foods, watch TV, and go to sleep, you will achieve that. If your daily goal is to make it home, exercise, work on your favorite projects all night, and wake up in the morning with an abundance of energy, you will achieve that too. (48)

So, if you live close to a gym and can afford it – get down there and get a membership. If you don't live close to a gym or can't afford it, then buy a book or some other type of program that will help you get started and stay committed. At the very least, get out and start walking – just move – your body and your mind will thank you for it.

A strong body makes a strong mind.
-- Thomas Jefferson

Until man duplicates a blade of grass, nature can laugh at his so-called
scientific knowledge.
-- Thomas A. Edison

Whatever occurs in the mind affects the body and vice versa.
The mind and the body cannot be considered independently.
When the two are out of sync,
both emotional and physical stress can erupt.
-- Hippocrates

A new scientific truth is not usually presented in a way to convince its
opponents. Rather, they die off, and a rising generation is
familiarized with the truth from the start.
-- Max Planck

Chapter Seven
A "Season" to Die

Driving into Memphis, I felt the presence of my father sitting next to me in the car. His presence was so strong, I was afraid to look for fear he would leave. I just wanted to hold on to how close I felt to him. Pulling up to the V.A. hospital, he left. After his presence was gone, the panic set in. If he was with me, did that mean he had died? How could this be happening? It just wasn't possible! He was still young, many prayers had been offered in his behalf – he just had to get better!

I parked the car, ran into the hospital and took the elevator up to the cancer wing. As I walked into his room and looked at him, it became obvious the blankets were still rising and falling with each breath he took. My mother was sitting next to his bed, so I suggested that she might want to go get something to eat while I sat with him. Sitting down and taking his hand in mine, he opened his eyes and said, "Hi, tootsie. I knew you were coming."

"How did you know?" I asked.

"Well, each day as I lay in this bed I try to imagine what each of my girls are doing and where they are. Then I try to spiritually spend some time with each one of you."

My father was dying from a malignant brain tumor; but I was too young and ignorant to understand what was happening. At the ripe old age of 22, I could not imagine life without my father. We had always been very close. He was my confidant, advisor and friend. He was one of the few people in the world who really understood me. So many prayers had been offered in his behalf, that to me, it was "black and white." He had to get better. Otherwise, I would have to question everything I believed. My mother tried to tell me she had an impression which told her she needed to prepare to go on alone, but I wouldn't listen. In fact, I was surprised at her lack of faith.

For the next few months I watched my father suffer through brain surgery, chemotherapy, radiation, losing his ability to speak or write. To gain four more months of life he gave up his quality of life.

To protect each other, I watched him and my mother play games, where they both pretended he wasn't dying and so none of us were able to openly share those last precious months with each other. Eventually, he became comatose, began to drown in his own fluids and passed away. My father was gone at the age of 53! I couldn't believe the physical, emotional and spiritual pain I suffered.

At the funeral home, kneeling beside his casket, I told him how much I loved him and how much I was going to miss him. He felt so close. It was as though I could feel him standing next to me, saying, "Tootsie, some day you will understand."

I drove the lead car out to the little country cemetery in the Ozark Mountains of Missouri where we buried him. The grave had been opened at the foot of a giant Oak tree. Everything was green and vibrant with the coming of spring. There was a beautiful grave side service; my mother was handed the folded flag that had lain over the casket representing a man who not only served his country during World War II, but a man who exemplified the word "patriotism." As everyone passed by the casket and left, I remained standing alone. I looked over at the man who was being paid to close my father's grave. Not only was he obviously drunk, but he still had a six-pack sitting beside him. I could not tolerate the thought of my father's grave being desecrated with beer cans, so I called my brother and husband back to the grave. Each of us grabbed a shovel and closed the grave ourselves, placing the flowers reverently on top; we said our final farewells.

When I got back home, I felt like I had to find some peace with what had happened; so I went to the scriptures, desperately searching for answers. I knew what all of the textbook answers were, but I needed more than that. One day, in my search, I came across a passage that seemed to leap off of the page. Spirit spoke to spirit and I received the answer I needed at that time. It read, ". . . dispute not, because ye see not, for ye receive no witness until after the trial of your faith" (Smith). I came to realize that I still had my whole life ahead of me. I still had to prove myself, to have my faith tested and strengthened; there were still many experiences to pass through and much to learn. For the time-being I was at peace.

The 13 years, following my father's death, would take me through many experiences which I could never have imagined. However, in the course of growing up and discovering more about life, I had begun to become pretty cynical about some things. One of those things is death. I figured if you are in the wrong place at the wrong time and something drastic happens, you are dead, period, end of discussion!

Since my husband, Steve is an airline pilot; he sometimes wanted me to come and join him on his lay-overs in different cities. I would rarely do it because I was afraid of leaving our children and having something happen to me – like dying in a plane accident. Steve told me, "There is a time to be born and a time to die and if it's not your time, you needn't fear." I replied, "Are you trying to tell me that if a plane falls 35,000 feet and kills everyone on board, it was 'time' for all of those people to go?"

His response, "Do you think that is above the organizational ability of the Lord?" Well, I didn't have an answer for that; but I wasn't going to take any unnecessary chances.

Sometimes, however, when we get too far off track, life has ways of teaching us valuable lessons. July 23, 1989 held one of those lessons for me: We had a good friend visiting us from Hawaii. At that time he was head of the math and science departments at BYU- Hawaii. He had agreed to give a lecture on some research he was doing on "worm holes" in space. We had about 35 people over for dinner that Sunday and then car-pooled into town for the lecture. We were living in Texas on some acreage about 15 miles from town. The roads were winding and wooded, with no streetlights. I was leading the caravan back home after an incredible lecture on science and religion, driving a suburban with a dear friend next to the passenger door and seven teenagers in the back two seats. My sister-in-law and her one-week old baby started to get in the front seat with me, but at the last minute changer her mind and got into another car. I was six months pregnant with our 12th child.

I was coming up to a sharp turn in the road when, all of a sudden, in my mind's eye, I saw something large and dark come through the windshield. Then someone said to me, "Slow down and pull over to the right." My friend, sitting next to me, was still carrying on our conversation, but I no longer heard her. It was almost as if I had stepped into another dimension. I made the sharp right turn in the road and began to accelerate. Again, someone said to me, "Slow down and pull over to the right." I could see another car coming down the road toward me and could no longer ignore the instructions that were being given to me. I put my foot on the brake and began to pull over to the right. Just as my headlights and the headlights of the oncoming car met, a deer came running out of the woods from the left; it jumped over the hood of the oncoming car and I caught its legs in mid flight with the front of the suburban, sending it through the windshield and into my face. Since I was already following the instructions I had been given, I easily came to a stop on the side of the road. At first I was in shock and didn't know what had happened or what to do.

Again, a voice said to me, "It was a deer. Put the car in park." I obeyed. "Turn the car off." I obeyed. "Get out of the car." I reached for the door handle with my left hand. I was told, "Don't use that arm. It is broken." I reached across with my right hand and opened the door.

I had a number of injuries which took 4 hours in the emergency room to repair. The E.R. doctor told Steve that he had seen accidents like this before; but he had never seen anyone live through it. Normally, if a deer hits you in the face, it snaps your neck and kills you. Glass from the windshield was embedded in my face and eyes. My left wrist was broken in three places (nothing was out of place, however, because I had been warned not to use it). All of the fingers on my left hand had to be sewn back together, along with a severed artery in my thumb. I had a huge bruise on my leg where I had caught the impact of the steering wheel, instead of the baby I was carrying. When I was finally taken to a room at 2:00 in the morning, Steve said, "Happy Birthday." It was my 35th.

I was in the wrong place at the wrong time, but it was not my "time" to go. I learned that there really is someone who cares about us; that knows what we are going through and will protect us, if we are willing to listen. Later, Steve held a family council and shared with our children how I had been guided and protected. One of them asked, "If the Holy Ghost could help Mom through this, why couldn't he stop it from happening?"

Steve explained, "The Holy Ghost is not sent to stop us from gaining experience. He is sent to help guide us safely through them."

The next 12 years would lead me to discover many truths which are kept hidden from most of us. In fact, you are reading about some of them in this book. I have been in awe as I have scrambled to accept, understand and implement them in my life.

In December of 2000 a couple from Washington called to see if I would help them. The wife had been told she only had a week left to live. She had found a lump in her breast three years before, and knew it was breast cancer, so she aggressively did what she could to get rid of it. The lump shrank in size; but it was not completely gone when she got busy with life again. She was a master herbalist, she knew about nutrition and health, but she was too busy. She was helping other people, but not living the laws herself. By the end of the summer of 2000, she was having difficulty walking so she went to see a doctor. He missed diagnosed her with multiple sclerosis and set up an appointment for her in December with a specialist. By October, she was bedridden. By Thanksgiving she was hallucinating, so her husband took her to an emergency room. They did two CT-scans and an MRI. When they were finished, the doctors told her husband they did not expect her to live more than a week to ten days. They said the cancer had metastasized to the bones. They were eaten alive and looked like Swiss cheese. She had multiple brain tumors, breast tumors, uterine tumors; she was eaten alive from head to toe with cancer. They took her home and called me.

I flew to Washington to see if there was anything I could do. When I walked into the house I saw Coke cans sitting around, along with a lot of other things that are very obviously not healthy.

At first I was angry! I thought, "Why have you done this? You knew better!" I soon came to understand that "knowing" is not enough. We have to learn how to live a "healthy" lifestyle. We have to have the self-control and commitment to make the necessary life-style changes. Dr. Christopher and many others, including myself, have taught that there are no incurable diseases – there are only incurable people because they will not do what they need to do to fix the problem. However, Kris taught me that there is an exception to this rule. If we wait too long to correct the problem, the damage can become too extensive. In other words, if a house were to catch on fire and we put the fire out while there is only smoke damage, then it is fairly easy to repair. If we wait until the fire has consumed the house before we call for help, then when the firemen arrive, what is left? The only thing left will be ashes and soot because the house has burned to the ground. It is the same with the body. If we let it become completely destroyed before we do anything about it, what is left? The muscles, the tissue, the bones, the blood – everything will be in the process of dying. Then it becomes a race against time. Will you be able to cleanse, nourish and rebuild fast enough to survive?

When she had come home from the hospital, they had sent medication home to help prevent seizures and lots of medication for pain. She didn't want to take it because she wanted to stay coherent. I ended up bringing her home to Utah to stay with my family where we were able to put her on fresh organic juices, distilled water, herbal teas, and green drinks. She lived four times as long as they predicted. Until the last 24 hours, she was coherent and relatively pain-free unless we moved her. She was able to say good-by to her parents, set her affairs in order, and be in control of what was done to her. Even in the stage she was in, it is totally amazing to me how much the body will respond to correct principles. Even in death, we can be helped.

In the month that I cared for her, I gained more insight into myself and this thing we call "death" than I ever have in my life. She was the same height as I am. She was one month younger, almost to the day. She weighed almost the exact same that I weighed. As I sat next to her bed, I quite often thought, "Except for the grace of God, there go I." It was a real wake-up call!

Life had been challenging. I wasn't doing all that I should have been doing. I was carrying around extra weight, wasn't eating the way I should and was totally out of shape. I recommitted to be an example of what I knew I should be doing.

About three months into working on my diet and exercise program, I started to do some heavy bleeding with my cycles. It continued to get worse until I was bleeding about three weeks out of every month, sometimes passing clots as large as the pad I was wearing. Quite often, I was unable to go into public, for fear of bleeding through all of my clothing. By the time it got this bad, I was home-schooling four of my children, working at an herb store, teaching classes and taking care of my midwife practice. I just didn't have the time or energy to deal with anything else.

Steve was getting frustrated with me. He said I was like a plumber that never fixed my own pipes. One Saturday night I hemorrhaged – covering myself, the bed and my husband in blood. Sunday morning Steve said he had had enough – he was taking me to an emergency room. He told me that I could take care of the problem any way I wanted to, but he wanted to know what the problem was. In the E.R. they took my vital signs, drew some blood, and did an ultrasound. The doctor then came into the room and told me that I needed to get a hold of my gynecologist to schedule a hysterectomy for the next day. When I started to question him about it, he said, "You have uterine fibroids. They are incurable. You can either schedule a hysterectomy for tomorrow or you will bleed to death. Those are your only two choices." He also went on to explain to me that they would not even take me into surgery until I was given a blood transfusion because my hematocrit was so low.

After leaving the hospital, I had a decision to make. My choice did not please a lot of people, including several of my children. They told me they would rather have me without a uterus than to not have me at all. I tried to explain to them that I could not go in for the surgery. It had nothing to do with "saving face" or "making a point." It just wasn't right for me. If one of them were in my situation and were to choose the surgery, they would have my support, but this was my situation and my choice was to go home.

In my case, I knew that my own lifestyle choices had caused this problem. I had just come through a decade of watching miracle after miracle, so I knew the body was capable of healing itself. In the final analysis, I told Steve that I had been given knowledge and light over the past ten years, and quite frankly, I was afraid that if I denied that light to take the easy way out, the light which I had been given would be taken away. "To thine own self be true" became a very important theme to me.

After Steve took me home I was too weak to do anything except lay in bed for two or three days. On the third day, Steve walked into our room and waxing Biblical he said, "Physician, heal thyself!"

I told him that I felt too weak to pick up a glass of water, much less do anything about the problem, so he called in reinforcements. A couple of our daughters came to help. I explained to them that I could only have live food to eat – mainly in the form of fresh juices. Everyday they were to bring me two to four ounces of wheat grass juice to drink and every night they juiced a full flat of wheat grass which they brought to me to douche with. This was done so that I could get the juice directly into the uterus.

Within three days the bleeding stopped. On about the tenth day I passed some tissue. After three weeks my gynecologist asked me to come in so he could test my hematocrit again. I agreed to see him. A normal hematocrit is considered to be between 25 and 35. Mine had dropped below 20. After three weeks of live food and wheat grass, it climbed up to a 27. His nurse would not believe the results. She said that under the best of conditions, it takes six months to a year to bring the blood back into a healthy range after it has fallen that low. The doctor just laughed and told her that my bag was full of all kinds of tricks. She did not think it was funny!

Since that time I have a light, three day period every 28 days and quite often pass fertility fluid like I did when I was 20.

When I reflect back 28 years to my father's death, I am grateful for all that I have learned and experienced. My views and ideas have changed a lot. I started out believing that life and death was all predestined – something spiritual which was only known to God. Then I went through a period of believing it was just "fate" – being in the wrong place at the wrong time. I have now come to understand that we have much more control than most of us realize. With the exception of some type of accident – we have the ability to choose how we will live out our lives, how active and productive they will be, and, in many instances, how long that life will last.

We were all sent here with a mission to perform, something only we can contribute to the world; lives that only we can touch. If we spend our lives being sick and tired, the chances are we are not going to accomplish all that we could have done.

It really is true – ". . . after the trial of your faith, all these things shall be made known unto you."

Section III

Women's Health

"Women's Health" Overview

Many women from all across the country talk to me about the same types of health concerns and problems. No matter what part of the country we are from – it seems we are all having similar challenges. Obviously, a book such as this one is not going to fix all of the problems we are facing, but I would like to answer some of the questions which have been the most common. Again, I have to remind you – these are only my opinions – taken from my own experiences.

Women are facing challenges in many areas of their lives – emotionally, psychologically, spiritually and physically. In order to obtain optimal health, we must take time to examine our lives and decide what we can do to correct as many of these issues as possible. Sometimes the challenge can seem over-whelming, so it is important to take it one step at a time. Map out a course for yourself and then follow through. If you slip behind, do not beat yourself up – just get up, and keep going.

Over the years of working with women, I have gained a tremendous respect for the attributes of womanhood. Many spend their lives in selfless service to others – putting the needs of those they love ahead of their own. Many are making incredible contributions to our society and the nation. We have come along way in the last few decades when it comes to opportunity, education, and letting our voices be heard.

In spite of this, many women are unhappy. I have to wonder if some of this restlessness is due to living in a world where our roles are no longer defined and therefore, it becomes a challenge to know where we fit into the grand scheme of things. Women have spent centuries fighting off domination by a male-driven society to gain their God-given rights of independence.

According to *Toxic Psychiatry,* Breggin tells us:

> Mental health professionals have a lower standard for a mature woman than for a mature man. Male psychology is equated with adult maturity. Female psychology is degraded as more childlike. Since this observation by Chesler, the problem has been found to be pervasive throughout academic disciplines as well, including psychology and philosophy, as shown in Carol Gilligan's *In a Different Voice* and in Marilyn French's *Beyond Power.*

Far more women than men develop 'careers' as mental
patients, spending substantial portions of their lives on
psychiatric drugs, in psychotherapy, or in mental hospitals.
Women may seek these psychiatric careers because it's
even more painful to be forced into the same humiliating
role within the home and because they desperately desire
the nurturing they cannot obtain in the family. I would add
that women are taught to see themselves as flawed or
inferior and that this identity fits in with being a chronic
mental patient.

Because women are far more restricted by society in
what they can do and how they can behave, women more
than men are easily diagnosed as deviant or mentally ill.
(323)

Unfortunately, in this fight for equality, women quite often think
they need to become like men in order to compete. Since this
section is on women, I would like to put forth the idea that women
already have the innate strength, intelligence, intuition, and ability
to triumph on their own merits. For example, in working with the
editor of this book, he made the comment, "You are an archetype."
Having no idea what he was talking about, I asked, "Is this a good
thing?" He replied, "Yes, it is timeless. For example, a woman's
innate, intuitive nurturing ability; it is something that has always
existed and will always exist. It just is."

Going to the internet, Wes, my son, found the definition of
archetype, according to Jung:

. . . humans have a 'preconscious psychic disposition that
enables a (man) to react in a human manner.' These
potentials for creation are actualized when they enter
consciousness as images. There is a very important
distinction between the 'unconscious, pre-existent
dispositon' and the 'archetypal image.' The archetype may
emerge into consciousness in myriads of variations. To put

it another way, there are a very few basic archetypes or patterns which exist at the unconscious level, but there are an infinite variety of specific images which point back to these few patterns. Since these potentials for significance are not under conscious control, we may tend to fear them and deny their existence through repression. This has been a marked tendency in Modern Man, the man created by the French Revolution, the man who seeks to lead a life that is totally rational and under conscious control.

One of the "types" Jung referred to is the "mother" archetype. He says:

> The mother archetype is a particularly good example. All of our ancestors had mothers. We have evolved in an environment that included a mother or mother-substitute. We would never have survived without our connection with a nurturing-one during our times as a helpless infant. It stands to reason that we are 'built' in a way that reflects that evolutionary environment: We come into this world ready to want mother, to seek her, to recognize her, to deal with her.
>
> So the mother archetype is our built-in ability to recognize a certain relationship, that of "mothering." . . . The mother archetype is symbolized by the primordial mother or 'earth mother' of mythology, by Eve and Mary in western traditions, and by less personal symbols such as the church, the nation, a forest, or the ocean. Someone whose own mother failed to satisfy the demands of the archetype may well be one that spends his or her life seeking comfort in the church, or in identification with 'the motherland,' or in meditating upon the figure of Mary, or in a life at sea.

Many of the ancient Indian cultures were matriarchal, meaning they were governed by a council of "mothers." The chief, the warriors, the hunters, in other words, the "protectors" and "providers" were men, but the governing decisions were made by women. This provided a much different governmental organization than the one we are used to. For instance, if there was a disagreement among tribes, a mother will do everything in her power to make sure her sons are not put into harm's way as in a battle, whereas a man might tend to react according to his temper and strength.

The point to all of this is: Instead of denying, repressing or fighting the "timeless" qualities of strength and intuitive abilities which women are innately endowed with, let's use them to the advantage of ourselves, our families, our communities, and, eventually to the whole planet. Men do not characteristically possess the same attributes as women. If we can learn how to tap into these intuitive abilities, our potentials are unlimited.

Women can often times be their own worse enemy. We look around ourselves and think that everyone else has it together. We look at super-moms and wonder how they do it. We look at super-career women and think we can never measure up. We look at athletic women and wish we had their energy – not to mention, their bodies. We look at beautiful women on TV and in the movies, then allow ourselves to feel inferior because we are not a super model. Psychologically and emotionally, we are defeating ourselves.

Physically, we are also challenged. Due to our busy schedules, most of us do not spend all day in the kitchen preparing fresh foods from our organic gardens to feed our families any more. Unfortunately, neither are the people who do prepare our foods, so how do we meet the challenges of a changing world as a woman?

In order to fix anything or to get where we want to be, we have to understand some things. The first one is – NO ONE has it all together. Everyone has room for improvement and everyone has challenges and sorrows in their lives that we can't see. We have to believe that each of us is important, each of us is unique, each of us has the ability to be happy and each of us deserves it. If we can believe this about ourselves, then we will also believe it applies to everyone else; which will not only give us the ability to lift ourselves, but the ability to lift everyone around us.

May your path be strewn with flowers, memories, friends, and happy hours.
May blessings come from heaven above to fill your life with peace and love.
-- Author Unknown

Where do feelings begin?
Many of our feelings were established before we were born.
-- Karol K. Truman

Rana Lee remembers the time she went to her doctor because her husband was
beating her. "The doctor," she told a congressional committee,
"prescribed 10 milligrams of Valium three times a day to calm me down. . .
He refilled it for five years, with no questions asked."
-- Washington Post Health, January 3, 1989

Chapter One
Challenges of Being a Woman

Even in ancient writings, we find women being described as independent; buying and selling land, making and selling products, taking care of a family, being described as someone strong and honorable.

Who can find a virtuous woman? For her price is far above rubies. The heart of her husband doth safely trust in her, so that he shall have no need of spoil. She will do him good and not evil all the days of her life. She seeketh wool, and flax, and worketh willingly with her hands. She is like the merchants' ships; she bringeth her food from afar. She riseth also while it is yet night, and giveth meat to her household, and a portion to her maidens. She considereth a field, and buyeth it; with the fruit of her hands she planteth a vineyard. She girdeth her loins with strength, and strengtheneth her arms. She perceiveth that her merchandise is good: her candle goeth not out by night. She layeth her hands to the spindle, and her hands hold the distaff. She stretcheth out her hand to the poor; yea, she reacheth forth her hands to the needy. She is not afraid of the snow for her household: for all her household are clothed with scarlet. She maketh herself coverings of tapestry; her clothing is silk and purple. Her husband is known in the gates, when he sitteth among the elders of the land. She maketh fine linen, and selleth it; and delivereth girdles unto the merchant. Strength and honour are her clothing; and she shall rejoice in time to come. She openeth her mouth with wisdom; and in her tongue is the law of kindness. She looketh well to the ways of her household, and eateth not the bread of idleness. Her children arise up, and call her blessed; her husband also, and he praiseth her. Many daughters have done virtuously, but thou excellest them all. Favour is deceitful, and beauty is vain; but a woman that feareth the Lord, she shall be praised. Give her of the fruit of her hands; and let her own works praise her in the gates. (Proverbs 31:10 – 31)

What an incredible time to be a woman! There are no limits to what we can do or what we can become. We have the freedom to choose our own destiny. We can gain as much education as we desire, become wives and mothers, have any career, own our own businesses; we can do or be anything we choose. As an herbalist and midwife, I talk and work with many women all over the country. Many recognize how incredibly blessed they are to be alive at this time. They are doing everything in their power to leave this planet a better place because they were here. Unfortunately, many others are dealing with serious depression due to the overwhelming situations in their lives. All women seem to have serious questions about sustaining their health.

There's a saying, "God couldn't be everywhere at once, so he created mothers." While so many women spend their lives in quiet service to those around them; their families, communities, churches, the needy, etc., quite often this is done at the expense of their own health. In order to be able to serve others, we must learn to take care of ourselves. Otherwise, the day will come when we won't be able to help anyone due to our own bad health. If we do not take the time to "fill our own cup," we will reach a day when we realize our cup is empty and there is nothing left to give. This applies to our physical, emotional, mental and spiritual health.

All of the wonderful blessings that can be ours also bring many challenges. Some women are trapped in abusive relationships, both mental and physical. Single moms struggle to make ends meets. Career women decide to start a family only to find out they are unable to conceive. Women become addicted to drugs and alcohol which not only destroys their own lives, but effects the lives of all those who love them. Women find themselves pregnant with unwanted pregnancies. Elderly women are widowed and find themselves alone and feeling abandoned. I wish I could say these problems are easy to fix. Unfortunately, they are not!

Several things must happen in order to solve any of these problems. The first one is a personal challenge - we have to recognize there is a problem. I am painfully aware that one section in an obscure book, such as this one, is not going to solve the world's problems. However, I have watched these patterns repeat themselves so often, I feel the need to take a few moments of your time to make some suggestions. If, these suggestions help even one person to change life for the better, then this book served it's purpose.

If you are in an abusive relationship that is destroying you, you must reach a point where you recognize the fact that you do not deserve this! No one does!! Your situation is not unique. You are being used. As soon as you recognize you have a problem, you need to carefully do something about it. There are many places you can go to seek help where it will be kept confidential. If you are in a situation where happiness seems impossible, then find enough strength to do something about it. There are many people out there waiting to help you – let them! You have unlimited potential and the ability to obtain joy and happiness in this life.

If you are a single mom, struggling to keep your head above water, then you are probably living with too much stress in your life which is keeping you and your children from being as happy as you could be. Take the time needed to look into the programs that are available to help you get an education or start your own business, so that you do not have to spend your life working for minimum wage. If it were possible, I would open a day care center full of love and free of charge to any mom who wanted to improve her situation. Of course, this is not possible, but there are many programs out there, churches and government to help you meet your goals. The sooner you get started on improving your situation, the sooner you will be able to relieve some of the stress you are having to live with and the sooner you and your children will be able to start enjoying life more. The path you have been given as a single mom is not easy, but it's also not impossible. Don't give up and think that life is over. Too many women honestly believe that their lives are over and can never hold any joy again. There are still tremendous opportunities for you to take advantage of. You have children who depend on you for support, love and stability. You can make a tremendous difference in their lives if you take an active part in them. Somehow, somewhere we need to join together to stop this pattern of dysfunctional families. The love of a good mother can go along way toward this goal. It is easy to become immersed in self-pity, depression, and bitterness, but where children are involved, we must find a way to rise above it. These are not attributes we want instilled in our children.

If you are addicted to drugs or alcohol, please, find a program to help you overcome your addiction. The people who produce drugs, alcohol and tobacco know that if you ever start using these products, you can be addicted for life. That means that for the rest of your life you will be putting money into their pockets unless you take control of the situation and seek help. There is absolutely nothing in any of these substances which ultimately ever helps you. They are extremely destructive physically, mentally and emotionally, not only for you, but for everyone who loves you or associates with you. Our lives affect many people. We are not islands unto ourselves. So many times we try to convince ourselves that what we do is our own problem, it doesn't effect anyone else, but it isn't true! Everything we do effects the lives around us, including future generations.

If you are using legal substances, such as antidepressants, take a serious look at what you are doing: Are you the happy, vibrant person you once were? Maybe there are solutions out there which can help you fix what is causing the depression without resorting to drugs which turn you into a zombie so that you just don't care any more. Please, understand that I am not passing judgment on you or anyone else. I am simply offering suggestions in response to questions I receive regularly. Like every other condition of the body, we are always further ahead to question what is causing the problem than we are when we merely treat the symptoms. Depression is a symptom; let's get to the cause and fix it.

If you find yourself pregnant with an unplanned or unwanted pregnancy, consider all of your choices very carefully. Years ago I read an article in *The Readers Digest* which was written by a nurse. She had worked in an abortion clinic – it was her job to listen for the heartbeat so that they would know when the baby was dead. The type of abortion they were performing was the kind where they go up into the uterus, cut the baby into pieces and then suction it out. While she was listening with the stethoscope, she heard the baby scream from inside the womb. She left that day and never returned. She wanted people to know that these are living human beings who feel pain just as we do.

Abortion need not be an option. There are many people who will tell you that it is your body and you have a right to choose what you do with it. The fact is you made your choice when you got pregnant. (Unless you were raped.) Now there are two bodies involved; yours and someone else. You do not have the right to choose whether someone else lives or dies.

Recently, one of my daughters sent me an E-mail showing the hand of a 21-week-old fetus reaching out of the uterus to grasp the finger of the surgeon who was performing invetro surgery to fix spinal bifida. At 21 weeks, the parents could have chosen to have the fetus aborted, but instead chose to try a new surgical technique to correct the problem. Even at this young age, the baby was able to reach out through the surgical incision to grasp the surgeon's finger as if to say, "thank you."

In *Feelings Buried Alive Never Die,* Karol Truman tells us:

> Recent research on infants shows that even at birth the child has mastered many sophisticated physical and psychological skills. It is increasingly clear that the infant develops these skills in the prenatal period. In *The Secret Life of the Unborn Child,* Dr. Thomas Verny tells us that the unborn child is not 'the passive, mindless creatures of the traditional pediatrics texts.'
>
> We now know that the unborn child is an aware, reacting human being who from the sixth month on (and perhaps even earlier) leads an active emotional life. Along with this startling finding we have made these discoveries: The fetus can see, hear, experience, taste and, on a primitive level, even learn in utero . . . Most importantly, he can feel – not with an adult's sophistication, but feel nonetheless.
>
> . . . Even more intriguing is evidence of the impact of the mother's and father's attitudes and feelings on their unborn child. Based on the findings of many other

researchers as well as his own experience as a psychoanalyst, Dr. Verny presents evidence that the attitude of the mother toward the pregnancy and the child, as well as toward her partner, have a profound effect on the psychological development of the child and on the birth experience. The mother, by her patterns of feeling and behavior, is the chief source of the stimuli which shape the fetus. (22-23)

Life is a sacred trust. If you find yourself in this position and feel it would be impossible for you to keep the baby, then seek out an agency who can help you place your child with one of the many thousands of couples waiting to adopt. If you are afraid, alone or unsure how to proceed, then please give us a call and we will do all we can to help you. There is a son or daughter growing in your womb who is anxious to see what this life is all about. We understand that sometimes there are circumstances which would prevent you from keeping this beautiful child, but we want you to understand that there are many who would be able to give this child all the love and attention he or she deserves. Please allow someone to help you. No one else ever needs to know, but this child deserves a chance.

If you have had a career and now want to have a child, but find you are unable to conceive, you are not alone. More and more women are having infertility problems due to our lifestyles and diets. Study the second section of this book carefully. It will probably be necessary to do some type of cleansing program to prepare your body for a pregnancy.

Unlike men, who produce new sperm all the time, women are born with the only eggs they will ever have. The older we get, the older our eggs get. An OB/Gyn told me once that if you put sperm in a Petri dish with the eggs of a 20-year-old, about 90% of them will become fertilized. If you repeat the same experiment with the eggs of a 30-year-old, about 50% will become fertilized and if you repeat it with a 40-year-old, only 10 -20% will become fertilized. The other problem is that as we age, our "fertile time" during the month becomes shorter and shorter.

So, do not give up; all is not lost. Just take the time to cleanse and nourish. Look in the "infertility" section of the "reference guide," do everything you can to strengthen the female organs, balance the hormones, alkalize the body and stick to as many live foods as possible.

If you are elderly, facing loneliness and feeling abandoned, there are many volunteer programs you can be involved with which bless the lives of others and gives you a new lease on life. Check with libraries and schools in your area to see if there are programs where you can read to children. Daycare centers quite often need grandmothers who are willing to give love and quality time to the children. If there is something you always wanted to learn, but never had the time to do it because you were busy with a career or a family; now is the time to do it. Learning something new is one of the best ways to feel young again, keeping our minds busy and active. It helps to give us a new lease on life. If you have children and grandchildren, then take an active part in remembering them on their birthdays and holidays. Be as much a part of their lives as you can be. You have a lot of experience and wisdom which can bless the members of your family. If your health is poor, then take the necessary steps now to "cleanse and nourish." It is never too late, as long as there is breath in your body. You can take steps to enhance the quality of your life. Know that we love you and appreciate you for the life you have shared with the world and the contributions you have made through your love and service. Wisdom and insight are still needed. If they are not appreciated where you are, then share them with those who will appreciate it.

There is a beautiful song written by Janice Kapp Perry, which can give us all food for thought. It is called: *The Woman You'll Be Someday*. Some key lines are:

> I see an old woman rocking there.
> The sun shining softly on her silver hair.
> I wonder the secrets she holds deep inside.
> Is she smiling or hiding a tear in her eye?
> She watches our day as her story unfolds,
> For you see, she is you, grown old.

And with every decision you make today.
You're creating the woman you'll be some day.
Be watchful young woman,
Choose well today!
Remember to live for the woman you'll be someday.

Wouldn't it be wonderful if we all lived this way? Sometimes I think we forget the sacrifice and service that have been given by our elderly citizens in their life times. The following story is an example of what I am referring to:

In 1980, working the graveyard shift in a nursing home in Arkansas, I noticed one of the ladies I cared for was having a hard time breathing. I went to the front desk to check on the problem. They informed me the doctor had already checked on her. She was not expected to live through the night. I asked if they had contacted her family. They said her son had left a notice with them saying that he did not want to be disturbed in the middle of the night for any reason. If his mother passed away, they could call him in the morning. I was mortified! How could any child do this to their mother? I don't care how many things she may have done wrong in her life. The truth is, none of us are perfect! She was there when he came into this world and, as far as I was concerned, he should have been there when she left it. I sat with her through the night between my rounds. When my shift was over, I ran home to make arrangements for the care of my children and then raced back to the nursing home. When I got there, her bed was being stripped. They told me she had passed away while I was gone. I can't express the sorrow I felt for her, her son and the grandchildren who could have shared this sacred moment with her. Unless we check out early, we are all going to grow old. Let's love and respect our elders the way we hope we will one day be loved and appreciated.

I state my opinions on each of these areas, knowing they may not be popular. The reason I have done this is because health involves more than just the physical aspects. I can tell women what herbs to use to help reduce depression, balance hormones, feed the female organs, and cure what might be considered an "incurable disease," but until we address the spiritual, emotional, and mental aspects of health, these herbs will not be sufficient to restore you to complete health. We have to stand on our own two feet and begin to take charge of our lives. We have to return to a natural, solid value system, realizing we have not been left on this planet alone. If we can learn to tie into a source "higher than our own," we will be able to find the strength to overcome whatever life brings us. Sometimes life becomes so difficult we have to just take it one step at a time. Then, before we know it, we can walk a whole block, then a mile, and eventually we will run the whole marathon.

Stop and remember the incredible potential you possess. Walk Tall! Know that you can do whatever you set your mind and heart to doing. You are loved much more than you realize and there are many who are willing and able to help you. Reach out and do it!

This year, Americans will spend more money on fast food
than on higher education.
-- The New Yorker

Be true when you are tempted,
Be true when you don't want to be,
Be true when it means standing alone from the rest of the world.
-- Ruth B. Wright

. . . Many studies since have discovered malnutrition in anywhere from twenty-five to fifty percent of patients in American and British hospitals. The doctor who carried out the Boston study, George L. Blackburn, has since stated that malnutrition is one of the most common causes of death among old people in hospitals.
-- Robert S. Mendelsohn, M.D.

Chapter Two
Common Health Concerns

In chapter one, we discussed some of the issues pertaining to mental and emotional health. In this chapter we will take a look at some of the common, physical health concerns of women.

Following are a list of common concerns addressed in the "reference guide," section IV: cancer, cramping, depression, hormonal imbalances, irregular periods, mastitis, menopause, miscarriage, PMS, uterine fibroids, vaginal infections, varicose veins, and weight loss.

In one of Dr. Christopher's lectures he tells of a woman who came to him with cervical cancer. The doctor had recommended a hysterectomy, but she felt there were more children who were to be born to her, so she went to Dr. Christopher and asked if there was anything she could do. He told her to go on the mucusless diet, the NuFem, Changease, wheat germ oil and to use the "Slant Board Routine."

She was faithful with her diet and the herbs for several weeks, but didn't notice a change. She went back to Dr. Christopher and asked him what the problem was. He told her to continue with her program and to keep cleansing. Several more weeks passed. Then, one day, when she was sitting on the toilet, she felt something fall out of her. It appeared to be swimming in the toilet, so she called her husband in to see it. He scooped it out and put it in a jar. They took their specimen to the doctor, who said, "This is the first time I have ever seen one of these in its whole state. We usually have to cut it up in pieces to get it out. This is a 'spider cancer.'"

Dr. Christopher made the point that there was no longer any toxins left in her system to live on, so it had simply let go and fallen out.

The "slant board routine" helps women who are dealing with problems such as: ovarian cysts, endometriosis, adhesions, cervical cancer, etc. . Just about anything can be used as a slant board: two or three folded bath towels which you can prop your hips up on in the bathtub, an ironing board or some other board where you can prop one end up about 18 in. off the ground, or a commercial slant board. You want to be in a head-down position with your hips elevated.

You need something to douche with: an enema bulb, a turkey baster, an enema bucket, or a commercial douche bag. The idea is to get fluid up in the vagina, so use what you have on hand. The herbal combinations you will need are:

Dr. Christopher's VB formula

Dr. Christopher's Yellow Dock Combination

Cocoa Butter

Castor Oil

The herbs in the VB are designed to "draw things out." The herbs in the Yellow Dock Combination are designed to "nourish." VB stands for Vaginal Bolus which is what you will need to make with the VB powder and cocoa butter.

Melt the cocoa butter on the stove, add enough VB powder to make a paste about the same consistency as Play-do or pie crust dough. Fill the cubicles of an ice cube tray with the VB mixture and put it in the freezer. When you need to use it, pop one of the cubes out of the tray and cut it into three pieces. The cocoa butter will melt at body temperature so you will be able to easily mold the pieces into the shape of a tampon.

The program Dr. Christopher recommended is this:

Monday morning	Insert 2 boluses
(you may want to wear a sanitary pad as there is always some leakage)	
Tuesday morning	Insert 1 or 2 more boluses
Tuesday evening	Slant Board Routine
	(see instructions below)
Wednesday morning	Insert 2 boluses
Thursday morning	Insert 1 or 2 more boluses
Thursday evening	Slant Board Routine
Friday morning	Insert 2 boluses
Saturday morning	Insert 1 or 2 more boluses
Saturday morning	Slant Board Routine
Sunday	Rest from your labors

Slant Board Routine

Make a quart of tea using the Yellow Dock combination. When your tea has cooled down to room temperature, put it into what ever you plan to douche with. Set your tea and castor oil next to your slant board. Put a couple of towel on the slant board as this can become messy. Lay on the slant board head down and douche with the Yellow Dock tea. The tea is going to do two things. First, it will flush out the boluses from the last two days. Second, we want to get the tea up into the uterus to nourish it. After you have flushed out the boluses, allow the rest of the tea to stay up inside. While you are still in this head down position, holding the tea inside, put some castor oil on the abdomen and massage – put your fingers above the pubic bone and draw them up toward the naval, then draw your hands in opposite directions toward the outside of the abdomen, then down and around so they meet back at the pubic bone.

Massaging helps to draw the Yellow Dock up into the uterus. It also helps to draw the organs back up where they belong, so this is very beneficial if you are dealing with a prolapsed uterus or incontinency due to a fallen bladder. The castor oil helps to break up any adhesions or other stagnant conditions. I recommend staying on the slant board for 15 to 20 minutes.

If you are dealing with a problem, like uterine fibroids, which is causing such severe bleeding you cannot keep the boluses in – then I would douche every night with 4 – 6 ounces of wheat grass juice until you get the problem under control. It is truly amazing how fast wheat grass can restore order where there is chaos.

Like all of the conditions we talk about, if you are dealing with a serious problem, you must get enough pure water to drink and stay on a live food diet in order to correct the problem. The herbs will do their part, but in order to correct what started the problem in the first place, you must clean up the body and remove the toxins.

Total health only comes when we are emotionally, mentally and physically well.

A wise woman renews herself.
In proper season, she develops her talents and continues her education.
She musters the discipline to reach her goals.
She dispels darkness and opens windows of truth to light her way.
-- Russell M. Nelson

Each of us comes into this world separately, one by one.
This is not an accident. I think it's the Lord's way of reminding us of the
infinite worth of each soul.
-- Dwan J. Young

Not in the clamor or the crowded street,
Not in the shouts and plaudits of the throng,
But in ourselves,
Our triumph and defeat.
-- Henry Wadsworth Longfellow

Chapter 3
How to Have a Healthy Pregnancy

I encourage all women to learn as much as they can about pregnancy, a special time in a woman's life. It is a time to reflect on your life and the life which is preparing to enter mortality. It's a time to be at peace – to communicate love and encouragement to the child within your womb. It's a time for you and your partner to become close and more considerate of each other.

Pregnancy is not a disease or an illness. It is a natural, incredible time of creation. We all marvel at the beauty of the first flowers we see in the springtime, the first blades of green grass poking up through the ground after being dormant all winter and the awesome splendor of the fruit trees in bloom. How much more marvelous and awesome is it to think of a brand new human being growing within your womb. The perfect little fingers and toes, the little button nose, the adorable little tummy and bottom, the beautiful eyelashes and hair all topped off by a unique personality with thoughts and ideas that have never been put together in just exactly this way before.

After 30 years of experience with both hospital and home birth – I am truly amazed at the difference between a traditional, contemporary pregnancy as compared to one where a woman takes responsibility for her own health and the health of her unborn child. In a traditional pregnancy women continue to eat the typical American diet, use prescription prenatal vitamins, along with subjecting themselves and their babies to countless tests and ultasounds which are considered routine. As a result, pregnancy, labor and birth are typically harder, longer and with many more complications.

If, however, a woman is willing to take responsibility for her own pregnancy, she can do a lot to reduce her chances of having any complications. Obviously, when you are dealing with "mother nature" there is no 100% guarantees, but you can achieve a degree of certainty. Many women who have taken this challenge to heart are amazed at the difference in their pregnancies.

When I first began my midwife practice, I noticed that most women's urine is very acidic. One day, while my children were gathered around, I said, "I wonder if it is possible to change the pH of someone's urine." One of my sons had a mother-in-law who worked in a hospital as a nurse, so one day he brought up the topic of pH in the urine. She very adamantly told him that you can not change the pH of urine – it is acidic. When he told me this I was excited because it seemed to me that if the urine of sick and dying people is always acidic, then, maybe the urine of healthy people shouldn't be. pH is measured on a scale where anything below a "7" is considered acidic, while everything above a "7" is considered alkaline. That is how I began to put the following program together. I soon discovered that you can indeed change the pH of the urine. In fact, that is one of the ways I know whether a woman is following the program or not, because when they do, their urine becomes a neutral "7" on the pH scale.

These instructions are the culmination of my years of experience – I have found they make a major difference in how well the pregnancy, labor and birth will go. Listed below is the instruction sheet I used in my midwife practice, followed by the explanations for each recommendation:

PREGNANCY INSTRUCTIONS
Supplements:

Vitalerbs .5 capsules 3x's/day with meals
Wheat Germ Oil . . . . 2 capsules 2x's/day
Liquid Chlorophyll . . . . 1 Tbsp 2x's/day
Tea . . . . 1 qt. / day
    Choice of:
    Dr. Christopher's Pregnancy Tea
    Red Raspberry Combination
        3 parts Red Raspberry Leaf
        1 part Comfrey
        1 part Alfalfa
    Red Raspberry Leaf
Pure Water (preferably distilled) . . . 2 qts/day
Organa Minerals . . . . 1 cap full/day

Dietary Suggestions:

Fruits	Nuts
Vegetables	Seeds
Grains	Legumes

(Organic, if possible – try to make 50% of diet raw)

NO – NO'S

| NO alcohol, drugs or cigarettes | NO red meat |
| NO carbonated drinks | AVOID sugar, dairy and processed foods |

Exercise:

25 Pelvic Rocks/day
50 Kegal exercises/day
Walk 1 mile/day
Remember to take time to breathe deeply each day

Explanations for Pregnancy Instructions:

Vitalerbs - Take 5 capsules of Vitalerbs or any other natural supplement made from whole plants with meals to make sure you are getting all of the vitamins they need. The reason for insisting these supplements come from whole foods/plants is because science is still in the process of learning what the body needs and how it processes it. For example: Several years ago, science discovered that women needed extra calcium, so women ran out to health food stores to buy calcium. Then science figured out that in order to assimilate calcium, we needed magnesium, so women ran out to buy calcium with magnesium. In recent years, scientific research has shown that in order to assimilate calcium, we need vitamin D. One day in Christopher's herb shop, I heard someone come in and ask for calcium with vitamin D. I wanted so badly to step forward and tell them it would be cheaper to just buy the calcium, step outside and take it in the sunlight, which would give them their vitamin D.

My point with all of this is: If we were to sit at the feet of the greatest scientist on earth and ask the question, "What vitamins, minerals, amino acids, etc. do we need to be healthy?" He might give us a list a foot long. If, however, we could sit at the feet of our Creator and ask the same question, His list might be four feet long. We just haven't discovered everything in the other three foot list yet.

Science is constantly learning, but the Creator knew what we would need and He put it all in the plants. When we take synthetic vitamins it is very hard, if not impossible, for our bodies to assimilate them. When we take them in their whole, organic state we have everything we need to assimilate them. Some prenatal vitamins can actually be toxic and doctors will advise against taking them in the first three months of pregnancy because they can cause nausea. It is best to stick with supplements which come from whole foods and /or plants.

Wheat Germ Oil – Take two wheat germ oil capsules twice per day until the last six weeks of pregnancy. Wheat germ oil is high in vitamin E which is essential for a healthy pregnancy. Often, referred to as the body's glue – it seems to help attach a strong placenta. In fact, this is why in the last six weeks, cut back to one capsule twice a day, so the placenta will be willing to let go when it is time. Wheat germ oil also helps to keep the hormones balanced, along with keeping the skin soft and pliable so that when the mother is ready to give birth, she will be more likely to stretch and not tear.

Liquid Chlorophyll – fresh wheat grass juice would actually be the first choice, but if you cannot juice every day, then use the bottled chlorophyll. Chlorophyll is like liquid plant blood. It is very similar to our blood, without the red corpuscles which we make in the marrow of our bones. It is wonderful for building healthy blood which helps moms to not become anemic.

Tea – Choose between three different teas, add lemon, mint or honey to help the flavor. If you don't enjoy it, you won't drink it. Make a quart when you get up in the morning, then enjoy ice tea throughout the day. These teas are extremely nutritious for the mother and the baby.

Water – In addition to the quart of tea, drink two quarts of pure water every day. There are times in the first and third trimester when you will feel like you are living in the bathroom because the baby is sitting on your bladder, but if you will do this, you will have a much better pregnancy and your kidneys will thank you.

Organa Minerals – This relatively new addition to my instructions is important because I have found that fewer and fewer women are getting enough trace minerals in their diet. Remember we are not rock eaters, so, if you are going to add minerals to your diet, make sure they are coming from an organic plant source.

Diet – Eat as many live, wholesome foods as possible. I suggest making 50% of the diet raw which is easy to do if you juice in the morning or eat fresh fruit, have a salad for lunch, then snack on fruits, vegetables, and nuts during the day.

NO-NO'S – Alcohol, drugs and cigarettes should be self-explanatory. If moms are not willing to give these things up, then they need to give birth in a hospital where they are prepared to take care of the emergencies.

Most women are not prepared to give up all meat. Therefore, stop the red meat and eat chicken and fish sparingly. I'm not trying to make vegetarians out of you. The problem is most people are getting grocery store meat, pumped full of steroids, immunizations, pesticides, etc. . Those chemicals can play havoc with the mother's and baby's chemistry. The other problem is that there seems to be a correlation between heavy meat eating and heavy bleeding, something we do not want to happen at home.

Carbonated drinks seem to be the hardest restriction. There is absolutely nothing in a carbonated drink which is good for us. Without taking the time here to go into the sugar, the colorings, the preservatives, the caffeine, the sugar substitutes, the high acidity, etc. – let's just look at the carbonation. When we breathe, we take in oxygen, when we exhale, we breathe out carbon dioxide or CO_2, a waste product of the body. Carbonated drinks are made with CO_2 – it's like drinking our own waste. We wouldn't sit down to an ice cold glass of urine, so why would we sit down to an ice cold glass of CO2? If this is not enough to persuade you, then just remember, moms – carbonation tends to give babies colic, so how many nights do you want to walk the floor?

Exercise – Do 25 pelvic rocks every night when you get into bed – just get on your hands and knees on your mattress or on the floor beside your bed and do them before you lay down to sleep. These are done by slowly rolling the hips under (arching the spine, which is sometimes known as a "cat stretch"). Bring the hips back up until the spine is straight. Repeat 25 times. Pelvic rocks are good for strengthening the lower back so the third trimester won't be so hard. They are also good for encouraging the baby to line up head down instead of breech.

The 50 kegals are to strengthen the muscles used during childbirth. These are done by squeezing the muscles you would use to shut off the flow of urine and then releasing them. Instead of trying to count out 50 kegals, I suggest each mom program herself like Pavlov's dog to something like the telephone or stop lights. Each time you come to a stop light or the phone rings, do five kegals. That way, by the end of the day, you will have done 50.

Walking a mile each day is not only good exercise, but it allows you some quiet time. Whenever the weather is appropriate, it also allows you time to commune with nature and hopefully, with your baby. Each child has the right to come into this world feeling wanted and loved, so don't hesitate to communicate these feelings to your baby. When the weather is not conducive to being outside, then go somewhere where there is climate control, such as a gym, an indoor track or the mall – just make sure you walk as often as you can.

Because of our hectic lifestyles, we don't take the time to breathe deeply each day. You and your baby both need the oxygen, so each day, take the time to expand your lungs with fresh air.

When people have become defensive and claim these instructions are unnecessary – I explain that I do not feel the need to push my thoughts or feelings on to anyone who is not receptive. It is my belief that all women should be free to give birth wherever and with whomever they feel the most comfortable. If that is in a hospital with a doctor – they have my complete support. If it is in a birthing center with nurse midwives – they have my complete support. If it is at home with a midwife – they have my complete support. However, if they want my help at home, then these are the instructions I insist on. The reason for this is that I am not into emergencies – I don't like the adrenaline rush and I am not willing to take any unnecessary chances with the lives of the mother or baby.

The second sheet of instructions I provided for my moms are on the "common discomforts of pregnancy." For ease of writing here – if these instructions have already been given in this book, I will refer you back to the page where they are written.

COMMON DISCOMFORTS OF PREGNANCY

Consider these your first line of defense – if they don't work, we will need to get a little more aggressive.

Nausea:
   a) use Nausea tea found on pg. 375
   b) Nausea can be caused by a lack of B vitamins – if this is the case, many women turn to a B complex supplement – another great source of the B complex is leafy greens and sprouts, especially alfalfa sprouts and wheat grass – you will also find B complex in fresh pineapple juice and fresh carrot Juice.
   c) sometimes there are cases where the body is creating too much bile – in these cases we use the Barberry LG to help regulate it
Bladder Infection:
   See Section IV, pg. 277
Charley Horse:
   See Section IV, pg. 323
Vaginal Infection:
   See Section IV, pg. 462

Stretch Marks:
> Wheat Germ Oil
> The wheat germ oil you are taking orally will help to reduce stretch marks by supplying the skin with the right type of oil to help make it soft. You can also apply the wheat germ oil directly to the skin.

Insomnia:
> See Section IV, pg. 421

Danger Signs in Pregnancy

Report to your doctor or midwife immediately if you notice:

1. Vaginal Bleeding:
   In the first trimester, it can indicate threatened, spontaneous or missed abortion (miscarriage), molar pregnancy or ectopic pregnancy. In the second trimester, can indicate placenta praevia or placental abruption. Likewise, during the third trimester, it may be due to placental abruption.

2. Blisters in the peritoneal or anal area during first trimester:
   This may be herpes virus, contact doctor or midwife so culture can be taken.

3. Severe pelvic or abdominal pain:
   In the first trimester, may indicate tubal pregnancy. In last trimester, may indicate placental abruption.

4. Persistent and severe mid-back pain:
   May indicate severe kidney infection.

5. Swelling of Hands and Face:
   Particularly if face looks puffy or coarse, may indicate pre-eclampsia

6. Severe headaches, blurry vision or epigastric (chest) pain:
   May indicate pre-eclamptic condition becoming critical. Notify midwife at once.

7. Gush of fluid from vagina:
   If in first or second trimester, may indicate miscarriage. If in late second or third trimester, may indicate premature delivery.

8. Regular uterine contractions before 37 weeks:
    May indicate impending premature birth.
9. Cessation of fetal movement:
    May indicate fetal demise. The baby should move approximately three times per hour. If less, or less than usual, report to doctor or midwife.

The last six weeks of pregnancy, I recommend taking Dr. Christopher's prenatal tea, more commonly known as the "6-week formula." The schedule goes like this:

6 weeks before due date: take one capsule 2 x's/day
5 weeks before due date: take one capsule 3 x's/day
4 weeks before due date: take two capsules 3 x's/day
3 weeks before due date: take three capsules 3 x's/day
Continue this dosage until birth.

We have all heard the stories about Indian women working in the field until time to have their babies. Then they step into the trees, squat, give birth to their baby, put it in a papoose, strap them in, and then go back to work. Even though these stories may be exaggerated, the fact is that Indian women were well aware and knew which herbs to take in order to prepare their body for childbirth. This is same idea behind the six-week formula.

As the body prepares the uterus and muscles for birth – there will be sporadic contractions. Sometimes they can even form into a pattern. The difference between these contractions and active labor is that these do not increase in intensity. However, they can be uncomfortable and annoying, especially if they are taking place at night. When this is the case, you need to cut back on the six-week formula or discontinue its use.

Also, cut the wheat germ oil back to one capsule twice a day. On the full dosage until birth, the placenta sometimes wants to hang on for a couple hours after the birth of the baby, even though its job is finished. If the dosage is cut back six weeks before birth, we don't seem to have this problem.

During the last two weeks of the pregnancy, I suggest that twice a day, after the woman goes to the bathroom, she rub the perineum with olive oil. This is to help prepare the pelvic floor for the birth by helping the perineum to stretch and not tear.

The ancestor of every action is a thought.
-- Ralph Waldo Emerson

The greatest need of the human heart is encouragement.
Let me whisper this secret in your ear:
Every time you try to encourage someone else,
Your soul will be flooded with a light and glow of peace and good cheer.
Try it next time when the gloom is heavy and the load is barren.
-- Susa Young Gates

I recall the news media carrying a story in the 1970's about a midwife who
successfully delivered sextuplets under a bus on a hot, dusty road in Mexico.
They were on the way to the hospital when the births occurred. The nurse
suggested they get back in the bus and continue to the hospital, but the husband
asked, "Why? Everything is all right. Let's turn around and go home!"
-- Polly Block

Chapter 4

Institutional & Natural Traditions of Childbirth

Any class or book you can find on relaxation, breathing techniques, focal points, etc. can be helpful in preparing you for labor and birth. Understand the reason labor is called labor is because it is hard work. Women have been having babies on this planet for over 6,000 years, evidently successfully because we are still here. Labor does not have to be some horrible, frightening, out-of-control event. However we do need to be prepared. You would not show up on the day of a marathon to run the race if you had not prepared for it. Without being in shape for the race, you would never make it to the finish line. In some ways, labor is like that. No matter what, sooner or later, the baby will come out whether you are ready for it or not, but if you are prepared, you can accomplish your task with grace and dignity, being in control when it happens.

Many women today choose not to be in control, but want everything to be planned and orchestrated. As soon as they go into labor, they report to the hospital for the epidural and wait until someone hands them their baby. Other women actually schedule the day they want to have their baby. These women report to the hospital to be hooked up to pitocin, a labor-inducing drug, and an epidural or arrange for a 'C' section when it is convenient for them and/or their doctor. Let me reiterate; I think each woman should deliver wherever, however, and with whomever they are comfortable. This chapter, however, is dedicated to those women who want more control.

Consider this fairly routine scenario, a young woman becomes pregnant, starts reading books and researching pregnancy, labor and delivery. She comes to understand that any medication taken during labor and delivery can affect her and her baby. She decides, after careful research, she wants to have this baby in a hospital, naturally. You can have an unmedicated birth in the hospital, but in the majority of cases, you can not have a "natural" childbirth. Typically, there are just too many rules, regulations, and contradictory conventions to allow this to happen.

So, our young woman decides she is going to have her baby "naturally." She attends as many classes as possible and does her homework, she learns some relaxation and breathing techniques. Her husband has never been around anyone in labor before, but is willing and anxious to help her in any way possible. The time arrives when she goes into labor. She is excited her day has finally arrived.

She reports to the hospital (because this is what all of us are taught to do – anything else would be irresponsible) and finds that she is about 3 cm. dilated. She and her partner are in high spirits and ready to get their baby here. When she checks into the hospital, she is required to remove her clothing, put on a hospital gown and climb into bed where the monitors can be attached. Two large straps are put around her abdomen – one is to monitor the baby's heartbeat and the second one is to monitor how regular and strong the contractions are. Usually, she will be required to stay in bed for an hour while the hospital personnel assess whether she really is in active labor. Vital signs will be taken, papers signed, blood drawn, dilation and effacement checked.

When the required amount of time has passed, our young mother will hopefully be admitted and allowed to get out of bed. Normally, she will be advised not to eat anything while she is in labor, in case she needs to be medicated later on. Now, she and her sweetheart are ready to do this. Unfortunately, there is not a lot to do when you are sitting in a hospital room, so they're attention becomes tediously focused on every little thing that is happening. Some time passes and she reaches 4 cm. She is now starting to experience active labor. The contractions become much stronger, her mood has changes, and she is gets restless. Her husband tells her, "Relax!" She reaches over, grabs his shirt and says, "Shut-up!"

Around this time, a nurse comes into the room and says, "Sweetheart, you do not need to suffer like this. We can give you something that will help you relax, take the edge off and it won't effect the baby." Let's face it, at this point, what fool in their right mind wouldn't jump at this chance?

Now the scenario falls into an all too familiar routine. In ordered to have any of the promised medication, the young lady has to have an IV started in case there is a reaction to the medication. She is put back into bed, usually on her back, the monitors are wrapped back around her, the IV is started and the medication is given. Unfortunately, the medication sedates and nauseates her. Instead of being on top of the contractions, she is now dosing off and waking in the middle of them. As the contractions continue to get stronger, she has lost most of her mobility due to the monitor straps, the IV and the medication, so it is much harder to get comfortable. Quite often, the medication slows down or stops the labor.

Then the doctor advises a pitocin drip to be given through the IV to help her labor progress. Pitocin alters the natural rhythm of the contractions and makes it doubly hard to stay on top of them. Our young woman can no longer deal with this (which is no surprise and should not be seen as a weakness on her part), so the epidural is started and the baby's monitor is screwed into the top of his or her head. If the epidural works correctly, she obtains blessed relief from her suffering. If it doesn't work correctly, it can be worse than before because it is all concentrated in the area that did not take. If the medication comes up too far, it causes a feeling of suffocation. If the spinal cord is accidentally punctured by the needle, it drains spinal fluid which causes severe headaches because brain floats on it. Nerves can be damaged as the epidural is administered, with all kinds of potential future back problems.

Let's assume, in this case, the epidural works properly. If it slows down the labor or stops it all together and the pitocin is not effective in helping with the dilation, then our young lady is an automatic "C" section. Assuming the labor continues to full dilation, our young woman will attempt to push her baby out. If she has never had a child before, she has no idea what muscles to use to accomplish this. Since she has no feeling of the sensations that her body is trying to relay to her, she must depend on the coaching of others. I have seen women bare down so hard that capillaries begin to break in their face, and yet, little progress is made in pushing the baby down. This is because they are using the wrong muscles in their effort. If the baby does not come down the canal in the allotted period of time or the baby begins to show distress from being in the birth canal too long – she is an automatic "C" section. With an epidural, doctors allow a 2 hour minimum time for pushing – in a home birth, pushing time is typically less than 30 minutes.

If she is able to move the baby down the birth canal, most doctors perform an episiotomy to help make the opening bigger to get the baby out. If she has moved the baby down far enough, but is having a difficult time pushing the baby out on her own, the doctor will go in with forceps (the salad spoons) or a vacuum to pull the baby out. In 1999, 20/20 reported on the amount of spinal cord damage, brain damage and death that can result from these procedures.

In many parts of the country, hospitals report one out of three births are taken "C" section. In some hospitals, it is actually one out of every two births. Does it make any sense at all that in the last 30 years we have come to a point where half of the babies being born to be cut out of their mothers?

Obviously, not all hospital births go like the one I just described. There are women who have very positive experiences having their babies in the hospital and if you are one of them, I am thrilled for you. The unfortunate truth is, the one I just described is very typical. These tend to be the ones who come to me to find out if they have alternatives. For instance, several years ago, a friend asked me to help with her daughter-in-law, the month before, her own daughter had given birth to her first child. Her daughter was a jogger and was in great shape. She had fallen into the scenario I just described. She came out of it with a "C" section. Now her daughter-in-law was in the same hospital going through the same scenario. The doctor had just been in the room – pronounced a "failure to progress" (hospitals expect you to dilate 1 cm./hour) and said they would have to do a "C" section. The mother knew this was too big of a coincidence. She asked me if I could help.

When I went in the room, she was hooked up to the monitors, the IV with the pitocin drip, and the epidural. The mothers and baby's vital signs looked good. When the doctor came back in the room, I said, "Her vital signs and the baby's vital signs look good. Would it be all right if we waited a couple more hours?" The doctor was furious, but he couldn't justify not waiting, so he said, "You have two hours," and left the room. After he left, we called the nurse in, and had the epidural shut off. Within a short time, she was able to feel her contractions. We worked with her, in an hour and a half, she gave birth to a beautiful, healthy baby vaginally. I have seen this "emergency" happen too many times.

By contrast, let me share a typical home birth experience. In the early stages of labor, mothers are busy with their daily routine, taking care of their children, fixing meals, taking walks, getting the baby's clothes laid out, eating, drinking and doing anything else they are comfortable doing. In the active phase of labor, some women continue to go about their normal activities, stopping to squat or brace themselves against a counter or wall while they breathe through contractions. Others feel more comfortable getting into a hot tub of water with ginger root or essential oils to help them relax. (A whirl pool tub, garden tub or birthing tub works best for this, the stomach is completely immersed in the water) Quite often, soothing music plays in the background. Depending on each women's personality and how the woman is working with the labor will depend on how much the midwives are involved in using comfort measures. During transition (the shortest, hardest part of labor) some women prefer to stay in the warm water – others will get on the bed or couch where they almost become trance-like as they reach inside themselves to find the strength they were given to focus on and accomplish this task. When it is time to push the baby out they will sit on a birthing stool, stay in the water, stay on the bed, get into a hands and knees position – whatever is most comfortable for the mother. The midwife talks the mother through the pushing, so she will stretch and not tear. When the baby is born, mother and baby rest comfortably in her bed where she begins to nurse the baby.

Consider one incredible birth by a woman in Idaho. I was called to the birth early in the morning to join another midwife. Mother fixes all of the children breakfast and gets them off to school, then went about cleaning her house. Every so often her breathing changes or she would lean against something as she contracted, but other than that, she went about her work, as usual. At lunchtime, she fed her five-year-old and toddler. Then she took him to kindergarten and laid the toddler down for a nap. After everyone was settled, she looked at us and said, "O.K., let's have a baby." We went into her room where she pushed out a baby about an hour later. When everyone came home from school, they were able to welcome their new sibling into the world. Now that was an organized woman!

Let's look at how labor works, along with some different techniques you can use to make labor more comfortable.

In order for your baby to come out, the cervix or doorway has to open up. Normally, the cervix is shaped kind of like the top of a coke bottle. It is long, thick and closed. In order for the baby to pass through, you must efface and dilate. Effacement means the cervix must become soft and flat. This is measured by percentages. Dilation means the cervix must open. This is measured in centimeters. For example, you might be 50% effaced and 3 centimeters dilated. In order to push your baby out, you need to be 100% effaced and 10 centimeters dilated.

During labor the uterus, a pear-shaped muscular organ contracts, pulling the cervix open. Most of the feeling associated with contractions is a tremendous amount of pressure; we tend to associate any strong sensation as pain. This is not to say there is no pain involved, but the majority of the sensations is one of pressure. If you can understand what is happening, it will help you to visualize and concentrate in a more effective manner. In understanding what is really happening, we can learn to work with the labor and not against it.

There are basically four phases to labor; early, active, transitional, and pushing. The early phase of labor goes from 0 cm. to approximately 3 cm. Contractions are relatively mild. Many women go to 3 cm. never knowing they are in labor. These contractions may last 30 seconds and be 5 to 20 minutes apart. During this stage of labor a woman is usually happy and excited. If this happens during the day, go for a nice walk, it is important to stay busy and active. This would be a good time for your "nesting" instinct to kick in, pull out the baby clothes, make last minute adjustments to the nursery, clean house. It is important during these early contractions to work on breathing techniques and relaxation until they are second nature to you.

The active phase of labor normally takes you from about 3 to 7 cm. These contractions last about 60 seconds and are usually 3 – 5 minutes apart. You can tell when a woman has hit this stage, even without checking her dilation because of the way her mood changes. This is where women begin to concentrate and focus on labor. This is hard work and takes a lot of concentration.

The transitional phase of labor is the most intense and, thankfully, the shortest phase of labor. This phase will finish taking you to 10 centimeters so your baby can be born. During this phase moods swing, tending toward impatience, being short-tempered and discouragement. Sometimes, feeling as though they "can't do this any more" and that "the baby will never come." This is usually a sign they are near the finish line.

However, at home, this phase typically takes on a different atmosphere. Quite often, I see women draw further into themselves. They may not want to be massaged or touched. They often appear to be sleeping, except that their breathing is very focused. For example, at one birth, a neighbor found out her friend was at 8 centimeters, so she came running over to check on her. As she came into the house, I put my finger to my lips. She needed quiet. She came in, saw her friend lying on the couch with her back to us as though she was a sleep. She motioned for me to follow her into the other room. She said, "I was told she was at 8 cm." I assured her she was. She said, "No way! I remember what that felt like. She can't be." I assured her this was pretty common. She left. A few minutes later the mother was ready to push her baby out. At home, this phase often becomes exactly what it is called – a transition – a time of going from labor contractions to delivering the baby. I think it only happens this way when a mother feels safe, secure, confident in what she is doing in her own environment.

In working with contractions, it is important to remember that every natural contraction has a beginning, a peak and an end. Once a contraction is gone, you do not ever have to do that one again. This simple, but when you are in labor it is important to remember that you will have a break between contractions. Otherwise, you can create what is known as the 'fear, tension, pain syndrome'. This happens when you fear the next contraction, remain tense until the next one begins which increases the pain, which causes greater fear and tension. It becomes a vicious cycle. Every contraction has a beginning, a peak, and an end!

Following is a list of "comfort measures to use for labor, birth, and post partum.

Comfort measures for labor, birth & post partum:

Relaxation – It is important to learn how to relax and understand where you carry your tension. I encourage women to do an exercise which helps them learn how to isolate different muscle groups – in the evening when you can relax with your partner, I suggest tightening all of the muscles in your body, then concentrate on relaxing one particular muscle group, such as one leg and foot. All the other muscles stay tense. When you can relax one muscle group, then work on two different groups, such as relaxing one arm and one leg, while everything else remains tense. This helps you to recognize tension, learn to relax it and how to isolate different muscle groups so when you are in labor you will be able to relax while the uterus tightens up to do its job. Your partners job is to watch for tension and to recognize the signs of how you carry it – wrinkled brow, hunched shoulders, hands held in a fist, feet stretched out straight, etc. If they see tension in your body, then they can gently touch that area – you learn to automatically let go of tension when you feels the touch (this eliminates the need to command her to relax, which is usually not received well in the middle of labor). This technique helps couples to work as a team without irritating or frustrating each other.

Breathing – Learn how to do several different types of breathing. Program yourself to take a "cleansing" breath at the beginning and end of each contraction, breathing in through the nose, filling the lungs, then breathing out through the mouth, accomplishing two things: First, it helps to level out the oxygen so you don't hyperventilate and second, it lets everyone in the room know that a contraction has started so that everyone's energy can be focused on supporting you through the contraction. During most of the labor, slow chest breathing is usually effective, breathing in through the nose, out through the mouth, slow and easy. These breaths are kept relatively shallow so the diaphragm is not pushed down on the uterus while it is working. Sometimes women relax better if they breathe deeply. Some women do better in transition if they can change their breathing to match the intensity of their labor, alternating three hes and a blow, so it would go something like this: he, he, he, ooooohhh, he, he, he, ooooohhh. Sometimes it helps to breathe through the peak of the contraction with short little blows, like blowing out candles in succession. Sometimes, it helps to have the mother drop her jaw, letting her mouth hang open, then groan out the pressure she is feeling by saying, "Ahhhhh." Everyone is different and it is important to be in tune with what works for you. Some women like to labor alone; others need a lot of help and encouragement. Most women appreciate some support through transition.

Healthy Snacks and Treats – The mother can eat and drink as much as she wants during labor so she will have the strength needed to do her job effectively. Some women do not like to eat because their digestive system stops working. If this is the case, encourage them to drink so they will stay hydrated.

Empty the Bladder – As labor advances – remind the mother to get up and empty her bladder. This will help the labor to progress and relieve the pressure on the uterus

Herbal Aids:

- Blue Cohosh – Blue cohosh can help get labor started – if a woman has reached her due date, the cervix is soft and ready, try blue cohosh. If the body is ready, it will help get the labor going. If the body is not ready, it probably won't help. Usually take 4 capsules or one dropper full every 20 minutes while walking. Do this for 2 – 4 hours unless you begin to develop a headache. This is the body's signal you have had enough.

- B&B Tincture in a vegetable glycerin base – This is also an effective way to get a labor going or to encourage a sluggish labor to move along. This combination contains blue and black cohosh. The blue cohosh stimulates the contractions and the black cohosh makes them more effective.

- Castor Oil – When a mother is past her due date, anxious about not starting her labor and her body is ready, then she can take an ounce of castor oil in juice. Normally, if the body is ready, in two to four hours the bowel cleans out and the contractions begin. This is effective because the castor oil causes the intestines to contract which irritates the uterus and causes it to contract.

- Horsetail Tincture – Calcium is a natural pain killer; given with a dropper under the tongue, it is high in organic calcium.

- Rescue Remedy - A Bach Flower remedy is used under the tongue, as often as needed, if the mother is feeling out of control or nervous

- Shock Tea – It will help with the chills, cold feet, the shakes, bleeding and any other signs of shock. It is also good for an energy boost. Made with hot water, lemon & honey to taste, along with 10 drops of cayenne tincture to every cup of water. My daughters always make a thermos full of this tea so it will be ready when we need it. Normally, this tastes pretty potent, but in labor it tends to match the intensity of the labor, so most mothers enjoy it.

- Shepherds Purse Tincture – A dropper full of shepherds purse under the tongue, as often as needed, for uterine bleeding.

- Evening Primrose Oil – Stubborn cervical lips move in order for the baby to be born, when massaged with evening primrose oil. A couple of capsules up under

the cervix melt and allow the oil to help melt away the cervix.
- Liquid Chlorophyll – If it has been a long labor and she needs an energy boost, give the mother an ounce or two of chlorophyll. This is also used after the birth if there has been any excess bleeding – in fact, if the bleeding has been heavy, drink a whole bottle in 4 - 6 hours.
- Red Raspberry Leaf Tea – at the onset of labor, we take one ounce of red raspberry leaves, pour one pint of boiling water over the leaves, cover, let steep for 30 minutes, strain. Drink as hot as possible. Often this can help to make labor shorter and easier. Then we make up regular Red Raspberry tea, using one teaspoon of herb to a cup of water to drink throughout the labor.
- St. Johns Wart or Afterease - Mothers use one of these tinctures after the birth for afterbirth pains.
- Fresh Ginger Root – Grate up two or three roots, put into a cloth diaper, rubber band the edges together and float in some warm bath water. Soaking in a tub of water with the fresh ginger root is very soothing and relaxing. Keep several wash cloths on hand to soak in cold water to put on the mother's forehead and neck, so she doesn't become light-headed due to the steam coming from the hot bath.
- Ginger Root Powder and Olive Oil – Keep a crock pot full of warm water for the pushing stage. Soak cotton diapers or wash cloths in this solution to use on the mother's perineum and legs while pushing.
- Post-Partum Bath – Put a hand full each of the following cut herbs in a cloth: comfrey, uva ursi, shepherds purse. Add 1/3 of a hand full of cut golden seal, along with 2 or 3 cloves of chopped garlic and 1/3 hand full of sea salt. Fold the cloth up and rubber band the top together. While filling up the bathtub with water, hold this cloth in the running water, so the herbs will steep into the tub. When full, drop the cloth in the bath water. Within the first 12 – 24 hours after the

birth, have the mother and baby soak in this tub of herbs. Allow the baby to soak for 5 – 10 minutes with the mother, then remove the baby and allow the mother to soak as long as she is comfortable. This bath is wonderful to start the healing process.

- X-Ceptic Tincture - dip a Q-tip into the tincture. Use this, twice a day, when the baby's diaper is changed, to clean all around the umbilical cord. Usually, if the baby has been in the herb bath, then had the X-Ceptic used on the cord – it will fall off in three or four days, instead of taking 7 – 10 days.

- BF&C™ Tea – while the mother is in labor, make a large batch of BF&C tea. Soak 4 sanitary pads in the tea and place them in the freezer. The rest of the tea is placed in a jar for the mothers use after the birth. The frozen pads are used for the first six to eight hours after the birth when the perineum is swollen and sore, to reduce swelling and begin healing. The rest of the tea is used in a Peri bottle, following the birth, each time the mother goes to the bathroom. Instead of wiping herself, she uses the Peri bottle to rinse herself off. This will help her to heal faster.

- INF - If there is any cause for concern about infection, take 4 INF capsules four times per day.

- Kid-E-Col – for use with the baby if it is having any problems with colic.

- Fresh Parsley – when the mother is finished nursing her baby (hopefully, this will be at least a year to 18 months after the birth) start cutting back the number of times you nurse until you are down to one feeding per day. When you are ready to completely dry up your milk, take some fresh parsley – bruise the leaves (this can be done by crushing it in your hands) – pack this on the breasts at night – drink a cup of parsley tea before going to bed. This will help to dry up the milk without becoming engorged.

Essential Oils:
- Lavender – can be used in bath water or in some massage oil to help with relaxation.
- Clary Sage – if the mother is feeling a sharp knife-like pain in the lower abdomen that she is having a hard time dealing with; soak a cloth diaper or hand towel in hot water, wring out, put several drops of Clary Sage on the warm, wet cloth and hold on the lower abdomen to help the pain.
- Gentle Baby - this is a wonderful combination to mix with massage oil to rub the mother's neck and shoulders with.
- Pain Away - we hold the bottle directly under the mother's nose so she can inhale the essence during contractions to help with relaxation.
- Olive Oil – can be used for massage on the body or feet. Also used on the perineum during pushing to help the mother stretch. This is what we recommend to rub on the baby's dry skin when they start peeling.

Reflexology:
- Heel – From Polly Block's *Birth Book,* we learn:

    the spot we are concerned with is found at the top center of the pad of the heel. As the uterus contracts, there is a corresponding, mild, sphincter like action in this spot on the heel. When the uterus contracts and puts pressure on the cervix to make it dilate, the uterine reflex opens, leaving a rather deep, fluidlike feeling within the spot on the heal. As the contraction reaches its peak and subsides, the muscle structure in the uterine reflex closes up and becomes firm again.

    When the reflex is worked in conjunction with rimming the cervix (past 3 ½ centimeters dilation), uniform thinning of the cervical rim – and therefore, labor, - is facilitated considerably. (274)

If you have a sluggish labor, working with this particular point on the foot will help to stimulate contractions and dilation.

Pressure Points:
- Sacrum Points – If you put your hands on your hips and slide them toward your back, your thumbs will naturally fall into these pressure points, located on both sides of the sacrum just below the last lumbar vertebrae. If you slide your thumbs around a little bit in this area, you will discover the indentions. Your thumbs will fit nicely into these points. Use your thumbs or the heel of your hands to apply pressure in this area during a contraction, relieves the pressure of the contraction, especially with back labor. The mother will be able to tell you if you are pushing in the right place and whether or not your need to push "harder."
- Knees – you can apply "counter pressure" during the contraction if the mother is in a tub of water, a sitting position , or laying on her side. Cup your hands around both of her knees with your thumb on the inside of the knee and your other four fingers on the outside of the knee – apply pressure with your thumb to the inside of the knee while pushing against the knee with your hand – this will push the upper leg toward the small of the back. Most mothers appreciate this counter pressure during a contraction; this can be especially helpful if someone is pushing on her back.

Other Helpful Hints:
- Birthing Ball –The mother can kneel on the bed or floor and lay across this large, inflatable exercise ball if she is suffering from back labor or the baby is not positioned quite right for birth, this will sometimes help. Have the mom put her full weight on the ball, then sit in front of her – take her shoulders and rock her back and forth, envisioning rocking her baby. As she rocks back and forth, it takes some of the pressure off of her back and encourages the baby to line up, head down, for birth. Some mothers enjoy sitting on the ball and bouncing during their contractions.

- Pelvic Rocks – Another method for back labor or for a baby who does not want to line up right is the pelvic rock as described in the "pregnancy instructions." These can be done on the floor, on the bed or in the bathtub with warm water.
- Walking – It is good for the mom to move around while she is in labor. It helps to take her mind off of the intensity of what she is experiencing; it helps the baby to line up correctly; it helps to keep the labor going and it puts gravity in your favor. We have taken many a midnight walk through our neighborhood in our nightgowns and robes.
- Massage – If the mother is having a hard time relaxing or is getting tired from a long labor, massage can bring some welcome relief to tired muscles, especially in the neck and shoulders.
- Reflex Combs – These are metal combs the mother holds in her hands with a pointed end which she can place in the center of her thumb, another reflex point which helps to stimulate contractions and helps take the edge off of the pressure.
- Back Labor – In *Back Labor No More,* an excellent book by Janie McCoy King, we learn about the physiology of back labor.

> Vectors travel in straight lines! Vectors don't go around corners. When they hit an obstruction, the result is PAIN. (83)

If you have ever experienced back labor or are a labor coach, this is an excellent book on the physics of back labor. The author shows how to lift the abdomen up so the pressure of the baby's head is removed from the back and lined up where it belongs.

Now, let's look at what happens as the mother reaches full dilation and is ready to start pushing.

There are several positions in which this can be done. If she has been laboring in the water and wishes to remain there, then the baby can be delivered in the water. (There is no concern for the baby drowning because it is coming from a water environment to a water environment and will not take a breath until you lift them from the water). If the mother wishes to squat, kneel, or be in a hands and knees position, there should be no problem in delivering the baby. Sometimes mothers like to sit on the toilet, however this can make it difficult for the midwife to reach the baby to help her. There is always the traditional way of laying on your back on a bed, grabbing your knees and delivering in a manner that is convenient for the attendants. My favorite spot is on the birthing stool.

The birthing stool allows a mother to get into a more natural squatting position and also allows plenty of room for the attendants to assist. Usually, women straddle the stool, plant their feet firmly on the floor, lean forward and take hold of the bars at the front of the stool. This makes it easy for the mother to work with the attendant, who can easily apply hot compresses and massage the perineum during the pushing stage and it puts the pressure of the birth in the right area. Unless there is a reason for the baby to be born quickly, let the mother listen to her body and push when it is comfortable. Most women will do well with short, controlled pushes which helps the perineum to stretch slowly. Most of the time, with this gradual, intermittent pushing and a little bit of counter pressure on the baby's head, we can avoid any tearing.

After the birth, the mother can immediately hold her baby and begin to nurse it. I do not usually cut the cord until it stops pulsating which may take 20 or 30 minutes. The cord is still sending nutrients and oxygen to the baby, so if you have one that is a little slow to take their first breath, it is O.K. because they are still receiving the oxygen they need.

After the cord has been cut, the placenta delivered and the mother put to bed, we make sure she has plenty of juice to drink and something to eat if she is hungry. If there has been any substantial amount of blood loss, we make sure she has plenty of chlorophyll to drink or wheatgrass to drink.

It is good to continue with the same good nutrition they used during their pregnancy. At a minimum, I like to see them continue with their herbal supplements and a quart of red raspberry leaf tea daily. When their milk comes in, if they are having a difficult time maintaining a good milk supply, they can add Blessed Thistle to their tea as this will help to increase the amount of milk they are producing.

The hardest part of a birth like this is convincing the mother that she needs time to rest and pamper herself for at least three days until her milk comes in. Whatever work or cleaning you have to do will still be there when you get ready to go back to work. If she can get extra help for a week or two that is even better. Quite often, they are on such a "high" after the birth, it is hard to keep them down. Whether this is your first baby or your tenth, you need to take the time to rest and get your strength back. This is also an important time for you and your family to bond with this little angel that has just entered your life. Enjoy this time. Help all of the siblings to be an integral part of this excitement and change. Cherish this time – take advantage of the moments. You will never get it back again. I have a needle-point hanging on my wall that says it all:

> Quiet down cobwebs,
> Dust go to sleep,
> I'm rocking my baby,
> And babies don't keep.

Our life is frittered away by detail.
SIMPLIFY, SIMPLIFY.
-- Thoreau

Home is an invention on which no one has improved.
-- Ann Douglas

A temperature of 98.6 degrees Fahrenheit is not the "normal" temperature for everyone. That is what most of us have been told all of our lives, but it simply isn't true. The 98.6-degree standard for body temperature is merely a statistical average, and "normal" for most people is either higher or lower than that. This is particularly true of children. Their "normal" temperatures, measured in carefully controlled studies, ranged from a low of 96.6 degrees to a high of 99.4. Very few of these healthy children registered temperatures of exactly 98.6 degrees.
-- Robert S. Mendelsohn, M.D.

Chapter Five
What if There's an Emergency?

No matter how many times I am privileged enough to be a part of the birth process, I never get over what a miracle it is! When my first daughter was born, a set of missionaries gave me the following poem, called:

Day-old Child
By: Carol Lynn Pearson

My day-old child lay in my arms, with my lips against his ear
I whispered strongly, "How I wish – I wish that you could hear;
I've a hundred wonderful things to say (A tiny cough and a nod),
Hurry, hurry, hurry and grow so I can tell you about God."
My day-old baby's mouth was still, my words only tickled his ear.
But a kind of light passed through his eyes,
and I saw this thought appear:
"How I wish I had a voice and words; I've a hundred things to say,
Before I forget I'd tell you of God – I left Him yesterday."

I want each couple I have had the privilege of working with, to know how much I appreciate them, admire them, and applaud them for their strength, courage, and sweet resolve to do whatever they have to do to provide a safe and peaceful Although each birth is different and unique, most of them have some common threads. The mother labors for a certain length of time, pushes her baby out and then rejoices in the miracle and love of her new child. The statistics from many countries have shown that good prenatal care and birth with a midwife is the safest way to have a baby. In fact, right now America ranks 22nd in infant and mother mortality rates. That means there are 21 other countries where it would be safer to have a baby. All of these countries use midwives except in high-risk-pregnancies, which are handled by doctors who can take care of emergencies.

People often ask me if we ever have emergencies in a home birth and, if we do, "How do we handle it at home?" I will be the first to admit that they can happen. This is one of the reasons it is so important for each couple to take responsibility for their own decisions. They need to study the statistics and the facts. Then search out their own feelings until they are comfortable. Decisions should not be based on money or pressure from others. They need to be united and at peace with their own intelligent decision.

There is a big difference between just deciding to stay home to have your baby without help versus a planned, intelligent decision to have a baby at home with a trained midwife. One couple who decided to have their baby at home on their own without any help from anyone turned into a tragic heartache. When the baby was born, it was not breathing, the father rushed it to the emergency room, but lost the baby. When he returned home to his wife, he found she had bled to death. I was not there and do not know all of the details, but I want to stress here that the type of birth I am talking about is one in which the parents have studied for themselves the pros and cons, have had good prenatal care, have been responsible for their health during the pregnancy, have chosen a competent midwife and then, have taken responsibility for that choice.

It is important to understand that 95% of home births are generally uneventful, in that there are no emergencies to worry about. The outcome is usually a healthy, happy mother and baby. It is also important to point out here that I have attended enough births to realize I am not the one in charge. Midwives are merely instruments to assist in the miraculous natural process of birth. Even though we need to learn all that we can in order to make intelligent decisions, we need to remember that a source higher than our own is in charge. No matter how much we learn, no matter how many degrees we obtain, if we ever think we have all the answers – some day, some where we are going to find out that we don't. Sooner or later, we will find ourselves in a position where we don't know what to do. In order to make it safely through these experiences we must learn to rely on all our best knowledge and a source higher than our own to guide us.

The following experiences are given to answer the question, "What would you do in case of an emergency?" The following four experiences are examples of some of those times when I was well aware that I was not in charge. I have purposely changed the names of these people to protect their privacy and the sacredness of their personal experiences.

Experience I
Bob and Sally

Bob and Sally came to me on a Sunday afternoon, asking if I would be willing to deliver their first child. I knew they did not believe in eating the same way we do. I also knew Sally's parents were adamantly opposed to home birth. Under these circumstances, I suggested they might want to consider having their first baby in a hospital. I told them we could look at having the second one at home after they had a better feel for what was going on. I told them they could fast and pray about it.

The next Sunday Bob told me he had fasted and prayed about it. He told me three nights in a row he had had the same dream. He said in the dream they are in a hospital having the baby. When the baby is born, the doctor comes out to tell Bob the baby is fine, but Sally did not make it. Bob said, "I just can't take her to a hospital."

When I asked Sally how she felt about this, she said,

"All of my life, I have had severe reactions to medication – I am really concerned that if anything goes wrong, I will be given medication which could cause a severe reaction. It really frightens me."

I asked her if she would be willing to follow the program I give to all of my ladies; she said she would. Her one request was that I schedule one appointment with my back-up doctor, so she could tell her parents she had seen a doctor.

When we went to the appointment with the doctor, he asked her if she had any concerns about the pregnancy. She told him her only concern was that she was hypoglycemic. He told her I would be able to handle that concern better than he could because there were a lot of things I could recommend nutritionally that he couldn't.

Throughout the whole pregnancy she was an angel. She took all of the herbs and oils, ate as many live foods as possible and gave up many things she was used to eating. She did everything she could to ensure her baby was born healthy and strong.

Sally went into labor on a Sunday morning. The labor progressed beautifully. In fact, if there was ever a labor which I wanted my unmarried daughters to be a part of, it would be this one because she handled it with such grace and dignity. When she was fully dilated and ready to push, I asked her if she wanted to give birth in the tub or on the bed. (I didn't have a birthing stool then). She said she wanted to get on the bed, so we helped her out of the tub and on to my bed. She began to push the baby down the birth canal. Everything was proceeding exactly the way it should.

As the baby's head crowned, bright red blood began coming out around the baby's head with each push. I began to get extremely concerned because I knew the placenta was detaching prematurely which meant the baby needed to be born immediately before his oxygen supply was cut off. I instructed Laura, my assistant, to give her some shepherds purse under the tongue, along with some shock tea to drink in order to slow this bleeding down.

Trying to decide what to do to speed up this birth, I watched the top of the baby's head completely rotate as he turned in the birth canal. Then the perineum began to bulge in my hand. For a split second, I thought about doing an episiotomy, but I didn't feel good about it. As I looked down at my hand, supporting this bulging perineum, I saw a blue ear sticking out. At first, my mind would not accept the fact that there was an ear in my hand so I reached over with my other hand to touch it. It was an ear and as I touched it with my other hand, the baby's whole head fell into my hand and his body slid into my other hand. He immediately started gasping for air and then began to cry.

It is extremely difficult to explain what happened. The bulge in the perineum was actually his body. When he rotated in the birth canal, either his shoulder or his elbow tore a hole in the bottom of the birth canal, allowing his body to drop onto the perineum. He was then lying in a "V" shape, with the top of his head showing at the opening to the birth canal, his bottom was sitting in my hand (bulging through the perineum) and his feet were up in the cervix. Juanita, my oldest daughter, called it the "bull-frog" effect. When a bull frog croaks, he blows his throat way out in front of him. Looking from the side at the perineum, this is what it looked like:

we could see the baby's head at the opening to the birth canal, then the perineum bulged out like a bull frog. His shoulder tore through the side of the perineum, allowing his ear to appear first in my hand before the rest of his head popped through, followed by his body, legs and feet.

As I held him, I noticed that the cord was completely white, which meant it was no longer supplying him with oxygen – he had been out of time. We kept the bleeding under control with herbs, so I covered Sally up and handed her the baby. No one else in the room knew what had happened except for Myrna and Juanita, who were by my side. I didn't say anything because I wanted them to bask in the joy of their first born son. However, I don't ever remember being so scared in my life. This baby had not come through the birth canal, he had torn his way out next to it. I didn't know how much damage may have been done. The adrenaline was really flowing. I went from shaking to feeling sick to my stomach to feeling like I was going to pass out. This couple happened to be members of my family – I was sick over what had just happened – I wasn't sure where I was going to go from here. I quietly asked Laura for a cup of the shock tea and drank it myself. That helped to calm some of the shaking and unsteadiness I was feeling. I was able to deliver the placenta through the same opening the baby had come through.

When I had finished delivering the placenta, I leaned over to Juanita and asked her to call Carol, a dear friend in Idaho, who is also a midwife. Juanita brought the phone to me, I stepped into the bathroom where no one could hear me and explained to Carol what had happened. She asked me if I wanted her to come down. I said yes – she said she would leave immediately, but it would still take three hours to get there. I thanked her and went back to the bedroom.

We got Sally and the baby all cleaned up, the bed made up fresh and all of the fun stuff like weighing and measuring out of the way. Family members were coming through congratulating them and they were truly basking in the joy of this miracle. I still hadn't explained to anyone what had happened. I did not want to put her through two exams, so I had decided to wait until Carol arrived before examining her.

A couple of times while I was watching her, I asked her if she was doing O.K. She would say, "Yes, I feel great, but I'm kind of sore." I thought to myself, "Yea, I'll bet you're sore!"

Just before Carol arrived, when everything was quiet, I explained to Bob and Sally what had happened. Sally's mother had warned her that if she had a child at home, something terrible would happen, so I was concerned about what her response would be. When I finished explaining everything to them, Sally looked up at me and said, "Well, I guess we know why we had to have him at home." Her sweet faith and support won a place in my heart forever. She never seemed to doubt or question, she simply knew she had done what she was destined to do. The strength and sweet serenity of women never ceases to amaze me.

When Carol arrived, it was the first time I had really been able to release all of the pent up emotions of what I had just been through. I met her at the top of the stairs and fell apart. She allowed me to cry while I explained that I had been afraid of losing both of them. She was extremely supportive until I made the following statement: "Maybe I shouldn't be doing this; maybe I am in over my head." Carol is about five feet tall, but when I made that statement, her spirit rose up to ten feet tall, she pointed her finger at me and said,

> I don't ever want to hear those words come out of your mouth again! That is just what the 'Advisary' wants you to think. Don't you recognize the legions of angels who have been by your side this day? That baby was given instructions on how to save his life and he obeyed them. Now you have a healthy mother and a beautiful healthy baby. Rejoice in the blessings around you and recognize the miracle which has just taken place!

After we examined Sally, we concluded there was nothing seriously damaged. The rectum was intact; the urethra was unharmed; no ligaments had been involved; there was simply a laceration which needed to be repaired. When you read the medical text books, they will tell you that if a baby does not come through the birth canal, they will take the path of least resistance which is normally the rectum. Because she had followed the program so carefully, her perineum was extremely soft and flexible which allowed him to tear through.

I asked Sally if she would like to go to the hospital where they could use anesthetics to numb the area. She said no. I agreed to try to help repair it at home, but told her if it became too painful she would need to go to the hospital. She agreed. We went back up to repair the hole in the bottom of the birth canal and then worked our way to the outside. We irrigated the area with mineral water mixed with lobelia tincture. Then numbed the area with an ice cube and put in stitches. Bob and his sister, Taunya talked and laughed with her the whole time we were working, along with using an essential oil blend, Pain Away. It was uncomfortable for her when we reached the outside stitches, but it cam be just as uncomfortable in the hospital with those particular stitches.

The next day I went to see my back-up doctor to ask him if there was anything else I could have done or if there was anything else they would have done in the hospital. He said that I was well aware of the fact that they are trained to cut. In this case, he said if they had started cutting, the pressure would have caused her to split wide open, probably into the rectum, which would have required major reconstructive surgery to repair. He said she was much better off at home. I was amazed at his candor. He said to bring her in for a 6-week post partum check-up and he would make sure everything had healed satisfactorily.

We put Sally on five BF&C capsules four times per day to help with the healing process. I also had her take four INF capsules four times per day to combat any possible infection, along with the normal Vitalerbs, and red raspberry tea. We told her she would have to spend two weeks in my bedroom because we didn't want her going up and down stairs or putting too much strain on the stitches. Three or four days later, she started getting cabin fever and wanted to join the rest of us downstairs, so she sat on her bottom and scooted down the stairs. When I checked her afterwards, I found she had torn out ¼ to 1/3 of the stitches which, of course, left a gaping hole. I didn't have the heart to put her through any more stitches, so I told her I would keep it packed with BF&C ointment to see if that would close it back up.

When I took her in for her six week check-up, the doctor sat on his stool looking at her, then turned to me and said, "Now, where did you say that baby came out?" It was almost impossible to see where the tear had been. There was just a thin, white line. At eight weeks post partum there was no sign at all.

Later, Sally's mother told her she had a similar thing happen when Sally was being born. That was why she was so concerned about a home birth. In her mother's case, however, they had cut, causing severe damage. Almost thirty years later, she still has problems caused by the birth.

This birth taught me that things do not always turn out the way I expect or want them to, but they usually turn out the way they should.

Experience II
Mike and Sue

Mike and Sue came to me to help deliver their first child, I got that all too familiar feeling that all was not right with this couple. However, they answered all of the questions correctly and agreed to do everything I asked them to do, so I accepted them.

The pregnancy progressed to the 30th of 40 weeks without any complications. Sue was doing everything I asked which was obvious by the improvement in her blood and urine over the course of her pregnancy. Earlier, in the 24th week she was measuring quite a bit larger than she should have at this stage. I suggested an ultra sound to check for twins or any other complications. They refused, saying they did not want any medical intervention. I said I would respect their wishes unless there were any more red flags.

Christmas day she was spotting and contracting. I put her to bed, gave her False Unicorn and Lobelia to prevent her from miscarrying, but had to explain to them that I definitely wanted an ultrasound done to assess the situation. I explained that we could have a partial abruption of the placenta, a placenta praevia, or several other possibilities that could become dangerous. They still did not want any intervention; but when I insisted, they agreed.

The ultrasound revealed a gestational age of 31 weeks and showed a normal pregnancy. The doctor who read the ultrasound called me to tell me that a partial separation will not necessarily show up on an ultrasound and he agreed with my assessment – it was his opinion that was the problem.

With all of the herbs and nutrition she was using to build a healthy placenta, I was surprised that this happened. In questioning her further, I discovered she had fallen against the tail gate of her husband's pick-up. This was beginning to make more sense – whether it was an accident or not, I wasn't sure, but, at least it explained why we were having this problem.

I put her on bed rest along with BF&C oil being rubbed into the abdomen over the placenta to help it heal, chlorophyll for the blood loss, cayenne to help stop the bleeding, extra wheat germ oil, and green drinks. She continued using all of her other herbs. Four days later, she was still bleeding, so I explained to her that his pregnancy had become "high risk." I wanted her to see a doctor. They refused, telling me this baby had to born at home. I told them if they wanted me to continue to help them, they would have to respect my wishes. They agreed and the appointment was set.

The doctor explained the risks involved, said the cervix was still closed, and scheduled an appointment in two weeks to see them again.

One week later at about 11:00 in the evening, Sue called and said she was contracting again. I asked her how close together they were. She told me they were about 30 minutes apart, but they were strong. I told her to soak in a tub of hot water with fresh ginger root and relax. If they didn't stop or got worse she was to call me. I didn't hear back from her, so I went to bed. At about 2:00 A.M., I got a call from Mike telling me there was some kind of fluid coming out of Sue. I told him to get her to the emergency room. About 10 minutes later the phone rang again and Mike said, "The child is born." My heart went up into my throat and I said, "Is she alive?" He said, "Yes, listen." He held the phone next to the baby and I could hear her screaming. It was music to my ears.

He told me that the EMTs were there and they were heading to the hospital.

I found out later, the baby was rooting (trying to nurse) on the way to the hospital. When they arrived, the doctor told them they were not equipped to keep a baby that young, so she would have to be life-flighted to Primary Children's Hospital. After examining the baby, however, they came back to Sue to tell her there was no reason to transfer her. She weighed in at 3 lbs. 3 oz., but she was perfectly healthy. The only problem she had was that she would forget to breathe, so they put a monitor on her. She was also having trouble maintaining her body temperature, which was taken care of with an incubator.

Mike and Sue told me they knew their baby was healthy because of all the herbs and nutrition she had used during the pregnancy. It truly is amazing the difference nutrition and exercise can make.

Experience III
Carl and Becky

Carl and Becky are two of the most vivacious, loving people I have ever had the privilege of working with. They were so excited to be pregnant and having their first child. I looked forward to seeing them every month; they were such a joy to be around!

Becky was a dance instructor in great shape. She was adamant about having a good home birth experience, so she was extremely faithful about her diet and supplements. She had a wonderful pregnancy and went into labor the day before her expected due date.

The labor was 15 hours long, not too uncommon for a first baby. It progressed well and she handled it beautifully. At the end of her labor she said something that exemplifies the incredible unselfish nature of women. As we discussed, transition is the most intense part of labor, where many women feel they can not do this any longer. Becky reached this stage, exhausted, tired of hurting, feeling intense pressure and out of motivation. Most of her active labor was spent in the birthing tub. At this point, she was leaning over the edge of the tub, with Carl pushing on her back to help relieve some of the pressure. She was fighting back the tears and told Carl she could not do this any more. Then she looked at me and said, "Where do you think my baby's spirit is right now?" I said, "Right here with you." Becky, in a pleading tone said, "Why won't he come?" I didn't know the answer, so I said, "Becky, life can be pretty challenging – maybe he is getting some last minute instructions." She looked at me through her agony, and said, "Then, I can wait."

I have to admit that tears flowed down my cheeks with love for the sweetest attributes that are so amazing in women. She no longer cared what she might have to pass through as long as it helped her child. It never ceases to amaze me as I watch these incredible women reach deep inside themselves to find an inner strength they never knew they had.

When it was time to push the baby out, she opted to get on the birthing stool. As the baby descended down the birth canal everything appeared to be going well, but my stomach tied in a knot and I thought, "Something is not right here." I pushed the thought aside. Becky worked with me, doing everything I asked her to do. Becky and Carl shed tears of joy as they talked to their beautiful little girl she delivered, with no tearing.

While they were holding the baby, I noticed Becky was bleeding more than usual, so we gave her some shepherd's purse and some shock tea. She lost what appeared to be a couple of blood clots, then said, "I feel funny, like I'm detached. I feel like I'm floating." We took her off of the birthing stool, laid her down, and put her on oxygen so she could get her equilibrium back. She began gushing more blood, in spite of the fact that the uterus felt like it had clamped down tight. We used more of the herbs, put ice on the uterus and got the baby to start nursing. Again, we were able to get the bleeding under control.

Another midwife who was with me, took hold of the cord to see if the placenta had detached. The cord came out with a small piece of membrane on it, but no placenta. I never pull very hard on the cord and have waited up to three hours for them to detach, so now I was really concerned. I looked more closely at what I had thought were blood clots and realized that they were actually pieces of the placenta. I put on another sterile glove to go into the uterus to get the rest of the placenta, but when I took hold of it, it felt like a dozen different pieces, completely fragmented. So I left it alone. I asked the other midwife if she had ever seen anything like this. She said she had not. I knew we had an extremely dangerous situation here, so I explained to Carl what was going on and asked him what he wanted to do. I recommended transporting to a hospital – he agreed.

When the ambulance arrived, they put Becky on a gurney and then reached for the baby. Juanita told them the baby was fine and would not be going. The EMT said, "I'm not leaving without the baby." When I heard the argument, I stood up, and informed the man that I was the one who had called because I had a mother with heavy bleeding, a retained placenta and she needed immediate medical attention. The baby was fine and would not be going anywhere. He became extremely indignant and said they would not leave unless the father signed a "release form." Carl said, "I'll sign it; just help my wife."

When we arrived at the hospital they had an IV going and were giving Becky platelets. The ER doctor was very kind, told me I had done a great job and that everything would be fine. He was extremely surprised we were able to get the bleeding under control. He said this gave them time to stabilize her blood pressure. When the OB/GYN arrived, it was a different story. He was so hateful everyone could feel it. Just before they took her into surgery to do a D&C, Becky said to me, "I'm cramping." I told her that was wonderful – just bare down. When the OB/GYN heard what I was saying, he ordered the nurses to get her in the O.R. .

Before Becky had come to the hospital, she asked me what had gone wrong. She told me she had been so faithful with her program that she didn't understand why this had happened. I told her I didn't know.

Carl was wonderful, told me how much he appreciated everything we had done. While we were sitting in the waiting room he revealed that five years ago, he was on heroine and other hard drugs. He said he had been clean for about four years. Then I began to understand what may have happened.

The first time the doctor came out, he talked to Becky's mother. He asked her if these kids had chosen to have their baby at home due to lack of insurance. She informed him they had excellent insurance, but they had studied it out and decided this was the way they wanted to go. His rebuttal, "If this does not stop, someone is going to die."

Her mother knew I was upset over what had happened, so she told me not to listen to a word he was saying. She told me she had worked in this very hospital for 15 years in labor and delivery. She told me, in that time, she had seen mothers and babies die with a doctor standing right next to them. She said if Becky had been in the hospital having her baby, she could have been one of them because they would not have done what we did to stop the bleeding. I was amazed and thankful for all of the support she was giving me.

The next time the doctor came out, he talked to Carl. He told them they did not have to use any instruments because he was able to remove it with his hands. That made perfect sense to me since it was obviously detaching before they took her in. As he walked past me, I asked him how she was doing. He looked at me hatefully and said he had had to put in a lot of stitches. I was shocked. The perineum was perfectly in tact the last time I had seen it. The next day when I saw her at home, she told me she did not have any stitches. He had merely wanted to degrade me in front of everyone in the waiting room. I honestly do not understand this type of mentality. Obviously, I felt like she needed their help or I wouldn't have recommended it. I expected more professionalism than that.

She was given a couple of units of blood at the hospital before they released her the next day. The doctor told her she was running on ¾ of a tank. He told her it would take 20 months or so for her to build her blood back up and get her original strength back. We put her on a bottle of chlorophyll a day for the first week along with her Vitalerbs and tea.

Again, they asked me what went wrong. I told them what my theory was, but I assured them it was only a theory. My first comment was to Carl. I told him I did not want him to ever look back on this birth with regret or remorse. As far as I was concerned, both of them had done everything they could to give their daughter a healthy start in life. He had supported his wife in every way possible, so, in my opinion, he should only look back on this experience with joy.

Then I explained to him that when you are dealing with hard drugs, they may actually affect the DNA, the chromosomes and many other aspects of pregnancy. In many cases, where there is a problem, you have a strong placenta and a baby with problems. In this case, we had a strong baby and a placenta with problems. Had we been given a choice between the two, I would definitely have chosen the scenario we got. This wonderful couple recognized the blessings that were theirs and set an incredible example for us all.

I saw her at six weeks post partum and she was doing great! She said she had her energy back and felt wonderful. In fact, her boss had offered her old job back and agreed to let her take the baby to work with her, so she was back working full time, taking care of her baby full time, and giving dance lessons. She certainly was not lacking energy as the doctor had dictated.

Experience IV
Robin and Charlotte

This experience is about opposites – the contrast between two similar events under completely different circumstances.

A young mother, Robin, was showing signs of pre-eclampsia (toxemia). On this particular morning, she came to my home for a check-up. Her blood pressure was dangerously high, the proteins in her urine were high and the cervix was not showing any signs of being ready for birth. I explained to her how dangerous her condition was and that we could not risk taking this any further at home. She was upset and begged me not to take her to the hospital. I told her, "I will stay with you through your birth, but we have to go to the hospital." Fortunately, I know a wonderful OB/GYN who was willing to work with us.

Checking into the hospital was not a pleasant experience. The nurse recorded her history as having had no prenatal care and being a high risk pregnancy. When the doctor arrived, he looked at the chart, turned to the nurse and asked, "If she didn't have any prenatal care, how did she know to come in?" The nurse stammered around until the doctor explained to her that the trick with any pregnancy is to have enough knowledge to know when goes out of the parameters of "normal." In this case, he said there was obviously good prenatal care and someone was experienced enough to know that it had become high-risk. The nurse changed her chart and the rest of the day was much more pleasant.

Robin was put on an IV. Drugs were administered to help stabilize her condition, so that she could deliver vaginally. The pitocin was started in order to get her labor going. She was adamant about not having any pain killers because she didn't want any more drugs than necessary going to her baby. Selflessly, this young girl, having her first baby with a "pit" labor, which is much more difficult than a normal labor and, yet, her first concern is for her unborn child. Women constantly are amazing.

Robin had to stay in the hospital bed, so the day was spent breathing through contractions. In the evening, another woman was brought into labor and delivery, having twins, two months early. All of a sudden, it seemed like the whole place was in commotion. Nurses, doctors and personnel from the nursery seemed to be running everywhere. The mother of twins was rushed into an operating room because they said they couldn't take a chance on her delivering vaginally. After the babies were delivered C-section, they were rushed off to the Neonatal Intensive Care Unit.

Shortly after these twins were born, I received a call from a dear friend and midwife who wanted to know if I could come and assist her in delivering a set of twins. Robin was doing fine, so she agreed to let Juanita stay with her while I ran to assist in this birth.

I raced to the other end of the valley, a 30 – 40 minute drive. When I arrived, the mother, Charlotte, was in the birthing tub, all of her other children were in bed asleep; the home was quiet and peaceful. The mother labored for another 10 or 15 minutes, then stood up and said, "It's time." With the help of her husband, she got out of the tub and on to the birthing stool. She pushed out the first baby, which the midwife handed to me. She was a little blue and not anxious to take her first breath, so I rubbed some cayenne ointment on her chest, which made her gasp and start to breathe – she immediately started turning pink and was handed to her mother. Charlotte sat on the stool holding her daughter and talking to her. I was in total awe of this incredible woman!

The second baby had been laying horizontally in the uterus, so when the first baby was born, the midwife reached inside and guided the second baby's head into position. After about 15 minutes, Charlotte handed the first baby to her husband and began to push again. Her second daughter was born, handed to me and started breathing almost immediately. The placentas were soon delivered. Charlotte and her babies were tucked into to her bed together, safe and warm. There was no blood, no fuss, no muss – incredible! How sweet, how serene, how peaceful the spirit was in that home.

With everyone tucked into bed, the midwife and I looked at the placentas. One of the placentas had a normal cord insertion – it was in the center of the placenta, securely attached. As we looked at the second one, the midwife said, "Oh, look, we had a miracle baby – she caught a hold at the last minute." The cord was what is called a "marginal insertion," meaning it was on the edge of the placenta – it also was a precarious insertion. Instead of being embedded in the placenta, it was attached by three small strands. If you held up the cord and looked at where it was attached to the placenta – it looked like the poles which hold up a Teepee.

Then, Juanita called and said I was needed back at the hospital. I went into the bedroom – gave that incredible mother a hug – got in the car and raced back across the valley. I arrived in time to coach Robin through her pushing stage. It was now past midnight. She had been laboring valiantly all day hooked up to machines, an IV and still had not been given anything for pain. The doctor did an episiotomy and she was able to push out her baby. The baby did not breathe right away, so they rushed it off to the nursery. Robin was not able to hold the baby or even get a good look at it. I couldn't help but think about the baby we had just delivered an hour before who just needed some cayenne.

Robin's placenta was delivered and the doctor sewed up the episiotomy. Unfortunately, she continued to bleed quite heavily. The doctor decided that maybe there was still a piece of the placenta inside, so he went back up to get it out. It was extremely difficult to coach her through this. She still had not been given any thing for pain; she had already had her baby; she had already been sewn back together. Now this man has to puts his hand back inside to scrape out pieces of the placenta. My heart was breaking for what she was going through. After he had removed the pieces from the uterus, he had to sew her back up again because the stitches had torn out. After he had sewn her back up for the second time, we took a look at the placenta. As soon as he saw what type of insertion it had, he looked at me and said,

"Oh, my gosh, do you know how dangerous this is? I cringe every time I see one. This is so dangerous – if one of those strands were to tear loose, it could cause a life-threatening situation for the mother and baby."

The insertion was the same Teepee I had seen earlier that evening. Again, I couldn't help but contrast his near panic to a sweet midwife who recognized a miracle baby.

Eventually, Robin's baby was considered stable enough to bring back to her, so that she could hold him and remember why she had just gone through this horrendous experience. I gave her a hug and headed for home.

At 2:00 in the morning, on the way home, I couldn't help but shed tears over the contrasts. Grateful the hospital helped with a potentially dangerous situation, but, oh, how grateful to be reminded of how much better it is when we allow nature to take its course. One location had been so full of fear, panic and stress – another, full of courage, love, serenity and peace.

Section IV

Reference Guide

Section IV
Reference Guide Overview

When we began taking responsible for our own health and the health of our children, we more or less drew an imaginary line in the sand. Our philosophy was: we can begin by taking care of relatively minor conditions at home, knowing we had the medical system to back us up, if we need it. As we saw how remarkable the body is at healing itself, when it is given the correct elements to work with, that line in the sand moved further and further away. In other words, as we realized we could naturally take care of most of the challenging conditions our family faced, we gained more confidence and greater faith in tackling serious conditions.

Some times when people have already tried everything they can medically and not found relief, they feel as though they have nothing to lose and are willing "to try anything." I always find it amazing that most people do not want to try anything as "radical" as herbs or changing their diet (we have become slaves to our dietary addictions, such as sugar, meat, the wrong kinds of fat, etc.) or other alternative health methods, but they will go in for open-heart surgery, chemotherapy, transplants, hysterectomies, etc. and not consider it radical. If you are facing an immediate life-threatening situation, I can understand why some of these things might be necessary, but if it is not immediately life-threatening, then it seems to me it would be much better to give the body a chance to correct the problem itself, knowing the medical alternatives will always be there if it doesn't work.

One of Steve's aunts said to me once, "All truth comes from God. Therefore, all of our technology and medicine comes from God." If all of our modern medicine was pure truth I would have to agree with her. Unfortunately, the medical schools are greatly influenced by the pharmaceuticals and I do not believe what they teach is pure truth.

In the following reference guide, I will try to list several different herbal combinations, essential oils, juices and other modalities I have seen work for each condition, so you will be able use what you have on hand. However, please keep in mind that what I am sharing with you comes from my own experiences – you will have to adapt each of these suggestions to your own experience – making adjustments for age, size and the conditions you are working with.

There are many reference books on the market that teach what each specific herb can be used for. That is not the intent of this book. Most people in our society want to be able to go to the store or order what they need. I will list some individual herbs, but in most cases, I will share the combinations I have seen work. These are the combinations we have had a lot of success with.

In some cases, you might choose to use only one of the aids and it will take care of the problem. In other cases, you may need to use several of the aids simultaneously in order to get the results you want.

Get in tune with what you are dealing with, listen to inspiration and then be as aggressive as you need to be to clear up the condition. I have found when you are dealing with bacteria, viruses, toxic conditions, degenerative conditions, etc.; you must be as aggressive as the condition you are dealing with or it will win. If, however, you will fight back just as aggressively with your diet, the herbs, hydrotherapy, reflexology, essential oils, massage, and whatever other modalities you have to work with, mixed with prayer, you will win!

The biggest problem I see with people who start using herbs is they are not aggressive enough! These are not drugs. The herbs and herbal combinations I am referring to in this book are safe. They do not have the same side effects as drugs do. We have to change the mentality of "take two and call me in the morning." Be aggressive! Know the action you are looking for and then do what you need to do to get it.

Included with many of the conditions, I will include personal experiences, so you can see how we handled similar crisis.

Again, let me remind you, I am sharing my own experiences and the experiences of others that I have been a witness to. My intention here is not to give you medical advice or to guarantee any type of particular result. Use your own judgment, educate yourself and then take responsibility for your own decisions and actions.

Remember, "God hath not given us the spirit of fear; but of power, and of love, and of a sound mind" (2 Timothy 1:7).

The three greatest letters in the English alphabet are N-O-W.
There is no time like the present. Begin now!
-- Sir Walter Scott

Vitality and beauty are gifts of nature for those who live according
to its laws.
-- Leonardo DaVinci

There is a principle which is a bar against all information,
which is a proof against all argument, and which cannot fail to keep a man
in everlasting ignorance. That principle is
condemnation before investigation.
-- Herbert Spencer

A

ABSCESS

As an abscess develops, it will get larger and larger until it bursts open and drains. Usually a bloody pus and sometimes solid matter drains from the open wound. Then, the infection needs to be cleared up and the area healed.

Herbal Aids:
- Dr. Christopher's INF formula – take two to four capsules every 2 - 4 hours depending on severity of infection.
- Echinacea & Golden Seal Combination – take two to four capsules every 2 – 4 hours depending on severity of infection
- Dr. Christopher's Black Ointment – apply black ointment over the abscess – cover with a gauze pad during the day and while sleeping – remove the pad morning and night to allow the abscess to drain – black ointment is designed to draw things to the surface.
- Dr. Christopher's BF&C Ointment – use after infection has drained to heal the area
- X-Ceptic Tincture – use to kill infection after abscess has drained

Other Modalities:
- Onion Poultice – apply thickly to help draw out whatever is causing the abscess – place an onion on a cookie sheet in the oven at about 250 degrees until it becomes soft and juicy – take out and slice – place warm, not hot, onion on affected area.

Experience:

My cat was about 12-years-old and developed a large abscess near his spine. He probably had been in a cat fight and the bite had gotten infected. We applied the Black ointment on the lump, covered it with gauze pads, wrapped an ace bandage around the cat and let him go.

A couple of days later he had a convulsion and seemed to be dying, so we took the ace bandage off to make him comfortable. When I pulled the gauze pads off, the black ointment had drawn everything to the surface and it began to drain. At least a cup full of fluid drained out of the abscess. After everything had drained out of it, the cat laid around for a couple of days, regained his strength and was fine.

ACNE

Acne, quite often, is caused by a poor diet. Since the skin is one of the channels of elimination, it sometimes manifests itself as acne as the body tries to rid itself of toxins. If this is the case, change the diet to live, wholesome foods - fruits, vegetables, grains, nuts, seeds, and legumes; raw and/or sprouted, whenever you can. Stay away from processed foods, processed sugars, deep-fried foods, artificial colorings, flavorings, etc. . Consider doing a three day juice cleanse, followed by the extended herbal cleanse, using the Herbal LB, the Barberry LG, the JuniPars, and the Red Clover combination.

If the condition is caused by the body becoming overly acidic, then you need to go to green drinks, green vegetables, chlorophyll, and lots of water to bring the body back into a balanced state. The skin also needs to be kept clean with a daily bath or shower and some type of exercise that will work up a good sweat to clean out the pores.

When acne is caused by changing hormones, we use herbal aids to help balance them.

Sometimes, however, acne is caused from picking up a parasite that manifests itself in skin eruptions. If your diet is good and you have tried the hormonal herbal aids, then I would seriously consider the parasite cleanse to flush the system of possible parasites. Be aware that most of us have parasites. Consider doing a spring cleaning once a year to get rid of them.

Herbal Aids:
- Red Raspberry and Blessed Thistle Tea – mix the cut Red Raspberry and cut Blessed Thistle half and half – use one teaspoon per cup of water – if the tea is too bitter to drink, then cut back on some of the Blessed Thistle as this is a bitter herb. You may add honey, lemon, peppermint or any other flavors that help you to better enjoy the tea. This tea could be made hot in the morning and then put in the refrigerator to use throughout the day as iced tea. It is good for both male and female to help balance the hormones. Best results have been seen when drinking three glasses per day.

- Dr. Christopher's Changease Capsules and Wheat germ Oil Capsules – take two capsules of each three times per day to help balance hormones.
- Dr. Christopher's Extended Herbal Cleanse – use Dr. Christopher's Herbal LB, Barberry LG, JuniPars, and the Red Clover Combination to cleanse the body of toxins. (See complete instructions for this cleanse in Section V).
- Parasite Cleanse - try the parasite cleanse from *A Cure For All Cancer* by Hulda Clark using Cloves, Wormwood and Black Walnut Hull Tincture in it's green state. (See Section V for complete instructions).
- Innerlight Alkalizer Pack - if the diet has been poor and the system is too acidic, then the Alkalizer Pack may help to neutralize the acidic condition. You may want to try Dr. Young's 10-day alkalizing program to help bring the body back into balance. (See Section V for complete instructions).

Essential Oils:
- Melaleuca alternifolia (tea tree oil) – "A clinical study found that Melaleuca alternifolia is equally effective as benzoyl peroxide for treating acne but with fewer side effects." (Young 478 Essential Oils).

ADENOIDS

The adenoids are part of the lymphoid tissue known as the tonsils. What we commonly refer to as the tonsils are oval bodies located at each side of the soft palate. The adenoids are located behind the nose on the back wall of the upper pharynx. They are often removed when the tonsils are removed. I do not believe that we came here with "spare parts." If the tonsils or adenoids are inflamed, then the same policy of cleanse and nourish comes into play. We have to clean out the toxins and then nourish the weakened tissue.

Herbal Aids:
- Mullein and Lobelia – use ¾ cup of cut Mullein and ¼ cup cut Lobelia in ½ gallon of water, preferably distilled – place the herbs in the water and gently simmer them on the stove – do not allow the water to boil – as the volume of the water decreases, the tea (decoction) will become stronger. Soak a cloth (cotton or wool) in the warm tea – wrap it around the throat and jaw line of the person with the swollen

adenoids – repeat this as often as necessary to bring down the swelling – keep the cloth moist and warm.
- X-ceptic Tincture - rub on to the throat and behind the ears to help kill the infection.
- Mullein Oil - rub on to the throat and behind the ears over the X-ceptic to help break up congestion and mucus.
- Dr. Christopher's INF Combination - take four capsules every two or three waking hours to kill infection.
- Echinacea - take four capsules every two or three waking hours to boost immune system.
- Echinacea and Golden Seal - take four capsules every two or three hours to boost immune system and kill infection.
- Kid-E-Well - take one or two dropper fulls every 2 hours to draw out congestion and boost the immune system.
- Kid-E-Cep - take one dropper full every two hours to kill infection. (Put this in juice or water for children as it is pretty strong)

Other Modalities:
- Hot Onion Poultice - place an onion on a cookie sheet in the oven at about 250 degrees until it becomes soft and juicy - take out and slice - place slices of warm (not hot) onion on chest and back
- Hot Steamy Showers – Stand in the shower with the water hitting your back and breathe in the steam to help open up the bronchial tubes and drain out the congestion.

Experience:

When my oldest grandson was about a year old, I got a frantic phone call early one morning from my son telling me that the doctor wanted to take my grandson into surgery and remove his adenoids. I had just seen him a couple of days before this and he had been fine. I asked, "What is going on?" My son explained that the day before, Stevie, my grandson, came down with a cold and last night he was having a hard time breathing, so they had taken him to the emergency room where he was admitted to the hospital. Now they wanted to remove his adenoids to help his breathing.

I left immediately for the hospital and when I arrived I suggested that my son and daughter-in-law go home and get a couple of hours sleep while I sat with Stevie in his hospital room. A little while later a nurse came in and told me that she needed to take Stevie to a room where they could start an IV because he was so dehydrated. I stood up with him to follow her and she said, "I'm sorry, parents are not allowed to go with me."

I said, "Well, that's O.K. because I'm not his parent, I'm his grandmother." She explained to me that no one was supposed to accompany her and I told her that wherever he went, I went. She could see that I was not going to let go of him, so she allowed me to carry him. When we got to the room to do the IV, there were three medical students waiting for us. The first one attempted to put the IV in his hand, unsuccessfully. The second one attempted to put it in his foot, unsuccessfully. The third one attempted to put it in his other hand, unsuccessfully. When they started to go around the circle again, I put a stop to it. I informed them that they were not going to use him as their guinea pig any longer and that I wanted someone in there who knew how to insert an IV into someone who is dehydrated. They called someone from life-flight and he put it in on the first try

When I got him back to the room, the doctor came in and told me that they wanted to take him to surgery, so I asked why. He told me that his adenoids were swollen and making it difficult for him to breathe so they wanted to remove them. I told him that two days ago, Stevie had been fine. In my opinion that meant that he had picked up a virus somewhere and that in a couple of days he would be fine again. The doctor said he was not willing to take that chance. I told him that I was and that he would not be going into surgery.

When the doctor left, a male nurse came in to see how we were doing. I told him everything that was going on. He seemed as frustrated as I was. I asked him how he put up with this nonsense and he said, "I try to help where I can with those who are willing to learn. The truth is if your daughter-in-law had known how to make an onion poultice, your grandson would not be in here." He then went on to tell me that when the pioneers came to Utah, they were losing a lot of their babies to croup. After they befriended the Indians, they learned how to gather wild onions, make a poultice and save a lot of their children. I didn't know very much about herbs at this time, but I have sure used a lot of onion poultices since then.

They monitored Stevie at the hospital for another 48 hours while the virus ran its course, his adenoids went back to normal and he was released to go home.

ADRENALS

The adrenals are two small glands located above the kidneys. They release several different hormones in the body. Sometimes when they are disfunctioning they can be a contributing factor to diabetes.

In cases of complete hysterectomy, where the ovaries have been removed, strengthening the adrenal glands will help them to take over and produce the hormones that are needed in the body. With a hysterectomy, also consider strengthening the thyroid as it too, helps in the production of hormones.

Herbal Aids:
- Dr. Christopher's Adrenetone - 2 capsules three times per day - more, if needed to cleanse and strengthen the adrenal glands

ALLERGIC REACTIONS

An allergic reaction occurs when the body reacts in a negative way to a substance it comes in contact with. The reaction may appear as a rash, swelling in a localized area, difficulty breathing, increased heart rate, etc. . An allergic reaction to something can be mild or it can be fatal, so it is something we need to counteract as quickly as possible.

Herbal Aids:
- Green Drinks - the system must be alkalized
- Chlorophyll - as much as needed depending on severity
- Dr. Christopher's Red Clover combination - use to cleanse blood – again the amount would depend on the severity of the reaction
- Echinacea - Again the dose will depend upon the severity, but,
     "Dr. Meyers of Pawnee City, Nebraska in the 1800's claimed that it was an anti-spasmodic and an antidote for blood-poisoning. He said in cases of poisoning, take two ounces three times per day and in cases of rattlesnakes take three

ounces three times a day till the swelling is gone. He claimed that this was an absolute cure within 24 hours" (Christopher 3 Newsletter).

- Activated Charcoal - take several capsules of charcoal to absorb poison and flush it out of the system
- Yellow Dock and Bugleweed - use 3 ounces of yellow dock root, cut and 3 ounces of bugleweed, cut - put into one pint of distilled water, boil ten minutes, strain and let stand until cold. This is given from a wineglass to a teacupful until the whole pint is consumed . Dr Shook wrote,

> "This life giving remedy (in arsenic poisoning) serves two purposes. The iron in yellow dock and the tannic acid in bugleweed pick up any soluble arsenic that may be in the stomach or intestines, and immediately convert it into insoluble iron arsenite or arsenate, which cannot be absorbed into the system. The bugleweed supports the heart and acts as a sedative to the sympathetic nervous system, thus conserving energy until the danger is past" (Christopher 3 Newsletter).

Although Dr. Shook was specifically referring to arsenic poisoning here, I would not hesitate to use this combination when the body is having a severe allergic reaction to something. In essence, it has been poisoned.

- Imucalm – In the *School of Natural Healing,* Dr. Christopher tells us,

> ". . . many times we believe that we are allergic to certain foods, plants or animals, but in reality our immune system may be just overreacting. This simple combination of marshmallow root and astragalus has made life easier for those who suffer from allergies, hay fever, asthma, rheumatoid arthritis or any hyperactive immune response." (597)

Experience:

One afternoon I received a call from Dr. Christopher's herb store telling me that they had a couple from Idaho looking for something for their daughter who was extremely ill. After listening to some of the details of her story, I told them to give the parents my number and if they needed help to call me.

About 9:00 that night I received a call from them. Tuesday afternoon their 20-year-old daughter had gone into a health clinic at school because she wasn't feeling well. The clinic told her she had strep throat and gave her some amoxicillin. She took two capsules and began feeling much worse, so her boyfriend took her to an emergency room at the hospital. They checked her and said she did not have strep, she had mono, so they gave her Arythimiacin. (Mono is caused by a virus, which cannot be helped by any kind of antibiotic). She only took one dose of this one and threw it up.

On Wednesday, she broke out in a rash, so her boyfriend took her back to the emergency room where they told him that a rash is quite common with mono. Later in the day, he noticed she was getting blisters in her mouth, so he called them again and was told not to worry about it.

On Thursday, she was much worse, so he called her parents in Idaho and told them what was going on. They came down immediately and since they weren't getting any co-operation from the medical community, they decided to try to find an alternative way to help their daughter.

Thursday night, when I first arrived at their daughter's home, they were attempting to do a "cold sheet treatment" which had been recommended to them to clean out the toxins. Normally, the "cold sheet" treatment is a wonderful way to clean toxins out of the system, especially in cases of pneumonia. However, you have to understand that this treatment uses the skin as its eliminatory channel by sweating out the toxins. Unfortunately, in this case, the skin was covered by what appeared to be a heavy rash with large water blisters forming on it. I strongly advised them not to continue with this treatment because the skin was not capable of sweating and so the "cold sheet treatment" would be ineffective and could do more harm than good.

At first I thought she might have small pox because of the way her skin looked. I had never seen anything like this before. Her eyes were glued shut; the skin was covered with this thick rash; there were huge water blisters on her face, throat, and torso and she was having a hard time swallowing and breathing. When these conditions seem overwhelming and extremely frightening, if you keep it simple and stick to the basic principles, you can still help to bring some relief. In cases of chicken pox, soaking in a tub with golden seal, burdock root, and yellow dock brings relief, so her parents put her in a warm tub with these herbs which were wrapped in a cloth diaper. Soaking in the tub also helps to fight dehydration by allowing the skin to draw in some of the moisture.

When she got out of the tub, her parents built a tent with a sheet and put a hot water vaporizer in it with eucalyptus oil to help open up her breathing passages. They also made a strong tea out of cut mullein and lobelia, soaked a cloth in the tea, and wrapped it around her neck to bring down the swelling so she could swallow. They rubbed her feet with olive oil, then packed a paste on the bottom of her feet made from putting chopped garlic into Vaseline, so her body could draw on the antibiotic properties of the garlic. She was given chlorophyll with an eye dropper so that it would be easier for her to swallow it.

Several times during the night, she was placed in the tub of water and the procedure was repeated. By morning the blisters were beginning to break which was extremely painful, so they added a cloth diaper filled with cut marshmallow to the water which was very soothing. (Marshmallow root is very slimy when wet and can be rubbed over sensitive tissue without tearing it or damaging it). When she got out of the tub, fresh aloe vera gel was applied to the tender skin where the blisters had broken.

In the morning, she sat up, drank three glasses of water and was very coherent, so we thought we were past the worse part of the crisis. I went home to get some sleep.

A couple of hours later, her mother called to tell me she was hallucinating. I told her that it could be caused from dehydration, so she was given more fluids. The sun can have a wonderful healing effect, so in the early afternoon she was taken outside to sit for a couple of minutes. She was extremely uncomfortable in the sun, however, so was brought back in the house. She was beginning to lose control of her bowels. By mid afternoon I could tell that her lungs were beginning to fill with fluid, so I told her parents that this was extremely serious and that I didn't know what else could be done at home because of the condition of her skin.

They were afraid to take her to the emergency room again because of the experiences of the last few days, so they called a friend of theirs, a pediatrician. He told them to take her to the lab, have some tests run and then he would call to let them know what to do. They took her to the lab and as soon as they got back to the house, he called and said he was sending an ambulance to pick her up. Before she left, I took her blood pressure which was still in a normal range.

When I met her parents at the hospital on Friday night, she had just been admitted to the intensive care unit. The parents were taken to a room to meet with the doctor. They invited me to join them. The first doctor who spoke with them told them that their daughter would probably not live through the night. Her lungs were filling with fluid and they fully expected her kidneys and heart to fail. As he talked with them, my heart sank and I felt physically ill because the doctor made it sound as though it was their fault. He said that she did have strep and because they had not followed through with the original medication, the infection had gone systemic. As he was talking, a second doctor came into the room who had done biopsies on the blisters. He told the parents, it would not have mattered when they brought her in because it would not have stopped what was happening. She was having a severe allergic reaction to the amoxicillin. Because her body was trying so hard to rid itself of this poison and to protect the vital organs, it had pushed it out through the skin, causing severe chemical burns on the head, neck and torso. What had looked like a thick rash was actually a severe burn. The second doctor agreed that she would probably not live through the night, but at least he helped them to understand it was not their fault. I was extremely grateful for his honesty. He recommended she be life-flighted to the nearest burn unit. They agreed and so she was transported.

I was extremely torn apart all week-end. I was also extremely frustrated that I did not have the knowledge or skills to deal with this situation. "Why was the body not able to correct itself? Why had the herbs failed? Was there anything else that could have been done?" Driving myself crazy with more questions than I had answers for, Sunday morning, Steve had had enough of my frustration and sorrow, so he called his brother in Alaska, who is a doctor.

Before I even finished telling him what had transpired or what the diagnosis was, he asked me some questions about the "rash" and about her ability to swallow. When I answered his questions, he told me that she had "Stephen Johnson Syndrome" and that it is fatal. He said, "Every medical student knows if you give someone an antibiotic and they develop a rash, you get them off of it immediately and pray that it does not develop into the full blown syndrome, because if it does, it is fatal." He asked me if we had intubated (put a tube down her throat) her and I said, "No, Charlie, I don't carry tubes around. We had to use the herbs." He said that was the most amazing thing he had ever heard. Normally once the throat closes the only way it can be opened is with a tube.

When I told him what her blood pressure had been before she was transported, he said that was also amazing because it indicated that she was not dehydrated. He then explained that by putting her in so many tubs of water with the herbs in it, the osmotic pressure of the bath water had been greater than the bodily fluids which had helped to hold them in. Our skin holds our fluids in -- when it is severely burned or missing, fluids leak out. He seemed truly amazed at what we had been able to accomplish with such a serious condition. I was still extremely frustrated and kept asking, "WHY? Why didn't the herbs work?" He finally said, "Are you kidding? Normally, by now she would be dead. They did work!" He explained to me that what we were dealing with was an iatrogenic (doctor induced) condition. This is much different than working with the natural conditions of the body. This was a case of poisoning and not just a matter of bringing the body back in to balance. I was grateful I had someone to help me understand what was going on. Where I saw complete failure, he saw amazing success!

Shortly after I hung up the phone, I received a call from the burn unit. Her mother was calling to tell me that she was still alive, but they were concerned because her kidneys appeared to be shutting down. She wanted to know if there was anything I could do to help. I told her that I doubted if I could do anything with her in an intensive care burn unit where she was being monitored 24 hours a day. She told me they had peeled all of the burned skin off, wrapped her in a plastic wrap to keep the fluids from running out of her body and that she was on paralyzing drugs to keep her from moving, lots of pain medication and amnesia medication so she would not remember anything. She said her feet were not affected and that we could work with them. I told her I would come up and see what we could do.

When I arrived, her mother told me they had a new machine which takes all of the blood out of the body, detoxifies it and then puts it back. Apparently, this is helping to save a lot of lives that would otherwise be lost due to this syndrome. I took some cayenne oil, Dr. Christopher's BF&C Oil and a small foot reflexology chart with me. The nurses said it would be all right to rub her feet as a comfort measure, so I used the cayenne oil to rub the reflexology point for the kidneys to stimulate them. Then I used the BF&C oil to help her body heal. I spent 5 ½ hours rubbing her feet, but by the time I left, her blood pressure and pulse had come way down and the catheter bag was filling up, which meant her kidneys were functioning. Apparently, even in serious situations, small measures can bring big results.

While I was at the hospital, they did something which was very disturbing to me. They decided to put a feeding tube down her throat so they could give her a protein drink. At the time I wondered how her bowels were going to function if she was on drugs to keep her paralyzed. Of course there was nothing I could say or do, but it just didn't make sense to me. About ten days later, her mother called to tell me they had taken her daughter into surgery for a bowel blockage. Sometimes I wonder where common sense has gone.

This story does not have a happy ending. This sweet girl suffered untold amounts of misery for two years and then passed away at home. The agony which she and her family went through is something I hope I never see again. When my older children were young, we used to call liquid amoxicillin, the bubble gum medicine – it is pink, tastes good and was prescribed for everything. I think it is important for us to understand that just because we get used to something being around does not make it harmless. These drugs are not candy. They can have some very serious side effects. They can even be fatal. There are no magic pills! We have to be very careful when it comes to our health and the health of our children. Let's be sure, before we use something that could be potentially lethal, that it really is necessary.

ALLERGIES

The best way to overcome allergies is to clean up the system and stop putting garbage back into it. The colon and respiratory system seem to be directly related to each other, so one of the first places to begin is in cleaning up the colon. As you cleanse the system and begin to rebuild it with herbs and good nutrition, you clear up the allergies.

Herbal Aids:
- Dr. Christopher's SHA Combination - take 2 capsules three times per day - more if it is allergy season
- Dr. Christopher's Extended Herbal Cleanse - use the Herbal LB, Barberry LG, JuniPars, Red Clover Combination - try for six months
  (See Section V)
- Three Day Juice Cleanse (See Section V)
- Alkalizer Pack - depending on the type of allergies you are suffering with, you may need to alkalize the system, this will help to speed up the process (Section V).
- Tahitian Noni Juice – if you are dealing with a skin allergy, quite often drinking Noni Juice and then applying it to the area helps to clear up the problem
- Imucalm – take as directed on bottle to help calm the immune system

Other Modalities:
- Colonics - if suffering with severe symptoms, you may need to cleanse the system quickly – try cleaning out the colon with a series of three to five colonics – then move to an herbal alternative, such as the Herbal LB or the Intestinal Formula 1.

Experience:
My husband, Steve, suffered from hay fever and allergies every spring and fall. Since he has been working so hard to control his diabetes with cleansing, diet, herbs, and exercise over the last few

years, one of the side effects is that his allergies have gone away too.

ANEMIA

Iron-deficient anemia is caused by not getting the right types of organic iron in the body. Anemia quite often occurs in women, causing them to be tired and weak. To combat this problem, doctors often give them a prescription for iron supplements. One of the leading causes of poisoning deaths in toddlers is due to getting into their mothers iron supplements. These are extremely toxic and very hard for the body to assimilate. I have found in working with women who are pregnant, if they will take their Vitalerbs and liquid chlorophyll, the anemia will usually turn around in a couple of days. Chlorophyll is essentially plant blood with everything our blood has except the red corpuscles, so it is an excellent way to help build strong, healthy blood.

Yellow Dock is high in organic iron and alfalfa has every mineral known to man in it. Green drinks are an excellent way to help build strong blood. We like to use Jurassic Green in unsweetened pineapple juice with bananas and ice to make a great slushy. The diet should include lots of fresh, green vegetables and plenty of exercise with fresh air and sunshine.

Herbal Aids:
- Liquid Chlorophyll – if fresh wheat grass juice is not available, then use a good quality liquid chlorophyll in it's place – this will usually be made from alfalfa – I have used a whole bottle over a twelve hour period in cases of hemorrhaging.
- Vitalerbs - 5 capsules three times per day with meals for added nutrition
- Dr. Christopher's Yellow Dock combination - 2 capsules three times per day or as needed
- Alfalfa - 4 capsules three times per day
- Jurassic Green or other good quality Green Drinks - 3 glasses per day

Juices:
- Wheat Grass Juice – Ann Wigmore tells us:

... in 1930, Dr. A Zin showed that an injection of chlorophyll increased the red blood cell count of animals with normal hemoglobin counts. Scientists J.H. Hughs and A.L. Latner of the University of Liverpool went one step further. In their study, reported in the Journal of Physiology in 1936, a number of animals were made anemic by daily bleeding. After their hemoglobin levels were reduced to less than half the norm, the animals were divided into ten groups. Five of the groups were fed various types of chlorophyll in their diet. The five groups of control animals did not receive any chlorophyll. Those animals receiving 'crude' or raw, unrefined chlorophyll were able to increase the speed of hemoglobin regeneration by more than 50 percent above average, to approximate their previous blood values in about two weeks. However, the group receiving synthetic chlorophyll showed no improvement in the speed of hemoglobin regeneration. In their report, the scientists concluded: 'It seems, therefore, that the animal body is capable of converting chlorophyll to hemoglobin.' (10)

Drink two to six ounces per day depending on how serious the anemia is.

- Beet Juice – In the *Juiceman*, we learn:

... it is no coincidence that ruby-red beets are beneficial to the blood. Old time raw foodists and herbalists have long known that the color or shape of a fruit or vegetable often conveys its healthful properties. Beets contain iron, calcium, sulfur, potassium, and chlorine. They also are a source of beta carotene and vitamin C. Their rich mineral makeup contributes directly to the well-being of the liver and gall bladder while building up blood corpuscles and cells and stimulating the activity of the lymph glands . . . Beet juice is potent stuff. Never drink it solo. Always dilute it with a milder juice such as apple, carrot, or cucumber. The juice of half a small beet is all that should be mixed with the juice of four apples. (Kordich 165)

APPENDICITIS

Dr. Christopher describes appendicitis:

Appendicitis is an inflammation of the appendix, sometimes resulting in rupture. The symptoms of appendicitis are an inflamed, painful condition of the appendix and the surrounding portion of the bowels. Other symptoms are nausea, pain and distress around the navel, constipation, quick pulse, and perhaps a rise in temperature to 100 or 102 degrees. There may be tenderness to the right of the naval and below, which is increased by pressure or movement. The patient frequently flexes the right knee to ease the pain. (35-36 Home)

When a doctor checks for appendicitis, they quite often push in on the sore area and then let go quickly. The patient will usually feel pain with the quick release of pressure.

Appendicitis can be life-threatening and is not anything to play with. Left untreated, it can be fatal. However, if you look at where the appendix is located, it becomes more obvious what is causing the problem. The appendix is that small gland at the bottom of the ascending colon, so you can see that if the colon becomes backed up with garbage and toxic matter, then it could cause the appendix to become inflamed. If you rush to the hospital and have the appendix removed, have you solved the problem?

Compare the appendix to a smoke detector in the house. If the house begins to burn and you remove the smoke detector, have you solved the problem? All you have done is remove the irritant. You don't have to listen to that horrible screeching sound, but it will not stop the house from burning down. The appendix is the same way. You can remove the irritant, but you haven't fixed the problem, you have only removed the smoke detector.

You have to clean up the problem; the diet needs to be changed to a mucusless diet, with plenty of water and fresh fruits and vegetables.

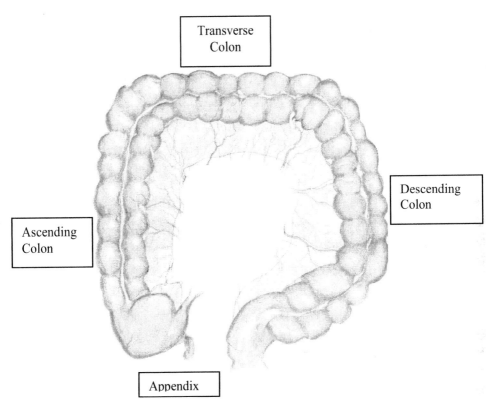

Transverse
Colon

Descending
Colon

Ascending
Colon

Appendix

Herbal Aids:
- Poultice - combine a tablespoon of granulated or powdered Lobelia with a large handful of granulated or crushed mullein leaves, and sprinkle with ginger. Mix the herbs into a paste by adding powdered Slippery Elm or corn meal - apply the poultice as warm as the patient can stand, leave on until cool, then repeat (Christopher 35-36 Home)
- Lobelia tincture - apply right over the inflamed appendix to help relieve pain
Other Modalities:
- Herbal enema - we like to use catnip - spearmint, white oak bark, bayberry, or wild alum root will also work – use every couple of hours, if needed, to clean the toxins from the colon.
- Castor oil fomentation - rub castor oil into the abdominal area and then alternate with a hot, wet towel and a cold, wet towel - check every 15 minutes or so to be sure that the skin remains oily - if the skin feels dry - apply more castor oil.

- Reflexology - look on a reflexology chart for the appendix area or look for the tender spot on their foot - using olive oil or lobelia tincture - rub the area to help stimulate the appendix to drain
- Liquid diet - during an attack of appendicitis, go on a completely liquid diet with water, herbal teas, and fresh fruit juices

Experience:
See Section I, Pg. 40

ARTERIOSCLEROSIS

Arteriosclerosis is a hardening of the arteries caused by a poor diet. Even a good exercise program will not stop arteriosclerosis if the diet is poor and high in the wrong type of fats, which is why there have been several famous athletes die of heart disease, even though they were extremely physically fit.

A good book to read on this subject is *Left For Dead* by Dick Quinn. Cayenne helps to increase circulation and feed the heart. Garlic helps to break down the plaque and Hawthorne Berries are a very specific herb to feed and rebuild the heart.

Herbal Aids:
- Cayenne and Garlic Capsules - 2 capsules of each three times per day
- Hawthorne Berry Syrup - 1 Tbsp three times per day
- Lots of Distilled Water to Drink - according to body weight, women should be drinking at least three quarts per day and men should be drinking one gallon

ARTHRITIS

We are constantly taking inorganic material into our bodies, which is then deposited in different areas, such as the joints. Distilled water is pure H2O; there is nothing else in it, so it is hungry for inorganic minerals. As it goes through our system, it gathers up the inorganic material and flushes it out.

Does distilled water leach organic minerals from our body? The answer is no! When we take organic vitamins and minerals into our body, they are immediately assimilated and used. They are not just sitting around, waiting to be flushed out. Again, diet and hydration are extremely important in clearing up arthritis.

Herbal Aids:
- Dr. Christopher's AR - 1 formula - use 2 capsules three times per day or as needed
- BF&C ointment and Professor Cayenne ointment on joints to help relieve pain and mend damage

Other Modalities:
- Drink distilled water (approximately 3 qts for women and 1 gal. for men per day) – this has actually been shown to help many people with arthritis because it helps to cleans out the minerals and other deposits in the joints which are causing a problem
- Apple Cider Vinegar fomentations - soak a cloth in hot apple cider vinegar - wrap around joints.

Experience:
a) In Section I, I share the experience I had with my mother and her arthritis. Five years after she moved in with us, she was doing great. She was off of all of her prescription medications and doing pretty much anything she wanted to do. She crocheted, she worked in the genealogy library, she cooked, she sewed and enjoyed much better health at 80, than she had at 75.

At the age of 78, we took her to a family reunion on Lake Powell. She was out riding a wave runner with me and having a great time.

However, she has gone back to most of her old habits again, and so, at the age of 86, she is suffering with a lot of arthritis and other problems. Many times I have seen people heal themselves of different conditions, only to let their guard down and return to the exact same things that caused the problem in the first place. My mother is a good example of this.

ASTHMA

Asthma is considered an auto-immune disease, which means the body is attacking itself and making it difficult to breathe. When treating asthma, take a close look at diet and water intake. Follow a good diet and try not to put any more garbage into the body.

Choose the treatments depending on how severe the asthma is and whether or not you are in the middle of an attack.

If you are in the middle of an attack, obviously, it is important to open the breathing passages as quickly as possible; using the hot steam in a shower, putting your head out of the open window of a moving car or by immediately using the emetics to clear the stomach and lungs. Once you have gotten past the initial attack, it is extremely important to clean up the system using wholesome foods and pure water in the diet, along with daily exercise and fresh air.

Herbal Aids:
- Cut Lobelia - one pint of boiling water over 1 tsp Lobelia - allow to steep a few minutes - drink several cups lukewarm until vomiting occurs - when stomach has been cleansed, drink a cup of hot spearmint or peppermint tea to settle the stomach
- Dr. Christopher's SHA formula - use 2 three times per day (more, if needed)
- Breathease - use 2 three times per day (more, if needed)
- Astragalus and Marshmallow - 2 capsules three times per day to calm immune system as asthma is an auto-immune disease
- Dr. Christopher's Extended herbal cleanse with LB, LG, JuniPars, and Red Clover Combination (See section V)
- Alkalizer Pack - Dr. Young's 10 day alkalizing cleanse using the prime Ph and the SuperGreens
- Asthma Formula - this is an asthma syrup to help expel mucus from the respiratory system - use a teaspoon or more, as needed
- Resp-free - 2 to 3 capsules three times per day with cup of comfrey tea to relieve irritation in the respiratory tract, lungs and bronchioles
Other Modalities:
- Diet – add more fresh, raw foods and stay away from as many processed foods as possible. From *Raw Family we read*:
. . . one day at school in gym class we ran a quarter of a mile. This really isn't far; sort of like running around the soccer field one time. I finished that race second to last. The very last girl walked. It wasn't that my legs couldn't run fast, it was that I couldn't breathe when I was running. It was my asthma. There were some nights I could not breathe at all, but I was sleeping and didn't notice. But my parents were really worried and talked about it in the morning. Then I thought, wow, maybe I should go on raw food.

I noticed how my mother and father had both lost weight. Not only did they look better, but they were gentler and had more energy. So, I decided that I would try it. I stopped cheating at school.

Soon we were running that quarter-mile again at school. Now I could run much more easily. I stopped breathing hard at night. I could move, I could go to gymnastics, and I could run and do all kinds of things I couldn't do before" (Boutenko 17-18).

- Water – In the *Bodies Many Cries for Water,* we read:

It is estimated that 12 million children suffer from asthma, and several thousand die every year. Let us declare an end to asthma in less than five years. Let us save children from the constant fear of suffocation because they do not recognize they are thirsty for water!

Histamine is an agent that, apart from its water regulatory role, has responsibilities in antibacterial, antiviral, and anti-foreign agents (chemicals and proteins) defense systems in the body. At a normal level of water content of the body, these actions are held at an imperceptive r unexaggerated level. At a dehydrated state of the body, to the point that the histamine activity becomes exaggerated for water regulation, an immune system activation of histamine-producing cells will release an exaggerated amount of the transmitter that is held in storage for its other functions.

It has been shown in animal models that histamine production in histamine-generating cells will decrease with an increase in the daily water intake. Both of these conditions should be regulated with an alert and determined increase in water intake. On average, these conditions respond after one to four weeks of water regulation of the body.

Mr. Peck, an asthmatic since childhood, who also became sensitive to all sorts of 'allergens,' is no longer in fear of these health problems. Mr. Pauris also testifies to the fact that his wife's allergic condition became less problematic. Jose Rivers, M.D., had for years suffered from allergies and asthma. He was severely allergic to cats. In fact, he would never go to a house where a cat was also kept. It seems he at one time got very sick after being exposed to a cat. As a result of using the new information about the relationship of dehydration to excess histamine production in the body, he has totally recovered from both of these conditions. To top it all, he now treats asthmatics with water and salt. (Batmanghelidj 115-116)

- Hot shower or hot tub of water - Remain in the hot steam for as long as possible (45min - 60 min) - sponge off with cool or cold water
- Hot fomentations of castor oil, comfrey, lobelia and mullein – placed over the stomach, spleen, liver, and lung areas
- Steam vaporizer with eucalyptus oil in the water
- Keep bowels open - may need to do a series of colonics in the beginning to get the bowel opened up
- Bathe daily
- Exercise daily - outdoors, if possible
- Keep good ventilation in sleeping room - sleep with a window partly open
- Put in an air purification system

Experience:

In the *School of Natural Healing,* we read about a dramatic case: One night there came a pounding at the door; when Dr. Christopher opened it, there were two young men, supporting a wizened old man who was struggling for every breath of air. Dr. Christopher recognized the wheezing sounds of asthma. "Please!" cried one of the young men. "Our regular doctor is out of town and we can't find his assistant. Can you help keep Pap alive?" Dr. Christopher settled the old man in a chair and gave him a cup of peppermint tea. The man had been sick with asthma for twenty-six years. For twenty of those it had been so severe that he could not hold a job. He could not lie down in bed because he choked up so much that he risked death. His sons built him a special chair to sleep in at night. The sons both worked to support the family's needs, including the high medical bills from this condition. The man required shots, respiratory therapy, and oxygen treatments, often more than twice a week.

Dr. Christopher helped the man sip the peppermint tea. Ten minutes later, he gave him a teaspoon of lobelia tincture. Ten minutes later, as the four of them talked, Dr. Christopher spooned in another dose, and ten minutes later, another. Dr. Christopher began to quietly gather pots, pans and buckets. Suddenly, the man began vomiting. From two till five in the morning he vomited the thick, sticky, blackened phlegm that had choked his airways. Because of the peppermint tea, his muscles were relaxed and he suffered no soreness form the hours of heaving.

Just after five o'clock, well before dawn, Dr. Christopher said, "You can take your father home now; he is finished with the treatment. He is fine now." The two rushed to their father's side to take him home, but he said, "You don't have to help me, boys. I'll walk." Dr. Christopher settled into bed for an hour's rest before starting the next day's work. The boys took the man home to his chair but he said, "Put me to bed, boys. I'm going to sleep tonight."

"You can't, Pap. It will kill you!"

But the father insisted and went to bed. He fell into a heavy sleep for thirty hours. When he woke up, after sleeping soundly for the first time in twenty years, he said, "I'm healed. I'm going out to get a job." He got a job as a gardener, and he never lost a day's work. He slept in a bed every night thereafter.

ATHLETE'S FOOT

Black walnut kills fungus, which causes athlete's foot. If it is too strong; then use BF&C which contains black walnut. Keep the feet clean and dry, using only clean socks when you need to wear shoes. Go bare-footed or wear sandals and let the foot air out.

Herbal Aids:
- Black Walnut Hull tincture - apply directly to affected area as an anti-fungal aid
- BF&C Oil or Ointment- apply directly to affected area – this has black walnut in it along with being very soothing and healing.
- Wheat Grass Juice – I wouldn't hesitate to apply fresh wheat grass juice to the area – it is very healing and soothing

Essential Oils:
- Melaleuca alternifolia (tea tree oil) – this can be diluted in a 50-50 blend with olive oil or massage oil – then applied directly to the feet – it could also be used directly in the bath water or as a foot bath to kill the fungus.

Life is either a daring adventure or nothing.
-- Helen Keller

Some of the world's greatest feats were accomplished by people not smart
enough to know they were impossible.
-- Doug Larsen

And Jesus continued: "God commanded your forefathers: 'Thou shalt not kill.'
But their heart was hardened and they killed. Then Moses desired that at least
they should not kill men, and he suffered them to kill beasts. And then the heart
of your forefathers was hardened yet more, and they killed men and beasts
likewise. But I do say to you: Kill neither men, nor beasts, nor yet the food
which goes into your mouth. For if you eat living food, the same will quicken
you, but if you kill your food, the dead food will kill you also. For life comes
only from life, and from death comes always death . . . ."
-- The Essene Gospel of Peace

B

BACK PAIN

Back pain can be extremely painful and debilitating! There are a lot of different reasons for back pain including injury to the spine or muscles, degenerative disks, pinched nerves, arthritis, etc. . Support good chiropractors and massage therapists for relief of pain and to help correct the problem. Once you have identified what the problem is and healed the damage, it is important that you implement some type of exercise program that will help to strengthen the muscles in the back in order to keep the spinal column in correct alignment.

Herbal Aids:
- Dr. Christopher's BF&C Ointment, Oil, or Fomentation - apply directly to sore area to help with healing process or soak in bath water made from the tea (see Section V)
- Professor Cayenne Deep Heating Balm - apply directly to area that is sore to relieve pain and bring more blood to the area to help with healing or apply directly over the BF&C formula to intensify the action of the BF&C.
- Lobelia Tincture – rub directly into sore muscles to help relax them.
- Anti-Spasmodic Tincture – rub directly on to muscles to stop spasms
- BF&C Capsules – 5 capsules three or four times per day for injuries (more if needed).

Other Modalities:
- A Good Chiropractor – there is no substitute for a good chiropractor who can relieve the pressure off of inflamed nerves.
- A Good Massage Therapist – this can be anyone from a professional therapist to a good friend or spouse who is willing to help – massage helps to bring blood to the area, it helps the muscles to relax and it adds the human touch, which in itself can be healing and soothing.
- Alternating Moist Heat (BF&C fomentation) and Cold – to bring down the inflammation, pain and swelling – do not use a dry heat source like a heating pad as it can actually increase the inflammation.

- Hydrotherapy – soak in a bathtub, shower or hot tub to help relax the muscles

Experience:

At the age of 16, I threw my lower back out for the first time running on a beach. Anticipating a dance festival that week and hardly able to walk, my mother took me to a chiropractor. He corrected the problem by bringing my lower back into alignment, relieving the pressure on the pinched nerves.

When I was 21-years-old, I was suffered a lot of pain in my lower back and again, could hardly walk, so my husband took me to an emergency room where they put me on pain killers and muscle relaxants. It did not correct the problem but made me so groggy I could not take care of my children, so I went back to the chiropractor and got some relief.

Around the age of 34, I found myself in a wheel chair for a short time due to inflammation and pain in my lower back. Again, a chiropractor helped me get back on my feet.

When I was 35-years-old, a deer come through the windshield and hit me in the face, causing a severe whiplash, which caused a lot of problems with my neck and shoulders. I continued to see massage therapists and chiropractors for relief.

After my last child was born, at the age of 39, I was in bad shape again. My chiropractor sent me to a neurosurgeon because the problem did not seem to be getting any better. In constant pain, every step I took was calculated and precarious because my back could seize up and send me falling to my knees.

The neurosurgeon told me that one of the disks in my lower back was completely gone – it was just bone on bone – and that two more were almost gone. He said the only thing he could do to help me was to take me into surgery and fuse the vertebrae together. I thanked him for the suggestion, but told him I knew people who had tried this route and it had not been very successful

– they were still in constant pain – so I told him I would continue to do what I was already doing.

A short time later, I discovered the School of Natural Healing, began studying, and changing my lifestyle. Around the age of 45, I started seeing a new chiropractor who wanted to take some X-rays of my back due to my history. When he looked at the X-rays, he commented on how good my spine looked for someone my age. He pointed out that there was only one disk that was a little bit smaller than normal in my lower back. I said, "Well, considering six years ago I didn't have one there at all, I think it looks pretty good." He said, "That is impossible. You cannot regenerate a new disk." I explained everything to him and told him if he would order my X-rays from six year before, he would be able to see for himself. He was totally amazed when he compared the X-rays.

I have come to believe that nothing is impossible. The body is an incredible mechanism that is always trying to bring itself back into balance and if it has the tools to work with, every cell in our body has the blue print to rebuild itself exactly the way it was before; even the disks in our spine. Ten years ago I could hardly walk. Today I can do anything I want to do – I can run with my grandchildren, play soccer, basketball, wrestle, pick them up – it is never too late to start turning things around for the better.

BED SORES

If you have someone who is suffering from bedsores, I would look into the quality of care they are receiving. Bedsores should not happen if a person is receiving the proper amount of care and attention, being turned often, so there is relief to the pressure areas they are lying on; unless there is a lack of circulation. If this is the problem, then circulation needs to be brought to the area so that the wounds can heal. You may need to look into an air mattress or water mattress to relieve the amount of pressure on the skin. The bedding needs to be kept clean and as soft as possible. Keep the room well ventilated and fresh.

Herbal Aids:
- Golden Seal, Myrrh, and Boric Acid – a good wash for bed sores is made of one teaspoonful each of golden seal, myrrh and boric acid added to a pint of boiling water.
- BF&C Ointment – apply directly to sore to help with healing
- Fresh Aloe Vera – remove the get from an Aloe Vera plant and put in wound to aid in healing.
- Burn Paste – made with Comfrey powder and equal parts of Wheat Germ Oil and raw Honey – place directly on or in sore.
- X-Ceptic Tincture – if the sores are showing any sign of becoming infected, use this tincture to clean them out – if the sores are extremely sensitive or painful, you might want to mix some X-Ceptic with your ointment as it can sting when applied alone.
- Cayenne Capsules or Tincture – sometimes bed sores can occur due to poor circulation – if this is the case, I would use 2 capsules or ½ to 1 tsp. of liquid in a glass of water two to three times per day to help increase circulation.
- Yarrow Bath – if the problem is due to circulation, I would soak the person in a hot tub of yarrow tea once per day to draw the circulation down into the hips and legs or to whatever area you are having problems with the pressure wounds – make sure you are using the Cayenne so that you have circulation to draw into the area.

Other Modalities:
- Keep the Person and all Bedding Clean and Dry
- Massage – will help to keep the circulation flowing and help prevent sores.
- Allow Sores to Air Out – it is imperative that you allow the sores to air out for a couple of hours every day.
- Sun Bathing – if the sores are bad, I would strongly recommend laying out in the sun for five to ten minutes every day with the sore completely exposed to the suns rays – the sun is an incredible healer – just be very careful not to fall asleep and burn.

Experience:

A friend of ours was involved in a gun accident which left him paralyzed from the waist down. Due to extremely poor circulation, he had some large pressure wounds on his hips and feet that would not heal. The doctors and nurses worked on the problem for seven months without any success. When they suggested amputating the legs due to the possibility of these sores becoming infected, this young couple called me and asked if I could help them.

After talking to them about what needed to be done, they put him on the following daily program:

- 2 oz. of wheat grass juice added to a powdered green drink
- glass of fresh apple juice
- glass of fresh carrot juice
- no meat or dairy
- wheat grass implant
- Lobelia tincture and BF&C oil rubbed into the spine
- Sun bath nude for five minutes on each side
- Herbal vitamin
- 2 Cayenne capsules 3 times per day
- Yarrow bath
- Clean wounds with X-Ceptic tincture
- Pack wound with Burn Paste or BF&C
- Allow wounds to air out at least two hours
- Massage
- Exercise – alternating days between resistance training with weights and pull-ups - cardio by 'running' in his wheelchair

Within two weeks the sores were healing for the first time, closing up and shrinking in size, but the most exciting result was that he began to have feeling in his legs again – something that no one expected to happen. As he followed this program the nerves began to wake up. It is too soon to tell what the final outcome will be, but I believe if he sticks with it there will come a time when he will walk again.

BLADDER INFECTION

Bladder infections can cause cramping, burning with urination, and a fever. I have never seen the following regime fail. There is an ingredient in Cranberries that keeps the bacteria from adhering to the bladder wall, the JuniPars and INF kills the infection, then the water flushes it out. In the first 24 to 48 hours, the person may notice a burning sensation when they urinate. This means the body is flushing the infection out and is actually a good sign. If the burning becomes too intense, try running some warm water in the bath tub, sit in it and urinate. This will dilute the urine and ease the burning sensation.

Herbal Aids:
- Dr. Christopher's JuniPars - take 2 capsules three times per day.
- Soloray Cranactin - take 1 capsule three times per day with the JuniPars
- INF Formula – for really stubborn infections, add 4 capsules of INF to the JuniPars and Cranactin
- Distilled Water – drink one gallon of water per day to flush out infection

Experience:
Sometimes we get so busy we don't take the time to explain all of the details of how the body works when we are trying to help someone. It can also be because we take too much for granted, assuming that they already know things that they may not understand. I discovered with a bladder infection we need to always make sure we take the time to explain all of the details.

My daughter's sister-in-law had been fighting a bladder infection for over a year with antibiotics and had not been successful in getting rid of it, so one day she asked Myrna what she would do. Myrna had her call me, I told her about the two JuniPars and one Cranactin three times per day. I was in a hurry to get to a class that I was teaching, so that was all I said about it. Three days later she called me again and said it wasn't helping. She was running a fever and feeling worse than ever. I was really surprised because I had never seen this fail, so I started going back over it with her. I said, "You're taking 2 JuniPars and 1 Cranactin three times per day with a gallon of water, right?"

She said, "Water? I don't like water. I've been taking them with my Dr Pepper."

She added the water to her regime and cleared up the bladder infection.

BLEEDING

Dr. Christopher taught that one of our best first aid herbs is cayenne pepper because it stops bleeding. We have found this to be true over and over. The reason Cayenne is so effective is because it equalizes the blood pressure throughout the body.

Shepherds Purse is considered an excellent herb to use for uterine bleeding. We use it at all of our births to help control bleeding.

Herbal Aids:
- Cayenne
  - o can be taken as a tsp. of powder in a glass of water
  - o can be taken in tincture form – either straight or in water
  - o can be taken in capsules – usually 3 or 4 of the 40,000 BTU – this method takes a little longer to work because you have to allow time for the capsules to dissolve
- Shepherd's Purse – ½ dropper full under the tongue as needed – is very specific for uterine bleeding, but will help with all types of bleeding

Experiences:
a) Section I, pg. 27
b) Section I, pg. 29
c) Section I, pg. 33
d) Section I, pg. 54

e) Section II, pg. 170
f) Section III, pg. 227
g) Section III, pg. 231
h) Section III, pg. 234
i) Section IV, pg. 343

BLOOD POISONING

Many people have with blood poisoning have a streak running up their leg and have been able to watch it go back down as the black ointment drew the infection back to the surface. In a case of blood poisoning, I use the INF formula to fight the infection and echinacea to boost the immune system. Any time you are trying to flush something out of the system, you need to be drinking lots of pure water.

Herbal Aids:
- Black Ointment – apply ointment directly on area to draw infection out
- INF Formula - take 4 capsules every two to three hours while awake to fight infection – more, if needed
- Echinacea – take four capsules every two to three hours while awake to boost immune system
- Echinacea & Goldenseal – take two to three capsules every two to three hours to fight infection and boost immune system
- Red Clover Combination - take three capsules twice a day to cleanse the blood (any time you are using a blood cleansing formula, you should make sure the liver is detoxed and the bowel is open)
- Herbal Enema – such as Catnip to help cleanse the colon

BLOOD PRESSURE

In a book called *Left for Dead,* Dick Quinn shares his experience of going through multiple procedures, including by-pass surgery to correct his high blood pressure and heart problems.

After he had gone through everything he could medically and still did not have his health back, he discovered cayenne and garlic. Cayenne increases circulation in the body and garlic tends to break down the plaque that builds up on the artery wall. Hawthorne berries are a very specific herb for the heart.

Those on high blood pressure medication should not go off of it cold-turkey. It can be extremely dangerous. When you have high blood pressure, it is an indication that somewhere in the body, cells are being deprived of oxygen. These cells send a message to the brain requesting more oxygen. The brain signals the heart to send out more blood, thus the blood pressure goes up. When you take blood pressure medication, that signal from the brain to the heart is blocked. However, the problem in the body has not been fixed, so the cells scream louder and the brain sends stronger and stronger signals. If you were to stop taking your blood pressure medication without reducing the dosage gradually, you would be a prime candidate for a stroke, which is considered a possible side effect of the medication.

As you change your diet to wholesome, live foods and use the herbs to strengthen your system, blood pressure automatically begins to come down and your doctor will reduce the dosage of your medication.

Herbal Aids:
- Cayenne – take two capsules three times per day to increase circulation
- Garlic – take 2 capsules three times per day to help open up the arteries by cleaning the arterial walls'
- Hawthorne Berry Syrup - take one or two Tbsp. three times per day to help strengthen the heart
- Chlorophyll – take one Tbsp. three times per day to help build healthy blood
- Dr. Christopher's BPE formula – two capsules three times per day (contains garlic and cayenne)

- Alkalizer Pack - like so many of our degenerative diseases, high blood pressure can be caused from diet and allowing the body to become too acidic

Other Modalities:
- Change your DIET – in order to cure this condition you must change your diet and get the proper exercise

BREAST INFECTION
(Mastitis)

Herbal Aids:
- Cut Mullein and Cut Lobelia – apply a fomentation (see Section V) of three parts Mullein to one part Lobelia to breast – keep warm and moist.
- Mullein & Lobelia Ointment - if you are in a situation where you cannot do the fomentation – rub the ointment onto the breast
- Professor Cayenne Ointment - if you are using the Mullein & Lobelia ointment, you could add a small amount of Cayenne ointment to keep it warm and help it to be absorbed
- INF Formula - take four capsules four times per day to fight infection – more, if needed
- Echinacea & Goldenseal – take four capsules four times per day to fight infection and boost the immune system – more, if needed

Other Modalities:
- Hot Shower – stand in hot shower – let the water run on breasts – this will help to relieve pain and allow milk to run out of the breast, which will help to relieve engorgement
- Hot Bath – lay in a hot bath with breast under the water – if your tub is not deep enough, then soak a wash cloth in hot water and lay it on the breast
- Nurse Baby – allow the baby to nurse in order to drain the breast. This can be very painful, but is a necessary part of healing. If it is too uncomfortable – try getting in a hot tub of water, slide down in the water so that most of the breast is in the water – have someone hand you the baby and nurse while in the water.

Experience:
When my children were born, I got mastitis several different times. I found that if I went on antibiotics, I was going to be extremely ill for three to four days. If I didn't go on antibiotics, I was going to be extremely ill for three to four days. Since I have learned about mullein and lobelia, I have not seen a case of mastitis last more than 24 hours. It is truly incredible how fast it will help to give relief.

BROKEN BONES

Herbal Aids:
- BF&C Capsules – five capsules three times per day, more, if needed – I have used up to a hundred per day, see experience 'd' below – if you have a toxic liver due to lots of drugs, medications, bad diet, etc., you may want to take two capsules of Barberry LG three times per day to cleanse the liver. (In all of the experiences below, using BF&C, the formula still contained comfrey – the FDA has now banned the use of comfrey in any formula which is taken internally, so, if you want the same results, you might want to consider getting some comfrey separately).
- BF&C or Comfrey – soak broken limb in a strong tea or decoction of BF&C or Comfrey for one hour morning and night.
- BF&C Ointment – when not soaking – keep BF&C Ointment or Oil on the break.
- Vitalerbs - five capsules three times per day with meals for added nutrition – more, if needed
- Comfrey Paste – if you know where some Comfrey is growing, you can take the leaves – put them in a blender with a little bit of water – blend them into a paste – put into plastic baggies – keep in the freezer – apply to wounds or broken bones whenever needed.

Other Modalities:
- A Tuning Fork – if you are somewhere that it is impossible to get an X-Ray, such as a remote camping trip and you want to know if the bone is broken – hit the tuning fork against something solid and get it vibrating – run the stem of the fork along the bone you suspect is broken – if the bone is intact the vibrating fork will not hurt, but if you come to a broken spot, the vibration will cause a sharp pain and you will know where the break is.

- Immobolize – the joint above and below where the broken bone is to stabilize it.
- Alternate Moist Heat and Cold – in the first 24 to 48 hours alternate moist heat and a cold pack to disperse the inflammation, pain and swelling.

Experiences:
a) See Section I, pg. 17
b) In Section I, pg. 22, I share Nathan's experience with his broken foot. The chiropractor who X-rayed the foot had told Nathan that he had a spiral break of the fifth metatarsal and the bone had rotated. He said he was legally obligated to tell Nathan that he needed to see an orthopedic doctor in order to have the bone pinned back into place so that it would heal correctly. Nathan decided to use the same methods that we had used for all of our other broken bones. He was successful and back doing everything he had done before within four weeks.

When I used to tell this story, people would ask me if I had ever had the foot X-rayed again to see how it healed. I used to tell people no, why would I do that? As long as it works and it isn't hurting him, why waste the money? Well, now I can tell everyone that it has been X-rayed again.

The next year was so crazy for us that I could not face the idea of ten different birthday parties, so I gathered our children together and told them that we were going to have two big birthday parties that year. One in the spring for everyone born in the first half of the year and one in the fall for everyone born in the second half of the year.

When we had the first birthday party, we rented one of those blow-up moon walks that children like to jump in at the carnivals. We had it in the front yard. I was rotating among five birthday parties and was unaware of the fact that Nathan and our chiropractor had discovered that it was great fun to jump out of the second story window into the moon walk. They were having a great time until the last jump when Nathan's sister fell across his foot and it could not rotate as he fell, so it broke. I sent the chiropractor and Nathan down to his office to X-ray the foot. When they got back, Wade told me that it was the same foot, different ·bone. However, he had shot the X-ray so that he could check the first break. He told me that no one would ever be able to tell that the bone had been broken. There was no sign of it. Now, I've seen enough X-rays to know that when there has been an old break, you can see it because of the scarring.

My point is this; time and time again I have watched the same phenomenon and have come to believe that scar tissue is a patch job. Our body does the best it can to patch us back together and so forms scar tissue. However, when the body has the right tools (nutrition which creates building blocks) to work it, it also has the blue print and will rebuild itself exactly the way it was before without scar tissue.

c) In the winter of 1998, Steve broke his leg right above the ankle. He is tall and thin so my normal method of making a half-cast wrapped with an Ace bandage did not work. I tried to putting a full cast on it, but then I had to cut it off each time I wanted to soak the leg. It was painful for him and difficult for me. Other people with broken legs wore braces held together with Velcro straps, so I went down to our local medical supply store and asked him if he carried the Velcro boots. My supplier told me he did not carry them because you have to go to an orthopedic surgeon and have them specially fitted. I said, "Well, I don't have an orthopedic surgeon. Could we look in the catalogs and see if I can order one?"

He said, "Why do you want one?" I said, "My husband has a broken leg."

"So, if your husband has a broken leg, why don't you have an orthopedic surgeon?" He asked.

I replied, "I can't see paying them a thousand dollars to do what I can do myself."

Well, he laughed and said we could check the catalog. We found them. When he filled out the order form – we saw how specially fitted they are – they came in small, medium, and large. The special fitting is determined by how tight you pull the Velcro.

d)   In March of 2000, Aaron, 15 at the time, was in a snow boarding accident. His experience was an exception to the rules I had been applying up to this point. With all of the broken bone experiences I have shared with you, we did not need to see a doctor and they healed beautifully. However, when you are dealing with a joint, it is difficult to stabilize the bones long enough for them to heal.

We were living in Montana at the time of this accident. Juanita, our oldest daughter, was getting married in Utah. We decided to take the family to Utah in two carloads. Steve and I took the first carload down on Wednesday. Aaron was suppose to come down in the second car on Thursday. When we arrived in Utah Wednesday evening, we called home to check in and found out that Aaron had been taken to the emergency room due to a severe snow boarding accident.

When I checked in, I was told that the doctor who had seen Aaron in the emergency room wanted me to call him at home. When I contacted him, he told me that Aaron had shattered his elbow and needed to go into surgery immediately. He said my sister-in-law and daughter would not let him do anything to Aaron so he had released Aaron with his X-rays, a splint and some pain killers. A dear friend of ours put him on a plane first thing Thursday morning and flew him down to us.

We were getting ready for Juanita's wedding in two days and now we had Aaron with a broken elbow heading into the weekend. I was extremely torn about what to do. All of the broken bones we had dealt with up to this point had responded extremely well to treatment with the herbs. However, this time the doctor had impressed upon me that if I did not take him into surgery he could be permanently disabled. The elbow was broken into three pieces, but at this point I did not completely understand the anatomy of what had happened.

I decided to care for Aaron through the weekend, then decide on Monday what we were going to do. We put Aaron on ten BF&C capsules every hour and six Vitalerbs on the half hour. That meant he was taking 100 BF&C capsules and 60 Vitalerb capsules per day. I massaged BF&C oil into the elbow several times a day along with alternating hot and cold packs over a BF&C fomentation. We used reflexology on his foot to help with the pain.

Within two days he was off of the pain killers and relatively comfortable. When he needed to get up and move around we put his arm in a sling. Saturday he was able to attend the wedding.

Monday morning I took him to a chiropractor whom I knew well to have him X-ray the arm again. It looked bad. He, too, recommended surgery and also suggested that I stop using the herbs because they would speed up the process of healing the bones in the wrong position.

I could see that, so far, what I had been doing did not seem to be lining the bones up correctly, so I called the orthopedic surgeon in Montana who had seen Aaron in the emergency room and scheduled surgery for Wednesday afternoon. I also stopped the herbs.

By Tuesday morning, Aaron was asking for pain killers again. I got thinking about the herbs I had been giving him. From previous experience, I know every cell has the blue print for where and how they are supposed to be – I also know they would not purposely line up wrong. I also came to understand that pain is the body's cry for help. When we give the body what it needs to heal – it stops screaming. I put him back on the herbs. Within a few hours, he did not need or want the pain killers any more. This is known as "biofeedback" – listening to what the body is trying to tell you.

It became obvious on Tuesday that we were not going to get back to Montana in time to do the lab work they required before surgery, so we called to reschedule and were told the doctor was leaving on vacation Thursday morning.

Tuesday afternoon I took Aaron down to the hotel hot tub. We soaked his arm in the hot water so that the soft tissue in his arm would relax. I gently tractioned it, extended it and flexed it. That evening I had it X-rayed again. It looked better, but still not good enough.

We called around Tuesday evening to find out which orthopedic surgeons were recommended in Utah. Two or three people recommended the same surgeon, so at 8:00 Wednesday morning we went to his office. I took all of the X-rays with me, explained our situation and was allowed to see one of the partners. He had another X-ray taken to see down into the elbow. When he had seen all of the X-rays, he asked me to explain what happened; he wanted to know why Aaron was calming sitting there without pain killers; and he wanted to know why we had waited a week. I told him about the wedding, the canceled surgery, and a little bit about what I had been doing.

He was furious and rude, starting with a guilt trip about how I had messed everything up by waiting too long. He insisted this was an extremely bad break and because of that he would not touch it. He recommended a partner, an elbow specialist who may take it, but this would be major surgery and Aaron would have to be in the hospital for at least three days, in a cast for several weeks and then go through months of physical therapy. Even after going through all of that, he doubted that Aaron would ever have complete, normal use of his arm.

The doctor called his partner to see if he would take the case. His partner told him he couldn't because he was leaving on vacation. There was one other orthopedic doctor in the office so I asked if I could speak to him. The doctor I had been talking to asked for my insurance carrier. When he found out that I didn't have any, he told me to wait out front and he would speak to the other doctor. Several minutes later he came out to the waiting room to tell me that no one in the office would take this case because it was too serious and without insurance he didn't think the hospital would take us. He said his advise was to go to the University of Utah and let the residents handle it. At the time I remember thinking, "Are you crazy? As an orthopedic surgeon, you won't accept the case because it is too serious and now you want me to turn my son over to students?!"

Aaron was surprised and upset about the doctor's unprofessional behavior. As we were leaving he told me not to worry about his arm, we could just go home and fix it. I appreciated his compassion for me and the simple faith he had in all that he has witnessed in his short life. I told him by the end of the day we would decide what to do. Some people in the family did not approve of what I was doing, so they took it upon themselves to call the state

Child Protective Services. Fortunately for us, I was unaware of this at the time and they were not able to locate us so no harm was done, but it is important for you, the reader, to understand that when you break with conventional wisdom there can be some serious opposition. You have to weigh your choices and consequences out carefully and then be willing to do whatever you have to do to protect yourself and your children.

Later that morning, in a friend's office, I told his receptionist what had happened. She told me she had an excellent pediatrician who we could call to get a recommendation. When we told the pediatricians receptionist which doctors we had already seen, she said those were the same ones they would normally recommend. When I explained how bad the elbow was broken, she told me about a doctor in Salt Lake City who specialized in just the elbow, shoulder and wrists.

We called the specialist and, after explaining everything again, his receptionist told us to be there at 4:30 and he would see us after he finished with all of his other appointments.

The doctor turned out to be a middle-aged, down-to-earth doctor, a refreshing change. I told him right up front that I did not want to offend him – I just wanted to be honest, explain everything I had done and tell him where I was coming from – I knew we were both tired after a long day and, quite frankly, I couldn't deal with any more egos. He said that was exactly what he wanted me to do. He was particularly interested in how Aaron was doing so well with such a severe injury and no pain killers. I told him everything. He seemed extremely interested in what I had done. He told me that a hundred years ago what I had done would have made the difference between having use of the arm again as opposed to never using it again. Then he said, "Let me show you what is going on here."

He took out a model of the arm and showed me how the humerus balloons out to form two condials when it reaches the elbow. There is a dished out area between these condials where the bones in the lower arm rotate back and forth as you flex and extend the arm. Aaron literally blew this area apart. The condials were split in half and broken off of the humerus so that they were floating free. There was also a large piece broken off at the bottom of the humerus where the condials should have been connected. All three pieces were floating free and every time Aaron made any movement at all, the bones were pushed apart.

The doctor told me that if there were no surgery performed, the arm would heal. However, it would not be able to heal correctly because of the movement of the bones. He said that if we immobilized it, it might heal perfectly, but the arm would freeze in that position and there would be very limited movement. He said, "If you will allow me to help you, we will stabilize the bones by pinning them in place. We will put a splint on Aaron's arm to support it while the trauma of the surgery heals. Then we can take the splint off and you can keep doing everything you are doing now which I feel will give him a good chance for complete recovery."

The doctor explained that it is pretty uncommon to see this type of injury in a young person. He said that you normally see this type of thing when a grown person is thrown from a car or other vehicle.

I asked him if there was a problem because we had waited so long and he assured me that was not a problem. Quite often in these type of injuries there are skin abrasions that have to heal before they can ever do the surgery.

I was so impressed with his kindness, his willingness to take the time to show us what was happening, and his attitude of wanting to help that I could have thrown my arms around him.

Steve brought up the fact that we didn't have insurance and asked him if that would be a problem. The doctor laughed, told us he had been doing this for a lot of years and that he wasn't worried about the money. That could all be worked out. The surgery was scheduled for Friday afternoon without any required lab work.

Before the surgery on Friday, the doctor explained to us that when an elbow explodes like this, the bones are crushed due to the impact of the accident. He said they normally have to do some bone grafting in order to pin the bones back together. He wanted to know if he should take the bone from the bone bank or from Aaron's wrist.

Aaron was in surgery for four and a half hours. When the doctor came to speak to us, he said that the injury was even worse than he had thought, but he had not had to do any bone grafts. He also said he was amazed at Aaron's fast healing. He wanted to keep Aaron in the hospital overnight to help him with pain, but if everything went well he could go home in the morning.

Even though the body had not been able to realign the bones due to the location and constant movement, I firmly believe that there were no bone grafts needed, because the BF&C and Vitalerbs had given the bones what they needed to pull all of the small pieces back together and regenerate themselves.

After surgery, when Aaron was put into the hospital room, the nurse told me the doctor had ordered a morphine drip because these are painful injuries. However, Aaron was doing so well, she had not set it up and told me she would only bring it in if we needed it. Over the next twelve hours, Aaron only needed two pain pills. He was released from the hospital and we went back to using ten BF&C capsules on the hour and six Vitalerbs on the half hour. Within two days he was off pain killers. If he forgot to take his supplements, his arm would begin to hurt again. Again, when the body is getting the nutrition and building blocks it needs, it is busy with the healing process. When it doesn't get what it needs, it screams for help.

Finally, on Wednesday, five days after the surgery, we took Aaron back to the doctor for another X-ray to be sure everything looked good before we took him home to Montana. I asked the doctor if we would be able to see new bone growth in the X-ray. He said it was way too soon, but when we looked at the X-ray, he was amazed to show me where the new bone was already forming.

Aaron stayed on the ten BF&C and six Vitalerbs for the first week after surgery. Ten days after the surgery I removed the stitches and he dropped to fifty BF&C and twenty Vitalerbs per day. Each day I rubbed the arm with BF&C oil, gently flexing and extending the arm, along with rotating it. The third week after surgery, I put him in a hot tub each day and worked the arm a little bit more.

Within a couple of months, Aaron has complete use of his arm.

BRONCHITIS

So many successful experiences have come from using the following program; some have been frightening and some have taken more time than others because it always comes back to being as aggressive as whatever it is you are battling. I want to share a couple of different ones here so you will know some of the things you can expect when using this program for colds, bronchitis, RSV, pneumonia – any type of upper respiratory infection.

Herbal Aids:
- X-Ceptic Tincture – rub onto throat, chest, and back
- to fight whatever is causing the problem.
- Mullein Oil – rub onto throat, chest and back over the X-Ceptic Tincture to break up congestion
- INF Formula – for anyone old enough to swallow capsules – take 4 every two to three hours to fight infection
- Echinacea – take 4 capsules or a dropper full of liquid (depending on age) every two to four hours while awake to boost immune system
- Echinacea & Golden Seal – take 4 capsules every two to four hours to fight infection and boost immune system
- Dr. Christopher's Anti-Plague - take as often as needed until condition is cleared up
- Kid-E-Well - take one to two droppers full every two hours while awake – more, if needed
- Cold Sheet Treatment – see Section V for complete instructions
- Enemas – use a room temperature Catnip enema to cleanse bowel or, if nauseated, use a green drink enema to put nutrition back into the system
- Onion Poultice – place whole onion in oven at low temperature (around 250 degrees) – leave in oven until it begins to get soft and juicy – slice, place on chest, making sure they are not hot enough to scald – secure with cloth or T-shirt.

Essential Oil:
- Tei Fu - put a couple of drops in the palm of your hand – rub your hands together to activate it – then cup your hands around your nose and inhale.
- Eucalyptus Oil – put into hot water vaporizer and steam into room
- Bronchitis Blend – Dr. Gary Young recommends this combination:
  - o 2 drops sage
  - o 4 drops myrrh
  - o 5 drops clove
  - o 6 drops ravensara
  - o 15 drops frankincense
  - Applications:
  - TOPICAL: . . . dilute 50:50 with massage oil
    - Apply 2-6 drops to neck and chest as needed.
    - COMPRESS, warm, on neck, chest, and upper back areas 1-3 times daily

INHALATION:
DIRECT, 5-10 times daily as needed
DIFFUSER, 15 minutes, 3-10 times daily as needed. . . also diffuse at night during sleep.
RECTAL;
RETENTION: Using any of the recommended blends, combine 20 drops with 1 tablespoon olive oil. Insert into rectum with bulb syringe and retain throughout the night. Repeat nightly for 2-3 days (411 Essential).

Experiences:

a) See Section I, pg. 61
b) See Section I, pg. 66
c) A dear friend, Janet, in Idaho who is a midwife, called one morning to tell me of three babies who were sick with some kind of a bronchial pneumonia which was caused by a virus in the area. She the medical route claimed at least one death due to this virus. There is nothing that can be done medically for a virus. They administer oxygen to help with breathing and intravenous fluids for dehydration, but they can't stop the virus. Some doctors will give antibiotics which do not help with a virus and actually causes harm because it shuts down the one defense the child has and that is the immune system. She asked if I would be willing to help.

I gathered up the herbs she would need and went to Idaho. We went to the homes of the first two children, showed the mothers how to steam the children in a hot bath or shower, how to rub the X-Ceptic on the chest, neck and back, followed by the mullein oil rubbed over the same area. X-Ceptic fights whatever is causing the problem, mullein oil helps break up the mucus which is causing the congestion. They gave their children Kid-E-Well orally to boost the immune system and bring the congestion out; an onion poultice was placed on their chest and a hot water vaporizer was started with eucalyptus oil. They were grateful for the help and the children were breathing much better when we left.

Arriving at the third home, I discovered that this baby was delivered just five weeks earlier. We showed the mother how to use the same things. In this case, since the baby was so young, we used the kitchen sink to bathe the baby. It was a double sink, so the mother ran some warm water in one side for the baby and then let just hot water run in the other side to create steam. After the bath,, she gave the baby a dropper full of Kid-E-Well and rubbed the X-Ceptic and mullein oil onto her throat, chest and back. She applied the onion poultice and then turned to talk to Janet while I got the baby dressed.

While I was dressing her, everything had begun to work and the congestion started to break up. Unfortunately, a young baby does not know how to cough things up. A large chunk of mucus broke loose in her chest and when she started to cough it up it became lodged in her throat. I held the baby head down on the palm of my hand, over my knee to try to help her dislodge it. I didn't want to alarm the mother, but while I was trying to help the baby, I felt her body go limp in my hand. She was not breathing. I called to Janet to come over to me for a minute. She saw what was happening and grabbed a bulb syringe to help suction out the baby's throat. She suctioned out part of the mucus, but the baby was still not breathing and was blue. Janet turned to the mother and said, "Call her back. She knows your voice."

The mother knelt down by the baby's head, called her by name and began to tell her how much she loved her. Pretty soon she gagged and started to cough so that we were able to get the rest of the mucus out. The mother followed through baby recovered beautifully.

The reason I shared this experience with you is because there are two things I hope you will come to understand. The first one is that you need to know what action you are looking for when you use these herbs. In this case, we were trying to break up and move out congestion. Herbs, hydrotherapy, and other modalities we were using worked. You then have to be prepared for the results, such as having the bulb syringe on hand. If we had lost that baby, the headlines the next day could have read, "Midwives Kill Baby With Herbs." The truth is, the herbs were doing exactly what they were supposed to do. It was up to us to be prepared to help them.

The second thing I want you to comprehend is this: no matter how much you study, no matter how many degrees you have on your wall – eventually you are going to run into something where you do not know what to do. During these times we have to learn to turn to a source higher than our own for answers. There is intelligence higher than our own in this universe and, if you are going to step out of your comfort zone, it is imperative that you learn how to draw on it. I can make you this promise – if you ever think you have all of the answers – someday, somewhere you are going to get in over your head and not know what to do – then who will you turn to? Help usually comes in one of two ways – either the right person shows up at the right time to help me through it or I "instinctively" am given the inspiration to do what it is I need to do.

d)   Returning from Idaho, another friend called from Arizona with her two-year-old suffering from the same type of virus. We told her what we had been doing to fight these viruses and she was able to help her daughter through it.

About a week later she called to say that her nine-year-old son had come down with the same thing, but was not recovering as quickly. We told her some conditions call for more aggression and to do more of what she was already doing. A couple of days later, she called to tell us she did not think he was going to live. He couldn't keep anything down, was extremely dehydrated and very ill. Without going into the details of why, they could not take their son to a hospital even if they had wanted to; so Steve and I left for Arizona.

To get more aggressive, the mother added some Jurassic Green enemas to get fluid and nutrition into her son. She gave him Kid-E-Cep along with the Kid-E-Well orally, put a garlic poultice on the bottoms of his feet, increased the frequency of the hot showers and used some essential oils to open up the bronchial tubes. Within three days he was up and around the house, watching television and getting his appetite back.

BURNS

Burn paste works beautifully on all types of burns: chemical, steam, hot water, sunburn, etc. . It is important to expose the burned area to the fresh air everyday and rebandage daily to allow the burn to air out; it needs oxygen to heal. They do not heal well if they are constantly covered with bandaging. The skin has to be allowed time to breathe.

Herbal Aids:
- Fresh Aloe Vera Gel – cut a leaf off of an Aloe Vera plant, slice it open and remove the get from inside – apply the gel directly on the burn being careful not to tear any blisters or the skin – if fresh aloe is not available, you can use a commercial aloe vera gel – just make sure it is pure aloe.
- Burn Paste – mix Comfrey or BF&C powder with equal parts of Wheat Germ Oil and raw Honey – make a thick paste – apply to burn being careful not to damage the tissue.
- BF&C Ointment – use in the final stages of healing to avoid scar tissue.

Essential Oils:
- Lavender Oil – put some lavender oil into a spray bottle full of water – spray directly on burn to soothe the burn and help with healing – extremely effective with sunburn.

Other Modalities:
- Pure Water – drink lots of water to help rehydrate the body and the skin
- Cool the Burn – as soon as a burn happens, it is important to cool the area off – use cold water, a cool cloth, snow, whatever you have available – just get it to stop burning
- Air Out – it is important to remove all gauze and

Experiences:
a) See Section I, pg. 68
b) When our son, Joseph was about eight-years-old, he was trying to make a hot drink for his younger sister in the microwave, and left it in too long. As he was climbing down off of the counter with the cup, he slipped and spilled it down his thigh. I heard him scream. When I got to him, I pulled his sweat pants off and the skin came with them. He had a bad second degree burn.

We put a cold, wet cloth on it to cool it off. Then we covered it with some fresh, aloe vera gel. We got him into bed and made the burn paste. He was in a lot of pain, so Kelly found the spot on his foot that correlated to the burn on his thigh and began to rub his foot. There were already quite a few "crystals" in his foot that she could feel breaking loose as she rubbed them. Within a few minutes she had relieved the pain enough that he could lay comfortably. We applied the burn paste and a gauze pad.

The burn was in a horse shoe shape, with the horse shoe being a severe second degree burn and the area around the horse shoe a first degree burn. The first few mornings when I unwrapped the burn to put more burn paste on it, most of the paste would be gone because the body absorbed it. After about three days I noticed that when I removed the gauze, the paste was gone where the horse shoe was, but all around the horse shoe was crusty with dried paste from the day before. The reason was that the first degree burn had healed and so the skin no longer needed the burn paste. It didn't draw it in any more and so it would just dry and stay where I put it. The second degree burn was still healing; so it continued to draw in the burn paste.

Another fascinating thing that we watched was how the body made new cells. About the third day when I removed the gauze pad, we noticed that inside the horse shoe was a whitish gelatin substance. When my mother saw it, she said, "Are you sure you know what you're doing?" I looked all around the burn for signs of infection such as streaks, inflammation, fever, etc. . I didn't see anything that would indicate an infection, so I said, "No, but his body does." I put more paste on it and covered it up.

Since that time, I have seen this substance many times. It is new cell growth! The thing I have never come to understand is why hospitals scrape and peel burns – if you scrub this new tissue away, you then have to do a skin graft to replace it. When I see this cell growth taking place I never disturb it. The body does a remarkable job in rebuilding the tissue.

Each day while the burn was healing, we would find a time when Joseph could watch a movie and be relatively still so we could take the bandaging off and let it air out without him injuring the tissue. It healed beautifully, leaving only a small scar which I tried to keep BF&C on, but Joe thought the scar was cool, so he still carries a small battle wound.

c) The following experience was sent to me by one of my students.

November 4, 1999, my granddaughter, Emilee, age 2, burned her feet on her mother's smooth-topped stove. She loves sweets and while her mother was putting things away in the refrigerator, she tried running across the stove to get into the cabinet that has the sweets.

When she screamed, her mother (Cynthia) turned and grabbed her off the stove and immediately put her feet in cold water. When she called me to see what to do. At this time, I had no idea how badly she was burned. I told her to get the heat out of her feet which she assured me she was doing. I asked her if she had aloe vera and she said no. I told her to get some and I also told her about the comfrey, wheat germ oil, and raw honey paste. She started giving Emilee Kid-E-Well to keep infection out.

The burns were so bad that she took her to the emergency room. Emilee had very bad 2nd degree burns.

This was a nightmare experience. In the emergency room, they handled Emilee roughly and all they were concerned about was how she got burned – apparently, burn feet is a common form of child abuse. She was finally give a shot of Demerol to kill the pain and they dressed her feet. Cynthia was told to see her doctor and to keep the bandage on. They also gave her Tylenol with codeine for the pain.

The next morning Cynthia called her 'health' friend and she came running over with ale vera and vitamin E oil. These really helped keep the pain down. The blisters were still forming at this time. Cynthia took Emilee to the doctor and all the doctor could say was they could put her feet in a whirltub, get the dead skin off and do a skin graft so she wouldn't scar. Cynthia was totally disgusted with this advice so she took Emilee home and called me. It was this call that finally made me realize just how badly Emilee was burned. I told Cynthia she had to find comfrey and make the burn paste. Through a health store she found cut comfrey leaves, the wheat germ oil and raw honey. She mixed these up and made the paste, using 100% cotton diapers as the bandage. Interesting note – she found aloe vera to be real effective for two days and then it was only effective after that as a moisturizer. The comfrey mixture was real rough looking due to the cut leaves. It looked like straw and dirt and was flaky and messy. There were places on Emilee's feet where it looked like it was embedded into the flesh. The feet started to heal with this mixture and Cynthia changed Emilee's bandages about 6 times a day and had to do a lot of vacuuming to keep this straw-like mixture off the floor and couch.

Cynthia took Emilee to the doctor again. The doctor was amazed at the healing that was taking place and made Cynthia bandage Emilee's foot because of the mixture she was using. The doctor still insisted that they go to a plastic surgeon. When Cynthia called me about it, I told her as long as there was no infection and the feet were healing, if I were her, I would keep bandaging them myself. She took this advice and Emilee healed a little bit each day.

Sixteen days later I visited California and saw Emilee's feet for the first time. I brought the powdered comfrey root with me, and Emilee's feet looked terrible. Black skin was hanging all over her feet. The blisters had popped so ther was a lot of raw flesh. They assured me she looked great! We decided to let her soak in the tub to remove as much dried skin and comfrey mixture as possible. When she got out of the tub we mixed the powdered comfrey, made a thick paste and bandaged it on her feet. Two days before I got there she would walk on just her heels for a few minutes each day. This was a great improvement from just sitting or crawling around and not letting anyone near her.

The next morning was incredible! We could not believe the healing that had taken place. With this new mixture, every day brought a new miracle. When I left a week later, all the open flesh and slimy looking white cells were closed over except for one small hole on the ball of her left foot – the foot with the worst burns and possibly 3rd degree burns. Two days later that hole was completely healed.

Four weeks after Emilee was burned, she refused to have her feet dressed and bandaged and insisted she be put in socks and shoes. She ran, jumped and danced. Cynthia listened to her wants and needs. When Emilee needed her bandages changed, she let Cynthia know. Emilee also let Cynthia know that it was time to stop bandaging her feet altogether, even though Cynthia wanted to bandage them a few more days.

The bottom of Emilee's feet have healed beautifully! The color is gradually changing from red to a beautiful soft pink.

We witnessed an absolute miracle! There is no scarring emotionally or physically with Emilee or her two sisters, ages 4 and 5, who had to go through the trauma. This experience has increased my testimony of herbs and of the God given design of our bodies to heal themselves given sufficient natural resources.

This letter was sent to me from Carolyne Eliason of Orem, Utah. I wish to extend a special thanks to her and her family for allowing me to include it in this book. Following are the before and after pictures of Emilee's feet. In this case, a picture truly is worth a thousand words.

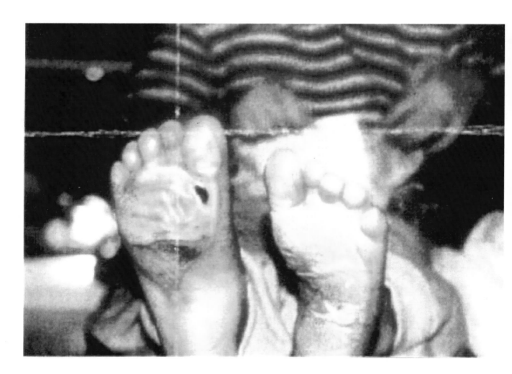

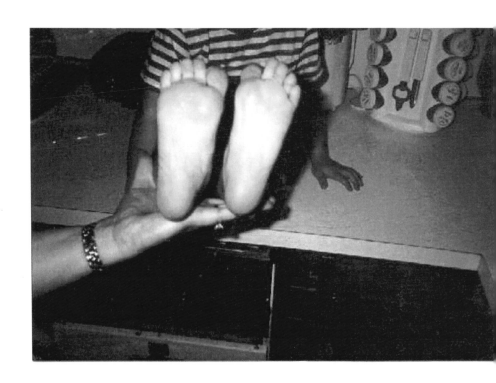

You cannot by reasoning correct a man of ill opinion which by
reasoning he never acquired.
-- Bacon

The word "vegetarian" is not derived from "vegetable," but from the Latin,
homo vegetus, meaning among the Romans - strong, robust, thoroughly healthy.
-- Paul Bragg

Dehydration of certain organs will result in certain symptoms which are often
misdiagnosed by physicians. The message is: drink your way to health with
volumes of pure water.
-- F. Batmanghelidj, M.D.

C

CANCER
(Incurable Diseases)

Cancer is not something to play with – if you play with cancer, it will kill you! If you suspect that you could have cancer, I would strongly recommend getting it diagnosed, so you will know what you are working with.

It is important to emphasize that if you choose to not follow conventional therapies, then you must be just as aggressive in using alternative therapies.

As you put a program together for yourself – remember the foundation. We "cleanse" and we "nourish." When we are dealing with cancer or any other potentially "incurable" disease, we have to be sure that our program is as strong as what we are trying to cure and that we stick with it long enough to accomplish what we are trying to do.

Herbal Aids:
- Arise and Shine Cleanse - see information below
- Dr. Schulz's 30-Day Safe Your Life Cleanse - see information below
- Dr. Christopher's Incurables Program - see information below
- The Stanley Burroughs Master Cleanse - see information below
- Alkalizer Pack - this formula helps to alkalize the body quickly
- Parasite Cleanse – whenever you have a condition as toxic as cancer – you will have parasites – see section V for instructions on doing this cleanse
- Vitamin E (antioxidants in general) – In the *Antioxidant Miracle* we are told why it is so important to get enough antioxidants in our diet:
  . . . free radical attack of lipids and proteins can also damage DNA, the genetic material within the cell, which can lead to cancer. Quenching free-radicals is not the only way vitamin E can keep cancer at bay. Each of the network antioxidants in general, and vitamin E in particular, appears to play a much greater role in regulating body systems than was ever believed possible. As is lipoic acid, vitamin E is involved in signaling pathways that turn on and off genes and regulate cell growth.

  In particular, researchers such as my friend and colleague Angelo Azzi, in Bern, Switzerland, have found that vitamin E inhibits protein kinase C activity, which activates enzymes that stimulate tumor growth. Numerous studies confirm that people who eat a diet rich in vitamin E and other antioxidants have significantly lower rates of cancer than those who don't.

Other studies have linked low levels of vitamin E to an increased risk of many different kinds of cancer, but especially prostate and lung cancer. (Packer 58)

- Chaparral Tea – Dr. Christopher teaches in the *School of Natural Healing:*

Chaparral or creosote bush is especially known for its use in cancer and arthritis. It was considered to be a cure-all by many Native Americans. It is a potent healer to the urethral tract and to the lymphatic system. It tones up the system and rebuilds the tissue. It cleanses the lower bowel and tones peristaltic muscles. It is very bitter, but for the needy and courageous, it works fast for difficult conditions.

Preparation:

Infusion: Use 1 tsp. of powdered herb to each cup full of water; put the appropriate quantity of the herb into a glass or stainless steel thermos bottle, fill it with boiling water, and immediately cork or cap; infuse for 24 hours, strain, and sweeten with honey; bottle and keep in a cool place. . . take 1 teacup full (6 to 8 oz) 3 times daily. (78)

- Barleans Flax Seed Oil – In a newsletter issued by Barleans, we read:

We want to save your life. We want you to live to 100 and beyond. But, first, we need to deal with the basics. That's why in the last few months we have explored the many benefits of consuming flax oil daily, focusing on this super food's omega-3 fatty acid content and scientific and medical evidence that documents how these essential fatty acids benefit children's intelligence and behavior, as well as reduce risk of cancer and heart disease.

. . . lignan precursors, compounds that are converted by flora in the colon to the lignans enerolactone and enterodiol. Lignans are one of the important foods that people can consume daily to minimize their risk of cancer and, also, to minimize its spread.

Since the early 1980's, lignans have come under increasing scientific scrutiny after studies suggested they may interfere with the development of breast, prostate, colon, and other cancers. Indeed, with cancer now striking greater than one in three Americans, perhaps lignans' greatest gift to humankind is their well-documented anti-cancer activity.

The mounting scientific evidence shows how important it is to consume a lignan-rich diet (and flax is ranked as perhaps the richest source of lignans in the diet today).

Persons who excrete high amounts of lignans in their urine (indicative of a high intake) have markedly lower cancer rates. . . We also have increasingly important human evidence – this from the University Department of Surgery, Queen Elizabeth II Medical Centre, Perth, Western Australia. In this case-control study, published in Lancet, women with newly diagnosed early breast cancer were interviewed by means of questionnaires, and a 72 hour urine collection and blood sample were taken. The urine samples were assayed for various plant constituents including the lignans enterodiol and enerrolactone. After adjustment for age at menarche, parity, alcohol intake, and total fat intake, high excretion of both equol (a plant estrogen) and enterolactone was associated with a 'substantial reduction in breast-cancer risk,' note the researchers. 'There is a substantial reduction in breast-cancer risk among women with a high intake (as measured by secretion) of phyto-oestrogens – particularly the isoflavonic phyto-oestrogen equol and the lignan enterolactone. These findings could be important in the prevention of breast cancer.'

Meanwhile, the researchers from the Department of Biomedical Sciences, Creighton University School of Medicine, Omaha, Nebraska, investigated the effect of dietary supplementation of flaxseed, the richest source of lignans, on experimental melanoma cells. Flax reduced tumor occurrence by up to 63%. The addition of flaxseed to the diet also caused a dose-dependent decrease in tumor area and volume, showing that it could be beneficial both in prevention and treatment. (Doctors Prescription 1)

Juices:

- Wheat Grass Juice – In the *Wheat Grass Book,* Wigmore states:

Dr. Otto Warburg, a German biochemist, won a Nobel prize for his study which revealed that cancer cells cannot exist in the presence of oxygen. Therefore, he surmised that any cancer therapy, if it were to work, would have to increase the oxygen content of the blood, especially at the site of the cancer.

Wheatgrass contains liquid oxygen.

In a conversation I had with Dr. Arthur Robinson, co-founder of the Linus Pauling Institute, he mentioned that it seems wheatgrass juice has a dilating effect on the blood vessels themselves. That is it makes the blood vessels larger so that blood can flow through them more easily. Increased circulation means better nutrition to the cells and more efficient removal of waste from them as well; both processes are important in terms of healing or rebuilding the body. (20)

- Fresh Green Drinks – any type of fresh or powdered green drink is going to help nourish and alkalize the body

- Apple Juice – One of the most effective blood purifiers known is the common apple. In *Herbal Home Health Care,* Christopher refers us to Dr. Shook:

> Dr. Edward E. Shook states in his *Advanced_Course,* Lesson 30, page 4: There is no other remedial agent or herb in the whole range of known therapeutic agents, that can compare with the apple tree and, although it would be difficult to say which of its many virtues is the greatest, we suggest that its abundance of nascent oxygen compound is probably the main reason why it is such a precious food, blood purifier, and unfailing remedy for so many forms of diseases. (152)

- Carrot Juice – In the *Juiceman,* Kordich shares the wonders of carrot juice:

> Today, the established medical community urges everyone to consume more vegetables with beta carotene as a guard against an array of cancers. Carrots are a great source of beta carotene . . . The American Cancer Society recommends three or four servings of these vegetables every week. The society states that the crucifers 'might reduce the incidence of colon, stomach and esophageal cancers. In animals, these vegetables have inhibited the effects of carcinogens.' Who can argue? I believe juicing is the ideal way to consume these valuable vegetables raw and in quantity so that the important nutrients get right to work. (18-19)

In the *Antioxidant Miracle,* we find added benefits to carrot juice:

> Alpha carotene (found in carrots) has been shown to be a potent cancer fighter; in fact, it can suppress the growth of cancerous tumors in animals far better than beta carotene.

> Women take note: Carrots can also help protect against stroke. According to the Harvard study of the food consumed by more than 87,000 female nurses, those who had five or more servings a week of carrots were 68 percent less likely to suffer a stroke than those who ate only one serving a month. (Packer 170-171)

Essential Oils:

- Raindrop Therapy – Taken from *Essential Oils,* Gary Young tells us about a therapy to help kill microbial agents in the body.

> I developed the Raindrop Technique (RT) during the 1980's based on my research with essential oils as antimicrobial agents, and prompted by some fascinating

information I learned from a Lakota medicine man from South Dakota. . . Essential oils are some of the most powerful inhibitors of microbes known, and, as such are an important new weapon in combating many types of tissue infections. . . A 2001 study I conducted with Diane Horne, Sue Chao, and colleagues at Weber State University in Ogden, Utah, found that oregano, thyme, peppermint, and basil exhibited very strong antimicrobial effects against pathogens such as Streptococcus pneumoniae, a major cause of illness in young children and death in elderly and immune-weakened patients. Many other studies confirm these findings.

My Raindrop Technique uses a sequence of highly antimicrobial essential oils synergistically combined to simultaneously kill the responsible viral agents and reduce inflammation. The principle single oils used include:
Oregano (Origanum compactum)
Thyme (Thymus vulgaris)
Basil or balsam fir (Ocimum basilicum or Abies balsamea)
Cypress (Cupressus sempervirens)
Wintergreen or Birch (Gaultheria procumbens or Betula alleghaniensis)
Marjoram (Origanum majorana)
Peppermint (Menthal piperita)
The oils are dispensed like little drops of rain from a height of about six inches above the back and very lightly massaged along the vertebrae and back muscles. Although the entire process takes about 45 minutes to complete, the oils will continue to work in the body for up to one week following treatment, with continued re-alignment taking place during this time. (207,211,212)

All though this technique is easy to do, the instructions are quite extensive and cannot be told simply in this space. To order an instructional video or to obtain complete instructions, please call our toll-free number at the back of this book or contact ESP directly at www.essentialscience.net or by calling toll-free 800-336-6308. I am sorry that the space is not available here to include the complete instructions, but I considered the benefits of this treatment to be worth including in this section.

Other Modalities:
-    Colonics – when you are cleansing quickly and heavily, quite often, the body cannot empty out the toxins as fast as you are releasing them – colon therapy can be a great aid in this situation by keeping the colon cleaned out and allowing somewhere for the toxins to go. If you do not allow for the escape of the toxins, they

will overload the liver and cycle back into the blood stream, causing you to suffer with the toxicity.

- Wheat Grass Implants – Ann Wigmore promotes implants as a way to get the wonderful alkalizing, and nutritional benefits of wheat grass directly into the body.

   Another way in which wheatgrass is used internally at the Hippocrates Institute is as a rectal implant or retention enema. In many people, the lower bowel has become a dumping ground, its walls encrusted with debris and bulging with bubble-like diverticula. The use of an enema to cleanse the colon, followed by a wheatgrass implant, helps stimulate peristaltic activity of the muscles that contract the colon wall. This helps to loosen deposits that may be seen later (after defecation) in the form of hardened black material and ropes or lumps of mucus. In addition, the high magnesium content of wheatgrass juice draws fat out of the colon wall and the liver. (92)

- Organa Minerals – the body can become extremely imbalanced when it is lacking trace minerals. Unfortunately, most of our produce, especially if it is not organic, lacks many of the minerals they used to have due to mineral deficient soil. This is a colloidal mineral supplement which is taken from organic mineral sources.

- Stop all Commercial Soaps & Shampoos – when your system becomes this toxic – it is in an overload situation, much like my father was in after radiation – just turning on a TV would cause him to become nauseated because he could not handle the radiation coming from the television – therefore, I would stop using anything that could possibly bring any more toxicity in contact with the body, such as: commercial soaps, shampoos, hair spray, make-up, lotions, perfumes, and especially deodorants and antiperspirants – the aluminum in antiperspirants has actually been linked to breast cancer.

- Sun Bathing – as we have already discussed in previous chapters, the sun is an incredible healer – if you are going to heal yourself of any serious disease – you need fresh air and sunshine – try sun-bathing nude for at least 5 minutes on each side every day.

- Acupuncture – if you have access to someone who is skilled in the art of Chinese acupuncture, it can be a great help in aligning the energy fields of the body and a great source for the easing and elimination of pain.

- Lymphatic Massage – most massage therapists will tell you that massage therapy is contra-indicated with cases of cancer – however, my feeling is just the opposite – if you are engaged in a heavy cleansing program, then massage can be a great aid in

getting the toxins to move so that you can eliminate them. Dr.
Schulz states:
> Massage the entire body every day with special emphasis
> on deep foot reflexology and all around the problem areas.
> Don't be afraid to touch your sore or sick parts. Put some life
> back in there. (48)

- Health Retreats – see section V for health retreats around the
  country where you can go to begin your healing process.
- Videos by Dr. Lorraine Day – anyone facing cancer needs to see
  these videos – my favorites are: *You Can't Improve on God* and
  Cancer Doesn't Scare Me Anymore

Cleansing – The body must be cleansed, if there is cancer
present; the body is in an extremely toxic condition. This cleanse
needs to be as aggressive as the condition you are fighting, so it
needs to be powerful. From my experience, there are four cleanses
I would recommend which can be done at home: The first one is:
The Arise and Shine Cleanse, which can be purchased in a box
with everything you will need to accomplish it. In his book,
Anderson states:

> . . . for even when there is success in curing one ailment, it
> is rarely more than a brief time before the 'patient'
> develops another ailment. This is because the symptom
> alone was treated, not the cause, not the mind, not the
> subconscious, and not the soul.

The present medical treatments for chronic and
degenerative disease are a contemptible disgrace, especially
with heart dis-ease and cancer. One prominent cancer
researcher, Dr. Hardin Jones, said, 'My studies have proved
conclusively that untreated cancer victims actually live up
to four times longer than treated individual . . . Beyond a
shadow of a doubt, radical surgery on cancer patients does
more harm than good.' Many medical studies, and even
textbooks, verify Dr. Jones' findings. For an example,
Yamada reveals in his medical textbook that there is no
indication at all that patients treated with chemotherapy
have any increase of survival. He also explains that even in
cases where tumors respond to treatments, there is no

indication of living longer. Then why use it? A medical textbook on hematology reveals that the use of chemotherapy for several dis-eases has caused serious, and often fatal, results. This textbook explains that the 'major risk' is the treatment rather than the dis-ease. Imagine, if you will, having a serious dis-ease that results in a high percentage of fatality, and then being treated with chemicals that cause an even higher fatality rate than the dis-ease. Now, does that make any sense at all?

According to Edward Griffin, author of *World Without Cancer* (a revealing and stimulating book that I urge you to read), when skin cancer is excluded, the average cure rate of cancer by medical doctors is 17%. Would you take your car to a mechanic if he claimed a mere 17% cure rate of transmissions? I would suggest it is time to consider other methods.

The medical religion claims no cure for cancer and, what's more, no one else can either. It's against the law – even for those who know the cure. Therefore, I hereby announce that I do not claim that my Program will cure cancer. Should you find your cancer disappearing when you use this system, I will not accept responsibility. You'll have to take the credit yourself.

The cure of cancer or any other dis-ease has been known for decades among a few rare health experts who understand dis-ease and its cause. But, it is also unlawful, in most states, for those experts to treat cancer unless they are M.D.'s. And even the M.D'.s who do understand are greatly hampered by our government and our medical authorities. What a crime against the American people! To think that there are those who can more adequately treat cancer by using non-conventional methods, but who are not legally permitted to do so!

I had better be careful here. I had better not say that all cancers can be cured. No dis-ease is curable if it's gone too far, or if the patient's attitude will not permit healing. But based on my studies and the people I've known who have conquered cancer, heart dis-ease, diabetes, and leukemia, and based on the numerous books I've read and health professionals I've talked to, the following is undeniably true: America must look to alternative healing methods if it wants to return to the healthy nation it once was. (17-19)

The second cleanse is Dr. Shultz's 30-Day Safe Your Life Program. In his "incurables" guide he says,

O.K. So you were diagnosed as 'Incurable' or 'Hopeless'. Well, so was I. All my doctors agreed that I would be dead by the age of 20 without their surgery. Well now they are all DEAD and I am very much ALIVE.

If you have any doubts about whether you can get well, then order a copy of my 'Miracle' - video tape immediately! Call 1-310-576-6565. On this video tape I will explain to you, in detail, how to prove your doctors are wrong and why you can heal yourself of anything. You will also see and hear the personal testimonies of many others just like you that against all the odds, created their own healing miracles.

The 4 week Incurables Program can save your life! I designed this program for people in my clinic who were written off by their doctors, and told, 'It's too late.' This program works So get up off your sick butt, hang up that call to Dr. Kivorkian and give me 110%. Take your life back into your own hands. You will be amazed at the miracle that will happen to you too. (41)

Schultz's program includes nine steps:

1. The morning nutritional drink
2. The intestinal detoxification program
3. The 5-day cleansing & detoxification program
4. Herbal formulae
5. The food program
6. The hydrotherapy program
7. The movement program
8. Additional routines
9. Final thoughts

Schultz continues:

> I know that the ages in the Old Testament of the Bible are correct. I know that we should live 300, 400, 500 years, maybe more. I don't know if you or I will achieve this in our lifetime but what about in 20 or 30 generations of better living!
>
> When we finally die after living a healthy natural lifestyle, what I have seen is we go not with pain, but a big smile on our face and in a room with our loved ones. Considering the screaming hospital death drama, my patients prefer a natural death. (49)

The third cleansing program is Dr. Christopher's Incurables Program. This program is laid out as a three week program, but can be continued as long as needed. During this time only fresh juices are being consumed – alternating fresh apple, carrot, and grape juice. This program also incorporates:

    a. Herbal formulas
    b. Deep breathing
    c. Natural fibers for clothes and bed covers
    d. Releasing Static Electricity
    e. Three Oil Massage
    f. Sunbathing
    g. Baths
    h. Herbal Fomentations
    i. Zonal Foot Therapy (Reflexology)

Christopher insists:

> There are no incurable diseases, but at times there are incurable patients. The Creator has given herbs and assisting wholistic therapies for every type of body malfunction. If they are used, benefits will come. But if they are not used as directed, they can be of no aid.
>
> Over the years, we have put together a healing program that has done miracles for those who have conscientiously used it. It has even brought people who were supposedly on their death beds back to a full and active life. Yet, this program yields no results unless the instructions are followed carefully.

No one can truly tell a patient that he or she has just so many days, weeks, or months to live. The scriptures plainly say that everything moves in its time and season; there is an hour to be born and an hour to die. We have seen cases where the person was told that he had only a few days to live, and many of these people are alive and well today, because they had faith to turn to the natural ways of healing and have been healed. (1)

The fourth cleanse is The Stanley Burroughs Master Cleanse – If you cannot afford to get a complete herbal cleanse or do not have access to them for whatever reasons, this cleanse is something that could easily be done at home without a lot of herbal combinations.   In *Essential Oils,* Gary Young includes the instructions for this cleanse:

a) before undertaking any extended fast or cleanse. The Master Cleanse is not a fast, but a cleansing program. A true fast consists only of water, while the Master Cleanse incorporates a mixture of lemon juice, maple syrup, and cayenne pepper that is consumed throughout the day and is a source of calories, vitamins, and minerals.

The Master Cleanse is ideal for anyone who is not diabetic and can safely cleanse for at least three to seven days. The ideal duration of a cleanse is one to three weeks. As with any program of caloric restriction, however, it is strongly recommended that you consult with your health care professional

Program:
- Take juice of ½ fresh lemon (preferably organic)
- Mix juice into 8 oz. of distilled water
- Add 1-2 tablespoons of grade B maple syrup
- Add up to 1/10th tsp. cayenne pepper (red)

Start with a pinch or two of cayenne and gradually increase to 1/10th tsp. Do not put cayenne pepper in capsules and take separate from the lemonade drink. It changes the action of the formula, and if sent directly to the stomach can cause inflammation and excessive mucous secretion. This may lead to sinusitis or to bowel mucous, and can even contribute to inflammatory bowel syndrome.

Drink as many 10 oz. glasses as required according to your body weight per day. If you weigh 100 pounds then you would drink half your weight in ounces which would be 50 ounces or 5 glasses.

Grade B maple syrup is one of the most balanced of all sugars, containing a balance of positive and negative ions. Grade B does not enter the bloodstream as rapidly as honey or sugar which is better for people who react adversely to sugars, (becoming restless, sleepless, and energetic after consuming sugar), or may be borderline or pre-diabetic. (Diabetics should substitute blackstrap molasses for the maple syrup, using up to ¼ tablespoon.) (If you have difficulties locating Grade B Syrup in your area, it is available through Creer Labs in Utah (801-465-5423)

Contrary to popular belief, lemon is not acidic in the body. It turns alkaline in the mouth. If an acid-like reaction is observed when using lemon with water, it is because of the minerals in the water. Distilled water will not react in this manner.

Cayenne pepper is a blood vessel dilator, a thermal warmer, and provides vitamin A. People who have type O blood tend to have poor circulation. As a result, their body temperature may drop during a cleanse. Because cayenne is an herb known for its ability to warm and restore circulation, it may be taken internally and used topically (especially on the feet, but in small amounts).

Cayenne pepper is also thermogenic. When used in a dietary program, it can facilitate an increase in the body's ability to burn fat.

For the deepest cleanse, it is recommended that you cleanse for at least two weeks. Exercise enhances the cleansing action of the program.

During the middle and later phases of the cleanse, the body chemistry changes, and energy levels may begin to increase. One may experience minor discomforts, such as headaches, upset stomach, or low energy, as toxins and parasites are released from the body. These symptoms will be short-lived.

It is important to have a positive attitude during cleansing or fasting. If you are unaccustomed to the process, you can prepare yourself by fasting one day a week. Sunday, or your Sabbath day, is a wonderful day for this purpose. The biggest obstacle to successful cleansing is fear of failure and not knowing what to expect.

To fast for 24 hours, it is easiest if you begin at noon and finish at noon on the following day or from one dinner to the next.

Again, drink plenty of water.

As you begin to fast, you may experience some unpleasant side effects of cleansing, such as headache, nausea, bloating, or irritability. These symptoms are part of the cleansing response and are often a result of toxins and waste matter being purged from the body which usually takes place within 12 to 36 hours.

If you experience these symptoms, you can cut back on your fluid intake, and turn to vegetable juices: carrot juice, carrot and celery – and 50/50 mixes, carrot with celery, spinach, and broccoli is really good. Carrot with a little apple juice or carrot, apple, and a little lemon juice is good to facilitate the continuation of the cleansing. Six ounces of carrot juice, one ounce of apple, and ½ ounce of lemon juice will help keep the pH steady, slow the diarrhea, and keep the cleansing action going.

If you are feeling nauseated and bloated, it is an indication of two possibilities: (1) poisons are being released at a very rapid rate and may be backing up into the liver. Keeping the liver cleansed and flushed is extremely important. So it would be good to take ledum essential oil in a capsule at night or early morning. Ledum has a very strong effect on the liver and kidneys as a diuretic and a bile duct dilator.

The second reason for feeling ill is that the colon may not be eliminating as well because of spastic colon, loss of peristalsis (the wavelike motion of the intestines that moves waste matter out of the body), and/or from prolapsing with restrictions from kinks, loops, or twists in the colon. Hydro Colon therapy is a powerful treatment for cleansing the body and assisting in restoring peristalsis. You can call a colon hydrotherapist or buy a colima board. Portable colon hydrotheryapy units that are available for use in the home are available from the Young Life Research Clinic (801) 489-8650. (218-220).

Nutrition – After you have cleansed the toxins from the body and alkalized the system – it is imperative that you assess what caused the cancer in the first place. While you are in the process of healing, stay on a "live" food diet, so the only thing you are putting into your body is "life." During the cleansing phase – at least for the first 30 days – stay on a liquid diet consisting of fresh juices, herbal teas and water.

In the *Wheatgrass Book,* Wigmore shares the research of Max Gerson, M.D., pioneer in the field of metabolic (nutritional) therapy against cancer, he said,

To remove the underlying cause and accomplish the cure of cancer means the re-establishment of the whole metabolism, especially of the liver . . . it is the filter for the entire digestive apparatus . . . the liver is the most important organ for our detoxification. (20)

One of the main reasons for a dysfunctional liver is a dysfunctional colon. Of the colon, Norman Walker, Ph.D., has written,

> Few of us realize that failure to effectively eliminate waste products from the body causes so much fermentation and putrefaction in the large intestine, or colon, that the neglected accumulation of such waste can, and frequently does, result in a lingering demise... the fact of the matter is that constipation is the number one affliction underlying nearly every ailment; it can be imputed to be the initial, primary cause of nearly every disturbance of the human system. (Frahm 37)

Too many people make the mistake of going right back to lifestyles that caused their problem in the first place. They cure themselves of what was trying to kill them, let down their guard, and then go back to their old lifestyle.

How many times have I seen this pattern repeat itself? Skeptics will then say they were never cured to begin with. The truth is, it is just like touching a hot stove – when you touch it, you get burned. If you heal the burn and then touch the hot stove again – you will get burned again because you didn't learn your lesson the first time.

Experiences:

a) I lost my father 28 years ago to a brain tumor. He went the medical route with surgery, chemotherapy, and radiation. He was gone in less than six months. Even though I knew none of the things I know now about nutrition or alternative health, I swore after watching what my father went through that no one else I loved and was responsible for would ever go through chemotherapy or radiation again. It did not make sense to me that you could cure an extremely sick person by poisoning and burning them. He had so much radiation in his system that if you turned a television on in the same room he was in, it would make him sick. If his life was extended at all, it certainly did not leave him with any quality of life

b) In 1997, I received a call from a young man whose father had the same type of cancer, in the same location that my father had. He said his father had gone through the surgery to have as much of the tumor removed as possible, but he did not want to go through the chemotherapy or radiation. He asked me if I would be willing to talk to his dad and tell him what I would do if I was faced with the same decisions.

I went to see his father, which was extremely difficult because he was suffering with a lot of the same things my father had gone through, such as: loss of speech, difficulty writing, etc. I told him that I would do Dr. Christopher's Incurables Program, the parasite cleanse from *A Cure For All Cancer* and that I would do a series of colonics to really get the colon cleaned out. I also recommended that he watch the videos, *You Can't Improve on God* and *Cancer Doesn't Scare Me Any More"* by Dr. Lorraine Day.

About two months later, his father called me and told me that he had just come back from getting an MRI to check on his progress. (Obviously, he was now speaking because I could understand him over the phone) He told me that the doctor was amazed because all of the swelling was gone in the brain and the cancer was almost completely gone. The doctor asked him how he managed to do this and still keep his hair. He told the doctor it was because he had not followed their program. He was extremely excited when he called and shared with me how he was singing again, playing the guitar, and enjoying his family. I was thrilled for him!

About four months later, his son called me to tell me the tumor was back, bigger than ever. He said that his dad was going back into surgery and he had agreed to do the chemotherapy and radiation. I asked him what had happened. I just couldn't imagine why the cancer would come back after he had so successfully beaten it. He explained that after the first MRI, his dad had felt like he was cured so he went back to his old eating habits and way of life.

c) In 1991, a friend of ours was married, became pregnant right away and nine months later had a healthy baby. When she went back for her six week check up they discovered cancer. She went through surgery, radiation and chemotherapy. They said she was cured. Two years later, she went back to the doctor because she wasn't feeling well and was told she had leukemia. They explained this can be one of the side effects of radiation. She fought it medically for two more years and then was gone.

d) Section II, pg. 164

As you can see, I have devoted a lot of space to this topic. It is one very dear to my heart and, it is my hope, that the information is this segment will be helpful to you or to someone you love. I have lost way too many friends to cancer, watching them be mutilated, radiated and poisoned. There has to be a better way! This is barbaric! We have to go to the cause and stop trying to treat the symptoms. We have to stop treating the fish and clean up the water. How many of us will continue to give up our lives because we are not willing to give up our addictions? In the case of cancer, we have to overcome our programming, our fears, our addictions, our lack of self-control and then take responsibility for our own health!

CANKER SORE

Canker sores are a symptom of a body that is out of balance and too acidic. Sores are a manifestation of the acidity. Diet is a major factor in cleaning up the sores and keeping them from returning. The body needs to be in a more alkaline state.

Herbal Aids:
-   Myrrh – put directly on sore to numb and heal
-   Dr. Christopher's Tooth Powder - brushing your teeth with the tooth powder will help to neutralize the acidity of the mouth
-   Red Raspberry Tea – drink three glasses per day

- L-Lysine – 500 mg three times daily on an empty stomach (Balch 126)
- Alkalizer Pack - helps to alkalize the body

Experience:

Our daughter, Juantia, used to have a lot of canker sores, but since she has used the herbal tooth powder she has not been bothered with them.

CAVITIES
(See Toothache)

CHARLIE HORSE

Charley horses (muscle cramps) are usually due to a lack of the right kind of calcium in the diet. Taking a commercial calcium supplement will not fix the problem because the body also needs magnesium, vitamin D and other components to utilize the calcium. Therefore, keep it in its whole state where it has not been isolated or chemically altered.

Herbal Aids:
- Wheat Grass Juice – drink two to four ounces daily
- Calc Tea - 2 or more capsules three times per day for additional calcium
- Professor Cayenne Ointment - rub directly on muscle which is cramping

CHICKEN POX

When a child breaks out with chicken pox, we need to help the body bring the toxins to the surface where they can be eliminated. A good way to do this is with moist heat, putting the child in to a bath of warm water with the herbs added to it and giving them lots of liquids to drink. A good outbreak of chicken pox when a child is young can actually be a blessing because they will develop immunity for life.

Herbal Aids:
-   Warm Catnip Enema – help clean out the colon and reduce fever.
-   Cut Burdock Root, Cut Golden Seal, and Cut Yellow Dock Root – place a hand full of each in a cloth diaper or dish towel, rubber band the top together, hold under running water as you fill bathtub, then float in bath water - soak child in tub.
-   Chickweed Ointment – apply directly to sores
-   Herbal Teas – Catnip and Peppermint, Red Raspberry Leaf, Yarrow – these would all be good teas to drink.

Other Modalities:
-   Drink lots of fluids – pure water, fruit juices, vegetable juices and herbal teas.

Experience:

When my three-year-old grand-daughter, Elizabeth came down with chicken pox, she had a really bad case of them. They were in her ears, her mouth, on her bottom – she was miserable. Our oldest son, Stephen was living in Texas at the time, so when Laura, his wife, called to find out what to do, I was having to talk to her over the phone from Utah and then just hope she could find the herbs she needed to take care of the problem. When she called the second day to tell me she could not find the herbs I had recommended, Elizabeth got on the phone and said, "Gaama, can you fix my boo boos?"

Well, of course, my heart melted and I was on the next fight to Houston with the herbs in hand. Laura met me at the airport hotel, so we immediately put Elizabeth into the bathtub with burdock root, golden seal and yellow dock root; several hand fulls of the dried herbs in a cloth diaper, folded up and then rubber banded at the top, so the ball of herbs could float in her bath water. By the time she got out, she had dumped the herbs into the water and was drawing pictures in them on the bottom of the tub. She stayed in the tub for a while because she was having a good time. When she got out, her mom put the chickweed ointment on each of the sores. I passed the herbs to Laura and went home and later reported Elizabeth was able to sleep comfortably and it was just a matter of waiting for everything to heal.

This scenario typically happens when herbs are used to heal chicken pox. They can pass through the virus quickly without a lot of undue suffering.

CIRCULATION

Many types of circulation problems come back to the same basic principles – make sure the veins and arteries are clean and healthy, then draw the circulation out to the extremities. Again, we are back to the principle of "cleanse and nourish." Most people think it needs to be much more complicated. We simply have to clean up our diet, exercise, and breathe!

Herbal Aids:
- Cayenne – taking ½ - 1 tsp. of powdered Cayenne in a glass of water or 2 capsules three times per day will help to increase circulation.
- Cayenne Ointment – rubbing Cayenne ointment into a problem area will help to bring circulation to that area.
- Garlic – if the circulation problem is due to clogged arteries, garlic (either fresh or in capsule form) can help to break up the plaque that is on the arterial walls.
- Yarrow – make a hot tea and soak the extremity that is having the problem in the tea. In the *School of Natural Healing,* Christopher tells us:

> . . . drinking hot yarrow tea and soaking in a hot bath or shower can also increase general circulation when ill, especially with any type of respiratory complaint, because hot yarrow tea is a diaphoretic and will cause you to perspire thus eliminating toxins and increasing the circulation. (233)

Other Modalities:
- Massage Therapy – this is a great way to increase circulation and move toxins through the lymph system
- Breathing – most of us are very shallow breathers because of the life-style we live – in order to carry oxygen throughout the body, we must take time to breathe deeply.
- Exercise – this body was intended to move and whne we live a sedentary life style, it can cause a lot of circulation problems – we need to MOVE!

Experiences:
   a) See Section I, pg. 71
   b) See Section II, pg. 160
   c) See Section IV, pg. 378
   d) A woman I had never seen before came into one of the classes I was teaching, sat in the back of the room, never making a comment throughout the whole class. After the class was ended, as everyone was leaving, she stayed in her seat. When I was ready to leave, I started to walk past her and as I did, she reached up, touched my arm and said, "Can you help me?"

   I said, "I don't know if I can or not, but I will try, what is the problem?"

   She pulled her pant legs up, showed me her legs, and said, "They want to amputate my legs."

   Her legs were hard, red, in some places white, and she had large open sores. When I asked her what had happened, she explained that a few years before she had been in an automobile accident. As a result, she had to have knee-replacement surgery. While her knees were healing, she had to keep her feet elevated for several weeks. When her knees had healed, the vein structure in her lower legs had atrophied and collapsed. She had been to several doctors to see if the problem could be fixed. She told me that she had spent thousands of dollars seeing different doctors, but each time was told, "We're sorry. Sometimes this happens, but there's nothing we can do about it." The last doctor she had seen, injected dye into her veins so they could see what had happened. When it went into her lower leg, she said you could see the dye disperse throughout the leg because the vein structure was gone. The doctor again said, "We're sorry. Sometimes this happens. There's nothing that can be done and when the gangrene sets in, we will have to amputate."

   Because of the other experiences we have had with circulation, we taught her how to take the Cayenne and Garlic orally. We then suggested soaking her feet and as much of the lower leg as possible in hot yarrow tea at night. We also told her that when she went to bed at night, she might want to rub in Dr. Christopher's BF&C oil to help heal the vein structure. After the BF&C, it would also be beneficial to rub in the Professor Cayenne ointment to help intensify the healing properties of the BF&C and to bring more circulation to the area.

Two weeks later, she came back to my class, walked up to the front of the room, pulled up her pant legs and said, "This is the first time in two years that I have had feeling in my legs!"

All of the sores, except the largest one were completely healed and the legs were both beginning to turn pink again. Isn't it amazing to think that something as simple as Cayenne, Garlic, BF&C™, and Yarrow could make the difference between healing your legs or losing them?

CIRCUMCISION

Samuel Butler said, "Mankind has always been ready to discuss matters in the inverse ratio to their importance, so that the more closely a question is felt to touch the heart of all of us, the more incumbent it is considered upon prudent people to profess that it does not exist."

In *Circumcision; the Hidden Trauma,* Dr. Goldman tells us:
Every day 3,500 circumcisions are performed in this country, one every twenty-five seconds. From a global perspective, most of the world rejects circumcision: over 80 percent of the world's males are intact (not circumcised). Most circumcised men are Muslim or Jewish. The United States is the only country in the world that circumcises most of its male infants for nonreligious reasons. (1-2)
What is circumcision?

The tip of the penis, a slightly enlarged region called the glans is shaped like an acorn. The edge of the glans is called the corona. In *Holistic Midwifery,* we read:

The glans is protected by a loosely fitting retractable covering of skin known as the prepuce or foreskin. Some cultures practice circumcision, the removal of the foreskin for religious, cultural or supposed hygienic reasons. This is usually done in infancy among Western peoples, but some African tribes include it in rites of puberty. Removal of the foreskin leaves the glans unprotected. In most instances, anesthesia is not used. (Frye 187)

Many people in the United States believe there are health benefits to circumcision; such as cleanliness and protection from various diseases. "However, the American Academy of Pediatrics has not found any proven medical benefit from circumcision" (Goldman 2), so why do we routinely have this surgery performed? Is this a painful procedure and are there any types of danger associated with it?

Circumcision may have started with a revelation given in Genesis to Abraham. As a part of the law of Moses the Lord said, "This is my covenant, which ye shall keep, between me and you and thy seed after thee; Every man child among you shall be circumcised" (17:10). The Jews still circumcise their children: they do not believe the law of Moses has been fulfilled. However, for those who believe Jesus Christ was the Savior of mankind, then the belief is that the law of Moses has been fulfilled. In Moroni 8:8 we read ". . . and the law of circumcision is done away in me." Because we don't understand the law has been fulfilled or because it is more important to us to have our sons be like their fathers, we continue to circumcise.

Let's take a look at what we are inflicting upon our sons by continuing this tradition. According to Marilyn Milos, who witnessed a circumcision during her training in nursing school:

We students filed into the newborn nursery to find a baby strapped spread-eagle to a plastic board on a counter top across the room. He was struggling against his restraints – tugging, whimpering, and then crying helplessly . . . I stroked his little head and spoke softly to him. He began to relax and was momentarily quiet. The silence was soon broken by a piercing scream – the baby's reaction to having his foreskin pinched and crushed as the doctor attached the clamp to his penis. The shriek intensified when the doctor inserted an instrument between the foreskin and the glans (head of the penis), tearing the two structures apart. The baby started shaking his head back and forth – the only part of his body free to move – as the doctor used another clamp to crush the foreskin lengthwise, which he then cut. This made the opening of the foreskin large enough to insert a circumcision instrument, the device used to protect the glans from being severed during the surgery. The baby began to gasp and choke, breathless from his shrill continuous screams . . . During the next stage of the surgery, the doctor crushed the foreskin against the circumcision instrument and then, finally, amputated it. The baby was limp, exhausted, spent. (Goldman 23)

Why do we just take it for granted in our culture that a male baby is born deformed? Why do we feel the need to change his appearance from what he is born with? If we are vain enough to want him to look like his father, are there possible complications we should be concerned with? In Polly Block's *Birth Book,* she tells us:

Although considered a minor surgical procedure, reported complications of neonatan circumcision include infection, hemorrhage, loss of penile skin, laceration of penile and scrotal skin, injury to the glans, urethral fistula, urinary retention, staphylococcal scalded skin syndrome, concealed penis, necrotizing fasciitis, Fournier's syndrome and sepsis. . . .

Elective newborn circumcision is a cruel procedure . . . The beliefs that infants "do not feel pain" or "won't remember it anyway" reflect concepts which cannot be substantiated and are barbaric . . . Marked flushing frequently occurs during circumcision and a propensity of newborn infants to wail and vomit under the stress of circumcision is well appreciated by nursery personnel. The alteration in pitch, the intensity of cry when the first crush and clamp is applied to the foreskin is unmistakable . . . .

. . . Questionable potential benefits including the facilitation of penile hygiene and diminution in the risk of cancer seem to be outweighed by the risks of hemorrhage, life threatening infection, and lack of cost effectiveness. The neglect of the operator to obtain informed consent and to perform a needlessly radical technique with apparent disregard for pain needs to be abandoned (423).

Dr. Mendelsohn sheds more light on some of the risks involved:

The first surgery was religious, and ninety percent of the surgery performed today is also religious. The Jewish ritual circumcision, or bris, has a place in Jewish law and culture. The bris is performed on the eighth day of life by a trained mohel who uses the same technique that has withstood more than 4,000 years of use. Ten men stand by to make sure he does it right, too. Modern Medicine's routine circumcision, however, takes place on the first or second day of life, when blood loss can be especially dangerous. It's performed by a surgeon, or an intern, or a medical student using the 'latest' technique. Where the bris ceremony includes pouring some wine in the infant's mouth, no anesthetic at all is used in Modern Medicine's ritual.

Routine circumcision of all males makes no sense outside of a religious framework. A circumcision is an operation, and its dangers are not inconsiderable. It's not altogether rare for a surgeon to get smart and use cautery instead of a knife – and to slip and burn off most of the penis (Mendelsohn 60).

Another question we might want to consider is: Is there emotional trauma to the infant, along with physical trauma? If this child comes into the world feeling warm and secure in his mother's arms, what must it be like for him, when she hands him over to a complete stranger who takes him to another room, strips him, straps him to a plastic board and performs this procedure, usually without anesthesia? The emotional bonding connecting the infant and mother is called "attachment." The importance of attachment has been well established for decades.

Studies have shown that circumcision can adversely affect mother-infant bonding . . . The parts of the brain needed for long-term memory have been identified. Anand and Hickey, in their often cited review of the literature on infant pain, report that these structures are well developed and functioning during the newborn period (Goldman 126 & 86).

Charles Konia, a psychiatrist in eastern Pennsylvania who helps people resolve past traumas reports:

I can tell you that from my clinical experience in treating patients who relived their circumcision as well as observing newborns being circumcised in the delivery room, it is a nightmarish experience. I shudder each time I witness patients going through the horror (Goldman 97),

Psychologist John Breeding recounts his personal therapy session during which he re-experienced his circumcision:

The emotional experience . . . was horrible. I felt overwhelming fear, sweating and shaking for long periods. Intense rage also came up at times. I wanted to protect myself, but I couldn't . . . I felt . . . terribly sad, engulfed in grief, despair and helplessness. I released emotionally for well over an hour and was finally spent, sad (Goldman 97).

It would appear from the research which has been done, that there is no good medical reason for routine circumcision. "According to one national survey, 33 percent of American obstetricians and pediatricians are personally opposed to circumcision" (Goldman 1). Unless the surgery is performed for religious reasons, we, as a nation, are unnecessarily mutilating our sons. The good news is that people appear to be waking up to this realization. "According to the National Center for Health Statistics, the circumcision rate has dropped from a peak of about 85 percent to about 60 percent nationally and to only about 35 percent in some areas of the country" (Goldman 1). According to many professionals this surgery is something that is causing a lot more harm than good. We need to carefully consider what we are doing and why we are doing it, before we subject our sons to the knife.

COLDS

Remember, the cold is the cure! There are toxins in the body that need to be eliminated. If we stop the symptoms, we merely drive the problem deeper. We need to help the body to eliminate.

Herbal Aids:
- Kid-E-Well – one to two droppers full every hour or two while awake
- X-Ceptic - rub on throat, chest, and back to kill virus or bacteria – if using on a young infant, you may to dilute with olive oil as it can sometimes be too strong on the bare skin – can also be taken internally with juice or water for severe cases.
- Mullein Oil – rub on throat, chest and back to help break up congestion
- Anti-Spasmodic Tincture - rub on throat, chest and back to help stop heavy coughing spasms.
- Vicks Vaporub - rubbed on chest and back at night to help with breathing and coughing – this ointment contains eucalyptus oil
- Echinacea – take a dropper full or 2-4 capsules every two hours to boost immune system
- Red Raspberry Leaf Tea – drink several cups per day
- Cayenne – at the first sign of a cold coming on – take two capsules – stand in to a hot, steamy shower for several minutes – take two more capsules – drink plenty of fluids – get into bed with a couple of warm blankets – by morning, quite often you will be able to sweat out the toxins and stop the cold before it gets started.
- Sen Sei Ointment – apply over sinuses to open and drain the congestion
- Onions – use onion poultice on chest to help with breathing – see section V for instructions
- Garlic – can be used for it's antibiotic properties – it can be taken internally or applied to the feet – rub the feet with olive oil – chop up fresh garlic – mix with Vaseline - pack on the bottom of the feet – wrap the feet to keep the garlic in place.
- Echinacea & Goldenseal Capsules – 2-4 capsules every two to three hours while awake
- Dr. Christopher's Anti-Plague - 1-2 Tbsp. every hour or two while awake.

Essential Oils:
- Eucalyptus Oil – put several drops into a hot water vaporizer – place in room next to the bed or couch – helps to open up breathing and slow down coughing

- TeiFu - put a few drops in palm of hand, rub hands together – hold cupped hands over nose – inhale – helps to open up sinuses.

Other Modalities:
- Hot, Steamy Baths or Showers – as often as needed to help open every thing up so that it can drain and you can breathe easier.
- Lots of Pure Water, Fresh Juices and Herbal Teas – drink lots of fluids
- Keep the Bowel Cleansed – make sure the bowel is open and cleansing – this can be done with fresh juices, herbal aids or with an enema

Experiences:
   a) Section I, pg. 37
   b) Section I, pg. 52
   c) Section I, pg. 60
   d) Section I, pg. 66
   e) Section IV, pg. 251
   f) Section IV, pg. 294

COLIC

Colic will usually manifest itself as abdominal pain or bloating due to intestinal gas. Quite often, a baby will draw their legs up and scream or cry because of the discomfort. Look to the diet. An infant should be nursing, if at all possible, and the mothers diet should be nutritious

Herbal Aids:
   4) Kid-E-Col - use ½ - 1 dropper full as needed – can be given straight, put on a pacifier or added to a bottle
   5) Catnip & Fennel Tincture – for older children or adults – use as much tea or tincture as needed.

Other Modalities:
   6) Castor Oil – rub oil on abdomen over intestines – apply a warm, wet cloth – every ten to twenty minutes check to see if the skin is still oily – if not, apply more oil – this is usually very soothing for an infant or small child that may be dealing with gas or constipation.
   7) Diet – if you are dealing with an infant who is nursing – you need to take a serious look at the mother's diet to see what is causing the problem.

Experiences:
  a) See Section IV, pg. 376
  b) See Section IV, pg. 382
  c) When our grandson, Noah was about three days old, he was crying almost continuously because he had not yet passed all of the meconium (black, tarry poop that newborns have) from his intestines. Our son made a small bottle with some sterile water and a dropper full of Catnip and Fennel Tincture. Within 30 minutes, he told me he had a 12-wipey mess to clean up and Noah was happy because he wasn't hurting any more.

COLITIS

Colitis is a painful inflammation of the colon or large intestine, especially its mucous membranes, characterized by diarrhea or constipation. More and more people suffer from this condition due to our faulty diets. We must clean up the system and get back to eating live, wholesome foods.

Herbal Aids:
  - Herbal LB – the bowel needs to be kept clean and healthy – meaning that the peristaltic action is working properly
  - Dr. Schulz's Intestinal Detoxification Program - using Intestinal Formula #1 and Intestinal Formula #2 – the first formula helps with peristaltic action – the second formula is like the scrub brush – it is milder and uses roughage to help get everything cleaned out and functioning again
  - Tea – Comfrey, Marshmallow or Slippery Elm – using all three together would be very soothing.

Juices:
  - Aloe Vera Juice – a good quality Aloe juice can be used to help heal the colon
  - Morinda Noni Juice - helps to heal
  - Wheat Grass Juice – drink 2-4 oz per day to help heal and cleanse

Other Modalities:
  - Diet – change to live, organic, wholesome foods and fresh juices.
  - Wheat Grass Implants – see Section V for instructions.

- Cookware – make sure you are cooking with glass or stainless steal – not aluminum or cast iron, as these can leach caustic chemicals into the food
- Chew thoroughly – make sure food is chewed completely and mixed with saliva before swallowing
- Colonics – helps to completely clean the colon out so it can heal
- Distilled Water – drink three to four quarts per day

CONSTIPATION

Colon rectal cancers are the number one cancer among men and women. Refined, processed, low fiber foods, animal fats, stress and our sedentary lifestyles cause a lot of problems for our eliminatory organs.

When a baby is born and nursed, we know that every time the baby eats, it will need to have it's diaper changed. My children and I used to say, "In with the new – out with the old."

Adult bowel movements should work the same way. If we eat two to three times per day, then we should eliminate two to three times per day. If we don't, then we are holding too many toxins in our body. After John Wayne passed away, we were listening to Paul Harvey tell "the rest of the story." He said that when they did the autopsy on John Wayne he was still carrying around 35 pounds of fecal matter. I have since discovered that this is not uncommon. Many people carry around more than this. Can you imagine how many toxins could filter back into your system from that amount of fecal matter?

As many diseases begin in the colon – it is extremely important to keep this system in good working order.

Herbal Aids:
- Dr. Christopher's Herbal LB - start with two capsules three times per day – increase dosage until you are having two to three bowel movements per day.
- Dr. Schulz's Intestinal Detoxification Program - use Intestinal Formulas #1 and #2 to regulate bowel movements
- Wheat Grass Implants – see Section V for instructions.
- Castor Oil – rub castor oil on abdomen, over intestines – lay a warm, wet towel over the oil – check abdomen every 15 minutes – if skin feels dry, apply more oil – continue for 1 – 2 hours

Juices:
- Fresh Juices – drink on a daily basis
- Wheat Grass Juice – drink 2-4 ounces per day
- Prune Juice – drink eight ounces in the morning

Other Modalities:
- Diet – this condition is caused from eating too many devitalized, processed foods.
- Water – drink three to four quarts per day
- Foot Stool – putting your feet up on a foot stool while sitting on the toilet puts the body in a more natural squatting position and can help with elimination.

Experience:

David Christopher often tells the story of a lady who came to see him with health problems. As he was talking to her, he asked her if she had regular bowel movements. She assured him that she did and continued on with the conversation. He knew by listening to what she had to say that the problem was due to improper elimination, so he asked her again, "Are you sure you have regular bowel movements?" Again, she said, "Yes! I do! Every month when I have my period, I have a bowel movement just as regular as clock work."

Obviously, this is not regularity. We should move our bowels daily, preferably more than once a day.

COUGH

Again, recognize coughing as a symptom - not as the disease, itself. Hot lemon and honey, hot water vaporizers, steamy showers will help bring relief while we work on cleaning the toxins (mucus) out of the body.

Herbal Aids:
- Hot Lemon and Honey – place lemon juice and honey (to taste) in the bottom of cup – pour in boiling water – stir – will soothe sore throat and relax coughing spasms
- Anti-spasmodic Tincture - rub on throat, chest and back to help relieve spasms
- Catnip Enema – keep the colon clean

-   Vicks Vaporub - rub on throat, chest and back to help with breathing and coughing
-   Dr. Christopher's Cough Syrup - will help to pull out mucus which is causing cough
-   Honey and Pine Needle Syrup – see Section V for instructions on how to make your own cough syrup
-   Anti-Plague - take as needed to clear up problem

Other Modalities:
-   Hot, Steamy Shower – remain in steam as long as possible to break up and drain congestion
-   Hot Water Vaporizer – put several drops of eucalyptus oil in water to help open up breathing
-   Fresh Air – open some windows to allow fresh air into the room
-   Cold Air – if you are dealing with croup – going from a hot shower to cold night air will help to stop the cough

Experiences:
a) See Section I, pg. 37
b) See Section I, pg. 52
c) See Section I, pg. 60
d) See Section I, pg. 66
e) See Section IV, pg. 251
f) See Section IV, pg. 294
g) See Section IV, pg. 340

CRAMPS
(Menstrual)

I have heard people recommend using Wild Yam cream throughout the month to help balance the hormones – many times this does seem to help. In a case where someone is suffering with cramps, I will use the cream to help bring temporary relief. However, I do not recommend using it daily. Quite often, if we give the body something it should be making on its own, such as progersterone – it will become dependent on the supply we give it – and stop manufacturing its own. Our body has an incredible way to check our inventory. If we have plenty of whatever it is looking for in stock, it does not supply us with any more. Then when we stop supplying it from an outside source, we find that we have an even greater imbalance than what we started with. Another concern I have is that some manufacturers are actually putting synthetic progesterone into their creams to make them more effective.

Once we have brought temporary relief for the pain, it is important to go to the source of the problem and correct it. Let's clean up the system – give the body what it needs to come back in to balance – then the problem will correct itself and you won't have to hurt any more.

Herbal Aids:
- Lobelia Tincture or Tea – can be taken internally or applied with hot, wet cloth as a fomentation over the abdomen
- Anti-Spasmodic Tincture - rub directly on abdomen
- Wild Yam Cream – applied directly to abdomen along with warm corn bag or other heat source such as a warm, wet towel.
- Dr. Christopher's NuFem, Changease, and Wheat Germ Oil Capsules – take two capsules of each three times per day – the NuFem helps to clean and rebuild the female organs – the Changease helps to supply the building blocks for the hormones our body needs to produce – the Wheat Germ Oil helps in the chemical production of the hormones.
- Fresh Ginger Root Bath – grate up fresh ginger root – put in a dish towel or cloth diaper – pull up sides, rubber band the top – float in a hot tub of water while you are soaking in it.
- Red Raspberry Leaf Tea – drink three glasses per day throughout the month to help nourish and balance the system.

Other Modalities:
- Diet – if you want permanent relief from these symptoms, you have to clean up the diet – get rid of the junk food!
- Douche – use 4-6 oz of fresh wheat grass juice – put 2-4 folded bath towels in tub – lay in tub with your hips elevated on the folded bath towels – douche with fresh wheat grass juice – remain in slant board position for 10 – 20 minutes – this will allow the wheat grass to go straight to the cervix and uterus to nourish and strengthen it.

Experiences:
   a) See Section I, pg. 25
   b) See Section IV, pg. 400
   c) When I was growing up, I had severe menstrual cramps. My mother had never had them before and so, in the beginning, my parents tended to think I had an over-active

imagination. I want to dispel this myth! It is not an over-active imagination, they are very real. I knew that at least one day of every month I was going to be laid up in bed in horrible pain. Most of the time I knew when they were coming and I would just stay home from school, but one time when I was in high school I was sitting in a science class when they hit. I must have been pretty pale, white-knuckled, etc. because after class the teacher came back to my desk and said, "You're cramping, aren't you? Who is your doctor?"

I grew up in a small country town in northern California. We had one old country doctor in town who was also the doctor for the high school, so he told me to call my mom and have her meet me at his office. The science teacher drove me to his office and when my mother came in, the doctor had her lay her hand on my abdomen so she could feel the spasms going on inside. He explained that the cramping was very real. The only thing he could do to help me was to prescribe muscle relaxants and pain killers. In order to help, they had to be strong enough to knock me out. I absolutely hated the feeling of being drugged, so I never took the medication.

After realizing this condition was real and painful, my mother made an appointment with an OB/Gyn. Unfortunately, when she took me to see him, he did not believe they were real either and put me through a horrible pelvic examination. After that experience, I decided I would rather suffer than ever go through anything like that again.

Because of my early experiences, I can truly empathize with anyone who suffers with severe menstrual cramping. The good news is that it is fixable! Most people have been able to completely eliminate their cramps within one to two cycles if they will just make a few changes in their diet, give their body the correct building blocks to build the hormones they need, then cleanse and nourish the female organs.

CRAMPS
(Muscle)

If the muscles are cramping due to injury or over-working them (such as the weekend warrior), then we use BF&C oil or ointment directly on the muscle followed by Professor Cayenne. The oil will get into the muscle faster than the ointment, but the body will be able to draw on the ointment for a longer period of time, so with serious injuries we sometimes use both.

If the muscle cramps are more like a "charlie horse," then we would take the Calc Tea orally and snack on raw almonds to help get some organic calcium into the body, lack of calcium can cause the muscles to cramp.

Herbal Aids:
-   Professor Cayenne Ointment - rub directly onto muscle
-   Dr. Christopher's Calc Tea Formula – take two or more capsules three times per day to supply the body with organic calcium
-   BF&C Oil or Ointment – rub directly on muscle to heal and mend
-   BF&C Capsules – if the cramping is due to an injury – take 5 or more capsules three times per day
-   Comfrey Tea – again, if due to an injury, Comfrey is a cell-proliferate - taken internally and/or soaking the injury in the tea will help to speed the healing process
-   Raw Almonds – snack on these as often as you like - another great source of calcium

Other Modalities:
-   Massage – using acupressure on the muscle which is cramping will help it to release – just rubbing the muscle will bring additional circulation to the area
-   Hydro-therapy – soaking in hot water or in a whirl pool tub will help to relax the muscles
-   Exercise – stretching exercises will help to release tight muscles

CROUP

Croup is different than any other cough and chances are if you have ever heard it, you will never forget it.   Dr. Christopher describes is as,

" . . . a childhood disease characterized by laborious and suffocative breathing and a harsh, brassy, crowing cough. Usually occurs at night, during the course of an upper respiratory infection. When the child takes a breath there is a whistling sound and often it sounds like he is strangling." (56 Herbal)

Quite often, the best relief will come from the cool night air or a cool mist vaporizer. Make sure if you are taking a child from a hot, steamy shower into the cold night air that you bundle them up in a blanket so they do not get pneumonia. The idea is to let them breathe the cool air, not expose their whole body to it. Someone once told me that the virus which causes croup cannot exist in the cold. I have never been able to verify this, but it would explain why the cool air is so helpful.

Herbal Aids:
- Catnip and Peppermint Tea – drink warm with a couple of drops of Lobelia tincture added to the tea
- Catnip enema – sometimes emptying the colon will help to relieve the symptoms of the respiratory system
- Anti-Spasmodic Tincture – rub on throat, chest and back to help relieve coughing spasms
- Vicks Vaporub – rub on throat, chest and back to help breathing and slow coughing
- Mullein Oil – rub on throat, chest and back to break up congestion
- Kid-E-Well - take 1-2 droppers full every hour to boost immune system and help bring out congestion
- Yarrow Tea – when taken warm – will act as a diaphoretic and cause the body to sweat which will help to eliminate toxins

Other Modalities:
- Fresh Air – do allow room to become stuffy – make sure there is a window open enough to allow fresh air into the room
- Cool Mist Vaporizer – with croup – cool mist tends to work better than the hot mist from a hot water vaporizer
- Hot, Steamy Shower - steaming in a hot shower and then going into the cool nigh air tends to open the respiratory system and help relieve the coughing – repeat as often as needed

Experiences:

Mother was born in the Ozark mountains of Arkansas in 1918. Her older brother died of croup before she was born. One night when she was a baby she came down with croup. My grandfather knew she was not going to live through the night, so he put my grandmother and mother into the buggy (horse-drawn) and headed for town to see the doctor. About half way into town, he realized that she was not going to live long enough to get to town because she was having so much difficulty breathing, so he pulled up to the cabin of a little old woman of African descent. My grandfather asked if there was anything she could do to help his baby. She grabbed a slab of meat, punched it full of holes, poured kerosene and turpentine on it, then wrapped it around my mother's throat. It opened everything up until she could breath and the crisis was over.

Dr. Christopher teaches that we should keep things simple and use what is in our own backyard. Again, the difference between life and death was a little bit of home remedy and common sense. I would also like to point out here that this was 1918 in the South. This woman had no reason or obligation to help my grandparents. However, along with the physical materials she used, this woman had enough compassion to take the time to help them in the middle of the night, thereby saving the life of my mother. She could not have known what kind of impact my mother's life would have or how that one act of service would affect generations to come.

CUTS

Amazingly, cuts can generally heal without any scarring at all if the body has the nutrients it needs to rebuild the tissue. Every cell in our body has a blue print for the way it is supposed to be and if it has the building blocks it needs, it will rebuild itself exactly the way it was originally.

Herbal Aids:
- Comfrey Leaves – depending on the circumstances – the leaves could be bruised, chewed up, made into a poultice or a tea – apply to wound
- BF&C - oil or ointment – apply directly to wound
- X-Ceptic Tincture - use to disinfect the wound – this is a strong tincture and can sometimes sting, so I usually put the BF&C™ directly in the wound and then put the X-Ceptic on the gauze or band aid.

Other Modalities:
- Stop the Bleeding – apply pressure until the bleeding stops – if the wound is deep or serious, I would give powdered Cayenne in water or Cayenne tincture to get the bleeding to stop
- Butterfly Strips – it is a good idea to keep something on hand to pull the sides together in case of deep cuts.

Experiences:
a) See Section I, pg. 27
b) I was making some Halloween costumes a couple of years ago, and, as usual, was racing the clock. I was cutting some material using a quilters ruler and a rotary cutter. I got in too big of a hurry and allowed the rotary cutter to jump the ruler, slicing my finger to the bone. I felt the blade go through the tissue, but did not experience any pain immediately. (The body always goes into a few moments of blessed shock where you don't feel it) I jumped up and started pacing the room with my finger pressed against my hip, saying, "This is going to hurt. This is going to hurt."

One of my daughters realized what I had done, so she ran for the Cayenne and gave me four capsules to control the bleeding, Once the bleeding slowed down, we packed it with BF&C ointment, soaked the gauze on the band aid with X-Ceptic and applied it over the BF&C.

Then the pain set in. For a few minutes I was not sure I was going to be able to handle it. Kelly, my daughter, told me to sit on the couch while she massaged the corresponding toe on my foot. Within a few minutes, the pain was gone. (The place she was massaging on my toe was painful, but not nearly as bad as the finger had been.)

It was so amazing to me that the reflexology could remove so much pain from my finger that quickly. I had seen this work on other family members before, but it was the first time I had experienced it first hand.

I kept the BF&C and X-Ceptic on the finger and allowed it to heal without stitches. Today there is just a thin white line to indicate where the razor went through my finger.

c) Joseph was creating some new invention one Sunday afternoon, when he came into the house as pale as a ghost and holding his hand. Myrna got to him first and I could tell by her expression it was bad.

Joe had been trying to cut the end off of a water hose, the knife had slipped and cut straight across the palm of his hand below his fingers. I had him move all of his fingers for me to make sure the tendons were all connected. We gave him three Cayenne capsules to stop the bleeding and then used the same techniques that we have used before.

I'm sure if we had taken him in, it probably would have required about twenty stitches to put his hand back together. Instead, we put the BF&C oil inside the cut, packed it with BF&C ointment, used butterfly strips to pull it together, and covered it in a gauze pad soaked with the X-Ceptic tincture.

It healed beautifully with just a thin white line for a scar. In fact, Joey was pretty disappointed because it didn't leave a cool scar.

A ship in a harbor is safe, but that is not what ships are built for.
-- John A. Shedd

Our doubts are traitors,
And make us lose the good we oft might win,
By fearing to attempt.
-- William Shakespeare

The minute you begin a natural diet, your body, mind and spirit will start to improve! In 11 short months you can build a whole, new, wonderful, youthful feeling body by fasting to clean out the half-dead cells and using natural foods to build new, youthful cells.
This is the great secret of life.
-- Paul C. Bragg N.D., Ph.D.

D

DEPRESSION

If you are on anti-depressant medication and want to get off of them, you must do it slowly and carefully. One of the many side effects of these drugs is suicidal tendencies. Talk to your doctor about how to wean yourself off of the drugs. Then go back to the foundation of "cleanse and nourish."

Herbal Aids:
- Vitalerbs - use some type of all natural herbal supplement to be sure you are getting enough vitamins and minerals every day
- Organa Minerals - make sure you have enough trace minerals in your diet
- MindTrac - 2 or more capsules three times per day – specifically formulated to help with depression
- PreTrac - 2 capsules three times per day to cleanse the liver
- Mem - formulated to help bring oxygen to the brain
- Changease and Wheat Germ Oil – 2 capsules of each three times per day to help balance hormones
- Cleanse – see 'cleansing' chapter for different ideas on how to cleanse the body

Essential Oils:
- Dr. Gary Young teaches:
    Diffusing or directly inhaling essential oils can have an immediate positive impact on moods. Olfaction is the only sense that can have direct effects on the limbic region of the brain. Studies at the University of Vienna have shown that some essential oils and their primary constituents (cineol) can stimulate blood flow and activity in the emotional regions of the brain.
    Clinical studies at the Department of Psychiatry at the Mie University of Medicine showed that lemon not only reduced depression but reduced stress when inhaled.
    Single Oils:
    Eucalyptus globules
    Lemon (Citrus limon)
    Jasmine (Jasminum officinale)
    Frankincense (Boswellia carteri) (336 Essential)

Other Modalities:
- Diet – stay away from preservatives, artificial sweeteners, processed foods, meat, and dairy products – all of these contain chemicals which can cause an imbalance in the body
- Cookware – use only glass or stainless steal – Alzheimer and other chemical imbalances are being linked to aluminum in the brain

- Exercise – try to get outside and walk in the fresh air every day – also try shuffling your bare feet through the grass – we take energy (electricity) into our bodies all the time - we literally can build up too much static electricity and sometimes just need to ground ourselves and release the excess energy
- Give Service to Others – you'll be surprised at how fast you can get your mind off of your own problems by helping someone else

Depression has hit epidemic proportions in this country. There are a great many reasons for depression. Due to lack of expertise and space, I would just like to touch on a few.

1. Diet – we are taking in way too many chemicals and dead, inorganic materials which is playing havoc with our chemistry. Chemical imbalances are very real – so is the depression which accompanies them. It is time to wake up and stop this trend.

2. Lack of exercise and fresh air – we live lives that are too sedentary which restricts circulation and does not allow us to keep the toxins moving so they can be eliminated. When we limit the time we spend outside, we miss out on so many of the 'love notes' left by our Creator for us to see, smell, hear and appreciate: the colors of the flowers, the unending shades of green, the songs of the birds, the smell of rain just before a storm, the rainbow, the sound of a child's laughter, the crashing of the waves as they hit the shore, the sound of a creek or river as it travels past us, the sight of a squirrel scurrying up a tree – we are on this planet for such a short time – let's not miss out on a moment of it!

3. Hormonal imbalances – quite often people, women especially, are put on anti-depressant medications when what they really needed to do was bring their hormones back into balance, which can be done with diet and numerous herbal aids.

4. Selfishness – too many people have been raised to think the world and everyone on it was put here to keep them entertained. Too often we think our self-worth can be measured by dollars and cents or by possessions – the one with the most toys wins. We need to look around

and see that there are many who are worse off than we are who could use our help. We each have unlimited potential to help others – let's do it!

5. Dissatisfaction with our lives – maybe we are not in the job we planned on having or never could finish our education. Maybe our marriage has failed, or we have had a child go astray or we are frustrated with our living conditions. It is not always easy to make lemonade out of lemons, but there is usually something which can be done to improve our situation. Even if it is just going out and getting a library card so that we can start learning something new. If the world is falling apart and there is nothing you can do about it, then change your focus – start learning something you enjoy, start working out and improving your body, do volunteer work – improve your health, which includes your mind and body – you will be surprised at how much better the world will appear to be.

6. Unyielding sorrow – if you cannot rise above the sorrow or depression that is weighing you down – seek professional help. Find someone who can help you lift the load and help you to heal – then learn how to let it go. This is quite often easier said than done, but it is possible to heal, to forgive and to move on.

Due to lack of space, I know this is over-simplifying the problem but the number of people, including children, who are walking around on mind-altering drugs is criminal! This is not fixing the problem. I lost track a long time ago of the number of people who have called me feeling desperate, and quite often suicidal, over the use of these drugs. To the best of my knowledge, they are all drug-free and functioning fine today. This does not mean they don't have bad days occasionally – we all do. It's part of being alive and gaining experience.

DIABETES

If there is one thing I have learned for sure over the last decade of living with a diabetic, it is that there are definitely no magic pills! If there were, I'm sure we would have found it by now because I think Steve has tried every supplement or program there is for diabetes. The second thing I have learned is if you truly want to cure this disease – you can not cheat!

The aids which I have listed above have all helped Steve with different symptoms and different conditions he has had to deal with. They have also helped him to not have to deal with some of the devastating side-effects of diabetes. However, the only two times I have seen him in complete control of his disease is during the 10 days he used the Alkalizer Pack and when he was on a completely raw diet. Steve did not stay "raw" long enough to keep his blood sugar normal. However, while he was "raw" his blood sugar was steadily declining and he was putting on weight, which meant his cells were actually taking in nutrition.

Diabetes is a controllable and curable condition, but it takes a strong commitment to change your life-style. It can be a very devastating disease because it affects every system in the body which is why it is well worth the effort to do whatever you need to do to cure it.

If you are a Type II diabetic, just making some dietary changes, getting enough daily exercise, and losing weight will probably be enough to correct the situation. However, if you are a Type I diabetic or insulin-dependent, it is going to take a lot more effort to get where you want to be. You really have to decide that living a long, healthy life is worth working for. If you don't, then you can look forward to a life filled with complications from your disease such as: loss of energy, loss of eyesight, impotence, neuropathy, poor circulation which can lead to amputation, kidney failure, heart disease, etc. .

Herbal Aids:
- Panc Tea - two or more capsules three times per day to strengthen the pancreas

- Barberry LG - two capsules three times per day to cleanse the liver
- Adrenetone - two capsules three times per day to strengthen adrenal glands
- Dr. Christopher's Extended Herbal Cleanse – mild cleanse which can easily be tolerated by diabetics
- Lipoic Acid – antioxidantd – In the *Antioxidant Miracle,* Packer discusses how important antioxidants are in the treatment of diabetes:

Diabetes is a serious disease that over time can cause a great deal of damage throughout the body. During the initial stages of diabetes, the microvascular system (the cells lining the blood vessels) is slightly damaged. As the disease progresses, however, the damage can become more severe, causing the blood vessels to leak, which can increase the risk of permanent nerve damage, kidney damage (nephropathy), heart disease, and blindness (retinopathy). Much of the destruction that is inflicted by this disease is either directly or indirectly caused by free radicals.

Diabetes is very much an oxidative stress disease – that is, people who are diabetic have significantly lower levels of antioxidants than normal. . . In order to stem the damage that can be inflicted by excess glucose, diabetes needs to be controlled as early as possible. Although lipoic acid is not a cure for diabetes, it appears to have a remarkably beneficial effect in terms of both controlling symptoms and preventing some of the serious problems that can arise down the road.

For more than twenty-five years, lopoic acid has been used in Germany to treat periphereal neuropathy caused by nerve damage at various sites of the body that can weaken muscles and cause a great deal of pain and discomfort. Peripheral nerve damage is directly related to a lack of antioxidants in nerve cells. Patients have reported a marked improvement in symptoms after being treated with high doses of lipoic acid (200 to 600 milligrams daily). . . Recently, Dr. Dan Ziegler and Dr. F. Arnold Gries at Heinrich Heine University in Dusseldorf had even more exciting news to report about lipoic acid. They found that treatment with lipoic acid actually stimulated the regeneration of nerve fibers in diabetics. In as little as three weeks of treatment, patients taking 600 milligrams of lipoic acid daily experienced a significant reduction in pain and numbness associated with neuropathy. (46-47)

- Herbal Eyebright - rinse eyes each night with sterile water in eye cup with 2-4 drops of Herbal Eyebright

- Barleans Flax Oil – In a Barleans newsletter, we see how important the right types of fats are:

Drawing much less attention is the careful dietary manipulation of fats and oils in achieving optimal diabetic health. A review of past and present scientific literature underscores the importance of avoiding certain fats while supplementing other fatty acids to meet these ends. It has been discovered that diabetics not only possess a malfunction of carbohydrate metabolism, but a malfunction of fat metabolism as well. Largely ignored, this condition is of paramount importance, because the majority of diabetic complications – neuropathy, retinopathy, impotence, heart disease and stroke – are a result of faulty fatty acid metabolism, coupled with chronic hyperglycemia. . . the wrong kinds of fats have been proven to cause insulin insensitivity, the cells inability to allow blood sugar to enter the cell. Specifically, the excess consumption of saturated fat and hydrogenated fats and oils contribute to insulin insensitivity.

. . . organic flaxseed oil contains twice the amount of Omega 3 fatty acids (57%) without the risks associated with fish oils. Studies confined to diabetics and Omega 3 fatty acids reveal the following:
1. decreased blood levels of tryglycerides
2. decreases of potent inflammatory mediators
3. decreased blood vise (enhanced circulation)
4. decreased risk of atherosclerosis
5. increases favorable fatty acids (HDL)
6. blood platelet aggregation (stickiness) to levels healthy controls
7. no significant changes in glucose

The book, *Fats that Heal, Fats that Kill*, Udo Erasmus, suggests an optimal dietary intake of 6 grams or 54 calories of Omega 3 fatty acids daily, although much higher levels may be indicated to achieve a therapeutic dose. Six grams of Omega 3 fatty acids is equal to approximately 1.5 tablespoons of flaxseed oil. (Beutler)

Vitamin E, which is found in abundance in wheat germ oil, is also a powerful antioxidant. A wide variety of foods, such as: apples, berries (especially blueberries), citrus fruits, cruciferous vegetables, garlic, onions, greens, red grapes, spinach, tomatoes, etc. contain antioxidants.

According to Packer in *Antioxidant Miracle:*

Ironically, despite all of the spectacular, high-tech medical break-throughs of the twentieth century, Americans are still two to four times more likely to die of lifestyle-related diseases such as heart disease, cancer, stroke, and diabetes than citizens of poor nations. Why? The answers often lie with what we are putting on our plates. (166)

Whether we are lacking trace minerals, antioxidants, vitamins, or any other nutrient, we can always look to our diet and life-style to find the reason why.

- Alkalizer Pack - helps to alkalize the body which quite often will bring the glucose levels into a normal range.

Essential Oils:
- Neuropathy Blend – We have used this blend successfully with Steve's diabetes. In *Essential Oils,* Young recommends:
  Mix in ½ oz. V-6 Mixing Oil or Massage Oil Base. Massage on location of tingling or numbness.
  10 drops juniper
  10 drops geranium
  10 drops helichrysum (336)

Juices:
- Wheat Grass Juice – drink 2-4 oz. per day and use for wheat grass implants – helps to alkalize and nourish the entire body
- Pancreas Rejuvenator – In the *Juiceman,* we find a great recipe for diabetes:
  What is good for the pancreas is good for the entire body. I recommend this juice to everyone.
  One serving – 8 ounces
  4 carrots
  1 apple
  4 – 5 lettuce leaves
  3 ounces of string beans
  (approximately ¾ cup)
  3 ounces brussels sprouts
  (approximately 3 – 4 sprouts)
  Trim the carrots and cut them into 2 to 3 inch pieces. Process the carrot pieces in the juicer and set aside. Cut the apple into wedges. Process the apple wedges, lettuce leaves, string beans, and sprouts in the juicer. Combine the juices and mix well. (126)

Other Modalities:
- DIET, DIET, DIET – this is by far the most important thing any diabetic can do, especially Type 1, if they want to be healed. In *Raw Family,* we learn how they handled a diagnosis of type 1 diabetes:
  When I learned about Sergei's diabetes, it awoke in me my mother's instinct, which appeared to be stronger than my

depression and disease. It saved his life, and mine too. When I heard the diagnosis "juvenile diabetes", I was so shocked and horrified that I lost my appetite for a couple of days. I remember thinking, "God! Why is this happening to my son?" That filled me with self-pity and increased my suffering. Deep inside I felt very strongly that to put Sergei on insulin would be completely wrong. I decided to do some research.

Since I had studied to be a medical nurse years ago in Russia, I decided to buy medical books. I read that blindness and kidney failure could occur as a result of using insulin, not from diabetes itself. Throughout all of these books there were many statements that there is not even the slightest chance of cure for this type of diabetes. For example, the American Diabetes Association Complete Guide to Diabetes said: "The only way to treat Type 1 diabetes is to give the body another source of insulin. Usually, this is done through injections of insulin. However, new experimental approaches also show some promise. Patients with Type 1 diabetes have experienced miraculous results from pancreas transplants." Reading these medical books only strengthened my decision not to put Sergei on insulin. We bought him a blood monitor, and he began checking his blood sugar several times a day.

I took Sergei off white sugar and white flour. However, this didn't make any difference in his blood tests. I didn't know what to do next. In the bookstore there was a sea of information, all of which was contradictory. I didn't have much time; the doctor threatened to report me to social services because I wouldn't put Sergei on insulin. I decided that I needed only the information that worked. I wanted to know how people become healthy.

That's when I started to notice how different people look. I saw that some people look much healthier than others. One day I overcame my embarrassment and began asking healthy-looking people what they knew about alternative treatments for diabetes.

Then one day at my bank, I got in line behind a radiant and happy woman. I asked her my question and she smiled. "Of course, the body can heal everything. I healed my colon cancer fifteen years ago." I invited her to lunch. Elisabeth smiled again: "I cannot eat your lunch, but we can talk." What Elisabeth said was shocking (what do mean, everything raw?). At the same time I had a very confident feeling inside myself.

Elisabeth answered all my questions, and gave me an old
book about raw food. No matter how scary everything
sounded, it made sense. My heart told me it was right...
Sergei's Teen Message – I am so lucky that I am a raw
fooder, because I am cured of my diabetes .... (20)

Experiences:
  a) Section I, pg. 56
  b) Section I, pg. 58
  c) There have been many people come to me at our booth
  during trade shows wanting to know what to do for
  diabetes. Of course, too many times they are looking for
  the magic bullet and, as we have discussed, there isn't one.
  During one particular show, we had this conversation: A
  couple came to the booth and asked, "What do you have to
  cure diabetes?"

I explained there were many things which would help,
but in order to cure it, there would have to be some lifestyle changes. The husband asked, "Do you mean I have to
give up my liquor?" (as he held a beer bottle in his hand)

I replied, "Yes, you do."

"Well, most of the time I water it down with soda, is
that O.K.?"

"No, you will have to give up the soda, too."

"Well, Lady, if I have to give up my liquor and my soda,
what's the sense in living?"

"If you don't, you won't be alive to worry about it."

Unfortunately, this is the attitude of a lot of people. If
they have to change their diet and their life style, it's just
not worth it. In cases like this, diabetes becomes an
incurable disease.

DIARRHEA

Diarrhea can sometimes be a sign of extreme constipation
where the bowel is so congested, only the liquid can pass by; or it
can be a sign the body is cleansing, using the digestive system as

its eliminatory channel. If the symptoms are severe or prolonged, it can cause dehydration, so the person needs to be given lots of liquids to replace the lost fluids.

Slippery Elm, made into a gruel, will usually help to slow the symptoms of diarrhea and is nutritious. This is what George Washington used to help keep his troops alive at Valley Forge.

Herbal Aids:
- Sunflowers – prepare a tea using the leaves – give a teaspoon at a time – be careful not to give too much or it will cause constipation
- Red Raspberry Leaf Tea – drink several cups per day – helps to calm the stomach and the intestines
- Yarrow Tea – when taken hot it is a diaphoretic herb which helps to sweat out toxins – when taken cold it becomes a diuretic which causes urination – both ways it helps to eliminate toxins
- Slippery Elm Gruel – mix powdered slippery elm with some warm water to make gruel – soothing to the intestines - brings consistency to bowel movements

DIZZINESS

Lots of different conditions cause light-headedness or dizziness. If it is due to poor circulation, then using Cayenne pepper will help to increase the circulation. Sometimes a mild whiplash or neck injury can cause dizziness due to pinched nerves or the spine being out of alignment. A good chiropractor can help to adjust the neck and spine to correct the problem. Many times, dizziness is due to an infection of the inner ear.

Herbal Aids:
- Cayenne – ½ tsp. of powdered Cayenne in a glass of water or 2-3 capsules
- B&B Tincture - put 3 or 4 drops of B&B with a couple drops of garlic oil into the ear- put a cotton ball in the ear to hold the fluids in – this will help feed any damaged nerves in the ear – it is also the easiest way to access the central nervous system

Other Modalities:
- Chiropractic Adjustment – check with a good chiropractor to make sure your spine is aligned correctly
- Treat for infection of inner ear – see ear ache

- Check blood pressure – sometimes low blood pressure can cause dizziness

Like so many other conditions, dizziness is a symptom of something else going on in the body. We need to "cleanse and nourish" and quite often the body will correct itself without us ever being fully aware of what the problem was.

If you have tried these suggestions and do not get any relief, you might want to have some tests run, such as a cat scan, to make sure there is not something causing pressure on the brain.

Few cases of eyestrain have been developed by looking
on the bright side of things.
-- Author Unknown

The difficult is done at once:
The impossible takes a little longer.
-- Armed Forces Motto

The greatest tragedy that comes to man is emotional depression,
the dulling of the intellect and the loss of initiative that comes
from nutritive failure.
-- Dr. James McLester, former AMA President

E

EARACHE

When my oldest children were young and I would take them to the doctor with ear infections, it always followed the same pattern. We started out with the bubble gum medicine (Amoxicilin). If that didn't clear it up, we went to Ceclor. If that didn't clear it up, they would start discussing surgery to put tubes in their ears. This still does not cure the problem, it only treats the symptoms. The infection is still there – it just gives it a place to drain.

If our children are suffering from recurring ear infections, then it is time to take a look at what they are putting in their bodies. Most parents are amazed at how fast the ear infections clear up just by getting their children off of dairy products. It has also been proven in numerous studies that babies who nurse have far less ear infections than babies who are bottle fed.

Among the most common ailments for which children are taken to the doctor are ear infections. Most ear infections are extremely easy to take care of at home. If they are caught early, using the garlic oil and mullein oil for two to three days will usually take care of the problem. Hold the bottle of oil under hot tap water until it is warm, then put a few drops of the garlic oil and then the mullein oil into the ear. Secure it with a cotton ball.

If you get a real nasty infection that is hard to clear up, you will usually be able to feel the swollen glands in the neck. Then make a decoction of three parts mullein and one part lobelia. Soak a cotton diaper in the decoction and wrap it around the throat and jaw line over the swollen glands. Keep the cloth warm and moist. This will help to bring the swelling in the glands down and allow the ear to drain. Using either mullein oil or Mullein & Lobelia ointment to lightly (this area will be extremely tender) massage over the eustachian tubes will also help the ear drain.

When strep and other infections strike quickly, the ear may build up so much pressure the ear drum will break. If you see blood and other liquid draining from the ear, do not put any thing else directly into the ear. Quite often when the ear drum ruptures, the pain will be relieved because the pressure is gone. The ear drum was designed to rupture when there is too much pressure behind it. When this happens, continue to treat the infection orally and use the X-Ceptic externally. When the infection is cleared up, the ear drum heals.

Let's get back to raising a healthy generation of children instead of spending thousands of dollars treating the symptoms of our degenerative lifestyles.

Herbal Aids:
- Warm Garlic Oil – two to six drops in ear depending upon age and size of person to help kill infection
- Warm Mullein Oil – two to six drops in ear to help break up congestion behind ear drum
- Warm Lobelia Tincture – two to six drops in ear to relax the ear drum and relieve pain
- Three parts cut Mullein and one part cut Lobelia – fomentation applied around jaw area and throat to help reduce swelling of glands that may be keeping the infection from draining.
- Mullein and Lobelia Ointment – can be used in place of the Mullein and Lobelia fomentation when traveling or when you do not have access to the dried herbs – can also be used to promote drainage of the ear by lightly massaging along the Eustachian tubes (basically, run your finger from behind the ear along the jaw line)
- Kid-E-Well - one to two dropper fulls every two hours to help bring out congestion and boost the immune system
- Kid-E-Cep - one dropper full every two to four hours to help kill infection. Kid-E-Cep is the X-Ceptic combination in a glycerin base so it tends to have a pretty strong taste. Because of this, I like to use the Kid-E-Well orally and the X-Ceptic externally. However, if it is a stubborn infection, I will add the Kid-E-Cep into my program orally. I usually add it to juice when I give it to a child.
- INF formula – four capsules every two to three hours for infection
- Echinacea – four capsules every two to three hours to boost immune system
- X-Ceptic Tincture – rubbed behind the ears and down the neck to help kill infection
- Echinacea and Golden Seal - four capsules every two to three hours to boost immune system and kill infection

Essential Oils:
- Eucalyptus Oil – use in hot water vaporizer to help open up the breathing passages and promote drainage
- Single Oils: Recommended by Gary Young in *Essential Oils:*
  Thyme linalol (Thymus vularis CT linalool)
  Lavender (Lavandula angustifolia)

Tea tree oil (Melaleuca alternifolia)
Helichrysum (Helichrysum italicum)
Roman Chamomile (Chamaemelum nobile)
Ravensara (Ravensara aromatica)
Peppermint (Mentha piperita)
Eucalyptus radiate

TOPICAL: DILUTE 50-50 in warm olive oil.
Apply 2 drops to a cotton swab. Using the swab, apply traces to the skin AROUND the opening of the ear, but not in it. Put 2-3 drops of the diluted essential oil on a piece of cotton and place it carefully over the ear opening. Leave in overnight. Additional relief may be obtained by placing a warm compress over the ear.

NOTE: Never put essential oils directly into the ear. (344-345)

Experiences:

a) Section I, pg. 28

b) When Juanita was 21, we went on a lecture tour down the east coast. During the trip, she developed a cold which immediately led to a severe ear infection. Of course, it happened on a weekend in a town that we were not familiar with. I had brought a lot of herbs with me, but had not brought enough of the ones I needed to help her. It finally got so bad, I took her to an emergency room because I felt helpless without the supplies I needed. (I have since learned not to leave home without all of the herbs that I think I might possibly need in an emergency).

The doctor told me that it looked like a strep infection. He said they can strike so fast that within a half hour the ear drum can break. He did a culture, gave us some antibiotics and sent us on our way. Juanita took the antibiotics along with using the herbs that I had on hand and more that I was able to pick up as we went. At night, in the hotel rooms, we would build a tent out of sheets to lay Juanita in with the hot water vaporizer. The ear drum broke, draining blood and pus for several days. A week later she was still extremely ill and battling this ear infection. I called back to the hospital to see what the culture had shown. They said it was not strep. I asked what it was and they said they didn't know, it might be viral. We worked with her body and were able to clear it up. We had to work with it constantly for about two weeks.

When we got home from the tour, Juanita had a letter waiting from a friend of hers who was serving as a missionary. She had come down with the same type of infection and had been hospitalized. The infection traveled up to the brain, so they transferred her to another hospital. After several weeks of treatment, she was finally sent home from her mission.

We were told about two other people with similar symptoms. One of them died and the other ended up with brain damage.

Ear infections can be serious, but most of them are extremely easy to clear up at home with very simple means. When they are stubborn and serious, we have still found that working with them at home seems to have the best results.

ECZEMA

Eczema is a symptom of something going on inside the body. The skin is merely an eliminatory channel. Again, we have to go back to the philosophy of "cleanse and nourish."

Herbal Aids:
- Parasite Cleanse – skin problems are quite often an indication of parasites – see section V
- Chickweed Ointment – use directly on affected skin to heal and help relieve itching
- Chickweed tea – if a large area of skin is affected, make a tea out of the bath water and soak in it
- Plantain Ointment – apply directly to affected skin to help draw out toxins
- Black Walnut Hull Tincture – if the affected area is caused by some type of fungus – use Black Walnut Hull tincture or tea on affected area

- BF&C - use the tea, ointment or oil on affected area to heal – also helps with fungus due to Black Walnut in formula
- Christopher's Extended Herbal Cleanse – remember, the skin is like our third kidney – if there is a problem on the skin, we need to consider cleaning out the body
- Morinda Noni Juice – take orally and apply directly to the skin – can also be added to bath water – have seen great success in using this product with skin conditions
- X-Ceptic Tincture - if you are dealing with a gram-positive bacteria such as staph, I would use the X-Ceptic™ tincture because it contains Myrrh – studies have shown that gram-positive bacteria, when placed in a Petri dish with Myrrh cannot survive

Other Modalities:
- DIET – the skin may be reacting to the toxins we are putting into the body – as always, take a good look at the diet

Experiences:

a) A couple of years ago, I went to Idaho to help a friend with some sick children. When I was getting ready to leave, her husband asked if I could help him with a problem. I told him I didn't know, but I would try. He lifted his pant leg up and showed me his leg. It was dry, scaly and covered in sores. Some of them were irritated and scabbed over where he had been scratching them. I knew he had worked with cattle most of his life, so I suggested that he might want to do a parasite cleanse.

He used the parasite cleanse found in Section V. A month after my visit, when I saw him again, he was anxious to show me his legs. They were completely healed. He told me this was the first time in 30 years they had been clear. I was totally amazed at how long he had been living with this problem. He said it had been embarrassing to go swimming, play basketball, or any other sport where his legs would show.

More than once, I have seen parasites manifest themselves through the skin, so if you are having a problem clearing up eczema, you might want to seriously consider doing some type of parasite cleanse.

b) While working with a mother through labor and delivery, I noticed that her sister who had come for the birth was suffering with some severe skin problems. After the baby was born and I was packing up to leave, I saw her sitting on the couch with both arms spread across the back of the couch with just a sheet draped over her. She was in tears and obviously miserable. Her face, neck, chest and arms were covered in some type of eczema. She said she had taken her infant son in to several specialists with a similar problem, but had been unable to clear it up. The baby was just as miserable as she was, fussing and clawing at his chest because it burned and itched so bad. Whatever the problem was – she had obviously gotten it from her son. I gave her a bottle of Noni juice and some literature on it – suggesting she might want to take it orally and bathe in it.

Noni is a fruit which comes from the Polynesian islands and has long been known for its healing powers. The research done on this fruit seems to indicate that somehow it has the ability to balance the body at a cellular level. The information I had read on it indicated that it had been used successfully with skin conditions, so I told her to give it a try and see what happens.

Within a few days, she was doing much better. She has continued to use this juice to cure both herself and her son.

EDEMA

Edema, swelling and bloating, is caused when the body starts to retain extra fluids. Wherever symptoms are located, the general problem is that fluid does not eliminate properly through the kidneys and skin.

In *Advanced Herbal Treatise,* we learn:

When sulfuric acid is generated within the organism, it immediately unites with water and swells up. This action produces heat, which expands the capillaries. The osmotic pressure forces the serum through the walls of the blood vessels, producing inflammation and dropsy. Hence the using of inorganic matter is always poisonous to the human organism in spite of all the apparent evidence to the contrary. (Shook 101)

Herbal Aids:
- JuniPars - two or more capsules three times per day to flush out fluids – the herbs in this formula act together as a diuretic
- Parsley – make into a tea – to be taken orally and used as a poultice on the areas that are retaining fluid

Experiences:
a) See Section I, pg. 18
b) See Section I, pg. 69
c) Taken from a Christopher newsletter, we read about an extreme case of edema:

A lady came into our weekly Tuesday night lecture a little late, after we had barely started. She asked if she could interrupt and tell something that had happened to her since the last lecture, a week ago. We said we'd be happy to hear her story, so she told us the reason she was a little late was because of a long distance phone call she had received.

Just after the last lecture, the Tuesday before, she received a call from her brother-in-law in Chicago. He told her that if she wanted to see her twin sister alive she had better fly back there immediately because the doctors had said she had only a day or two to live.

Our student took a few days off form work and arrived in Chicago on the following Friday. She went in to see her sister and would not have recognized her if she hadn't been told who it was. Her sister was so badly swollen from edema (dropsy) that she seemed to be only a bloated, unrecognizable mass of flesh. She had been under doctors' care for a number of months, and they had been unable to give her anything but temporary aid from the water accumulation. Now they were utterly baffled and had, at the family's request, sent her home from the hospital to die (being given a day or two or slightly more grace).

The sick and suffering twin was in a coma, not recognizing anyone and our student cried when she saw her favorite sister lying there helpless, with little school children needing their mother so much, so she asked the husband if he would allow her to use an herbal routine she had heard about at a lecture recently. He said the family's doctor was just waiting for her to die anyway, so go ahead!

Our lady found a little health food store nearby and bought some parsley root and glycerin (this was animal glycerin, we now use vegetable glycerin, which is superior).

When she got back, she made up parsley root tea (one teaspoon of herb to a cup of water, or one ounce of herb to the pint of water), making up about one gallon of the tea. (Steam distilled water is 30% more efficient than tap water and is our choice).

One quart of the tea was used straight to give to this patient orally, and three quarts of the parsley root tea was mixed with equal parts of glycerin (making six quarts of the mixture) for fomentations.

They would give a cup of parsley tea each one half hour to the patient to drink and the heated combination (of parsley and glycerin) was used as a fomentation over the badly swollen legs, arms and abdomen. This was done by soaking white flannel cloths and laying them over the areas. (Use cotton or wool, never use synthetic cloth).

As the patient lay there so helpless, her sister remembered instructions given to follow the progress of the treatment. She was to lift the corner of the cloth, after the fomentation had been on for a short time, and watch to see if the pores were starting to take the water from swollen areas. She said that as she looked it was like seeing hundreds of little springs coming from the body. She had made this trip and was walking by faith, using a formula she did not know about or had ever used before. She had just heard of it at our lecture that previous Tuesday. She had to fly back to work on Monday, so she left all the instructions with the husband to continue on with the program that had been started.

After work Tuesday she rushed home to get ready for the regular Tuesday night herb lecture and the phone rang. It was her brother-in-law from Chicago. He said, "There is someone here who would like to talk to you." He put his wife on the phone. Even though she had laid helpless for months and part of the time in a semi-conscious condition, she was on the phone now, so happy she was crying. The swelling had gone down, and she was recovering rapidly – in fact, she said she got the children's breakfast and fixed their school lunches that day and was so grateful 'to be a mother again'—not a dying patient. There were not many dry eyes in the lecture room that Tuesday night when she finished her story.

ELEPHANTITIS
(See Parasites)

EYESIGHT
(Poor vision)

The Herbal Eyebright formula feeds the eye, brings circulation to the area and helps to cleanse it. Using proper exercises will also help to strengthen the eyes. There are doctors who have actually been able to cure cases of near-sightedness and far-sightedness with daily eye exercises. (See section V)

Herbal Aids:
-   Herbal Eyebright Formula - three to five drops in eye cup of warm sterile water, exercise eyes under the water at least two times per day.

Juices:
- Carrot Juice – one or more glasses per day
- Eye Exercises – see Section V

Experiences:
a) See Section I, pg. 56
b) Last spring we rescued a baby raccoon and bottle fed her. When a raccoon is born their eyes and ears remain closed for two to four weeks. When she was about four weeks old, they opened up, but she still ran in to things and walked off the back of the couch. Her eyes were white, so I took her to a veterinarian to find out what the problem was. She told me the baby had cataracts. Apparently her mother had gotten into something toxic, causing the baby to be born blind. The doctor told me that if I ever wanted her to see normally, I would have to take her to a specialist at the age of four months to have laser surgery done on her eyes. As time passed her eyes seem to clear up, so when she was about three months old I took her back to the veterinarian to have her checked. She told me there was no sign of the cataracts. She said that apparently all she needed was good nutrition and a clean environment for the body to dissolve the problem on its own.

This experience just made it even more clear to me why so many older people end up with cataracts. It is just one more place where the mucus and toxins build up after a life time of poor eating and exposure to toxins.

In *Why Suffer,* Ann Wigmore points out how necessary it is for you to become the guardian of your own food supply, as the food processors are now permitted by Washington authorities to "preserve" the elements for "life" by dangerous radiation processes. She says,

> When this ill-advised destruction of all 'life' in food is complete – and that day will come rapidly because the public is unaware of the dire consequences of such a condition – this country will experience, as one alarmed, nationally-known

radiometrist suggested, 'a calamity worse than a host of atom bombs.'(25)

The loss of sight in our later years is just one of many calamities which befall us due to this type of degenerative diet.

c) In *School of Natural Healing,* we are told how Christopher had success with the Herbal Eyebright formula:

> An elderly man in Fort Worth, Texas, suffered from both glaucoma and cataracts – and was healed completely with the formula. A Michigan woman used it for ten days and removed cataracts on both eyes. A woman in Kentucky, who had lost 80 percent of her sight due to a subretinal hemorrhage, had her sight completely restored. A California woman had the beginnings of cataracts when the gel broke in both her eyes. Her vision failed, and her eyes were so dry that she had to lift her eyelids with her fingers each morning. With Herbal Eyebright, both eyes healed and the cataracts dissolved.
>
> One Missouri baby had been born with Coloboma; one eye was smaller than the other. Three leading specialists proclaimed the blindness to be permanent. The mother began patiently using Herbal Eyebright with a dropper in each of his eyes. Within three months, this supposedly blind baby was reaching for objects. By the age of three, he ran freely, his vision perfect.
>
> Another couple had a baby born without optic nerves. Dr. Christopher knew that giving sight to such a child was almost impossible. But he knew that the formula could cause no harm, so he recommended Herbal Eyebright in the eyes and given internally, and B&B tincture dropped in the ears and given internally. Six months later, the same couple brought the child to a lecture. He chased balls across the room and picked them up; he had normal sight. (xxiv)

It is never too late to be what you might have been.
-- George Elliot

Remember that when you help one organ, every other organ benefits also.
-- Dr. Bernard Jensen

A fast can help you heal with greater speed; cleanse your liver, kidneys and colon; purify your blood; help you lose excess weight and water; flush out toxins; clear the eyes and tongue, and cleanse the breath.
-- James F. Balch, M.D.

F

FATIGUE

Suffering from chronic fatigue means the body is out of balance. It is having a hard time coping with the strain we have placed on it. It has to be brought back into an alkaline state and supplied with the nutrition and live enzymes it needs in order to function.

Along with cleansing and nourishing, we need to increase circulation by moving! Most of our lifestyles are too sedentary. Our bodies were meant to move. Our lymph system does not have a pump like the heart. We move lymph by moving out muscles. If we do not have some form of exercise our muscles will begin to atrophy and store too many acids. We need to have live wholesome nutrition, lots of fresh air, and exercise in order to feel energized.

Fatigue grows from lack of sleep. Fresh air, nutrition and exercise will help us to rest better.

We are constantly taking energy into our bodies. We run on electricity. Then we wear synthetic clothes, synthetic shoes, walk on synthetic carpets and we never get ourselves grounded out. This literally leaves us felling "wired" because we have so much static electricity built up inside us. If we will periodically take time to remove our shoes and shuffle through the grass for twenty or more minutes, it will help us to ground ourselves so that we can relax and rest.

Accordingly, in *The Healing Herbs* Dr. Christopher taught:

Fatigue is usually caused through not bringing oxygen into the body rapidly enough either through diet or through proper breathing, or oftimes by being in congested areas where you do not have good air to breathe. To bring oxygen into the body is very important because, unless the oxygen (which is the breath of life itself) gets to every cell, them waste materials accumulate. These waste materials sludge up the body, causing it to slow down to the point of drowsiness and fatigue. (59)

Herbal Aids:
- Vitalerbs – use some type of whole food or herbal supplement with your meals to insure you are getting enough nutrients in your meals
- Organa Minerals - drink a cap full daily to insure you are getting enough trace minerals in your diet
- Liquid Chlorophyll – if fresh wheat grass is not available, use Chlorophyll to build strong blood
- Yellow Dock Combination™ - two or more capsules three times per day to help with anemia
- Cayenne Pepper – two capsules three times per day to increase circulation
- Cleansing – use some type of cleansing program to clean toxins out of the body
- Alkalizer Pack - the body is too acidic – need to bring it back into balance
- Changease - two capsules three times per day with wheat germ oil to help balance the hormones
- NuFem - two capsules three times per day to help cleanse and rebuild the female organs
- Wheat Germ Oil Capsules – one Tablespoon or two capsules three times per day to supply the body with proper fats along with vitamin E or in conjunction with Changease to help balance the hormones
- Relaxease - two or more capsules in the evening to help you sleep better

Juices:
- Wheat Grass Juice – two to four ounces per day orally to help boost energy levels
- Green Drinks – drink one to three glasses per day of a good quality powdered green drink
- Vegetable Juices – In the *Juiceman,* we find a recipe for a Pick-Me-Up Energy Cocktail:
    Our boys drink this to revive their energy. Linda and I drink it after they have gotten their energy back!
    6 Carrots
    5 Sprigs of Parsley
    Trim the carrots and cut them into 2 to 3 inch pieces. Process the carrot pieces and parsley in the juicer. (Kordich 127)

Other Modalities:
- Diet – we build life with life – clean up the diet
- Exercise – walk, swim, bike, use a rebounder – just MOVE
- Fresh Air – as much as possible every day

- Walk Bare Foot – go outside bare-footed, shuffle your feet through the grass – this will help to ground you while getting rid of excess static electricity

FEVER

In our home, we do not take Tylenol, aspirin or anything else to bring a fever down. A fever is the body's way of activating the immune system and waging its battle. The basic rule of thumb we try to keep in mind is: Moist heat heals: Dry heat can kill. When working with a fever, we make sure we keep it moist by drinking plenty of fluids, steaming in hot showers, and drinking yarrow tea to cause sweating.

The Creator knew what He was doing when He put this body together, so I have to ask you, "Is the body working?" If it is, then let's help it accomplish what it is trying to do. Just like the example of the decongestants and cough syrups, trying to stop a fever is thwarting what the body is trying to accomplish and may drive the problem deeper.

Parents ask me what to do in case of a convulsion due to high fever. Personally, I have never seen or heard of a child having a convulsion when this program is followed. However, a fever convulsion is the body's safety mechanism. If there is a dry fever and it gets too high, this would be a way for the body to bring the fever down quickly. The exception to this rule would be if there has been a head injury of some kind which would cause the body's thermostat (for lack of a better word) to be off.

Herbal Aids:
- Yarrow Tea – taken hot – will cause sweating
- Cold Sheet Treatment – see Section V for instructions
- INF Formula – two to four capsules every two hours to kill infection
- Echinacea – two to four capsules every two hours to boost immune system
- Echinacea and Golden Seal – two to four capsules every two hours to boost immune system and kill infection
- Kid-E- Well – one to three dropper fulls every hour to boost immune system and clean out toxins

- Catnip Enema – allow enema to cool to room temperature - cleans out colon, puts moisture back into body, reduces body temperature
- Cayenne – take two capsules, get into a hot shower, take two more capsules, pile on the blankets – sweat out the toxins

Juices:
- Drink lots of fluids – water, juices, herbal teas, fruit popsicles, - whatever you can handle to get fluid into the body

Other Modalities:
- Hot Shower or Bath – help the body keep a moist heat going by getting into a steamy shower or bath as many times as needed through the day and/or night
- Rest – allow the body time to focus its energy on whatever it is trying to flush out

Experiences:
a) Section I, pg. 12
b) Section I, pg. 37
c) Section I, pg. 66
d) Section I, pg. 71
e) Section I, pg. 78
f) Section II, pg. 136
g) Section IV, pg. 251
h) Section IV, pg. 294
i) Section IV, pg. 360

FIBROIDS
(UTERINE)

Most doctors will tell you that uterine fibroids are incurable. If they are causing too many problems – such as heavy bleeding – the recommendation will be a hysterectomy. Under "experience" see how I dealt with mine – many people since my experience have had the same results.

Herbal Aids:
- Wheat Grass – drink two to four ounces per day – juice a full flat every night to douche with

Other Modalities:
- Diet – at a bare minimum – stay away from meat and dairy until

this problem is under control – the body can not heal this condition when it is having to deal with all of the extra chemicals in your diet

Experience:
a) See Section II, pg. 170

FLATULENCE

Gas in the intestinal tract is caused by poor digestion. This can be caused by eating too many processed foods which do not supply the body with needed enzymes, poor food combinations, hasty eating or not chewing food properly

In *Why Suffer,* Wigmore teaches:

. . . that the natural theory of digestion is not a chemical process, but the action of the live and helpful bacteria that thrive in the digestive juices and feed on the live foods, but these are largely ineffectual with the dead and inorganic intakes that have become the dietary habit of so much of humanity, and thus 90% of it is dumped into the colon, for the purpose of elimination and here is where most health troubles begin.

Herbal Aids:
- Catnip & Fennel Tincture – use by the dropper full to help relieve bloated feeling and disperse gas
- Gaseze - two or more capsules to help relieve gas
- Herbal LB – two or more capsules three times per day to clean out the colon
- Intestinal Formula I - one or more capsules at bedtime to clean out colon
- Dr. Christopher's Extended Herbal Cleanse - use to clean out and strengthen vital organs
- Alkalizer Pack - helps to alkalize the system and remove excess acid
- Castor Oil – rub externally on abdomen over intestines – apply warm, moist heat – when skin feels dry, apply more oil – continue for a couple of hours until bowel cleans out
- Kid-E-Col – children formula – give by the dropper full to relieve bloating and gas

Other Modalities:
- Diet – clean it up!
- Colonics – will help to clean out old debris which may be causing the problem

Experience:
   a) Section IV, pg. 334
   b) Section IV, pg. 377

FLU

To expel the flu, we use lots of fluids and rest. The body needs to be able to flush the toxins out and regain its strength. Diaphoretic herbs, such as yarrow help to sweat out the toxins.

Herbal Aids:
- Red Raspberry Leaf Tea – several glasses per day to nourish and calm the stomach
- Peppermint Tea – use to settle stomach
- Slippery Elm Gruel – mix powdered slippery elm with warm water to form gruel – helps to settle stomach and calm intestines
- Kid-E-Well - one to three dropper fulls every hour to boost immune system and draw out toxins
- Echinacea – one dropper full or 2 – 4 capsules every two hours to boost immune system
- Ginger Bath – put fresh, grated ginger root into a cloth diaper or dish towel, rubber band the top and let float in bath water or put powdered ginger directly into the water
- Yarrow Tea – drink hot to help sweat out toxins
- Catnip Enema – can be used to clean out colon and/or it can be used as a way to get fluid back into the body when someone is too nauseated to hold any fluid down
- Nausea Tea –
   1 tsp. Cloves
   1 tsp. Turkey Rhubarb powder
   1 tsp. Cinnamon
   1 ounce Spearmint
   Simmer the first three herbs in one pint of water for 5 min; pour this decoction over the spearmint; put lid on tightly and let this infuse until cool; strain. Take 2 tablespoons to ¼ cup full every ½ hour until nausea subsides.

Juices:
- Drink lots of fluids – it is important to stay hydrated – if it is hard to hold anything down – try juice popsicles or ice cubes
- Vegetable Broth or Soups – stay on a liquid diet until symptoms have subsided

Other Modalities:
- Rest – allow your energy to be focused on getting better – do not over do it

FOOD POISONING

Food poisoning, a very painful condition, causes the intestines to cramp and it can cause gas and bloating. Toxins need to be removed either by throwing up and/or pushing it through the intestines.

We have used this procedure to bring relief on many occasions with excellent results.

Herbal Aids:
- Lobelia – if the food is still in the stomach causing
- discomfort – use as much Lobelia tincture or tea as needed to induce vomiting
- Catnip & Fennel tincture – use a dropper full every few minutes until relief from bloating is obtained
- Catnip Enema – clean out the bowel
- Castor Oil Fomentation – rub castor oil on the abdomen, over intestines – cover with warm, wet towel – allow oil to soak into the skin – check every 10 or 15 minutes to be sure the abdomen is still oily- if it feels dry, apply more oil

Other Modalities:
- Reflexology – by massaging the reflex points for the ascending, transcending and descending colon, you can help the toxins to move out.

Experiences:
a) A good friend of ours called at about 11:00 one night complaining of food poisoning. He said he had had it before and he knew the symptoms. I could tell by the sound of his voice he was in a lot of pain. He told me he couldn't stand up straight and that he had to get better because he had an important appointment the next day.

We gathered up a few supplies and went to see him. I asked him if he had tried to throw it up. He said he had tried, but the problem had moved down into the intestines.

We started some Catnip tea. In the mean time, he took a dropper full of Catnip and Fennel tincture every 15 or 20 minutes. He rubbed his abdomen down with castor oil and we placed a hot, wet towel over it. (if you have access to a microwave – get your towel wet, wring it out and put it in the microwave for a couple of minutes) We then used olive oil to rub his feet. We massaged up the ascending colon reflex area, across the transverse colon and down the descending colon. His feet were extremely tender in those areas. We repeated this procedure for a couple of hours; the catnip and fennel orally, the castor oil with moist hot packs on the abdomen and massaging the reflex points on the feet. We knew we were making progress by the amount of gas that began to pass.

When the catnip tea had steeped and cooled, he took a dropper full of Lobelia tincture orally and then went to the bathroom to do a catnip enema. When he got to the bathroom, he threw up everything in his stomach. He did the catnip enema, retained it as long as possible and then cleaned out his intestines.

After all those hours of hurting so bad, he came down the stairs standing up straight saying that he felt wonderful. In fact, he couldn't believe the contrast between how bad he had been feeling before and how wonderful he felt after he got the problem cleaned out.

b)   We took the family to a 4th of July picnic in town. The children were having a great time eating all of the junk (hot dogs, pizza, soda, etc.) that was available. Just before time for the fire works to start, Megan came to me doubled up with a stomach ache. I sent her in to use the bathroom to see if that would help. It didn't, she was still crying, so I took her home. When we got there I coated her abdomen in castor oil, covered it with a warm, wet wash cloth, gave her some Kid-E-Col and rubbed her feet.

In about an hour she went to the bathroom and passed what was causing the problem.

FROST BITE

In *The Human Body in Health and Disease,* frostbite is described as:
> Exposure to cold, particularly to moist cold, may result in frostbite, which can cause permanent local tissue damage. The areas most likely to be affected by frostbite are the face, ears, and extremities. The causes of damage include the formation of ice crystals and the reduction of blood supply to the area. Necrosis (death) of the tissues with gangrene can result. (297)

Herbal Aids:
- Cayenne Pepper – take two or more capsules three times per day to increase circulation throughout the body (by putting a little bit of cayenne pepper in your socks and gloves, you may be able to avoid getting frost bite)
- Yarrow Tea – soak the extremity in warm yarrow tea twice per day to draw circulation to that particular area
- BF&C Ointment, Tea, or Oil – soak the extremity in the tea or keep the oil or ointment rubbed on the area in order to heal the tissue
- Professor Cayenne Ointment – rub the cayenne ointment over the BF&C to help bring circulation to the area and to speed up the action of the BF&C.

Experience:
When Wade came home from Africa with frostbite, his big toes were black. He got back to the states wearing thongs. When I saw his toes I said, "Wade, we need to fix those."

Wade is extremely educated, and has a photographic memory. We often tease him about being a human encyclopedia. One time we were talking about lichens and he gave us a beautiful 20 minute discourse on lichens. Well, when I mentioned that we needed to fix his toes he told me all the reasons why we couldn't do that. He explained to me that the tissue and nerves are dead and it is a medically accepted fact that with frostbite you either leave it alone or amputate it. Somehow that didn't make sense to me. It seems that there should be a happy medium somewhere; so I told him if it was all dead it shouldn't matter what we did to it. He finally agreed, so Myrna (my daughter) and I went to work on them.

We peeled off the dead, black tissue, then massaged the toes with Professor Cayenne ointment to bring the circulation to the area. About ten minutes into the massage, Kelly, who is attending massage therapy school, came into the room. When she saw what we were doing she said, "Mom, don't you know that it is contraindicated to massage frost bite?"

I said, "Really? Then what are you supposed to do with it?" She said, "You either amputate it or leave it alone."

Gosh, where have I heard that before? I explained to her that if this were a fresh frostbite I would agree with her because we would be dealing with frozen meat and could definitely damage the tissue. However, a week after the fact, I figured they had had plenty of time to thaw out and we were pretty safe. I also mentioned that I thought there should be a happy medium between such drastic measures. Sometimes I am truly amazed at how much we just accept as truth without using our own common sense.

After we massaged the toes for 20 or 30 minutes, we packed them in BF&C ointment. I gave him four Cayenne capsules and some cut yarrow when he left. I suggested he take two of the Cayenne capsules, a hot shower and then two more Cayenne capsules to help increase the circulation in his body. Then I suggested that he soak his feet in some hot yarrow tea in order to draw the circulation to that area, then pack them in the BF&C and Professor Cayenne ointments. The BF&C was to help rebuild the tissue while the Professor Cayenne would help to bring circulation to the area which would feed the tissue and aid in the healing.

The next day Wade was back at the house and he looked terrible. I asked him how his toes were doing and he said, "Intellectually, I can tell you they are doing much better." I asked what he meant by that. He told me he was exhausted because he had not slept all night due to the fact that his toes were killing him!

I was excited and said, "Wade, that's wonderful! That means the nerves are regenerating!"

He stayed with the program and his toes healed completely. Affirming, that every cell in our body has the blueprint for rebuilding itself. It just needs the correct nutrients to work with.

There is truth in the saying that man becomes what he eats.
-- Ghandi

Don't let life discourage you; everyone who got where he is had
to be where he was.
-- R.L. Evans

I will not try to tell you everything I have learned in the past 35 years, for I have studied continually, and it is impossible to present it all in a short treatise. Sometimes I feel so stupid that I feel you can put it all in a nut-shell very quickly, yet it seems like the more you study, the more research you do, the more inadequate you feel. I wasn't always this way, for, as a very young man, I was going to change the world. I knew everything. You could ask me anything and I could give you an answer. I'm glad I'm over that stage.
-- John R. Christopher

G

GALLBLADDER

Gallstones are a dietary condition which can be treated and cured at home, but if the same lifestyle and diet choices are made, the condition will continue to come back. If left untreated, gallstones can become extremely painful and life-threatening.

Herbal Aids:
- Olive Oil – 4 oz. four times per day with lemon juice to help soften stones
- Christopher's Extended Herbal Cleanse - see Section V
- Catnip Enema – clear toxins out of the colon
- Catnip & Fennel Tincture – use one dropper full, as needed, to relieve bloated feeling.
- Dr. Christopher's Barberry LG – this is a liver/gallbladder formula designed to help cleanse and rebuild the liver and gallbladder
- Castor Oil – rub into skin over the area of the gallbladder

Juices:
- Three Day Juice Cleanse – see Section V
- Fresh Lemon Juice – 4 oz. four times per day with olive oil to help break up stones

Experiences:
a) My sister-in-laws mother had just come from the doctor and said the doctor wanted to remove her gallbladder because it was full of stones. She wanted to know if there was anything else she could do. I told her about the gallbladder cleanse that Jethro Kloss has in *Back to Eden*. She was having a lot of discomfort due to bloating, so I told her about the Catnip and Fennel tincture. My sister-in-law worked with her for three days while she passed hundreds of stones. She was able to clear out her gallbladder and avoid surgery.

Jethro Kloss recommends using 4 oz. of lemon juice with 4 oz. of olive oil four times per day. Dr. Christopher recommended doing this in conjunction with a three day juice cleanse. Because it can be extremely dangerous to have a stone get caught in the bile duct, I also recommend rubbing castor oil into the skin over the gallbladder to further help soften the stones.

b) A man in one of our classes told me that he had also used the gallbladder cleanse successfully. His problem was that as the gallbladder healed it would go into spasms. We recommended rubbing the antispasmodic™ tincture into the skin over the gallbladder and, if necessary, use the tincture orally. This seemed to relieve the spasms.

GANGRENE

Gangrene is a condition where part of the body actually dies due to lack of circulation. If the blood stream is clean and the circulation is good, gangrene cannot set in, so it becomes essential to bring circulation to the area.

Herbal Aids:
- Marshmallow Root Tea – soak the afflicted area with marshmallow root tea, covering the area with tea as hot as the patient can take and leave it there for long periods of time. Soaking works faster than the poultice or the tea, but drinking the tea along with the soak will speed the action (Christopher 27 School).
- Cayenne – two capsules three times per day to increase circulation
- Yarrow – soak area an hour in the morning and an hour in the evening to draw circulation to the area
- Colonics or Enemas – cleanse the bowel

Experience:
See Section IV, pgs. 326

GAS
(See Flatulence)

GLANDS
(Swollen)

Three parts Mullein and one part Lobelia is the formula that seems to work best with swollen glands. A fomentation works the fastest, but, if you are in a situation, such as traveling, where you cannot make the tea, then using the Mullein and Lobelia ointment is also effective.   The area needs to be kept warm and moist. Professor Cayenne ointment works to create heat. I have also used my own body heat by holding my fingers on the ointment after rubbing the ointment onto one of the children's glands. Sometimes when you are traveling, you have to become pretty creative.

If you do happen to have any of the dried herbs with you while you are away from home, you can call room service and ask for a pot of hot water to make tea. They will bring you a teapot of hot water and then you can steep your herbs.

Herbal Aids:
- Mullein Leaf and Lobelia, cut – use three parts Mullein to one part Lobelia to make a decoction – place about ¾ cup of Mullein to ¼ cup of Lobelia in 2 quarts of distilled water – simmer on the stove – do not boil – as volume of the liquid decreases, the strength of your tea increases – soak a cloth in decoction – apply to swollen glands – keep the cloth warm and moist
- Mullein and Lobelia Ointment – rub onto swollen glands to reduce swelling

Experiences:
a) Section I, pgs. 28
b) Section I, pgs. 69
c) Section IV, pg. 281
d) Section IV, pg. 360

In order to a realist you must believe in miracles.
-- Henry C. Bailey

Wisdom begins in wonder.
-- Socrates

Time is
Too slow for those who wait,
Too swift for those who fear,
Too long for those who grieve,
Too short for those who rejoice,
But for those who Love
Time is not.
-- Henry Van Dyke

H

HAIR LOSS

Most people consider hair loss a genetic problem. Genetics does play a role, but it seems strange to me that when peoples have been found hidden away in undiscovered areas of the mountains, they not only seem to live unusually long lives, but they die with all of their hair and their teeth. Gorillas also seem to live much longer lives than we do when they are left in the wild. They are almost complete vegetarians and they, too, die with all of their teeth and all of their hair. It makes me wonder how much of this we have brought on ourselves by our degenerative diets and lifestyles.

After women have a baby, they quite often go through a stage where the hair falls out as they wash it or brush it, a temporary condition as the hormones balance themselves out.

The vitality or lack of vitality in our hair is a reflection of the condition of the body. The amount of water we drink, our diet, the amount of exercise and fresh air we receive all have an effect on our hair. The blood needs to be clean and healthy as this is what carries in nutrition and carries away waste.

Herbal Aids:
- Three Oil Massage – See Section V
- Hormonal Imbalance – See Section IV, pg. 400
- Bayberry – ". . . use a strong decoction and rub in well at night; wash off in the morning, brush the hair thoroughly and apply again (add a few drops of lavender oil). This will quickly stop falling hair and remove dandruff." (Christopher 146 School)

HAY FEVER
(See Allergies)

HEADACHE

Headaches can be caused by many different things. In 1995, the Nutrient Research Foundation did a study on cayenne with people who suffered with chronic headaches or migraines. Among the group who suffered with headaches, 85% reported definite improvement, 14% reported complete remission and 15% said no improvement after taking cayenne pepper. Among the group that suffered with migraines, 100% reported definite improvement and 9% reported complete remission.

Like so many other symptoms, a headache is merely a signal telling us there is a problem in the body. We need to figure out what the problem is and clean it up. It can be as simple as constipation or not getting enough water to drink.

We do not keep drugs in our house, so we have had to learn how to deal with headaches without reaching for aspirin or any other type of conventional pain killer. Two of the positive aspects of this type of treatment is we have discovered we can control the pain without drugs and we are extremely motivated to figure out what is causing the headache.

Herbal Aids:
- Cayenne Capsules or Powder – two capsules or ½ - 1 tsp. of Cayenne powder in water three times per day to increase circulation to the head
- Lobelia Tincture – 1 -2 dropper fulls of tincture as a relaxant
- Professor Cayenne Ointment - rub onto temples and base of head, lay in a quiet room for 20 – 30 minutes – if the headache is due to sore or tense muscles, rub the ointment into the muscles
- Paineze - two or more capsules when needed for pain
- SenSei - rub ointment over sinuses for relief of sinus headache, relax in a quiet room for 20 – 30 minutes
- Herbal Eyebright Formula - put 2 – 4 drops in an eye cup full of sterile water, rinse eyes morning and night for relief of eye strain.
- Chamomile Tea – drink as much as needed to relieve headache

Essential Oils:
- Lavender oil – place several drops of lavender into a hot tub of water to relax and help relieve tension headaches

Other Modalities:
- Eye Glasses – have eyes checked to see if there is a vision problem
- Massage – if the muscles are tense, get a good massage to relax the muscles
- Water – drink lots of pure water – a headache can actually be a sign of dehydration
- Chiropractic Adjustment – sometimes headaches can be caused from the back being out of alignment and pinching nerves in the spine

- Colonics – headaches can definitely be caused by too many toxins in the bowel

HEART TROUBLE

Cayenne, garlic and hawthorn berries are specifically for the heart. Cayenne helps to increase circulation; garlic helps clean up the arterial walls and Hawthorne berries help strengthen and rebuild the heart. If you suspect some type of degeneration, do a parasite cleanse. There are many parasites our technology cannot pick up which can be very damaging to the heart. If the condition involves a "hole in the heart" or some other type of deformity, use BF&C or comfrey fomentations to help the heart mend and rebuild itself

It is said that Dr. Christopher never lost a heart attack patient because he always administered cayenne immediately. He would put the cayenne into a cup of hot water, making a tea out of it, so it would get into the blood stream quickly.

To show what a miracle worker cayenne really is, Dr. Christopher related the experiment performed by medical doctors in the eastern United States – and printed in the medical journals.

They put some live heart tissue in a beaker filled with distilled water, and fed it nothing but Cayenne pepper, cleaning off sediments periodically and adding nothing else but distilled water to replace that which was lost from evaporation. During the experiment, they would have to trim the tissue every few days, because it would grow so rapidly! Having no control glands (pituitary and pineal), the tissue just continued to grow rapidly. They kept this tissue alive for fifteen years. After the doctor doing the experiment died, his associates kept it alive for two more years before destroying it for analysis. This shows the tremendous regenerative and healing power of Cayenne, especially upon the heart. (4 Newletter)

Herbal Aids:
- Cayenne Pepper – 1 tsp. in a glass of hot water or 2

capsules three times per day to increase circulation and strengthen
the heart
- Garlic – two capsules three times per day to strengthen veins and
  arteries
- Hawthorne Berry Syrup - one or more tablespoons three times per
  day to feed and strengthen the heart
- Cleanses – do some type of cleanse to clean the excess toxins from
  the body so the heart is not having to work over time
- Parasite Cleanse – see Section V
- BF&C fomentations – make a decoction of BF&C or Comfrey –
  soak a cloth in it – place over the heart – keep the fomentation
  warm and moist

Other Modalities:
- DIET, DIET, DIET – clean it up!!
- EXERCISE – get some!

Following is the story of a heart surgeon, Dr. Willix, who decided
he wasn't curing his patients, he was simply prolonging their
death:

I had to learn about the secret key to good health by
going through an experience that quite literally changed my
life. I don't want to go through anything like that again,
but I'm grateful for the experience. I believe that it helped
save my life – and the lives of my patients. It prompted me
to put down my knife after years of being one of the
country's leading cardiac surgeons . . . and take a whole
new approach to medicine.

That approach was revolutionary when I started it a
decade ago. Today more and more doctors are catching on,
but it's going to take a long time for that great ocean liner
of traditional medicine to steer back on course. In the
meantime, millions of Americans are going to die of
cancer, lung disease, and heart disease – when instead they
might have lived to a healthy 120 or more.

. . . I was a stressed-out, 225 pound heart surgeon with a
smoking habit that should have killed me. . . When I got to
medical school, I learned a lot about the sick. In fact, I
picked up a prescription for bad health the day I walked
through the doors of the University of Missouri, hell-bent

on being a "success". I worked day and night. I wanted to know everything – and I wanted to know it better than anyone.

Then after four grueling years of medical school, I got my medical degree and headed for the University of Michigan Medical Center for my residency in surgery. This resident program was well-known, prestigious, and tough to get into. Only 24 young doctors were admitted to my class. As it turned out, it was even tougher to stay in the program. As many as 16 of the 24 in my class were asked to leave because they didn't measure up to the program's high standards.

That was in the 1960's and back then "traditional medicine" was opening up a fantastic brave new world in surgery.

. . . But I didn't want to be just any surgeon. I wanted to be the Top Gun: a heart surgeon. That's what the big pioneers wanted to be in those days, because, for the first time, we were attempting to perform surgery on an open heart.

. . . After finishing my residency, I devoted my professional life to this brave new world of open-heart surgery.

I moved to South Dakota, where I developed the first heart-surgery program in the state and became the only board certified cardiac surgeon in all of South Dakota. I received accolades and awards. I had my own practice. The money was good. In fact, I was getting rich. I had a wife and two children. I had a big home. An expensive car. I had all the things that proved I was a huge success. Right? Well, maybe . . .

Meanwhile, my personal life was going to hell. And so was my health. While I was working as a big-shot surgeon, my weight shot up to 225 pounds. I smoked a pack-and-a-half a day. I ate anything and everything I could get my hands on. I'd have two or three highballs, whenever I didn't have patients to care for. I spent almost 24 hours a day indoors, working. I had a "fluorescent tan." I wasn't enjoying life; I was careening toward an early death. . .

Today I know that, somewhere deep down inside me, the realization was growing: What I was doing as a surgeon was NOT really improving peoples' health. The truth was that many of my patients were dying – as were the patients of every other heart surgeon. But I wasn't quite ready to face that. Like most other cardiac surgeons, I was deep in 'doctor denial.'

You have to understand that it's extremely difficult for a doctor to admit that what he or she is doing isn't really saving lives. Our rigorous years of medical training teach us that we ARE saving lives. That's what our careers are all about. And we have to believe that going into an operating room. You wouldn't want a surgeon with second thoughts about his abilities operating on you, would you? Of course not!

I'd probably performed more than a thousand coronary bypass operations. But I was beginning to find that a great many of my patients were back on the operating table within three to five years. Many of the others were dead.

And even those who "got well" were never the same again. The sad fact was that in all my years as a doctor, I never saw anyone go through cardiac surgery and come out the same. There are personality changes, memory loss . . . a transformation happens in the operating room that changes the patient forever.

These thoughts must have been running through my head on the day I had the experience that turned my life around.

The day began like any other. I woke up from my cot in the hospital locker room that all doctors used. (We kept cots there for the workaholics like me). I woke up, lit up a cigarette, found a cup of coffee, and went over the first chart of the morning. Heart attack victim.

The patient was a man in his middle 50s. His name sounded familiar, but I didn't think much of it at the time. I looked down the list of risk factors: overweight, smoker, stressful job, workaholic. Of course, now, I realize that every one of those risk factors applied to me. At the time, I didn't think about it. I kept reading. After all, my job was to replace a valve in his heart . . . not internalize the case history.

In the operating room, the other doctors and nurses were preparing this guy. . . They were basically sawing the guy's chest in half. That's what we have to do in open-heart surgery. Then, they stopped his heart and kept him alive with tubes and wires that ran into the heart-lung machine. When they had done all that, they were ready for me. The big man on campus. The surgeon. I scrubbed, got into my latex gloves, and picked up my scalpel as I had hundreds of times before. And I prepared to replace the valve.

And then it happened -- . . . it hit me. I knew this man. He'd been on that same table just a few months before. And I thought of all my other heart patients who'd come across my table more than once. They had a lot in common.

MY HEART PATIENTS WERE A LOT LIKE ME
- Almost all my heart patients were over 45
- Nearly every one was a smoker
- They were all overweight
- Most were classic workaholics
- Some drank too much
- Most didn't have time for their families
- Nearly every one was unhappy and depressed
- They didn't take care of themselves
- They didn't enjoy life
- They were at high risk for – early death

I looked down at that man who was unconscious, with all kinds of tubes running in and out of him. His chest was pulled apart. His heart was hooked up to a big machine. His family was hugging and crying in the waiting room, not knowing if they'd ever see him alive again. I couldn't even tell you for sure at that moment that he'd ever go home again – much less stay alive much longer. He was in terrible shape. He was as near death as one can be without being six feet under. And for the first time, at age 34, I realized that I would soon be in that same situation if I didn't do something quickly to change my life.

. . . I forced myself to realize what my subconscious already knew: Heart surgery didn't cure my patients – it just prolonged their deaths. That man had already been on my operating table once – and this time, he easily might not make it off alive. I hadn't helped him get his health back . . . I'd just slowed down his death.

I knew then that the same slow death awaited me – if I continued to treat my body and my health the way I had been. I'd be flat on my back in the O.R. Just one more patient who didn't care enough about himself to protect his health.

At that moment . . . it all came together. It 'clicked.' I realized that what I was doing as a doctor really wasn't improving my patients' health. I wasn't telling them how to regain their health . . . I was trying to "fix" them after they had broken down. I was like some sort of glorified auto mechanic. Except that instead of working on cars, I was working on human bodies. Unfortunately, the human body doesn't work the way a car does. It's far more complex.

The awful truth was . . . my patients who went through surgery ended up going home – if they were lucky! – and resuming the same old bad habits that brought them to my operating room in the first place.

I had known this all along. But for some reason, until that moment, it hadn't sunk in! My patients were going back out and doing the very same things that led to their heart disease. What chance did they have to get healthy?

I finished surgery that day. And although I didn't realize it at the time . . . that was the beginning of the end of my career as a surgeon. I was about to hang up my knife for good. That moment in the operating room convinced me that I could no longer in good conscience continue to practice medicine the way I had been taught in medical school. I knew I had to change my life and my outlook.

I successfully replaced this man's valve, and then I vowed I was going to teach him – and myself – how to get healthy. I wanted both of us to learn how to enjoy life to the fullest possible extent and to stay healthy at the same time. I didn't want to let heart disease, or cancer, or lung disease kill either one of us – and I knew I didn't EVER want to be on that table in the O.R.

I went home that day a changed person. But my change was just beginning. I knew there was something I had to find. Something inside me that held the answer.

In a lot of ways, our grandparents and great-grandparents were far wiser than we are today. They had faith in Mother Nature. They knew there were foods you could eat that were good for you . . . they knew that spending time in the great outdoors was healthy.

What happened to all their good advice?

Well, in the 20th century, we doctors got a little arrogant. We thought we could invent pills and surgical procedures that would do a far better job than nature could do. We thought relying on natural cures was "old-fashioned." In addition, I think we all had a certain fear that natural cures might put us out of business.

I'm the first to say that some surgical procedures . . . and some pills . . . save lives. But there are a lot of surgeries and a lot of prescriptions that are truly unnecessary. In fact, there are some that are downright dangerous.

These are things I couldn't have said before I had the experience I described. It took me some time – and a lot of research – to see the truth because it went against nearly all of my high-tech medical training.

The day after I had the experience in that Operating Room, I started researching the ways – other than surgery – that might help me keep my heart patients from having to go under the knife. I wanted to find a way to get them back to health.

. . . at the time I started putting together the results of all this research, I had a group of patients in my care who were on their way to surgery . . . or heart attacks. Whichever came first. Each of them had been diagnosed with clogged arteries. Each of them had been told he or she should undergo surgery.

And all of them were in pretty rough shape. Some couldn't walk up a flight of stairs without wheezing. Some were smokers. Most had no energy for sex. In some cases, the drugs they took made a satisfying sex life impossible. Some were depressed. Several were workaholics. Not one of them was living the life he or she wanted to be living.

I vowed to come up with a strategy that would get them – and me – healthy again.

. . . I asked each of my patients to stop smoking . . . and give me one year. I told them I thought I could help them keep from having either surgery or heart attacks.

And so, these patients and I embarked on our campaign to get healthy.

There were basically four parts to it. The first was information. We set up a system for letting one another know about the results of the latest medical research on the body's ability to heal itself . . .

The second part of our campaign was to put our bodies back to work for us.

. . . We started taking walks together. You have to understand that at first, not all my patients could walk very far at all. It was an effort for some of them to walk even one block. But after just a few days, every one of them got stronger.

. . . Then, we moved on to lifting small weights. . . Some of us began riding bicycles again, for the first time since we were teenagers. It was like taking 25 years off our lives!

. . . My patients reported they were interested in sex again.

. . . The third part of our campaign involved changes in the way we looked at food – and vitamins. Because the foods we eat . . . and the vitamins we give our bodies . . . play an extremely important role in the level of health we enjoy.

. . . The fourth part of our campaign was to get rid of some of the stress in our lives. Each of us approached this challenge differently. Some members of the group started going to church. Others began taking time out of each day to meditate. Some just cut back the number of hours they spent at work. . .

. . . we all went through the medical tests designed to determine our state of health. We underwent all of them – treadmill tests, cholesterol tests, blood tests, etc. And sure enough, the medical tests proved what we already suspected: All seven of us were much healthier than we'd been when we started. After just one year of healthier lifestyles, not one of my patients needed surgery! And most had been able to stop taking their expensive prescription drugs.

. . . As a result of all the time I spent working with my team of patients, I was inspired to continue on my own health program. My progress came so quickly and it made me feel so much better about myself that I wanted to step it up a notch.

I went running – for the first time in about 20 years. Then, with the encouragement of a friend, I entered a three-mile race. I felt terrible after that first competition, because I was still out of shape. But I decided to keep at it.

I began jogging on a regular basis. I don't recommend this for everyone, because it is so strenuous. But it worked for me. My weight dropped to 165 pounds! I felt incredible.

Within six months, I entered my first marathon – a distance of 26.2 miles. And finally, in 1984, I fulfilled a dream of competing in the Ironman Triathalon in Hawaii.

. . . My experience had a dramatic impact on my life. It liberated me from traditional unhealthy ways of thinking. But the bottom line is that it taught me that I have much greater control over my health and my life than I had believed. And I've seen this same transformation in many of my patients. . . I believe Mother Nature, in her eminent wisdom, provided us with almost everything we need to stay healthy. Of course, if something catastrophic happens, we may still need a hospital. But when it comes to retaining the good health we were born with . . . Mother Nature has most of the answers (Willix 3-40).

It should go without saying, by now, if you are going to work on a serious heart condition, you must be serious about using a good diet, good supplements and a good exercise program. An excellent book to read on this subject is *Left for Dead* by Dick Quinn.

Experience:
a) Section I, pg. 36

HEARING LOSS

In *Herbal Home Health Care,* Dr. Christopher put together a wonderful herbal combination to help restore hearing and repair nerve damage in the central nervous system.

When this procedure is used as explained here, it can be an aid in assisting an improvement of poor equilibrium, failure of hearing, aiding the motor nerve, etc. With an eye dropper insert into each ear at night four to six drops of oil of garlic and four to six drops of the following herb tincture, B&B, plugging ears overnight with cotton, six days a week, four to six months, or as needed. On the seventh day, flush ears with a small ear syringe using warm apple cider vinegar and distilled water half and half. (178)

Herbal Aids:
- B&B Tincture - put 4 – 6 drops in each ear at night
- Garlic Oil – put 4 – 6 drops in each ear at night

HEMORRHAGE

Hemorrhaging is very serious bleeding. Using these herbs and good first aid techniques can help to keep the bleeding under control while you get additional help .

Herbal Aids:
- Cayenne
  - 1 tsp. of powder in a glass of water
  - use tincture straight or in water
  - 2-4 capsules
- Shepherds Purse Tincture – dropper full under the tongue as needed
- Shock Tea – use during labor and childbirth or any time someone is displaying signs of shock
  - made with a cup of hot water
  - lemon and honey to taste
  - ten or more drops of Cayenne tincture

Other Modalities:
- Apply Pressure – when dealing with a wound
- Ice – in the case of uterine bleeding, putting ice on the uterus will sometimes help to restrict the blood flow
- Bimanual Compression – in severe cases of uterine bleeding after childbirth – if the placenta has been delivered – you may need to put a fist up in the birth canal against the cervix and then apply pressure externally on the top of the uterus, so that the uterus is compressed between both hands (hopefully, you will have a midwife present who knows how to do this procedure)

Experiences:
a) Section I, pg. 54
b) Section II, pg. 170
c) Section III, pg. 227

d) Section III, pg. 234

e) A friend of ours called us about a serious nosebleed. She had already taken several Cayenne capsules and it hadn't stopped, so I suggested putting some Professor Cayenne™ directly on her nose and then using some ice to restrict the blood flow. This seemed to bring it under control.

Two or three more times, something would trigger this serious nose bleed. Each time she was able to bring it under control with Cayenne and pressure. When she went to the doctor to see what was causing the problem, he told her she had an open vein hanging in her nose just like an open hose. He was amazed she had been able to control the bleeding at all.

HEMORRHOIDS

Bowel movements have to be kept soft in order for hemorrhoids to heal. This can be done with fresh juices, raw foods with lots of roughage, and/or herbal stool softeners. Each time the bowels move, the hemorrhoids need to be pushed back up inside with the BF&C ointment. If they are extremely sore and swollen (like after childbirth), then wearing a sanitary pad which has been soaked in BF&C tea, and frozen may be helpful. Cold tends to take the swelling down and help numb them.

Herbal Aids:
- Hemorrhoid Sitz Bath – make into a tea and then sit in it to shrink hemorrhoids
- BF&C ointment – use directly on hemorrhoids
- Enema – use the Yellow Dock Combination in a syringe to inject rectally – see "Slant Board Routine", pg 194.
- Herbal LB - take two or more capsules three times per day until you are having at least two comfortable bowel movements per day
- BF&C Pad – make BF&C tea – dip a sanitary pad into it – lay on wax paper on a cookie sheet – put into freezer – when frozen, use to help shrink swelling

Other Modalities:
- Diet – Wrong diet, overeating, intoxicating liquors, tobacco, spices of various kinds, white bread, sugar, fried foods, and all acid

forming foods which cause fermentation. This wrong, devitalized diet causes constipation, clogs the liver, causes an impure blood stream, and irritates the stomach and intestines. Taking of ordinary purgatives that are on the market is also a cause, as they irritate the membranous lining of the bowels and intestines (Kloss 481).
- Ice Pack – helps to reduce inflammation
- Foot Stool – keep near toilet to put your feet up on – this puts the body in a more natural squatting position and relieves the pressure on the hemorrhoids

HIGH BLOOD PRESSURE
(See Blood Pressure)

HORMONAL IMBALANCE

Many people suffer from hormonal imbalances, with symptoms including mood swings, weight gain, headaches, bloating, menstrual cramps, agitation, depression, and many others. Again, most of these problems can be traced right back to diet! Part of the problem is not getting enough live, raw foods in the diet along with enough pure water. Another problem is that a lot of our foods are missing many of the important nutrients because of poor soil conditions. If you are eating too much meat and dairy, the chemicals you are taking in are reeking havoc with your chemical balance.

When dealing with teenagers, I tend to use the teas. If you will make up a gallon of the red raspberry and/or blessed thistle tea in the morning – keep it in the refrigerator, they will learn to enjoy drinking iced tea.

Women should take two capsules each of the NuFem, Changease, and Wheat Germ Oil three times per day.

So many women today are being put on synthetic hormone replacement therapy. There are several problems with these programs. First, it is extremely difficult to know how much of each hormone may be out of balance in the body, so how can you know what to "replace" it with? Second, when you give the body something it should be making itself, it will quit making it.

Thirdly, the source of these synthetic hormones is frightening. We would be much further ahead to give the body what it needs and let it do what it was created to do.

Men can use the same formula or Dr. Christopher recommends the False Unicorn and Lobelia formula taken with wheat germ oil, especially in cases where a couple is dealing with infertility problems. Like so many other conditions, depending on the seriousness of the problem, you may need to look at cleansing and alkalizing the whole system.

Herbal Aids:
- Changease Capsules – two capsules three times per day with Wheat Germ Oil to help balance hormones. In the *School of Natural Healing,* we learn that Dr Christopher based this formula on false unicorn. Following are his recommendations:
  > He recommended it for puberty, pregnancy, nursing and menopause, including 'male menopause.' The herbs in Changease provide precursors to hormones, which the body can easily convert to the hormones that it requires. Synthetic hormones, on the other hand, cannot be completely assimilated by the body. They may be stored in the body tissues, with potentially serious side effects. (xxi)
- Wheat Germ Oil – take two capsules or one tablespoon three times per day
- NuFem - two capsules three times per day to cleanse and rebuild female organs
- Cleansing – use some type of cleansing program to cleanse excess chemicals from body
- Red Raspberry Leaf Tea – drink three glasses per day
- Red Raspberry Leaf and Blessed Thistle Tea – drink three glasses per day
- False Unicorn and Lobelia - two capsules three times per day
- Wheat Grass Juice – drink two to four ounces per day
- Barleans Essentially for Women Oils – this is a combination of oils which include flax and evening primrose oil – many times we are not getting enough of the right kinds of fat in our diet to produce the hormones we need
- Organa Minerals - one cap full per day in water or juice to get enough trace minerals in the diet

Juices:
- Rejuvenator – From the *Sunfood Diet,* Wolfe shares the recipe for a juice to help rejuvenate us:

1 bunch of kale
4-6 ribs of celery
1 cucumber
1 burdock root
1-2 apples (optional)

   Burdock root is a blood purifier and an excellent base to help the body create hormones. Burdock contains one of the highest amounts of organic iron in any food. Kale provides a dense source of alkaline minerals. Cucumber and celery soften the taste. Apples may be added to sweeten (although better results occur without them). This is, all-around, the most effective juice combination I have found. This is a great juice to drink everyday. (478)

Other Modalities:
  - Diet – more live foods and less processed material
  - Water – drink at least three quarts of water per day

Experiences:

a) Section II, pg. 170
b) Section IV, pg. 347
c) Shortly after I started studying with "The School of Natural Healing" I wanted to correct my own hormone imbalance. My periods were extremely irregular. In fact, I was so messed up, that I thought I might be going into menopause.

   In order to find out what was going on, I went to a doctor and asked him to do some blood tests to see if that was actually the case. When the test results came back, he said I had the blood work of a twenty year old and was no where near menopause. Then I knew my hormones were definitely out of balance.

   I began using the NuFem and Changease formulas with a tablespoon of Wheat Germ Oil three times per day. The problem came when I found out what Wheat Germ oil tastes like – it was some of the nastiest stuff I had ever tried to choke down. I even tried dipping fresh cucumbers and tomatoes in it, but all I succeeded in doing was ruining perfectly good produce, so I stopped using the Wheat Germ oil and just used the herbs.

After a couple of months, I really hadn't seen much improvement with my condition. This was frustrating because every other Dr. Christopher formula I had ever used seemed to work quickly and well. I didn't understand how he could have been so inspired with the other formulas and fail so miserably with the womens formulas. I finally went to one of the instructors at the school to see what his opinion was. He pointed out that I was not following the instructions – I was not using the Wheat Germ oil. In order for the body to take the precursors or building blocks from the Changease and chemically convert them into hormones, it needs the Wheat Germ oil. I soon discovered that some genius had put Wheat Germ oil into capsules, so I began using them and found that when I followed the complete instructions – I was able to get the promised results.

HYPERACTIVITY

This topic is one of my "pet peeves." When I was a young child I know I had enough energy for ten children. The reason I know this is because my memory is full of phrases such as: "Would you slow down?" "Would you be careful?" "Watch where you're going!" "You're like a bull in a China closet!" "Be quiet!" "Be careful!"

Well, you get the idea. My point is this – if I had not been born with that kind of energy, I would never have been able to raise 13 children along with all of the strays we took in along the way, teach classes, serve in the community, deliver babies, serve in my church, give lectures around the country, write this book, etc., etc. .

When I teach classes on this subject, I often put a list of careers on the board, such as: school teacher, plumber, astronaut, computer technician, football player, baker, hair dresser. Then I ask the question: Which of these careers is the right one? Obviously, the answer is; ALL OF THEM. Each one is different. Each one is unique and each one takes a different type of personality to fill it. The world needs all of them. Therefore, why are we so intent on making clones out of all of our children by drugging them?

Herbal Aids:
- Herbal or Whole Food Supplement – it is extremely difficult for a growing child to get all of the vitamins and minerals they need out of food which is grown in depleted soils, so you need to find supplements which are made from whole foods or whole plants – not something that is chemically formulated in a factory
- MindTrac - two or more capsules three times per day to help calm and balance chemistry
- PreTrac - two or more capsules three times per day to help cleanse the liver
- Kid-E-Trac - 1 – 3 dropper fulls three times per day (MindTrac in a vegetable glycerin base for children)

Juices:
- Wheat Grass Juice – put 1 – 2 ounces into pineapple juice, apple juice or any other kind of juice children will enjoy – I like to use unsweetened pineapple, a fresh banana, fresh wheat grass juice, and some ice cubes to make a smoothie – the children love it
- Fresh Fruit & Vegetable Juices – give them as much concentrated, fresh nutrition as you can possibly work into their diet

Other Modalities:
- Diet – stay away from processed foods and sugars as much as possible
- Exercise – make sure these children have a constructive way to release their energy – give them plenty of exercise in the fresh air

Experience:
a) When Juanita, our daughter, was doing her student teaching for her degree in elementary education, she taught in a class where 65% of the children were on Ritalin. This is absolutely criminal! The schools get extra money when the children are placed on drugs, so, naturally, they have a vested interest in making sure that as many as possible are taking them. In this particular school there was a lot of poverty, one parent homes and other problems creating dysfunctional families. The problem was not that these children needed drugs, they needed to be loved. They

needed someone to pay attention to them. They needed
something decent to eat.

In *Toxic Psychiatry,* Dr Breggin shares his views on Ritalin:

> . . . we do know that stimulants are highly addictive
> and often abused as illegal drugs, called speed and
> uppers. The Drug Enforcement Administration
> (DEA) put Ritalin and other psychostimulants in
> Class II, along with morphine, barbiturates, and
> other prescription drugs that have a high potential
> for addiction or abuse. Goodman and Gilman's
> 'The Pharmacological Basis of Therapeutics
> (1985)' points out that Ritalin is "structurally
> related to amphetamine" and says simply, 'Its
> pharmacological properties are essentially the same
> as those of the amphetamines' (p.586). It considers
> Ritalin among the highly addictive drugs.
>
> . . . In the 1960's and early 1970's an epidemic
> of psychostimulant abuse spread over America and
> a number of other industrial nations. In response
> the Health, Education and Welfare, published a
> large compendium or 150 studies dealing with the
> abuse of amphetamines and related drugs, including
> Ritalin, making clear the seriousness of the then-
> rising epidemic and the government's concern about
> stemming it. Yet estimates of the size of that
> epidemic of drug abuse do not approach the
> highwater mark of up to one million children now
> taking Ritalin.
>
> One study in the compendium, authored by
> P.H.Connell and reprinted from the 1966 journal of
> the American Medical Association, states that the
> regular ingestion of only two or three tablets a day
> constitutes abuse and that the self-abuser 'would
> certainly be better off without them.' This limited
> use of the medication, described as abuse, is
> exceeded frequently in the routine treatment of
> children.

    . . . The drugging of children seems to garner far more public sympathy than the forced drugging of adults. On June 10, 1988, Ted Koppel's 'ABC News Nightline' estimated that 800,000 children were taking Ritalin and that its production had doubled in recent years. The subject of the show is nine-year-old Casey Jesson, whose school system told him to take Ritalin as a part of its 'educational plan.' When Casey's parents protested, the New Hampshire Department of Education upheld the school's decision.

    The superintendent of schools appeared on 'Nightline' to affirm the school's right to insist on medication. What other alternative did Superintendent Brown offer the parents? "They have the right to withdraw their child from school."

    Intimidating parents into drugging their children is a common practice around the United States, especially among the poor and minority groups. There are cases in which schools have obtained Ritalin and given it to children without parental knowledge or permission. (306-312)

b) In addition to hyper-activity, I have a real problem with all of the labels that are being placed on our children. I have found that what some people term "attention deficit" is nothing more than an intelligent child who is bored to death. If you place that same child in front of a computer game or an Nintendo, they can play for hours. That is not an attention problem. It is a problem of not being challenged enough.

    Again, from *Toxic Psychiatry*, we read about the effects of using drugs to treat these problems:

    . . . There is reason to be concerned about brain tissue shrinkage as a result of long-term Ritalin therapy, similar to that associated with neuroleptic treatment. A 1986 study by Henry Nasrallah and his colleagues of 'Cortical Atrophy in Young

Adults with a History of Hyperactivity,' published in *Psychiatric Research*, found the brain pathology in more than half of twenty-four young adults. Since all of the patients had been treated with psychostimulants, 'cortical atrophy may be a long-term adverse effect of this treatment' (p. 245). One study is suggestive rather than conclusive, but there remains a cause for concern. It bears repeating that the use of any potent psychoactive drug is not good for the brain.

Our difficulty in raising children often is complicated by the stresses of our own adult lives. Many parents, especially single mothers, live in poverty; many families grow up amid racism; and all children and adults suffer from the effects of sexism and male supremacy. Many marriages are torn by conflicts that frighten and confuse the children.

When our children finally go off to school, it is often to a more unsatisfactory situation than the one at home within the family. Typically children are forced to endure long, boring hours in regimented classrooms that give almost no attention to their personal needs or unique attributes. In many schools children are beaten and humiliated as a means of control.

Child abuse and neglect are rampant. Instead of covering up this tragedy with diagnoses, drugs, and hospitals, psychiatry should be leading the society toward a more sympathetic understanding of the plight of children. Given what we've seen in this book, there's no chance that the profession can make such a turnaround in the imaginable future. (308 & 314)

We need to recognize that each of our children are unique and different. Thank goodness!! They all need to be fed good, wholesome food, they need to be loved and they need to be anxiously engaged in positive challenges. If they have a lot of extra energy, then learn how to help them channel it in a positive way. These are the "shakers and movers" of tomorrow. Let's make sure they are ready to move the world in a positive direction. Ritalin is the only drug I know of that went from the street to the doctor's office, instead of the other way around. Think twice or ten times before committing these precious lives to a life-time of drugs.

Many candles can be kindled from one candle
without diminishing it.
-- The Midrash

We make a living by what we get,
but we make a life by what we give.
-- Winston Churchhill

Considering the joylessness of many schools with their authoritarian structures,
It is fair to speculate that hyperactivity may be a "normal" response
-- indeed, even a healthy reaction --
to an intolerable situation.
-- J. Larry Brown and Stephen R. Bing (1976)

I

INFERTILITY

According to recent statistics this problem is affecting one out of every six couples. Like so many other conditions, there can be many reasons for this problem. Nutrition is definitely one of them. I have seen several couples who had had infertility problems for years be able to conceive after one or two cycles just by changing their diets and balancing their hormones. If our bodies become too acidic, vaginal fluid actually kills sperm before it fertilizes the egg. If a man's body is too acidic or out of balance, it can yield a low sperm count or cause the sperm to be too weak.

If you are having a difficult time achieving a pregnancy, the first problem I would address is diet and using the supplements needed to bring the hormones into balance. If you still do not become pregnant after two to four cycles, then I would start "charting." In order to do this, you will need to get a basal thermometer. Put the thermometer by your bed, so when you wake up in the morning, before you get up or do anything else, you can reach for the thermometer and take your temperature. Record your results daily, making sure you note it to the tenth of a degree. You will notice that somewhere during the month your temperature goes up and stays up until just before your period starts again. That rise in temperature signifies you have ovulated. Unfortunately, the best time to get pregnant was probably the day before you saw the rise, so it is important to chart for more than one month in order to see your pattern.

Taking Charge of Your Fertility by Toni Weschler explains how to chart your basal temperature, along with the changes in your vaginal fluid during your cycles, and the different positions of the cervix. It is an excellent book to help you discover your fertile time. Women are only fertile for a short time each month. Depending on your age, it could range from a couple of hours to four days, so it is important to know this time.

If you are planning on becoming pregnant soon – start now with the nutrition and exercise you need to stay healthy and to give your baby the nutrition he or she will need during your pregnancy.

Herbal Aids:
- NuFem, Changease, & Wheat Germ Oil – two capsules of each three times per day to balance hormones
- VB and Yellow Dock Combination - see Section V for instructions on how to do "Slant Board Routine."
- Herbal Supplements – find a good supplement made from herbs and/or whole foods
- Red Raspberry Leaf Tea – drink three or more glasses per day
- False Unicorn & Lobelia - take two capsules three times per day with Wheat Germ oil
- Organa Minerals - make sure you are getting enough trace minerals in your diet
- Barleans Essentially for Women - make sure your are getting the right kinds of fats and oils in your diet

Juices:
- Wheat Grass Juice – drink two to four ounces per day – may want to douche with the juice routinely to strengthen the uterus and female organs

Other Modalities:
- Diet – incorporate more live foods and juices
- Exercise – get in some form of exercise every day
- Water – drink at least three quarts of pure water per day
- Charting – see explanation above

Experience:
a) When I got married, it took me over a year to get pregnant with my first child. I was beginning to think I would never be able to have any children, so I went to a gynecologist to find out what the problem was. Before putting me through any extensive testing, he gave me a prescription for some powder that I was to mix with warm water and douche with before making love. The first month I used it, I became pregnant. He explained it was to neutralize the acid in the vaginal fluid. How grateful I am for a doctor who kept it simple.

IMMUNIZATIONS

Since the late 1950's most children who have grown up in the United States, have marched down like obedient sheep to their doctor or health clinic to receive all of the required immunizations, being taught that failure to do so is irresponsible. It is not uncommon to have a child run a fever of a 104 and above, or to see a child's leg become extremely swollen and painful, only to have a doctor tell you this is a normal reaction to an immunization.

Today parents are beginning to ask whether or not they should immunize their children. Study out the pros and cons of available research before making a decision that could have a powerful impact on your child's life. We should not assume that the billboards we see along the freeway, "Immunize by two, it's up to you" are the last words on the subject.

Questions we might want to ask are: Do immunizations really protect my child against disease? Are they safe and what are the risks to my child if I don't immunize him/her?

As a parent searching for some of these answers, Neal Z. Miller wrote a book entitled *Vaccines: Are They Really Safe and Effective?* It was time for his children to be immunized and he decided to explore the issue before blindly subjecting his children to these procedures. He said,

> In an earlier draft of this book I included two personal and highly emotional accounts from anguished parents describing how a particular vaccine damaged their child. Some critics voiced disapproval at this practice, claiming an appeal to the emotions has no place in a fact-finding search. However, . . . the truth has been obscured for too long. I don't see anything wrong with permitting my readers to feel their pain. In fact, I hope you become as outraged as I am. Real children are being damaged and dying, and real parents are having to cope with their disabilities and deaths. (14)

In this quote, Miller is referring to children being damaged and dying. Why is this happening if immunizations are safe and effective?

In *Confessions of a Medical Heretic,* Dr. Robert S. Mendelsohn says,

> If you follow the sounds of medical-governmental drum-beating in favor of a 'preventive' procedure, you'll more

often than not find yourself in the midst of one or more of the Church's least safe and effective sacraments. For instance, with some immunizations the danger in taking the shot may out weigh that of not taking it. (143)

According to the VAERS (Vaccine Adverse Effects Reporting System), they receive about 1,000 reports of serious adverse reactions to vaccinations annually, some 1% (112+) of which are deaths from vaccine reactions (Nat'l Technical Information Service 2).

Well, maybe if vaccinations are really effective, it might be worth a 1% chance of death to risk the vaccination. However, according to the Dayton Daily News:

> The FDA estimates that only 10% of adverse reactions are reported. In fact, the NVIC reported that: in New York, only one out of 40 doctor's offices (2.5%) confirmed that they report a death or injury following vaccinations, -- 97.5% of vaccine related deaths and disabilities go unreported there – these findings suggest that vaccine deaths actually occurring each year may well be over 1,000. (Severyn 8)

Why are we willing to take these kinds of chances with our children? Are these immunizations really for their best good? Maybe we take these chances due to our ignorance or maybe due to deceit on the part of those we trust.

Doctors and scientists on the staff of the National Institute of Health during the 1950's were well aware that the Salk vaccine was ineffective and deadly. Some frankly stated that it was,

> . . . worthless as a preventive and dangerous to take. They refused to vaccinate their own children. Even Dr. Salk himself was quoted as saying: "When you inoculate children with a polio vaccine you don't sleep well for two or three weeks." But the National Foundation for Infantile Paralysis, and pharmaceutical companies with a large investment in the vaccine (i.e. Parke-Davis), coerced the U.S. Public Health Service into signing a false proclamation claiming the vaccine was safe and 100 percent effective. (Miller 21)

In 1976, Jonas Salk, creator of the killed-virus vaccine used throughout the 1950's, testified that the live-virus vaccine (used almost exclusively in the United States since the early 1960's) was, "the principle, if not sole cause" of all reported polio cases in the United States since 1961. "The virus remains in the throat for one to two weeks and in the feces for up to tow months. Thus, vaccine recipients are at risk, and are potentially contagious, as long as fecal excretion continues" (Miller 21).

We have all heard on the news that immunizations have definitely been linked to autism. Is it possible that other disorders and diseases could also be linked to childhood immunizations? Medical historian, researcher and author Harris Coulter revealed that childhood immunizations are:

> . . . causing a low-grade encephalitis in infants on a much wider scale than public health authorities were willing to admit, about 15-20% of all children. He points out that the sequelae (conditions known to result from a disease) of encephalitis (inflammation of the brain, a known side-effect of vaccinations); autism, learning disorders, sexual disorders, asthma, crib death, diabetes, obesity, and impulsive violence are precisely the disorders which afflict contemporary society. Many of these conditions were formerly relatively rare, but they have become more common as childhood vaccination programs have expanded. Coulter also points out that ". . . pertussis toxoid is used to create encephalitis in lab animals." (Phillips 10)

SIDS (sudden infant death syndrome) is found to have a close correlation to immunizations. According to Dr. Mendelsohn in *Confessions of a Medical Heretic:*

> One study found the peak incidence of SIDS occurred at the ages of 2 and 4 months in the U.S., precisely when the first two routine immunizations are given, while another found a clear pattern of correlation extending three weeks after immunization . . . while another researcher's studies led to the conclusion that half of SIDS cases, that would be 2500 to 5000 infant deaths in the U.S. each year . . . are caused by vaccines. (143)

If truly half of all SIDS deaths are being caused due to immunizations, this is a very significant number!

Even in cases where death does not result, they report other significant consequences. Another doctor's report for attorneys found that 1 in 300 DPT immunizations resulted in seizures (Community Relations 3). Let's turn again to Dr. Mendelsohn:

> Diptheria, once an important cause of disease and death, has all but disappeared. Yet immunizations continue. Even when a rare outbreak of diphtheria does occur, the immunization can be of questionable value. During a 1969 outbreak of diphtheria in Chicago, four of the sixteen victims had been 'fully immunized against the disease,' according to the Chicago Board of Health. Five others had received one or more doses of the vaccine, and two of these people had tested at full immunity. In another report of diphtheria cases, three of which were fatal, one person who died and fourteen out of twenty-three carriers had been fully immunized. (143)

If we can assume these immunizations are dangerous, then what are the risks involved in not taking them? The British medical Journal reports:

> . . . that England actually saw a drop in pertussis deaths when vaccination rates dropped form 80% to 30% in the mid 70's. His study of pertussis vaccine efficacy and toxicity around the world found that 'pertussis –associated mortality is currently very low in industrialized countries and no difference can be discerned when countries with high, low, and zero immunization rates were compared.' He also found that England, Wales and W. Germany had more pertussis fatalities in 1970 when the immunization rate was high than during the last half of 1980, when rates had fallen. (Rabo)

It was reported in the McLavaney newsletter, after the Gulf War, that the only country who was not suffering from "Gulf War Syndrome" was France. They were also the only country in the war that did not immunize their soldiers.

We are often told that measles is a dangerous disease to allow our children to have, so we give them the MMR vaccine. However in a report from the Department of Internal Medicine we learn:

We are finding in the U.S. that the apparent paradox is that as measles immunization rates rise to high levels in a population, measles becomes a disease of immunized persons. Among school-aged children, measles outbreaks have occurred in schools with vaccination levels of greater than 98 percent. They have occurred in all parts of the country, including areas that had not reported measles for years. The CDC even reported a measles outbreak in a documented 100 percent vaccinated population. (4)

If we decide that these routine immunizations are not effective and can be downright dangerous, should we be concerned about our children contracting these diseases and are there things we can do to help prevent the diseases from happening?

According to the Center for Disease Control:

Most childhood infectious diseases have few serious consequences in today's modern world, conservative CDC statistics for Pertussis during 1992-1994 indicate a 99.8% recovery rate. In fact, when hundreds of Pertussis cases occurred in Chicago in the fall 1993 outbreak, an infectious disease expert from Cincinnati Children's Hospital said the disease was very mild, no one died, and no one went to the intensive care unit. (Phillips 8)

During the polio epidemic of 1948, Dr. Benjamin Sandler, a nutritional expert at the Oteen Veterans' Hospital, detailed a relationship between polio and an excessive consumption of sugar and starches. He compiled records of the countries with high sugar intake and high rates of polio. He claimed that such foods dehydrate the cells and leech calcium from the nerves, muscles, bones, and teeth. (A serious calcium deficiency precedes polio) Researchers know that polio strikes with the greatest intensity during the hot summer months. Dr. Sandler observed that children consume greater amounts of ice cream, soda, and sweets in hot weather. In 1949, before the polio season, he warned the residents of N. Carolina through newspaper and radio to decrease consumption of these products. During that summer N. Carolina residents reduced their intake of sugar by 90% and polio decreased by 90%. In 1948, there were 2,498 cases of polio. In 1949, there were 229 cases of polio. The powerful Rockefeller Milk Trust, sold frozen products to N.C., then combined forces with the Coca Cola power merchants and convinced the people that Sandler's findings were a myth and the polio figures a fluke. In 1950, sales and polio were back to "normal."

Why do we never hear about any of these complications or dangers? In his book, Neal Miller reports:

In spite of these findings, I was even more shocked to learn that many powerful individuals with the organized medical profession – the Medical-Industrial complex – including influential members of the World Health Organization (WHO), the American Medical Association (AMA), the American Academy of Pediatrics (AAP), the Federal Centers for Disease Control (CDC), the Food and Drug Administration (FDA), major medical journals, hospitals, health professors, scientists, coroners, and the vaccine manufacturers, are aware of much of this information as well, but appear to have an implicit agreement to obscure the facts, minimize the truth, and deceive the public.(13-14)

In *Vaccination Myths,* we learn:

Pharmaceutical companies have been allowed to use 'gag orders' as a leverage tool in vaccine damage legal settlements to prevent disclosure of information to the public about vaccination dangers. It is also interesting to note that insurance companies (who do the best liability studies) refuse to cover vaccine adverse reactions. Profits appear to dictate both the pharmaceutical and insurance companies' positions. (Phillips 13)

How do we measure the practicality of vaccinations when full disclosure of the facts, including knowledge of the immediate and long-term consequences of the shots, is not permitted? Many doctors, scientists, and legalized drug companies sincerely believe they've outwitted Mother Nature. Yet, how many experimental drugs have the medical and scientific communities endorsed –

thalidomide, Agent Orange – only to regret it years later? When we look at the statistics in medical reports and books written by concerned doctors, it becomes clear there is cause for concern. Statistics reveal immunizations are not risk-free. In fact, they may cause more harm than good.

Bechamp's research confirms terrain or environment is everything. Our children come in contact with toxins, including bacteria and viruses all the time. Whether they become sick or not depends on what type of environment we are creating inside their body. Is the fish bowl clean?

When making the decision of whether or not to vaccinate your children – make sure you do your homework – get on the internet, read books, talk to other people – then, make an informed, educated decision based on your particular circumstances.

IMPETIGO

Impetigo is not something we see a lot in the West due to our dry climate. However, when we lived in the South where there is a humid climate, we saw it quite often. One of the easiest places for it to start is on a baby's bottom because it tends to stay moist and is usually enclosed by some type of plastic diaper. Using Slippery Elm powder on the bottom will help to keep it dry. If you do get impetigo in this area, leave the diaper off and let it air out as much as possible.

Impetigo spreads rapidly, and must be treated as soon as the first crusty sore appears. It is caused by a fungus, so black walnut hull tincture is one of the best ways to treat it because it has anti-fungal properties. If it is too strong and causes too much of a burning sensation, then try using the BF&C oil or ointment which contains Black Walnut hulls. Garlic oil and the X-Ceptic tincture also help to kill the fungus.

Herbal Aids:
- Black Walnut Hull Tincture – place directly on sores
- BF&C oil or ointment – place directly on sores
- Garlic oil – place directly on sores

- X-Ceptic Tincture - place directly on sores
- Slippery Elm Powder – use on baby's bottom to absorb moisture

Experience:

a) A friend of ours gathered some Black Walnut hulls together to treat her son's impetigo. Unfortunately, the hulls she gathered were still green. She put the hulls directly on his skin and was surprised at how much he cried and fussed over the burning. (Green Black Walnut hulls are very acidic. This is when they are high in anti-parasitic properties) She said that his skin turned black and came off. Underneath was beautiful pink skin without any impetigo.

IMPOTENCY

Many things can cause male impotency; the typical American diet being one of them. Men tend to eat a lot of meat and dairy products – with all the chemicals they contain. Other factors can come from disease, surgery, psychosomatic problems, prescription drugs, etc. . Impotency is a devastating condition for most men and many of the women who share their lives. You need to understand when the body is having a hard time surviving, the first thing it will shut down is it's ability to reproduce. Women stop ovulating; and men have sperm and/or erection problems. Most mammals have this safety mechanism so we do not bring young into a stressed or unsafe environment. It is not necessary to our own survival so the body uses it's energy in other areas to try and keep us alive. The good news is; like so many other conditions, if we go back to the principle of "cleanse and nourish," we can restore the body to health and enjoy all of the benefits which go with it.

Herbal Aids:
- Male Formula - use 1 - 2 dropper fulls three times per day – works best if used consistently over a period of 3 – 4 months

- Super Ginseng Blend Tonic - use 1 – 2 dropper fulls three to four times daily – best if used consistently, 1 or 2 bottles   According to Richard Schultz:
  Ginseng is one of the most praised and revered herbs on the planet. People have been killed and wars fought for it. . . It contains rare essential trace elements and is a powerful tonic to increase energy, vitality and stimulates sexuality.   It is famous for giving strength to the weak. (26)
- Cleansing – impotency is a sign that the body is not functioning properly – you need to look at cleansing the whole body
- Cayenne – use three times per day to help with circulation
- Morinda Tahitian Noni Juice - drink 2 – 4 ounces per day

Other Modalities:

- DIET – In the *Sunfood Diet,* Wolfe shares some of the foods which increase sexuality:
  Male sexual fluids have extraordinarily high levels of trace minerals.   For males, excessive ejaculation – 'spilling the seed' – without nutritionally replacing what is lost, drains minerals and life-force energy from they body, which causes premature aging, leads to an accelerated loss of hair in men, and contributes to impotence.   Men can replace sexual fluids by specifically eating nuts, seeds, seaweeds, avocados, olives, garlic, onions, and hot peppers.   Breathing pure air and sunbathing nude will also restore sexual fluids and energy.
  Due to the mineral deficit and toxicity caused by the standard diet, men often experience a 'crash' or a mood swing after ejaculation, which is typically not pleasing to the sexual partner. This will reverse and may be totally eliminated once the diet is purified by eating a healthy balance of raw plant foods. (358-359)
- Neuropathy – see Diabetes – may need to add an antioxidant to your diet – check out essential oils

INSECT STINGS AND BITES

If you keep plantain ointment in a herbal 1st aid kit when you are camping or hiking, it is an excellent herb for drawing the poison out of a bee sting or insect bite.

Herbal Aids:

- Plantain, fresh or ointment – put directly on the sting or bite to draw out poison and stop the stinging
- X-Ceptic Tincture – put directly on problem to kill infection

- Black Ointment - put directly on problem to draw out toxins
- INF Formula – take 4 capsules every 2 – 3 hours to fight infection
- Echinacea & Golden Seal – take 4 capsules every 2 – 3 hours to boost immune system and fight infection

Experiences:
a) Section I, pg. 25
b) Section I, pg. 29

INSOMNIA

If you are mostly sedentary, working with your brain, but not necessarily doing anything physical, then you need to make sure you work your body everyday. Examine your life - we were meant to move – the body needs to feel tired in order to get a good nights rest. If your mind is still wired when it should be resting – then figure out a way to turn it off, so that you can rest peacefully.

Herbal Aids:
- Sleepeze - two or more capsules to help relax
- Professor Cayenne Ointment - apply to tight or sore muscles

Essential Oils:
- Lavender Oil – put several drops in warm bath or directly on pillow
- Cedar Wood, St. John's Wart, Roman Chamomile – there are many essential oils which have a calming effect on the mind – consider investing in an essential oil diffuser which puts the oils directly into the air, then experiment with several different scents until you find the ones that work best for you.

Other Modalities:
- Exercise – try to get some vigorous exercise every day so the body will be tired and ready to rest
- Walk Barefoot – shuffle your feet through the grass to ground out any excess static electricity you may be carrying around
- Fresh Air – leave a bedroom window partially open to let fresh air in the room while you sleep
- Massage – massage therapy is a wonderful way to help you relax

ITCHING

Itching is merely a symptom – not the problem. Determine what is causing the problem - it could be the detergent which is being used, a new soap on the skin, an allergic reaction to something that has been eaten, a parasite problem. Itching can be caused by something as simple as not getting enough water or the right kinds of oils and fats in our diet. Again, we go back to the basics.

Herbal Aids:
- Chickweed Ointment – apply directly to problem area
- Fresh Plantain or Plantain Ointment – apply directly to problem area
- Parasite Cleanse – see section V for instructions
- Olive Oil – rub into affected skin
- Flax oil, Wheat Germ Oil, Evening Primrose oil – incorporate some type of oil into your diet so that the skin stays soft

Other Modalities:
- Water – drink plenty of water so the skin does not become dehydrated
- Diet – use nuts, avocados, olive oil and other good sources of fats for healthy skin

A closed mind is a dying mind.
-- Edna Ferber

If you think education is expensive, try ignorance.
-- Derek Bok

Our greatest glory is not in ever falling,
But to rise every time we fall.
-- Confucius

A clay pot sitting in the sun will always be a clay pot.
It has to go through the white heat of the furnace to become porcelain.
-- Mildred Struven

J

JAUNDICE

The majority of breast-fed babies develop jaundice. Normally, it is nothing to worry about. The baby will begin to look like it has a suntan or you may notice that the whites of the eyes are beginning to turn yellow. Make sure the baby is getting plenty of fluids, which means it should be nursing at least every two to four hours. Two or more times a day, remove the baby's clothes and let him lie in the direct sun for a couple of minutes on each side.

If you are concerned that it is getting worse or not clearing up fast enough, then use the Catnip & Fennel in a couple ounces of sterile water or the Kid-E-Col directly in the mouth. If the problem continues to worsen and the baby's stomach is getting yellow, your health care professionals offer special lights which can be brought to your home.

Herbal Aids:
- Kid-E-Col - put a few drops directly into the baby's mouth, on a pacifier, or in a bottle
- Catnip & Fennel Tincture – put a dropper full into a couple ounces of sterile water and give in a bottle
- Barberry LG - in the case of an adult – cleanse the liver using as much as you need to get the job done

Other Modalities:
- Direct Sunshine – expose the baby, without clothes on, to as much direct sunlight as possible without allowing them to burn
- Nurse on demand – nurse your baby as much as possible to help flush out the problem (this should be at least every 3 – 4 hours)

JUNGLE ULCERS

Nathan had a great deal of success in Africa, helping the natives with jungle ulcers.

Herbal Aids:
- BF&C ointment and Plantain Ointment – Nathan found that combining these two ointments worked well to clear up these sores – apply directly to wound
- BF&C ointment and Black ointment - he used this combination if the ulceration was under the skin, forming more of an abscess – apply directly to inflamed area.

It's kind of fun to do the impossible.
-- Walt Disney

An eye for an eye only ends up making the whole world blind.
-- Mahatma Ghandi

God gave His creatures light, air & water open to the skies;
Man locks him in a stifling lair, then wonders why his brother dies.
-- Oliver Wendell Holmes

Every child comes with the message that God is not yet
discouraged of man.
-- Tagore

L

LEUKEMIA
(See Cancer)

LICE

Lice are scavengers that live on toxic material. If the body is in an alkaline state, the bowel is clean and the blood is pure, then there is nothing for them.

Herbal Aids:
- Apple Cider Vinegar – bathe area
- Oil of Garlic – bathe area
- Walnut tea – bathe area
- Apple Cider Vinegar – In *Herbal Home Health Care,* Christopher shares a way to get some quick relief:

    For quick relief (working on the effect) is to bathe the head or body parts covered with lice with straight apple cider vinegar, oil of garlic or walnut leaf, bark or nut husk tea.

    When lice are detected in the family, see that in addition to working on the cause (cleaning the bowel and blood stream) and staying on a mucusless diet, work on the effect itself as suggested here. See that fresh clothes – inner and outer clothing – are changed daily. All of these clothes should be washed with a good biodegradable soap with a cup or more of apple cider vinegar to each washer full of clothes. Change the bed linen each day. Spray the room with tea made of six parts chaparral, three parts black walnut leaf or bark, one part lobelia and to each pint of the spray add some lavender oil or oil of mint to give fragrance.

    We must remember one thing, a clean house and clean body are not to the liking of our scavenger friends; lice, mites, fleas, etc. (100)

Essential Oils:
- In *Aromatherapy for Women,* Tisserand gives us this recipe:

    Combine these oils – 25 drops of Rosemary, 12 drops Eucalyptus, 13 drops Geranium, 25 drops Lavender, in 75 ml. base oil – Lice have now become resistant to certain chemicals which would once have been fatal to them. They also seem to have become more tenacious. Lice can remain alive for more than 10 hours just by clinging to a single strand of hair, and it really is unwise to borrow another person's hairbrush. Head lice seem to survive for long periods of time under water, and no matter how much swimming, diving, showering and hair washing one does, it is almost impossible to drown them. . . Using the combination of essential oils to combat the problem will not only kill the lice within two hours, but will cost a fraction of the price of a chemist-preparation, and will leave your hair healthy and lustrous. Make up the recipe and section the hair, carefully applying the mixture to the hair roots and scalp. Stroke the mixture through the rest of the hair, and pile it on top of your head, wrapping a long sheet of cling film carefully around your head to ensure that all the hair is securely trapped inside. This is a little difficult to do by yourself, and if you cannot get a helping hand, I would recommend that you remove the cling film from its cardboard dispenser, and wrap the film around the head going over the ears, gradually working toward the center of your head. When all of your hair is covered by cling film, you can tuck the plastic behind your ears. (98-99)

Experience:

a) When we lived in Texas, years ago, my daughters came home from school with head lice. I used the commercial brands of insecticide to get rid of them, along with hours and hours of combing through their long hair to get all of the eggs. (this is where the terms 'fine tooth comb' and 'nit-picking' come from) When I put the younger children in the tub, I asked one of my older daughters to wash her brothers hair with the lice shampoo while I went to get something. He fought her and got it in his eyes. When I heard the screaming, I ran back to the bathroom and found him with a nose bleed. These shampoos have some extremely caustic chemicals in them and should be used with caution.

Low Blood Pressure
(Hypotension)

In *Back to Eden,* Kloss gives us a good definition for this condition:

The diagnosis of low blood pressure must be made with care. In adults the blood pressure is usually considered low if it is below 110/70. But many healthy adults consistently have a systolic pressure (the highest number) of 90 to 100 mm/Hg. (388)

If, however, the blood pressure stays consistently lower than this, with fatigue, dizziness and/or lethargy, then these are things we can use and/or do to help increase the vitality.

Herbal Aids:
- Kloss recommends:
  Increase the circulation by means of deep breathing, hot baths, and cold morning baths, thoroughly rubbing with a coarse towel when drying. Any one of the following herbs, mixed with a very little red pepper, will greatly increase the vitality: hyssop, golden seal, vervain, prickly ash, blue cohosh, gentian, wood betony, burnet, and skullcap. (388)

The moment a man begins to question the meaning
and value of life he is sick.
-- Sigmund Freud (1937)

Those who are saying it cannot be done,
Should not interrupt those who are doing it.
-- Unknown

Warnings About a Miracle Drug
A swift and sweeping popularity is often followed by a stinging backlash. This
is as true for medical therapies as it is for hit TV series and fashionable
restaurants. The latest example: Prozac . . . .
-- Time, July 30, 1990

M

MASTITIS
(See Breasts)

MEMORY

Like the rest of our body, the brain needs oxygen and nutrition to function properly. In the *School of Natural Healing* book, a dramatic story is told of a couple who went to Dr. Christopher for help with their son.

> . . . A family brought in a fifteen year old boy who had constant epileptic seizures, as many as twenty-five in one day! He could not be left unattended, and the family had hired nurses to watch him day and night. The epilepsy created roaring noises inside his head, and in an attempt to stop it, the boy pounded his head against the walls until blood poured from his ears, nose, and mouth. No doctors throughout the state could help in the condition. The boy could not talk and had never attended school. He was diagnosed as severely retarded and doctors recommended institutionalization. Instead, the family came to Dr. Christopher in a last attempt for help.
>
> Dr. Christopher recommended the mucusless diet and therapeutic massage. Then he came up with two herbal combinations to build and strengthen the nervous system. (B&B and Relax-Eze) He showed the parents how to make the teas and give them to the boy. Within six months, this boy, who had been thought retarded was speaking, and had tutors brought in twice a week to keep up with him in his learning! Instead of being handicapped, he was actually brilliant. Within a few months, he was at the normal level for his age. He enrolled in school, seizure-free from then on. (xiii – xiv)

Herbal Aids:
- MEM - two or more capsules as often as needed – the herbs in this formula help carry oxygen and nutrition to the brain to help restore memory and strengthen thought processes
- Bee Power - two or more capsules three times per day for added energy

- B&B Tincture - use 4 – 6 drops in each ear at night – put a cotton ball in each ear – this helps to feed the central nervous system
- Relax-Eze - used to rebuild nerves and reduce irritation of the central nervous system, soothes spasms, and relieves pain

Experiences:

a) When I was finishing the Master Herbalist program, I taught and attended the Master Herbalist seminar, which lasts for a week. Due to a lot going on in my life, I had not had very much sleep. On Friday night I was going over all of my notes for the final exam on Saturday morning. I was so tired I could hardly remember my own name and I thought, "This is wonderful. Here I am teaching at the seminar and tomorrow I'm going to fail the exam."

At about 11:00 that night, Juanita brought me 4 MEM capsules and four Bee Power capsules with a glass of Jurassic Green. She explained to me that this was her secret weapon for taking tests in college. I went over my notes for a couple more hours and then fell into bed exhausted.

The next morning when I got up I did the same thing – 4 MEM, 4 Bee Power with a glass of Jurassic Green. It was truly amazing! It was as though a fog lifted from my brain. If I had ever seen it or heard it, I could recall it. I was very grateful to have learned Juanita's secret.

MENOPAUSE
(See Hormone Imbalance)

MENSTRUATION
(See Cramping (Menstrual))

MIGRAINE HEADACHES
(See Headaches)

MISCARRIAGE

Be aware, when using the following formula, it is going to help the body accomplish whatever it needs to do. If the baby is healthy and the pregnancy is viable, then it will help stop the miscarriage. However, if there is something wrong with the baby or the pregnancy is not viable, then it will help the body to abort the fetus. It is important to understand this principle because if you are using this formula to stop a miscarriage from happening – you need to understand it may have the opposite effect. It may help the body to flush the pregnancy because there is something wrong.

Dr. Christopher calls lobelia the "thinking herb." It's job is to go into the system and assess the situation, then help the body to accomplish what needs to be done. I have used this formula successfully with many women who were spotting and cramping with a threatened miscarriage

Herbal Aids:
- False Unicorn & Lobelia - take 2 capsules every ½ hour until bleeding stops or becomes worse – then take 2 capsules every hour for rest of day – then take 2 capsules three times per day

Other Modalities:
- Bed Rest – stay down – rest until cramping and bleeding subside
- Pregnancy Nutrition – see Section III, pg.

Experiences:
a) Section I, pg. 32
b) Section III, pg. 231

MUMPS
(See Glands)

For the truly faithful no miracle is necessary.
For those who doubt, no miracle is sufficient.
-- Nancy Gibbs

Children have more need of models than of critics.
-- Joseph Joubert (1754 – 1822)

If you believe that you can do a thing, or if you believe you cannot,
in either case, you are right.
-- Henry Ford

It is easy to substitute our will for that of the child by means of suggestion or
coercion; but when we have done this we have robbed him of his greatest right,
the right to construct his own personality.
-- Maria Montessori (1870 – 1952)

N

NAUSEA
(See Flu)

NEUROPATHY
(See Diabetes)

NOSEBLEED
(See Hemorrhage)

For every disciplined effort there is a multiple reward.
-- Jim Rohn

Love cures people – both the ones who give it and the ones who receive it.
-- Dr. Karl Menninger

If fifty million people say a foolish thing, it is still a foolish thing.
-- Anatole France

The heights by great men reached and kept,
Were not attained by sudden flight,
But they, while their companions slept,
Were toiling upward in the night.
-- Henry Wadsworth Longfellow

O

OBESITY

It is not necessary to go on a "diet" to lose weight, at least not in the way most people think of a "diet." You can eat all of the food you want and lose weight if you will eat the right kinds of food! The easiest way to get started is to do a three day juice cleanse – then move into a raw food diet. As you cleanse, you will find that you eat about 1/3 of the amount you used to eat and you will eliminate about three times as much. The reason for this is that as you clean the eliminatory channels, the body is able to uptake more nutrition. One of the reasons we gain weight is because we are hungry all the time due to not getting the nutrients we need because the intestines are so clogged with toxins.

Herbal Aids:
- Cleanse – use a good cleansing program to get started
- Supplement – use a good herbal or whole food supplement to make sure you are getting the nutrients you need
- Organa Minerals - use a cap full per day to make sure you are getting all of the trace minerals you need
- Oils – I recommend using some type of oil supplements to make sure you are getting the right kinds of fats and to help curb your craving for anything greasy – my favorites are the Especially for Women and the Especially for Men made by Barleans
- Wheat Grass Juice – drink 2 – 4 ounces per day

Other Modalities:
- Diet – use a completely raw food diet for the fastest results
- Exercise – if you want to sculpt your body and look good after you lose the weight, then you need to make exercise part of your daily program
- Water – it is essential to drink enough water in order for the weight to come off

In the *Wheatgrass Book,* Wigmore shares one of the side benefits of wheatgrass and a live-food diet:

One of the most satisfying discoveries I have made since beginning my work in nutrition is the dramatic weight loss obtainable while using wheatgrass and the Hippocrates Diet. The Hippocrates Diet consists of vegetables, fresh fruits, sprouts, baby greens, sea vegetables, and sprouted seeds, nuts, and grains, all eaten raw and prepared in tasty combinations.

. . . Wheatgrass helps dieters by speeding up blood circulation and metabolic rate, and by enhancing digestive powers, thereby melting the excess fat in the body. If you take a moment to consider the many roles played by enzymes, you will realize that if you lose one pound (or gain another one) it will be because of the activity (or lack of it) of the enzymes in your food and body.

. . . The effectiveness of live foods and fresh juices, especially wheatgrass juice, has bankrupted many complex theories about why we become fat and how to reduce quickly. At the Hippocrates Health Institute, I have never stressed weight loss because it is as natural to wheatgrass and the living foods diet as swimming is to a duck. Nevertheless, among our guests at the Institute, the average weight loss per week is between four and fifteen pounds. I am convinced that the rich supply of enzymes in wheatgrass and live foods is the deciding factor. (59)

In the *Miracle of Fasting,* Braggs shares his thoughts on obesity:

Insurance figures accurately show that overweight people are short-lived and are more susceptible to many chronic diseases because of their unnatural overweight condition. Any way you look at it, excess weight is dangerous! Today, obesity is steadily on the increase worldwide. First, in America we have an abundance of food and fast food restaurants. The average person puts way too much food into their stomach for the sheer joy of eating. Eating is America's most popular indoor and outdoor sport! Family gatherings call for many varieties of food. . . .

Coffee breaks encourage people to snack between meals. TV invites people to snack as they gaze at the idiot box that promotes crime and evilness. Plus people are constantly eating sweets, ice cream, shakes, hot dogs, hamburgers, French fries, pizza and many other varieties of food even between meals. Then there are the buffets, banquets, benefit dinners, etc. that promote overeating.

We live in a mechanical age. We load heavy amounts of food into our bodies and never burn it up with exercise and physical activities. The automobile has replaced walking. We are a nation of sitters. Our children sit for hours in school and then in front of the TV. People spend hours at computers, attending movies, concerts, athletic events and musicals. This unhealthy, sedentary life contributes to being overweight.

. . . There are so many reducing diets that it's frustrating and confusing for people to know which one to follow. In my opinion, the fast is the only natural and scientific way to achieve reasonable weight reduction. Let me give you some of my reasons why I believe fasting is the perfect way to reduce. After the first 2 or 3 days of fasting you are no longer hungry. From the 3rd day on there is no craving for food. . . But after you fast for 2 or 3 days, all hunger fades away, the stomach shrinks and it actually becomes a very pleasant experience. You start to breathe easier, feel lighter, move easier and think more clearly.

I have seen many overweight people lose 7 to 20 pounds and more the first 7 – 10 days of fasting. After the loss of this excess weight, there is a special inner feeling of well-being and increased physical and mental energy! Of course, every human is different. Some people only lose 1 or 2 pounds a day on a fast while some will lose as many as 5 pounds. (114-115)

Fasting, combined with a good, wholesome diet is a good way to trim down and regulate your weight. However, as previously mentioned do not try to do any type of long fast without working up to it and having supervision.

Most folks are about as happy as they make up their minds to be.
-- Abraham Lincoln

In the last analysis, great human achievement rests on perfect physical health.
-- Emerson

Every man who has ever been earnest to preserve his higher poetic faculties in the best condition, has been particularly inclined to abstain from animal food, or from much food of any kind.
--Henry David Thoreau

If you can surround yourself with people who will never let you settle for less than you can be, you have the greatest gift that anyone can hope for. Association is a powerful tool. Make sure the people you surround yourself with make you a better person by your association with them.
-- Anthony Robbins

P

PARASITES

The truth is most of us have parasites of one kind or another. We come in contact with them all the time. They are garbage collectors who come in to help keep our systems clean. If our bodies are alkalized and clean, they cannot live in us because there is nothing for them to live on.

Some parasites, however, can be real trouble makers and those are the ones we usually hear about. The first parasite cleanse listed below is good to use in the spring with the whole family for some good spring cleaning. If, however, there is a health problem being caused because of parasites or maybe there is a severe health problem such as cancer where parasites are just along for the ride, then the second parasite cleanse is much stronger.

Herbal Aids:
- VF Syrup with Peppermint & Senna Tea – one teaspoon of the VF syrup each morning and night for three days. On the fourth day, drink one cup of Peppermint and Senna tea. Rest two days, then repeat two more times.
- Wormwood, Cloves and Black Walnut Hull Tincture (green) – See Section V – parasite cleanse

Experiences:
a) Section I, pg. 36
b) Section IV, pg. 362
c) When Wade came back from Africa he had Elephantitis, which is caused by a parasite that gets into the lymph system. The lymph begins to back up in different areas, causing the area to become enlarged. He was concerned about not doing something medical about the problem because once the skin becomes enlarged, it does not usually go back down. In spite of his concern, he decided to try herbs since he was having so much success treating the frost bite and the jungle ulcers. He used the second parasite cleanse mentioned above with wormwood, cloves and black walnut tincture which completely cleared up the problem.

PERIODS
(See Cramps (Menstrual))

PINK EYE

We have used these remedies successfully many times for colds and infections in the eye.

Herbal Aids:
- Herbal Eyebright Formula - put two or three drops into an eye cup full of sterile water – use an eye dropper to put a couple of drops in eye three times per day
- Eyebright Tea – use warm tea made from the eyebright herb to wash accumulated mucus from the eye – especially when they are glued shut
- Mother's Breast Milk – if you have an infant with a cold or infection in the eye – just squirt a couple of drops of your own breast milk into the eye

Experiences:
  a) Section I, pg. 26

PLEURISY

Pleurisy can be an extremely painful condition. By using these herbs and treatments, you can clear up the problem, but if it becomes chronic – you must change your diet. Also, remember to breathe deeply every day to fill your lungs with oxygen.

In *School of Natural Healing,* we find the cause of pleurisy:

> The cause of pleurisy is mucus forming in a weak area caused by the failure to breathe deeply. It is common where there is general debility of the body, especially in the lung area. (Christopher 43)

Herbal Aids:
- Pleurisy Root Tea – "1 tsp. of dry herb to a cup of water – pleurisy root alone is very effective if taken freely." (Kloss 527)
- Yarrow, Pleurisy Root & Cayenne – "a specific cure for pleurisy can be made by steeping one tablespoon of yarrow, one tablespoon

pleurisy root, and a pinch of cayenne in a quart of boiling water, let steep, take warm – a large swallow every hour. This has been known to cure many cases." (Kloss 526)
- Echinacea – four capsules every two hours to boost immune system

Other Modalities:
- Diet – stay away from all mucus-forming substances
- Water – drink three to four quarts of pure water daily
- Hydrotherapy – take hot, steamy showers or baths to help break up mucus and sweat out toxins

PMS
(See Hormone Imbalance)

PNEUMONIA

Pneumonia can be a very serious condition. When it is viral pneumonia, there are no antibiotics which help, so it becomes especially critical to know how to assist the body in cleaning toxins out. The cold sheet treatment is very specific for treating pneumonia, but it requires someone to assist and help the person who is ill. We have used this treatment many times and have witnessed incredible results.

Herbal Aids:
- INF Formula – 4 capsules every 2 hours to fight infection
- Echinacea – 4 capsules every 2 hours to fight infection
- Echinacea & Golden Seal – 4 capsules every 2 hours to boost immune system and fight infection
- X-Ceptic Tincture – rub on chest and back to help fight infection
- Mullein Oil – rub on chest and back to help break up congestion
- Onion Poultice – see Section V for instructions
- Garlic Paste – chop up fresh garlic and mix with petroleum jelly to form a paste – massage the feet with olive oil – pack the bottom of the feet with the paste – wrap the foot and put on a big sock to hold in place – this allows the body to draw on the antibiotic properties of the garlic
- The Cold Sheet Treatment – see Section V for instructions
- Anti-Plague - use 1 Tbsp as often as needed

Other Modalities:
- Hydrotherapy – four to eight hot, steamy showers per day to open up pores, open up respiratory system, and break up congestion
- Hot water vaporizer with Eucalyptus oil – build a tent and place the vaporizer inside with the person who is ill to help open up breathing passages
- Liquid Diet – use fruit juices, herbal teas, vegetable broths & juices

Experiences:
a) Section I, pgs. 12
b) Section I, pg. 52
c) Things take on a new perspective when you experience them first hand. In Sacramento, lecturing one weekend, I got sick with some type of bronchial pneumonia. Even though I know better, I had gotten caught up in a ridiculous schedule and was not taking care of myself the way I should have been. I wasn't eating right, getting enough sleep or exercising.

Anyway, my children knew I had gotten pretty sick, so when I flew home Sunday afternoon, they had everything prepared to administer the cold sheet treatment. In spite of the fact that I think they enjoyed getting back at me, I was extremely grateful for their help. I was able to sweat out most of the toxins that night and get back on my feet in a couple of days, instead of a couple of weeks.

PROSTATE

The prostate gland is a walnut-sized gland which produces a thin, milky fluid that acts to nourish sperm and provide part of the substance which forms semen. It surrounds the junction of the vas deferens and the urethra, which is why there is difficulty in urinating when it becomes swollen. Like so many other conditions we have discussed, a lot of the problem with the prostate can be traced back to diet and lifestyle. Vasectomy can cause a lot of prostate infections and problems. The prostate has to drain toxins that become backed up or they can cause chronic infections.

Herbal Aids:
- Prospalmetto - two or more capsules three times per day to reduce swelling, strengthen and tone the prostate
- Prospallate – ". . . two or more capsules three times per day to help dissolve kidney stones, kill infection and clear sedimentation in the prostate gland" (Christopher xviii School).
- Prostate Formula – ". . . the herbs in these formulae reduce swelling and inflammation in the prostate and promote the flow of urine – 1 to 2 dropperfuls 3 times daily. Works best if used with the foundational programs, and especially getting off of all animal products" (Shulze 26).
- Mullein and Lobelia Fomentations – see Glands, pg. 384

To live is to change, and to be perfect is to have changed often.
-- John Henry Newman

Thomas Edison tried 10,000 types of filaments for the electric light bulb before he found the one which worked.

Do you want to succeed? Then, double your failure rate.
Success lies on the far side of failure.
-- Thomas Watson, Sr., founder of IBM

People do not lack courage,
they simply are overburdened by an abundance of conformity.
Persistence requires courage, while quitting requires conformity.
-- David Wolfe

R

RINGWORM

Ringworm is caused by a fungus. When scratched, it can spread rapidly. Apply these herbs directly on affected area to clear up the problem and then look to the internal condition of the body to "cleanse and nourish."

Herbal Aids:
- Black Walnut Hull Tincture – rub directly on affected area
- Garlic Oil – rub directly on affected area
- Golden Seal & Myrrh – for ringworm of the scalp, Jethro Kloss recommends using the following solution morning and night:

    When ringworm occurs on the scalp, the hair falls out, leaving a small, round, scaly area. . . Ringworm of the scalp may be difficult to cure. The hair should be shampooed with a good quality of soap. . . every morning and evening moisten the spots with the following solution: 1 teaspoon golden seal: ½ teaspoon myrrh, steeped in a pint of boiling water. Daily application of wet dressings with boric acid is good. (419)

And God said: Behold, I have given you every herb bearing seed which is upon the face of the earth, and every tree, in which is the fruit of a tree yielding seed, to be your food.
-- Genesis 1:29

Your food determines in a large measure how long you shall live – how much you shall enjoy life, and how successful your life will be.
-- Dr. Kirschner

. . . doctors believe in surgery. There's a certain fascination in "going under the knife," and doctors take every advantage of it to get people there. After all, surgery is an element of Progress, and Progress separates us from those who came before us and from those we are surpassing. In America, what can be done will be done. Whether something should be done is beside the point. As long as we can build the tools and do it, it must be the right thing to do. So not only do we have coronary by passes, tonsillectomies, and radical mastectomies
-- but transsexual surgery as well.
-- Robert S. Mendelsohn, M.D.

S

SEIZURES
(See Memory)

SINUS

Sinus infections can be extremely painful. Unfortunately, once you have had a severe sinus infection, it causes a weakness which makes you prone to them each time you catch a cold. Learning how to use these precious herbs can make it easy to clear the infections up quite rapidly.

Herbal Aids:
- See Headaches
- Fresh Horseradish – grate up some fresh Horseradish – inhale the fumes to open up the sinuses
- Fresh Onion – the same thing can be done with an onion – grate it up and inhale the wonderful aroma
- Cayenne Pepper – take a few granules of cayenne pepper on to the end of your finger – snuff them up your nose – you will feel it go up your nose, through the sinus and back down the throat
- INF™ - take 4 capsules every two hours to fight infection
- Echinacea & Goldenseal – take 4 capsules every two hours to fight infection and boost immune system
- SenSei - rub ointment over sinuses to open them up

Other Modalities:
- Hot Showers – standing in a hot, steamy shower will help to open up the sinuses and allow them to drain. Putting a hot, wet washcloth over the sinuses will help to open them up and bring a lot of relief for the pain

Experience:
a) Wade's roommates are good friends and felt very comfortable about teasing me, "Rain, snow, sleet or dark of night, when you're in trouble, just call Dr. Mom."

His teasing was all in good fun, but when I was putting everything away to go home, he asked me if I had anything in my little bag to help him. He told me he had not been able to breathe on one side of his nose for years. I smiled and said, "I might have."

I told him a little bit of cayenne might help. He wanted to try it, so I told him how to do it. Instead of putting just a couple of granules on his finger like I had explained to him; he licked his finger, stuck it into the powder, put his finger up to his nostril and sniffed as hard as he could. As soon as he did, his eyes got big and wide, he started running around the room and yelling, "I'm dying!" We were all laughing so hard tears flowed freely. After about the third time he told me he was dying, I said, "No, you're not. If you were, you wouldn't be able to yell so loud."

His eyes were watering, his face was flushed, and being so dramatic we felt like it was adequate pay back for all of his torment. As I was leaving, he looked at me, totally amazed and said, "Hey, I can breathe."

SPRAINS
(See Broken Bones)

STRETCH MARKS

Even old stretch marks can be helped by consistently applying wheat germ oil or vitamin E oil directly on them – the process heals much faster if you are also using them internally.

Herbal Aids:
- Wheat Germ Oil – taking this supplement orally and applying directly on the abdomen during pregnancy will minimize the amount and severity of stretch marks – getting enough of the right types of oils in the body helps the skin to be much more pliable
- Barleans The Essential Woman - using a good oil supplement in your daily diet helps to keep the skin soft, young looking and maintain it's ability to stretch and shrink without creating stretch marks

STY

Sties, though irritating and painful, will usually clear up in a very short time using the Eyebright formula. Start out with just a couple of drops of the tincture in the water until they adjust to the burning sensation of the cayenne. After using the formula a couple of times, increase the amount, if needed.

Herbal Aids:
- Herbal Eyebright Formula – put 2 – 4 drops of tincture in an eye cup full of warm, sterile water – place eye cup over the eye and bathe the eye three times per day, opening and closing the eye while under the water

SUNBURN

Sunburns are painful, extremely damaging to the tissue, and can put the body into shock. Treating this condition requires staying out of the sun, resting, and putting lots of fluids back into the body.

Herbal Aids:
- Aloe Vera Gel – apply generous amount of aloe vera gel to the burn – either from the plant or a good commercial gel that is straight aloe vera
- Burn Paste – see Burns, pg. 297

Essential Oils:
- Lavender Oil – put several drops of Lavender oil into a spray bottle with water – spray onto burn to relieve pain and help with healing
- Water – drink lots of fluids to replace what was lost due to the damaged tissue

Experience:
a) When Steve was stationed in Guam, my children and I were out playing on the beach. I made sure they were all covered in suntan lotion so they would not burn, but I thought I would go a while without any so I could get a tan. Unfortunately, a little while turned into a longer time than I had planned. I ended up scorched! I spent several days laying around naked under a sheet, with chills, because I couldn't stand to have anything touch my skin. I drank a lot of fluids and went through several bottles of aloe vera gel. The bottom line with sunburn is "an ounce of prevention is worth a pound of cure.

No milk available on the market today, in any part of the United States,
is free of pesticide residues.
-- Congressional Hearing

Profanity is the effort of a feeble mind to express itself forcibly.
-- Spencer W. Kimball

The higher your energy level, the more efficient your body. The more efficient
your body, the better you feel and the more you will use your talent to produce
outstanding results.
-- Anthony Robbins

Overeating habits and weight gain are related to eating demineralized foods.
The richer a food is in minerals, the more difficult it becomes to overeat it.
When food is eaten raw, it gives a stronger signal to stop eating. This is called
the aliesthetic taste change.
-- David Wolfe

T

THRUSH

Thrush is caused by a yeast infection. Bayberry tea is one of the easiest ways to clear this up in infants. If you are nursing, you need to work on your diet and drink bayberry, so you can flush yeast out of your system.

Herbal Aids:
- Bayberry, cut – make a tea – put in a spray bottle – squirt right into the baby's mouth on the thrush – if it is an adult, gargle with the tea and drink 1 – 2 tablespoons every hour until you get relief
- X-Ceptic - dip a Q-tip into the tincture – apply directly on the thrush – just remember, this formula has cayenne in it, so I would not use it on an infant unless there was no other alternative

THYROID

The thyroid is a gland and so responds well to mullein and lobelia. The herbs in the Kelp T formula are designed to assist in controlling metabolism and to strengthen the thyroid. Kelp is a very specific herb for feeding the thyroid.

Herbal Aids:
- Mullein & Lobelia ointment or fomentation – see Glands, pg. apply a warm fomentation or ointment each night
- Kelp T Combination - two or more capsules three times per day

TONSILLITIS

Tonsils are one of the first lines of defense we have in our immune system. We did not come here with spare parts and the tonsils are no exception. They are glands and so respond well to mullein and lobelia fomentations. It is important that you stay on the herbs long enough to kill the infection, using them for a week to ten days, even if the swelling is down and you are feeling better.

Herbal Aids:
- Mullein & Lobelia – use three parts Mullein to one part Lobelia for a fomentation (see Glands)
- Mullein & Lobelia tea – drink ½ cup of mullein & lobelia tea morning and night (3 parts Mullein to 1 part Lobelia)

- Cayenne, Garlic & Honey – chop up a fresh garlic clove – put into a tablespoon of honey with a pinch of cayenne – mix together and swallow
- X-Ceptic - rub on neck and up behind the ears – can be taken internally
- INF Formula – take 4 or more capsules every two hours to fight infection
- Echinacea – 4 or more capsules every two hours to boost immune system
- Echinacea & Golden Seal – 4 or more capsules every two hours to boost immune system and fight infection
- Red Raspberry Leaf Tea – drink several glasses per day
- Kid-E-Well - 1 to 3 droppers full every hour while awake
- Kid-E-Cep – 1 – 3 droppers full every 4 hours for infection

Other Modalities:
- Liquid Diet - drink lots of water, juices and herbal teas

In the *School of Natural Healing,* Christopher shares how important the tonsils are:

> Many health practitioners believe that they can improve on the creation of God by removing what they deem as 'useless' or 'harmful' organs. Tonsils should NEVER be removed, rather the body should be cleansed of the toxins which are creating the problem. The tonsils are very vital to the body, as is any other organ. They are the last refinery that guards the reproductive system from toxic wastes in the body. Removing the tonsils will lessen fertility, and the likelihood of trouble in the prostate glands and ovaries, etc. is greatly increased. (307)

TOOTHACHE

Sometimes a toothache can be caused by something stuck down between the teeth or in the gum, such as a popcorn husk. In this case, a good flossing clears up the problem. If a cavity is caught soon enough, people have been able to fix the teeth by using the tooth powder – the cavity has actually filled back in. (You may need to add comfrey as the FDA has banned the use of comfrey in all products used orally) If, however, there is serious decay in the tooth, the herbs help give relief until the problem can be fixed by a dentist.

Herbal Aids:
- Dr. Christopher's Tooth Powder - brush with the powder – if gum is infected, mix tooth powder with X-Ceptic tincture and a little Slippery Elm powder to form a paste – pack gum and tooth with paste
- X-Ceptic Tincture – put directly on tooth or gum for infection or mix with tooth powder to form paste
- Horsetail – this herb is high in organic calcium – when a baby is teething, rub horsetail tincture directly on gums to help teeth break through – when our children have been cutting their wisdom teeth, they often pack them with horsetail to relieve the discomfort
- Calc Tea Formula - 2 or more capsules three times per day for additionally calcium

Essential Oils:
- Clove Oil – rub onto tooth and gum to relieve pain
  – can also be added into paste
- Myrrh Oil – rub onto tooth or add to paste to relieve pain and aid in healing

Wolfe, in *Sunfood Diet* points out how we have dated ourselves with our teeth:

> One of the ways anthropologists date human fossils is by looking at skull teeth. The more modern the fossil, the more tooth decay. Analyses of striations on fossilized teeth show no decay or premature wear when hominids ate a raw-vegan diet. Most paleontologists agree that tooth decay coincided with the discovery of fire and accelerated with the advent of agriculture.
>
> An unbalanced, cooked diet lacking in alkaline minerals (calcium, magnesium, silicon) and high in sugar and acid-forming minerals (phosphorus, chlorine) damages teeth formation. Because teeth begin to be formed in the pre-natal stage, the diet of the mother has a life-long influence. Due to improper nutrition, the body does not have the energy or minerals with which to properly control the eruption of teeth into the mouth. Poor nutrition results in crowded and malformed teeth, along with an altered bite.

These structural dental challenges begin essentially as birth defects and are exacerbated by continuous improper nutrition. T.C. Fry reported in an article entitled, *The Myth of Health in America,* which appeared in Dr. Shelton's *Hygienic Review* (37:7, p. 150-152) that 98.5% of the U.S. population suffers from dental problems of one type or another. These may often be reversed and corrected in one or more generations of eating significantly more mineral-rich organic green-leafed vegetables. (297)

Apparently, this problem can be corrected in the same way it was caused – through diet, as we see in the *Raw Family:*

- . . . When I went on raw foods, I had eight fillings in my teeth. I remember that when mom was taking me to the dentist to fill cavities, those teeth were very tender. The doctor couldn't even touch them. After I had stayed on raw food for some months, the fillings started to pop out. I was surprised my teeth were not tender.

I went to my mom and said, 'My teeth are rotting from this diet.' She said, 'Let's wait for a couple of weeks and see what happens.'

Within a couple of weeks my teeth began to fill with enamel. It was yellowish, then it whitened, and then it hardened. A couple of months later I had the same new teeth as before I ever had a cavity. Now I have all my teeth completely restored. You may look into my mouth. But you cannot say which tooth ever had a cavity; they restored completely. (Boutenko 23)

Experiences:

a) From the *Christopher Newsletter* we find another example of regeneration:

My oldest daughter, age 13 now, had a dental cavity at age 7 (the only dental cavity among our six children), We had the cavity drilled out and a filling put in by our local dentist. Two years later, the filling came out and a hole was left in her tooth. Nothing more was done about it except the herbal calcium formula that you recommend in your book,

The School of Natural Healing, made up of: comfrey, horsetail, oatstraw, and lobelia. This combination of herbs has been used very consistently by the entire family over the last two years. We have recently discovered that the hole where the filling was, is now completely grown over and is absolutely unnoticeable even under close inspection. – Malta, Ohio

b) One morning, bright and early, a friend showed up wanting to know if I could help her daughter. The night before her daughter had broken off her front tooth. The mother had kept the broken piece in a bowl of BF&C tea. She showed me how the tooth was still pink where the nerve hole was. She wanted to see if we could get the tooth to regenerate itself, so we mixed some BF&C powder with wheat germ oil and made a paste. We decided to use the BF&C paste as a glue to cement the tooth back on - we took a gelatin capsule, pulled it apart, put the broken piece in half of the capsule and slipped it up over the tooth. We then put a couple of drops of water on the capsule so it would shrivel up and seal the tooth like shrink wrap. At night, after her daughter had gone to sleep, the mother would use a band aid to tape the tooth, securing the tape to her daughter's lip to hold it in place.

She gave her daughter BF&C orally and kept the tooth bathed in it for about 10 days. At the end of that time, they were going out of town, so she found a dentist who was willing to let her pack the tooth in BF&C before he reattached it with a special holding compound that would not kill the tooth. The dentist told her it would not work, but was willing to go along with her. The last time I saw the tooth, you could see the pink lines going between the two pieces where it was regenerating itself. I'm not sure what the final outcome was, but it was fascinating to watch how healthy that tooth remained as long as it was being fed the proper nutrients for growth and life.

No one can make you feel inferior without your consent.
-- Eleanor Roosevelt

The ultimate measure of a man is not where he stands in moments of comfort
but where he stands at times of challenge and controversy.
-- Martin Luther King, Jr.

Is it so bad then to be misunderstood?
Pythagoras was misunderstood,
And Socrates, and Jesus, and Luther,
And Copernicus, and Galileo, and Newton,
And every pure and wise spirit that ever took flesh.
To be great is to be misunderstood.
-- Ralph Waldo Emerson

U

ULCERS

The Human Body in Health and Disease, describes ulcers as:
> . . . an area of the skin or mucous membrane in which the tissues are gradually destroyed. An ulcer may be caused by the acid in gastric juice. Peptic ulcers occur in the mucous membrane of the esophagus, stomach, or duodenum and are most common in persons between the ages of 30 and 45. (Wood 280)

In *Sunfood Diet,* we read:
> Studies done by Dr. Garnet Cheney, who at one time headed the Cancer Division of Stanford Medical School, revealed the value of glutamine in healing ulcers. Dr. Cheney administered 1 quart (1 liter) of cabbage/celery/carrot juice a day to 65 ulcer sufferers. Within 3 weeks 63 of the patients were healed and 2 retained only minimum symptoms. (89)

Herbal Aids:
- Cayenne Pepper – 2 capsules three times per day or ½ to 1 tsp. in a glass of water two to three times per day

Juices:
- Cabbage Juice – juice a head of cabbage and drink it each morning
- Anti-Ulcer Cabbage Cocktail – From the *Juiceman,* we find this wonderful recipe:
  > This juice may soothe your stomach and calm you frazzled nerves. When the going gets tough, head for the juicer.
  > ½ tomato
  > 1 (4-inch) wedge of green cabbage
  > 2 stalks of celery
  > Cut the tomato into narrow wedges. Cut the cabbage into narrow wedges. Cut the celery into 2 to 3-inch pieces. Process the vegetables in the juicer (Kordich 85).

Experiences:
a) When I was first married many years ago, my husband had bleeding ulcers. My father gave me a juicer and told me if I would juice a head of cabbage every morning and give it to him, it would cure his ulcers. I followed his instructions and within two weeks the ulcers were gone and never gave him any more problems.

b) From the *Christopher Newsletter,* we find another testimonial for the power of cayenne:

A lady had been attending our herbal lecture series for some time. One day she told us about her husband's severe case of stomach ulcers. The recommendation from their doctor was to have part of his stomach removed, but he said he would rather suffer the pain than risk such an operation. He also refused his wife's suggestion to try cayenne, ridiculing her studies.

When he would see me in town, he would bellow, 'Hello, Doc! Killed anybody with cayenne, today?' He became so obnoxious, I avoided him when I could.

Months went by and one day I saw him coming down the street toward me. I tried to avoid him but he came 'head on'. This time I was amazed because there were no cutting remarks or sarcasm. In fact, he was very apologetic and asked if he could talk to me for a minute, and then told me this story: He had come home from work one night, "sick enough to die", with stomach ulcers. His wife was not home. He was in such pain he wanted to commit suicide. He went to the medicine cabinet to find some kind of medicine poisonous and deadly enough to kill him. But he discovered his wife had thrown out all of the old bottles of pharmaceutical medicine. All that was left in the medicine cabinet were some herbs and a large container of cayenne pepper. He was so angry that, upon seeing the cayenne, he figured it in a large dose would kill him by burning him up. He took a heaping tablespoon of cayenne in a glass of hot water, gulped it down and rushed into the bedroom. He fell upon the bed and covered his head with a pillow so the neighbors couldn't hear his 'dying screams.'

The next thing he knew his wife was shaking him awake the next morning. She told him he had slept all night (instead of being up every half hour for anti-acid tablets). To his amazement he discovered that the pain was gone, for the first time in months. He continued using cayenne three times a day faithfully. (2)

UTERINE FIBROIDS
(See Fibroids)

Pure water is the best drink for a wise man.
-- Henry David Thoreau

Great spirits have always encountered violent opposition from mediocre minds.
-- Albert Einstein

Correcting oneself is correcting the hole world. The sun is simply bright.
It does not correct anyone. Because it shines, the whole world is full of light.
Transforming yourself is a means of giving light to the whole world.
-- Ramana Maharshi

The awareness of human separation, without reunion by love – is the source of
shame. It is at the same time the source of quilt and anxiety. The deepest need
of man, then, is the need to overcome his separateness, to leave the prison of his
aloneness. The absolute failure to achieve this aim means insanity. . . .
-- Erich Fromm, *The Art of Loving* (1956)

V

VAGINAL INFECTIONS

You can usually tell a yeast infection by the discharge which resembles cottage cheese, causes burning and itching externally and has an odor to it. Other vaginal infections tend to have a different type of discharge.

Herbal Aids:
- Garlic Douche – peel 8 – 10 cloves of garlic – put them in a blender with a small amount of water – blend them up – strain through cheese cloth – take 1/3 of strained garlic and put it into a pint of warm water or tea – douche
- Black Walnut – if the infection is being caused by yeast – you can put some black walnut tincture on a tampon and insert in to the vagina to kill the yeast
- Liquid Acidophilus – keep in the refrigerator – apply to sanitary pad – wear next to skin to relieve itching and burning
- Bayberry Tea – Drink tea to flush out yeast – the tea is pretty bitter, so take 1 – 2 Tablespoons every hour throughout the day or 3 glasses per day.
- Golden Seal Douche – make a tea – use as a douche – golden seal has wonderful antibiotic properties

Essential Oils:
- Bolus – this recipe was shared with me by a dear friend and midwife, Melody Pendleton – it is used to clear up vaginal infections of all types, including step B. You will need:
  o 2 ½ ounces Cocoa Butter (1/2 jar)
  o 30 – 45 drops Tea Tree Oil
  o 30 – 45 drops Oregano Oil
  o freezer bag or heavy-duty sandwich bag

Put cocoa butter in freezer bag – hold over boiling water to melt butter – add tea tree oil and oregano oil to butter – the butter will begin to harden almost immediately (if you live in a warm climate, you may need to set the bag in the refrigerator for a couple of minutes) – before the butter hardens completely, lay the bag on the counter so you can spread the butter out and flatten it (keeping it in the bag) – using the edge of a credit card or drivers license, make creases in the butter to form fingers vertically and horizontally – this will make about 25 suppositories. Keep the bag in the refrigerator or freezer – when you need to use them, break off a piece about the size of your little finger – insert vaginally at bedtime.

Melody recommends that mothers use these for two weeks every night before they give birth if they need to clear up a yeast infection or if they are concerned about or have tested positive for Strep B.

After a birth, one of her women tested positive for Strep F – she used the suppositories at night, then douched with Golden Seal in the morning which cleared up the problem.

This basic recipe can be altered depending on what the problem is. For example, if you are suffering with hemorrhoids, you could add white oak bark, uva ursi, garlic and/or comfrey to the recipe – then insert the suppository rectally to help shrink, heal and bring relief.

- Douche – In *Essential Oils,* Dr. Young recommends a douche:
  Douche with . . . a mixture of 2 drops oregano, 1 drop thyme and 5 drops Melrose in 1 Tbsp. V-6 Mixing Oil. Shake well. Mix 2 drops oregano, 1 drop thyme, 5 drops Melissa into 1Tbsp. of V-6 Mixing Oil for use in retention douche. (371)

VARICOSE VEINS

Poor diet contributor to varicose veins just as it is to most degenerative conditions. If the diet is corrected, the herbs and nutrition will help to strengthen and heal the varicosities.

Herbal Aids:
- Cayenne Pepper – 2 capsules 2 -3 times per day to increase circulation
- BF&C Oil or Ointment – rub on to veins several times per day to strengthen and heal
- Calc Tea Formula – 2 or more capsules three times per day – contains organic calcium
- White Oak Bark Tea – make a strong batch of tea - soak the legs in the tea or paint it on the legs at night or soak a pair of cotton stocking in the tea and wear them to bed – this works as an astringent which helps to tight the tissue
- Organa Minerals - varicose veins can sometimes be a result of the lack of trace minerals in the diet – I have had a lot of success in my midwife practice with varicosities just by adding minerals to the diet
- Hemorrhoid Sitz Bath – if you have varicose veins in the vaginal or perineal areas – the combination of herbs in this sitz bath will help to tighten and reduce the swelling

Juices:
- In *Raw Juice Therapy,* Lust instructs us:
  Varicose veins are the result of diets rich in concentrated starches and sugars, which cause deposits to form in the wall structure of the veins (valves). (102)

He recommends the following juices:
      Carrot & Beet – Carrot 8 ounces, Beet 8 ounces (preferable)
      Carrot, Celery & Parsley - Carrot 6 ounces, Celery 6 ounces,
                      Parsley 2 ounces
      Carrot, Beet, Cucumber - Carrot 6 ounces, Beet 5 ounces,
                      Cucumber 5 ounces
      Watercress – 8 ounces (twice daily)

Experience:
    a) Section IV, pgs. 326

VIRUS

Experience:
    a) Section I, pg. 66
    b) Section IV, pg. 251
    c) Section IV, pgs. 294

Bless your uneasiness as a sign that there is still life in you.
-- Dag Hammarskjold (1956)

Wisdom does not show itself so much in precept as in life –
a firmness of mind and mastery of the appetite.
-- Seneca

In nature there are neither rewards or punishments – there are consequences!
-- Robert Ingersoll

Water flows through every single part of your body, cleansing and nourishing it.
But the wrong kind of water – with inorganic minerals, harmful toxins,
chemicals, and other contaminants can pollute, clog and gradually turn every
part of your body to stone.
-- Paul C. Bragg, N.D., Ph.D

W

WARTS

Warts are a fairly easy problem to eliminate. The secret is not letting oxygen get to it while you are killing it. When using garlic oil, be careful not to let it get on the surrounding skin as it can blister it.

Herbal Aids:
- Garlic Oil – apply directly to wart – keep covered
- Dandelion Milk – pick a dandelion out of the yard – apply the white, milky substance that is in the stem directly to the wart – keep covered

WEIGHT CONTROL
(See Obesity)

WHOOPING COUGH
(See Section I, pg. 60)

WORMS
(See Parasites)

Section V

Practical Applications / "How To"

How to: Herbal Applications Overview

In this section, I will put a simplified version of each of the programs or techniques referred to throughout this book. When I first began studying herbal medicine, it would be extremely frustrating to look up something, only to have it refer to a poultice or fomentation and not know what that was or how to do it. I hope this section will fill in those holes for you so that you will be able to do any application you need to do. The reason I am giving the simplified version is because there have literally been books written on many of these individual topics and programs. The books which contain the complete programs will be listed on the "Works Cited" page at the end of this book. The topics covered in the first chapter are:

Cold Sheet Treatment
Decoction
Extended Herbal Cleanse
Eye Exercises
Fomentation
Honey & Pine Needle Syrup
Dr. Christopher's Incurables Program
Infusion
Parasite Program
Poultice
Ten Day Challenge
Three Day Juice Cleanse
Three Oil Massage
Wheat Grass Implants

In chapter two I will include a list of most of the herbal combinations contained in this book, along with a list of the herbs contained within each combination. This way you will be able to compare the ingredients listed with something you might already have on hand. Check with your local health food store to see if they carry these combinations. If you cannot find any of these combinations or something similar, then call our 800 number or check on our website for a free catalog.

In chapter three I will list some of the "retreats" around the country who use natural alternatives to "cleanse and nourish."

Don't Quit
Author Unknown

When things go wrong, as they sometimes will,
When the road you're trudging seems all uphill,
When the funds are low and the debts are high,
And you want to smile, but instead you sigh,
When care is pressing you down a bit,
Rest if you must, but don't you quit.

For life is strange with its twists and turns,
As every one of us sometimes learns,
And many failures turn about,
When they might have won, had they stuck it out.

So don't give up though the pace seems slow,
You may succeed with another blow;
Success is failure turned inside out,
It's the silver tint of the clouds of doubt.

And you never can tell how close you are,
It may be near when it seems so far.
So stick to the fight when you're hardest hit,
It's when things seem worst that you must not quit.

Chapter One

Programs and Techniques

Cold Sheet Treatment

In *Herbal Home Health Care,* Dr. Christopher gives the instructions for the Cold Sheet Treatment:

This program will take a little time and effort for the one doing the nursing. If you are desirous of seeing a sick friend, patient, or loved one healed, you will never regret the time spent, for this has saved many lives of people who were given up as hopeless, left to die, but were brought back, with this program to good health.

Step One: Give the patient an enema, using an herb to assist if available: catnip, sage, red raspberry or some other type made into an infusion and administered cold. A cold enema will cause the anus and rectal area to contract and retain the fluid until it reaches body temperature or, because of fever, higher before it will cause the rectal area to relax and allow voiding of the fluid and fecal matter. This allows the liquid to stay in the body longer and soak in more old dried waste matter loose.

Step two: A garlic injection. In herbology an injection is never a needle; it is a syringe type application. Into a pint of one-half apple cider vinegar and one-half distilled water, cold, blend in finely grated garlic, or use a garlic press or regular blender. Have the garlic liquid still thin enough that the liquid will pass through the orifice of the syringe. If in a blender just drop in cloves of peeled garlic, one at a time, until the proper amount is used to let it still flow from the syringe without clogging. Insert the garlic tea you have already prepared in advance into the rectum of the patient with the syringe (a pint for adult or less for children), encouraging the patient to retain as long as possible before voiding. Keep patient well covered while waiting. You will find it is easier for the patient to hold in the liquid if lying on a slant board, or with buttocks elevated with pillows.

Step three: The patient is placed in a bathtub, full of hot water, as hot as is possible (without blistering or scalding the flesh, of course) The tub has been prepared before their entering the water by adding three very fine diaphoretic herbs, namely an ounce or more of cayenne, an ounce or more of ginger and an ounce or more of dry mustard. These and the other herbs used in this program should always be on hand.

These three herbs will assist greatly in speeding up the perspiring of the patient and this is very important. This program (or idea) is to build an artificial fever or increase the fever they already have to a higher degree. This is being done to bring an incubation condition into place, to cause the disease germs to multiply as rapidly as is possible. The germs are God's gift to the sick to be used to speed up a healing. The germ is a scavenger that lives on toxins, mucous, poisons, and filth. They are nature's perfect garbage men. We should work with them, not against them. With the moist incubation they multiply faster and faster. To live they must eat and the only thing they can consume is the filth of the body. When all the garbage is cleaned up they leave, because they have nothing more to live on.

A germ cannot consume, or live on, good live cell structure. If they could then we should have a great fear! But after cleaning out the body of our sickness, which is accumulated waste, the germ finishes its job and leaves us with a healing climax.

. . . We want to build the fever as fast as possible with moisture. Dry fever is a killer, causing infantile paralysis, brain fever, etc., but moist fever can go much higher and if used properly, by working with the germs, can only do good as the 'Maker' of this human body intended.

Step four: to assist increasing the fever, we give the patient diaphoretic teas; this can be any good sweating tea such as yarrow (our favorite), blessed thistle, chamomile, pleurisy root, boneset, thyme, and many other good diaphoretic herbs.

When the patient sweats in the tub a long time, they become thirsty. Do not give cold drinks, give hot yarrow or one of the other type-unsweetened-but stay with one type of tea to drink if possible. Have them drink as much as possible.

During the sweating scene, the patient may get lightheaded and feel like fainting. If so, place a cold towel or washcloth on the forehead. Leave the patient in the hot tub as long as is possible, then have him step out, or lift him out, of the hot tub, and now . . . .

Step five: Wrap a large double white sheet, dripping wet from being soaked in cold water, around the standing patient. With just the head and feet protruding, the sheet is pinned down the side. The patient, thus wrapped, is put into a bed that has been prepared by having a rubber or plastic sheet protecting the mattress, with a cotton sheet over it. Then a dry cotton sheet covers the patient (still wrapped, of course, in the cold wet sheet), and natural fiber blankets are put over the top sheet for warmth and to help continue the sweating routine.

Step six: you have already prepared some garlic paste. This is made by blending crushed or finely grated, peeled buttons of fresh garlic into Vaseline about half and half. The low vibration Vaseline will not be absorbed into the skin, as will a hydrous lanolin or vitamin and ointment. The Vaseline holds the garlic in suspension where the high vibration ointments would be absorbed and leave the garlic exposed to the bare skin to thus blister it.

Before applying the garlic paste, the feet, from the ankles down, must be thoroughly massaged with olive oil. Allow as much of this oil to be absorbed into the skin as possible, covering the sole, sides and entire foot area. After the oiling is accomplished, the next step is to use about one-half inch thick or more of the garlic paste and spread it on gauze or cotton or wool cloth and apply over the entire sole of the foot. Do not allow the paste to get up on the sides or top of the foot – only on the sole! The purpose of being on the sole is that this is the area where the major part of reflexology (zonal therapy) is applied, and here is where the nerve ends form the entire body – including all the organs, can be controlled. The garlic will, by being applied to the soles of the feet, be able to disperse its oxygen-carrying power (the breath of life) throughout the body for healing.

Use two-inch gauze, or torn white cotton strips as a bandage to hold the garlic paste on the sole of the foot. When this is in place, gently pull over the foot and bandage a large cotton or wool white sock to aid in holding it on.

Put the bandaged feet back under the cold wet sheet and pin the bottom of the sheet together so the patient will be in a wet sack. The reason for using a large double sheet (instead of small) is because it will allow the patient to roll or turn around as we often do at night without being too closely confined.

Step seven: After the patient awakens from the deep sleep he has had, take him out of the bed and sponge him down thoroughly with warm apple cider vinegar and distilled water half and half. This is to remove from the skin the sticky poison mucous that has worked its way out of the body, for some of it is still in the pores and coats the skin. Sponging off the body this way will allow the body to breathe again through the skin. With the pore plugged up it means the doors and windows (pores) of the temple are shut and stagnation can start setting in again.

Step eight: . . . give the patient fresh fruit or vegetable juices or bottled or fresh grape juice, apple juice, etc., with no additives.

Do not mix juices, but let them drink (chew) as much of any one kind as they desire, or feel comfortable with. If a change of juice is desired, wait at least one half hour before using a different one.

Step nine: After a bad siege of body malfunction, it is wise to instruct the patient why he was in this condition and what to do from this point on so there will not be a reoccurrence of the disease. (67 – 75)

Corn Bag

Basic instructions: Sew two 7" by 10" squares of pillow ticking together like a pillow and fill it with dried field corn (do not use popcorn). Sew the opening closed. When you put the bag in the microwave for two minutes, it will hold the heat for about 45 minutes.

These bags can be made in any size – long and thin for the spine, moon-shaped for the neck. They can also be filled with rice or flax seeds. Some people like to use essential oils on the contents, so each time the bag is heated, the oils are activated.

Decoction

A decoction is used when you want your solution to be stronger than a normal tea. It is made by putting the dried herb into cold water and simmering on the stove, usually for several hours. The proportions are generally 1 ounce of dried herb to 1 ½ pints of water, but this can vary and you need to use your own judgment on how strong you want the decoction to be. As the volume of your liquid decreases, the strength of your tea increases. It is important not to allow this to boil, as it will kill the medicinal properties of the herb. If you decrease your volume of liquid by a half (for example, 2 qts down to 1 qt.) you will increase the medicinal strength of your tea approximately seven times.

Dr. Christopher's Extended Herbal Cleanse

Taken from the *Three Day Cleanse, Mucusless Diet & Herbal Combinations:*

> When we are dealing with long-standing health problems we cannot expect to totally cleanse or cure the body with one or so three-day cleansing routines. Therefore, to rid the body of chronic conditions or to prevent their occurrence, an extended herbal cleanse is an excellent path to follow. This should be used in conjunction with the aforementioned mucusless diet.
> 1. Take the following herbal formulas:
>   Herbal LB (Lower Bowel Formula)
>   2 capsules – upon rising in the morning

(more, if needed)

2 capsules – 1 hour before lunch

2 capsules – before retiring for the night

Barberry LG (Liver and Gallbladder formula)

2 capsules – 30 minutes before each meal

JuniPars (Kidney and Bladder formula)

2 capsules – midmorning

2 capsules – midafternoon

IMPORTANT – Use the first 3 formulas (Herbal LB, Barberry LG, & JuniPars) for about 2 weeks. . . THEN, simply add the Red Clover combination to the daily routine.

Red Clover combination (Blood purifying formula)

2 capsules – 1 hour after each meal

2. Tailor this program to your individual body's needs.

3. Drink about 8 – 16 glasses of pure distilled water a day between meals.

4. Follow the 'mucusless diet' as close as possible. This is important! (Christopher 15)

Eye Exercises

Taken from *Self Help Vision Care* by Dr. Deborah E. Banker, we are given the following advice:

Most visual problems which can be corrected by glasses are caused by an abnormality in the shape of the eye due to excessive amounts of pressure from the outside of the eye from the extraocular muscles. The superior and inferior obliques, when contracted too much, lengthen the eye. The rectus muscles, when contracted too much, shorten the eye.

Another muscle, which is a circular muscle inside the eye called the 'ciliary body,' focuses the lens and allows us to see at Near. If this fatigues with the lack of proper use and age, people need magnifying glasses, or Bifocals.

Though glasses in the beginning may seem to help, in the long run they weaken the eyes. It is better to teach people methods which actually strengthen the focusing ability of the eye.

As your eyes improve, your glasses must be weakened to give your eye a challenge to focus on their own and to grow stronger and focus better. People improve approximately a quarter of a diopter per month, or as much as 3 diopers in a year with fifteen minutes of work each day. Obviously more work will cause faster changes, i.e. a whole day or several days in a row. (forward)

Dr. Banker has created a whole program of exercises to help people strengthen their eyes to the point of no longer needing their glasses. It would be impossible and unethical to present her whole program here, but for further information, contact:

Deborah E. Banker, M.D.
23852 Pacific Coast Hwy
Suite 342
Malibu, CA 90265
310-317-2119

Fomentation

Soak a cotton diaper or similar material in hot tea or decoction, lightly wring it out, and place as hot as possible without causing blistering on the affected area. Keep the fomentation moist and warm by placing plastic and then some heat source, such as a corn bag, over the fomentation.

Honey & Pine Needle Syrup

A dear friend shared this recipe with me. It is meant to be used as a cough syrup or for sore throats. In the spring when the bright green, new pine needles come out – pick just the fresh, new green needles and fill a quart jar. Then cover the needles with raw honey, put the lid on the jar and set on a fence post or somewhere in the sun for a couple of months. The honey will draw the medicinal properties out of the pine needles. After 45 – 60 days, strain the honey off of the needles and store in a cool, dark place.

Dr. Christopher's Incurables Program

Taken from *Curing the Incurables,* Dr. Christopher shares his program for any type of persistent chronic condition:

The following suggestions are for a persisting chronic condition, not an acute one requiring emergency treatments.

Week One – drink as much fresh carrot juice as desired. Some people are satisfied with a quart while others need a gallon or more. Drink by chewing an eight-ounce glass or more each hour during the day for six days the first week.

Drink one cup or more of slippery elm gruel each day. The liquid can be as thin or thick as desired. With this herb, you take the powder and carefully mix it with enough water (preferably distilled) to form a paste because it does no mix easily. Then thin it to desired consistency by adding more water. A little honey can be added if preferred. In addition, drink one cup or more of comfrey leaf or root tea each day. Twenty minutes before or after drinking the juice, tea or gruel, drink as much steam-distilled water as desired.

. . . we also help the body rebuild by the use of herbal formulas. One cup or more of BF&C should be used for the rebuilding of cells in flesh, cartilage and bones. Also, take one cup three times a day of the Red Clover combination.

Take the following every day with some liquid:

-   Two or more #0 capsules of LB, three times a day. This is for regularity, as solids are not now cleansing the bowels.
-   Two or more #0 capsules of Relax-ease three times a day. This formula contains herbal nerviness.
-   Two or more #0 capsules of Panc Tea three times a day. This assists the LB.
-   Two or more #0 capsules of Calc Tea three times a day. This formula is a good source of herbal calcium

Breathing With Depth: The Lord put into us the breath of life, but we have to keep it there. Shallow breathing is not much life, but full breathing is the full breath of life. Learn to breathe deeply, as is taught in yoga, to get the breath of life into the upper lobes of the lungs.

Clothing: Synthetic cloth strangles and chokes the body and is a barrier to oxygen – the breath of life. We should use only natural fibers for the clothes we wear and also for our bed covers. Never use synthetic cloth for straining herbal drinks or for fomentations and bandaging. Use only natural fibers such as cotton, wool, linen or silk.

Releasing Static Electricity: Walk or jog barefooted on the lawn to get rid of the static electricity in the body and to allow new electrical vibration to come from the atmosphere. This is pure universal electricity that operates all the parts and organs of the body. It cannot come if static electricity is present, which should be grounded through the feet to keep a continual flow on hand.

Three Oil Massage: For the first two days, massage the patient with castor oil, using a clockwise circular motion from the top of the head to the bottom of the feet, always working toward the heart. The next two days use olive oil, ad the last two days of the week massage with wheat germ oil. By using the skin as a filtering agent, the castor oil cleans and flushes the skin. It also goes into the blood stream, aiding in the removal of mucous and toxins from the inner body. The olive oil is a complete food itself and will penetrate into the body to feed and rebuild muscles, flesh and the entire system. Wheat germ oil is a healing oil, high in vitamin E, valuable in rejuvenating the body. On the seventh day, rest the patient, using no foods, herbs or juice, only steam-distilled water as much as is desired.

Sunbath: Immediately after the massage, have the patient take a sunbath each day in the nude, not through glass but in direct sun. Only allow two minutes on the fron t and two minutes on the back the first day. Add two minutes front and back each day but no more. In six days you will be up to twelve minutes front and twelve minutes back. Do not sunbathe between eleven in the morning and one o'clock in the afternoon, that is, not at high noon. If it is a cloudy or cold day, use a sunlamp, but do not allow to burn.

The sun is the world's greatest doctor but must be used by building up the exposed time in the sun gradually so as to not burn. Do not be alarmed by articles in national publications each spring, warning people to avoid sunbathing, saying it is cancer-forming. The sun cannot cause cancer. When you do not gradually increase the use of it but lie in the sun for long lengths of time and burn, certainly it is dangerous for it will cause a severe toxic burn. But it is not cancer-forming. If cancer is already in the blood stream and the body, the sun can ripen it and bring it to the surface, but that is the only way skin cancer can result from the sun.

Baths: Each day the patient should have a hot bath followed by a cold shower or cold bath. No soap should be used for the bath unless it is a good biodegradable body cleanser. Each day before the bath, give a dry skin brushing (always toward the heart), using a natural bristle brush. Sixty percent of all of our breathing is done through the skin, so it must be kept clean with water and brushing. The skin is our 'second set of kidneys' and must be kept in good condition.

Herbal Fomentations: We use an herbal fomentation each night of the six days of the week. It should cover the head area (hair line), down the spine, all the way down to the end of the tailbone. Make a cap fit down to the ears (or use a cotton or wool skull cap) and stitch a flannel strip four or five inches wide down the back over the spine area. After wetting the fomentation cloth with BF&C and lightly wringing it out, cover it with a plastic over the head (shower cap, etc.) and a strip down over the spine. The moisture will go into the body and not the bedding or mattress. The fomentation down the back can be held into place with sweatshirt and shorts.

To aid the motor nerve and spinal cord, use the B&B tincture, inserting with an eye dropper four to six drops of oil of garlic and four to six drops of B&B into each ear six nights a week. Plug the ears with cotton overnight, and on the seventh day flush out the ears with half and half warm apple cider vinegar and distilled water. Repeat this each week during the program.

Zonal Foot Massage (Reflexology): If possible, use zonal therapy on the feet three times a week, leaving one day in between such as Monday, Wednesday, Friday. Zonal therapy will greatly speed up the program. You may find a number of good books on zone therapy at libraries or health food stores.

Week Two: The second week will be the same as the first except, instead of fresh carrot juice, substitute apple juice. Freshly made apple juice is best. If you don not have a juicer or fresh apples are not available, use a bottled apple juice that has had nothing added. Use canned only in an emergency. Do not use frozen juice, as nearly all frozen juices have additives. During the second week use the three oil massages, sunbaths, zonal therapy, fomentations, etc. . With the sunbaths add two minutes front and back onto the final total of the last week.

On the day of fast, there may be some physical reactions because you have reached a cleansing cycle. Toxic poisons break up in the body, accumulating for disposal and causing some upset. Do not be alarmed, for with some people it is more pronounced than with others. This same cyclical reaction can happen in any healing program in the third week, seventh week, seventh month and seventh year. The longer spasms occur in the major cycles and can be more pronounced, by far, than the minor cycles. If a cleansing crisis occurs during this short time, be happy with it and smile through the tears, for it shows the program is working well.

Week Three: Again repeat the full complete program, except instead of carrot or apple juice, during the third week use grape juice. Freshly made is best from dark grapes (concord preferred), juice from organically grown grapes found in some health stores, or any of the standard brands in bottles such as Welch's, Church's, etc. . Be sure in the bottled juice there are no additives (preservatives or sugar). It can be pasteurized but not frozen.

Week Four and On: Continue to rotate the three juices each week as before. This program is life-sustaining as the patient is taking rapid-healing and wholesome food. If the patient desires more solid food, just add one solid meal each day. This meal should consist of a good fresh vegetable combination salad (as many raw, fresh vegetables as you desire). If a salad dressing is desired, use a natural one, such as one made with fresh olive oil, apple cider vinegar or lemon juice, and, if desired, a small amount of honey, grated fresh onion and garlic to taste, savory salad herbs, coarse freshly ground black pepper, etc. .

A small serving of presoaked, low-heated grain may also be added. This is done by taking the whole uncracked grain (wheat, rye, millet, buckwheat, barley or whole oat groats) and soaking it with distilled water. Soak in a cool place so it won't sour, up to twenty hours, depending on the hardness of the grain. Then low-heat it is a stainless steal or Pyrex double boiler for twelve to fourteen hours. Use a food thermometer and do not allow the temperature to rise over 130 degrees. If you use a crockpot, equip it with a dimmer switch or some other type of control so it will not overheat.

In whole live grain you have nearly every known vitamin and mineral known to mankind, but this live food must not be killed by overheating.

On this type of food a person can live to a ripe, healthy old age. As the individual improves in health, a larger variety of fruits, vegetables, grains, nuts and seeds can by used. Later, all the lentils, beans and harder seed types with longer soaking and more low-heating can be added. With these, and low-heated grains, delicious casseroles may be created. . . use no salt, sugar, eggs, meats, breads, milk or milk products. In a short time you will find the hidden hunger will leave by using the food recommended. The cravings will disappear and will be replaced with a cozy, unbloated, satisfied fullness that will bring ease and peace. (3-7)

Infusion

This is a fancy word for tea. It is usually made with 1 tsp. of dried herb to a cup of water. The herb is placed in the bottom of a cup, boiling water is poured over it, then allow it to steep for 15 – 20 minutes, strain, enjoy.

Parasite Killing Program

Taken from a *Cure for All Cancer,* Hulda Clark shares a wonderful parasite program:

1. Black Walnut Hull Tincture Extra Strength
    Day 1: Take one drop. Put it in ½ cup of water. Sip it on an empty stomach such as before a meal.
    Day 2: Take 2 drops in ½ cup water same as above.
    Day 3: Take 3 drops in ½ cup water same as above.
    Day 4: Take 4 drops in ½ cup water same as above.
    Day 5: Take 5 drops in ½ cup water same as above.
    Day 6: Take 2 tsp. all together in ¼ cup water. Sip it, don't gulp it. Get it down within 15 minutes. (If you are over 150 pounds, take 2 ½ tsp. If you are over 200 pounds, take 3 tsp.)

    This dose kills any remaining stages throughout the body, including the bowel contents, a location unreachable by a smaller dose or by electric current. The alcohol in the tincture can make you slightly woozy for several minutes. Simply stay seated until you are comfortable again. You may put the tincture in lukewarm water to help evaporate some of the alcohol, but do not use hot water because that may damage its parasiticide power. Then take niacinamide 500 mg. to counteract the toxicity of the alcohol. You could also feel a slight nausea for a few minutes. Walk in the fresh air or simply rest until it passes. You may add more water or honey or a spice to make it more palatable.

For a year: take 2 tsp. Black Walnut Hull Tincture Extra Strength once a week. This is to kill any parasite stages you pick up from your family, friends, or pets.

2. Wormwood Capsules (should contain 200-300 mg. of wormwood)

Day 1: Take 1 capsule before supper with water

Day 2: Take 1 capsule before supper

Day 3: Take 2 capsules before supper

Day 4: Take 2 capsules before supper.

Continue increasing this way to day 14, whereupon you are up to seven capsules. You take the capsules all in a single dose (you may take a few at a time until they are all gone). Then you do 2 more days of 7 capsules each. After this, you take 7 capsules once a week forever, as it states in the Maintenance Parasite Program. Try not to get interrupted before the 6th day, so you know the adult intestinal flukes are dead. After this, you may proceed more slowly if you wish. Many persons with sensitive stomachs prefer to stay longer on each dose instead of increasing according to this schedule. You may choose the pace after the sixth day.

3. Cloves:

Fill size 00 capsules with fresh ground cloves: if this size is not available, use size 0 or 000. In a pinch, buy gelatin capsules and empty them or empty other vitamin capsules. You may be able to purchase fresh ground cloves that are already encapsulated; they should be about 500 mg. Grocery store ground cloves do not work! Either grind them yourself or check our sources.

Day 1: Take one capsule 3 times a day before meals.

Day 2: Take two capsules 3 times a day.

Days 3, 4, 5, 6, 7, 8, 9, 10: Take three capsules 3 times a day

After Day 10: Take 3 capsules all together once a week forever, as in the Maintenance Parasite Program. (19-22)

Poultice

Let's use the definition of a poultice taken from *Herbal Home Health Care:*

A poultice is an herbal preparation of a soft, semi-liquid mass made of some cohesive substance mixed with water, apple cider vinegar or other substances, and used for supplying heat and moisture to an area, or to act as a local stimulant. Have the herbs ground or granulated. When using fine powder, just use enough moisture to make a thick paste; and when using the granulated meal (or flaxseed meal). If fresh green leaves are used, simply heat, bruise, triturate or chop them finely, and apply to the affected parts. Poultices are excellent for enlarged or inflamed glands (neck, breast, groin, prostate, etc.) and also for eruptions, boils, carbuncles, and abscesses. (169)

Dr. Robert Young's 10-Day Challenge

This cleanse was submitted by Innerlight International and is used to alkalize the system quickly:

Once the basics of the diet are understood, one is ready to take control and make positive changes. It is time to begin the process of detoxification and cleansing. The most effective way that many individuals begin the healing process is with a 'cleanse.'

Cleansing is a holistic approach to allowing the body to heal itself, naturally. The first step to correcting the pH imbalance is to remove the debris that has built up in the body and provide the raw materials, or building blocks for repair. . . this is not a fast! Vegetable juices and soups, water with Prime pH, essential oils, and SuperGreens are recommended.

. . . Granted, each individual's body responds differently to various stimuli. Therefore, one must decide how many days to follow the cleanse, individually. Generally, a seven to ten day cleanse is recommended. This ensures that the body has rid itself of harmful toxins, adequately cleansed the system and weaned itself off sugar and other acid-forming foods which are difficult to eliminate from the diet.

Upon termination of the cleanse, one will find it is much easier to avoid the types of foods that are not recommended on an alkaline diet, like sugar, meat, coffee, etc. . It may be a challenge to pass up these foods during the start of the cleanse, but once completed, the body has almost 'forgotten' the sweet taste of these foods and finds enjoyment in subtler, more natural tastes.

During the cleanse, you intake should consist of the following:

1. Freshly juiced, green vegetables – kale, spinach, parsley, celery, cucumber, broccoli, wheat grass, cabbage, barley grass, collard greens, okra, etc. . If this is one's only intake, drink 8-12, 8 oz. glasses per day, in addition to 64 oz. to one gallon of water. If using SuperGreens in addition to fresh juice, drink 2-3 glasses a day. If juice is not available, try the soup recipes listed below. It is vital that enough energy and nutrients are provided so that the body ca heal itself. An example serving of juiced greens: 1 cucumber, 1 stalk celery, 1/3 bunch parsley, a handful of alfalfa sprouts, and some spinach or kale leaves.

2. Innerlight's SuperGreens Powder (and Prime pH) – This green juice powder consists of 49 different vegetables, grasses and herbs, combined to increase energy, detoxify the system, decrease appetite, and strengthen immune function to prevent disease and illness. SuperGreens is highly alkalizing, a great source of vitamins and minerals each day. During a cleanse, one should drink a minimum of 3 quarts of distilled water, a

teaspoon of the powder in each quart per day. Another quart of more of pure water should be consumed each day, with additional Super Greens added if desired. All water, even distilled or reverse-osmosis, should have Prime pH drops added to increase oxygen and alkalinity. Approximately 3 drops of Prime pH to 8 oz. water, 6 drops to 32 oz., 12 drops to 64 oz., and 24 drops to 1 gallon of water should be added. In summary, one should drink at least a gallon of water, adding at least three teaspoons of SuperGreens and 24 drops of Prime pH each day.

3.   Raw, pureed soups – These soups help the body combat toxins and can be very anti-fungal. Ingredients like garlic, onion, green vegetables, and vegetable broth are detoxifying and increae the effectiveness of the cleanse. Raw soups supply energy in a form that is easy for the body to utilize; it doesn't have to expend energy to obtain it during digestion. One to two bowls/day during a cleanse is suggested.

4.   Essential Oils – These high-quality oils may be added to juices, soups, or taken in gelcap form. Among the most highly recommended are: primrose, flax seed, borage, olive oil, or a blend such as Udo's Choice, Perfected Oil Blend. About 2-3 Tbsp/day is recommended.

5.   Innerlight Recipes:

Popeye Soup

Serves 4-6

10 minutes to prepare

This is a wonderfully alkalizing soup because of the cucumbers and greens. I serve it warm with a fresh tortilla for dipping.

1 avocado

1 cup water or vegetable stock (Pacific Foods of Oregon)

2 cucumbers unwaxed
1 cup fresh raw spinach
1 green onions
1 clove garlic
1/3 red bell pepper
Braggs Aminos to taste
Mid Eastern Spices ½ to 1 tsp.
Curry seasoning ½ to 1 tsp.
Zip ½ tsp.
4 spearmint leaves
fresh lime to taste
In a Vita Mix or blender add the avocado and ½ of the water or stock and puree, then add the rest of the ingredients (except the mint leaves) one at a time, blending to desired thickness and thinning with the remaining water if desired. Add Braggs to taste and flavor with spices and lime juice to your desire. Sometimes I add a couple of miced sundried tomatoes too! Experiment.

Dr. Christopher's 3 Day Juice Cleanse
Taken from *Dr. Christopher's 3 Day Cleanse and Mucusless Diet* pamphlet:
Supplies you will need:
54 ounces or 2 quarts prune juice
9 ounces olive oil
3 gallons selected cleansing juice (apple, carrot, citrus, or grape, etc.)
3 gallons water (preferably distilled)
Cleansing Steps:
Step one: Prune juice
16 oz. or more upon arising in the morning
Step two: Olive oil
One or two tablespoons three times a day
Step three:

8 ounces of fluid every 30 minutes, alternating 8 ounces of juice with 8 ounces of distilled water

Suggested Time Schedule:

7:30 am. - 16 oz. prune juice and 1-2 Tbsp. olive oil

8:00 am – 8 oz. or more cleansing juice

8:30 am – 8 oz. or more distilled water

9:00 am – 8 oz. or more juice

9:30 am – 8 oz. or more water

Continue alternating juice and water every half hour until noon.

12:00 pm – 8 oz. or more juice and 1-2 Tbsp. olive oil. Continue alternating juice and water every half hour until 5:00 pm.

5:00 pm – 8 oz. or more juice and 1-2 Tbsp. olive oil. Continue alternating juice and water every half hour until early evening.

8:00 pm – 8 oz. water every hour until retiring.

Remember:

One juice for three days. Select any juice (apple, carrot, citrus, tomato, etc.) but use it only for the entire three days.

Juice only. Do not eat anything during the three day cleanse, except matching fruit or vegetable with cleansing juice, apple with apple juice, etc.

Chew your juice. Make sure to swish each mouthful of juice thoroughly.

Constipation. Use more prune juice or take the lower bowel formula if you develop constipation during the cleanse.

3-Day house cleaning. Repeat your juice detoxification for three consecutive days.

Fourth day and on. After three days of juice cleansing, begin to take vegetable juices and vegetables and fruit, preferably raw.

Becoming weak. You will probably feel somewhat weak during or after this detoxification as your body uses all its energy to houseclean.

Enema. If there is the slightest tendency toward appendicitis, take a high enema, but only use enemas in cases of emergencies and not as a crutch for an inactive bowel.

Continued fast. Once you have completed several three day juice cleanses, you can fast one to three more days using only distilled water.

Cleansing symptoms. As your body begins to cleanse, you will probably experience periodic aches and pains as your body cleanses out its toxins and poisons, but this results in faster cleansing and quicker healing. (6)

Three Oil Massage

This massage is taken from a handout received in one of my classes at the School of Natural Healing to help prevent hair loss:

1. In the morning wash hair with Grandpa's pine tar soap. Pine kills fungus growth (use biodegradable soap when washing).
2. Rinse soap out of hair with the Desert Herb combination tea concentrate: chaparral, desert sage, and yarrow. Yarrow will restore the hair to its original color.
3. At night massage the head thoroughly (make sure the scalp is loose) with one of the following oils:

   Night 1 and 2: Castor oil

   Night 3 and 4: Olive oil

   Night 5 and 6: Wheat germ oil

   After the massage cover the scalp with hot Turkish towel and let the oil penetrate. Rest on the 7th night and repeat each week until done.
4. Take no less than a tablespoon of wheat germ oil three times a day, six days a week.
5. Follow the live food diet to speed up this procedure.
6. Use the slant board or gravity boots to get more circulation to the head. The head is like the attic that never gets cleaned out.

Cayenne extract can be used before the oil massage to greatly increase circulation of the scalp. This alone puts an immediate stop to falling hair. Use with caution – hot head.

If the hair follicles have been damaged by burning or acid or radiation, use the BF&C combination as a fomentation on the scalp.

This program has promoted hair growth (fuzz) in as little as 3 weeks to 5 months.

Wheat Grass Implants

Taken from the *Wheatgrass Book,* Ann Wigmore recommends:

In an implant, fresh wheatgrass is inserted into the rectum and retained there for about twenty minutes before being expelled. Implants are especially helpful in the case of illness, serious or otherwise, as they stimulate a rapid cleansing of the lower bowel. In my opinion, wheatgrass implants are safer than the coffee enemas used by many health clinic, because wheatgrass does not introduce unwanted caffeine.

. . . If you are planning to use wheatgrass implants, it is best to perform an enema before you do so. Early in the morning is probably the best time to do both.

To use wheatgrass juice implants as a purge, simply fill a sterilized infant enema syringe with one to two ounces of fresh juice and insert it into the rectum. A couple of minutes later, the bowels will move hurriedly. Try another one to two ounce implant and also let it out if it wants to come. The second attempt will probably carry more fecal matter with it. A third implant, of two to six ounces, will usually be retained with ease. Hold it until you feel the urge to eliminate, generally about twenty minutes later. There is no danger of reabsorbing toxins if you have purged the colon first with other implants or enemas. You may even be surprised to find that your body has absorbed all the juice after twenty minutes. (92-93)

It is for you to travel the path, not outside power can do it for you. It is as detrimental to have some outside force travel the path for you as it would be to tear open a cocoon before the butterfly has emerged. You have to free yourself through persistence, and in the struggle to obtain your freedom, you will have acquired the strength to fly.
-- David Wolfe

Why all this cooking when there really is no cook like old Sol? Cooked food is dead food – and remember, the whiter the bread the sooner we are dead! Every attempt to improve on natural food must prove a failure, and Nature will react at first acutely to any interference with her beneficent laws of health. And if we continue to disobey her laws by drugs or even surgery, the symptoms may disappear for a while only to reappear in chronic or fatal diseases. . . Man is the only creature that cooks his food, and he is more subject to disease than any wild creature that dines on unfired food. Tradition, gluttony, and increasing desire for strong stimulants have caused man to prefer cooked food, which has seriously weakened his digestive organs. This is because cooked food can be swallowed so easily without chewing, whereas thorough mastication is essential to good health.
-- Dugald Semple,

Chapter Two
Herbal Combinations

The following formulas are the most common combinations mentioned in this book.   Check the ingredients and see if something you have on hand is close.

A

Adrenetone – mullein, lobelia, Siberian ginseng, gotu kola, hawthorn berries, cayenne, and ginger

Anti-plaque – fresh garlic juice, apple cider vinegar, glycerine, honey, fresh comfrey root, wormwood, lobelia, marshmallow root, oak bark, black walnut bark, mullein leaf, skullcap and uva ursi

Anti-spasmodic tincture – skullcap, lobelia, cayenne, valerian root, skunk cabbage, myrrh gum and blue cohosh in an alcohol base

Ar-1 – Brigham tea, hydrangea root, yucca, chaparral, lobelia, burdock root, sarsaparilla, wild lettuce, valerian, wormwood, cayenne, black cohosh, and black walnut

Asthma formula – comfrey, mullein and garlic in a vegetable glycerine base

AT-GS – (anti-gas) fennel, wild yam, catnip, ginger, peppermint, spearmint, papaya and lobelia

B

Barberry LG – barberry or Oregon grape root, wild yam, cramp bark, fennel seed, ginger, catnip and peppermint

B&B – blue cohosh, black cohosh, blue vervain, skullcap, lobelia And either alcohol or vegetable glycerin as a base

Bee Power – Siberian ginseng, bee pollen, licorice root, gotu kola, Brigham tea, yerba mate, and ginger root

BF&C (Bone, Flesh & Cartilage) – oak bark, marshmallow root, mullein herb, wormwood, lobelia, skullcap, comfrey root, walnut bark (or leaves) and gravel root

Black ointment – chaparral, comfrey, red clover blossoms, pine tar, mullein, beeswax, lobelia, golden seal, marshmallow root, plantain, olive oil, mutton tallow, chickweed and poke root

BPE – ginger, cayenne, golden seal, ginseng, parsley and garlic

C

Calc tea – horsetail grass, oat straw, comfrey root and lobelia
Changease – black cohosh, sarsaparilla, ginseng, licorice, false
    unicorn, holy thistle and squaw vine

F

False Unicorn & Lobelia – False unicorn and lobelia

H

Hawthorn Berry Syrup – hawthorne berry juice concentrate using
    grape brandy ad glycerine as aids and preservatives
Herbal Eyebright – bayberry bark, eyebright herb, golden seal root,
    red raspberry leaves and cayenne
Herbal LB – barberry bark, cascara sagrada bark, cayenne, ginger,
    lobelia herb and/or seeds, red raspberry leaves, Turkey
    rhubarb root, fennel and golden seal root
Herbal Tooth Powder – oak bark, comfrey root, horsetail grass,
    lobelia, cloves and peppermint

I

Immucalm – marshmallow and astragalus
INF formula – plantain, black walnut, golden seal root, bugle
    weed, marshmallow root and lobelia
Intestinal Corrective formula #1 – curacao and cape aloe leaf,
    Senna leaves and pods, cascara sagrada aged bark, barberry
    root bark, ginger rhizome, garlic bulb and African bird
    pepper
Intestinal Corrective formula #2 – flax seed, apple fruit pectin,
    pharmaceutical grade bentonite clay, psyllium seed and
    husk, slippery elm inner bar, marshmallow root, fennel
    seed and activated willow charcoal

J

JuniPars – juniper berries, parsley, uva ursi, marshmallow root, lobelia, ginger, and golden seal

Jurassic Green – alfalfa, barley grass and wheat grass

K

Kelp combination – parsley, watercress, kelp, Irish moss, romaine lettuce, turnip tops, and Iceland moss

Kid-e-calc – horsetail grass, oat straw, comfrey root, lobelia and vegetable glycerin

Kid-e-cep – oak bark, golden seal root, myrrh, comfrey, garlic, capsicum in a vegetable glycerine base

Kid-e-col – catnip and fennel in a glycerine base

Kid-e-mune – echinacea, calendula and red clover blossoms in either an alcohol or glycerine base

Kid-e-soothe – marshmallow root and astragalus in a vegetable glycerine base

Kid-e-well – echinacea, yarrow, elder flowers, peppermint and vegetable glycerin

N

NuFem – golden seal root, blessed thistle, cayenne, cramp bark, false unicorn root, ginger, red raspberry leaves, squaw vine and uva ursi

M

Male formula – wild American "Blue Ridge" ginseng root, Chinese and Korean ginseng roots, Siberian ginseng root, saw palmetto berry, sarsaparilla root, Yohimbe bark, oat seed, kola nut and ginger rhizome

MEM – blue vervain, gotu kola, Brigham tea, ginkgo, blessed thistle, cayenne, ginger root, and lobelia

MindTrac – skullcap, valerian extract, Oregon grape root, barley grass, alfalfa, kamut (wheat grass), St. John's wart extract, mullein leaf, lobelia, gotu kola, ginkgo extract, sarsaparilla and dandelion

P

Panc Tea – golden seal, uva ursi, cayenne, cedar berries, licorice root and mullein

Pre-natal tea – (6-week formula) squaw vine, holy thistle, black cohosh, pennyroyal, false unicorn, raspberry leaves and lobelia

Prospallate – cayenne, ginger, golden seal root, gravel root or queen of the meadow root, juniper berries, marshmallow root, parsley root or herb, uva ursi leaves and ginseng

Prospalmetto – saw palmetto, mullein and ginkgo

R

Red clover combination – red clover blossoms, chaparral, licorice root, poke root, peach bark, Oregon grape root, stillingia, cascara sagrada, sarsaparilla, prickly ash bark, burdock root, and buckthorn bark

Relax-eze – black cohosh, capsicum, hops flowers, lobelia, skullcap, valerian, wood betony and mistletoe

Resp-free – comfrey root, mullein, chickweed, marshmallow root and lobelia

S

SenSei balm – olive oil and natural oils of cassia, eucalyptus, cajeput, pure menthol and camphor crystals and other fragrant natural oils

SHA – brigham tea, marshmallow root, golden seal root, chaparral, burdock root, parsley root, lobelia and cayenne

Super Ginseng Blend tonic – wild American "Blue Ridge" ginseng root, Chinese and Korean ginseng roots, Siberian ginseng root, and Brazilian ginseng root

SuperGreens – Kamut grass, barley grass, lemon grass, shavegrass, wheat grass, alfalfa leaf, dandelion leaf, bilberry leaf, black walnut leaf, blackberry leaf, plantain leaf, red raspberry leaf, blueberry leaf, boldo leaf, goldenseal leaf, papaya bark, marshmallow root, cornsilk, rosemary, ale whole leaf conc., oat grass, soy sprout conc., kale, spinach, okra, cabbage, celery, parsley leaf, broccoli, watercress, alfalfa juice conc., turmeric, tomato, peppermint leaf, spearmint leaf, wintergreen leaf, sage, thyme, rosemary leaf, high frequency mineral complex

V

VB Powder – squaw vine herb, slippery elm bar, yellow dock root, comfrey root, marshmallow root, chickweed herb, golden seal root and mullein leaves

VF Syrup – wormwood, American wormseed, tame sage, fennel, malefern and papaya

Vitalerbs – alfalfa, dandelion, kelp, purple dulce, spirulina, Irish moss, rose hips, beet, nutritional yeast, cayenne, blue violet, oatstraw, ginger barley and flash-dried wheat grass juice

X

X-ceptic – oak bark, golden seal root, myrrh, comfrey, garlic and capsicum in a grain alcohol base

Y

Yellow Dock combination – oak bark, mullein, yellow dock root, walnut bark or leaves, comfrey root, lobelia and marshmallow root

Man is a spiritual being, so when anyone undertakes to heal himself with herbs, he is involving himself with this spiritual energy and force (which some termed "Vital Force.") One cannot induce healing into his body without himself being compatible to the vibrations of the life forces in the herbs he uses. So the use of herbs in healing does involve some faith. The spirit force and energy in man governs the living physical body function. This directive power is resident in the tissue units (i.e. the individual cells) and the term "cell intelligence" is descriptive of its directive function therein. This governing intelligence presides over the bioplasm of the cell, much like the brain does consciously over the body system – directing the bioplasm activities in selection, absorption, disintegration, assimilation, conversion, etc., of the available nutritive or therapeutic elements that are needed in order to facilitate or carry on the normal systemal functions. This spiritual force, acting through the instrumentation of the bioplasma, selects from the blood plasma (as it circulates) the helpful elements that are made available in the system, and it rejects and eliminates that which is deemed to be harmful or useless. This spiritual intelligence always seeks the welfare of the cell and the system as a whole, opposing the invasion of harmful substances and excreting the waste that stifles or interferes with restorative principle, unless the tissue is beyond repair – and even then, the tissue is equipped to perform its own internal surgery and housecleaning IF the proper elemental materials are supplied. So you can see there is a very VITAL INTERRELATIONSHIP between the spiritual and the physical states of man.

-- John R. Christopher, N.D.

Chapter Three
Health Retreats

These are just a few of the health retreats in the United States which are based on wheat grass juice, raw foods, and other natural modalities. Check the internet for retreats in your local area or call and talk to any of the ones listed here for further help and guidance.

Ann Wigmore Foundation
P.O. Box 399
San Sidel, NM   87049
505-552-0595
This is a retreat and healing center that encourages raw plant foods to heal the body.

The Assembly of Yahweh Wellness Center
7881 Columbia Highway
Eaton Rapids, MI   48827
517-663-1637
This center uses the Ann Wigmore philosophy of raw foods and wheatgrass. It is located on 80 acres just south of Lansing, MI.

Creative Health Institute
112 West Union City Rd.
Union City, MI   49094
517-278-6260
This center offers a 2-week cleansing and detoxification program as outlined by Ann Wigmore.
This retreat is 3 hours from Chicago.

East County Holistic Care
3168 Florine Drive
Lemon Grove, CA   91945
619-589-7546
This center is located 2 blocks from the Optimum Health Institute in San Diego. They specialize in colon hydrotherapy, lymphatic drain, and massage therapy.

Eden Retreats
Nature's First Law

P.O. Box 900202
San Diego, CA 92190
888-729-3663
Nature's First Law and David Wolfe host several raw-food retreats each year.

Hippocrates Health Institute
1443 Palmdale Court
West Palm Beach, FL 33411
800-842-2125
This is a healing retreat run by Brian Clement emphasizing the use of raw plant foods in the tradition of Ann Wigmore.

L.O.V.E. – I.N.G.
(Longevity from Organic Vegetarian Enzymatic Indigenous/Indoor Nutriceutical Garden)
P.O. Box 1556
Mt. Ida, AR 71957
870-867-4521
This resort is situated on 90 acres in the Ouchita National forest.

Optimum Health Institute
6970 Central Avenue
Lemon Grove, CA 91945
619-464-3346
This is one of the best detox institutes in the U.S. They offer 1,2, 3, and 4 week programs. 100% raw food is served and they are affordable.

Optimum Health Institute
Rt. 1, Box 339-J
Cedar Creek, TX 98612
512-303-4817
Similar to one in California.

Rest or Your Life Retreat
P.O. Box 102

Barksdale, TX   78828
830-234-3488
This retreat is run by two medical doctors. It is designed for rest
and relaxation.

Tree of Life Rejuvenation Center
P.O. Box 778
Patagonia, AZ   85624
520-394-2520
This retreat was founded by a raw-foodist, Dr. Gabriel Cousens.

Young Life Research Clinic Institute of Natural Medicine
713 W. 1300 N.
Springville, UT   84663
801-489-8650
This center was founded by Gary Young of Young Living
Essential Oils. Treatment is overseen by a medical doctor.

Works Cited

Anderson, Richard N.D., N.M.D. *Cleanse & Purify Thyself: "And I Will Exalt Thee To the Throne of Power"*.Mt. Shasta: Christobe Publishing. 2000.

Atwood, Mary Dean. *Spirit Herbs: Native American Healing.* New York: Sterling Publishing Company. 1998.

Balch, James F., M.D. and Phyllis A. Balch, C.N.C. *Prescription for NUTRITIONAL HEALING: A Practical A-Z Reference to Drug-free Remedies Using Vitamins, Minerals, Herbs & Food Supplements.* Garden City Park: Avery Publishing Group Inc. 1990.

Batmanghelidj, F., M.D. *Your Bodies Many Cries For Water: You Are Not Sick, You are Thirsty.* Vienna: Global Health Solutions, Inc. 1997.

Beutler, Jade. *Diabetic Care: The Fatty Acid Answer.Provided Courtesy of Barlean's Organic Oils.* 2000.

Block, Polly. *Polly's Birth Book.* American Fork: Heartspun Publishers. 1984.

Boutenko, Victoria, Igor, Sergei and Valya. *Raw Family: A true story of awakening.* Ashland: Raw Family Publishing. 2000.

Bragg, Paul C., N.D., Ph.D., and Patricia Bragg, N.D., Ph.D. *The Miracle of Fasting: Proven Throughout History For Physical, Mental & Spiritual Rejuvenation.* Santa Barbara: Health Science, Forty-eighth Edition MMI.

Breggin, Peter, Dr. *Toxic Psychiatry.* New York: St. Martin's Press.1994.

Christopher, David. *Herbal Legacy of Courage.* Springville: Christopher Publications, Inc. 1990.

Christopher, John R. *Healing Herbs: Basic Course.* Springville: Christopher Publications, Inc. 1955.

Christopher, John R., Dr. *Curing the Incurables: A Home Therapy Program.* Springville: Christopher Publications, Inc. 1996.

Christopher, John R., N.D., M.H. *Dr. Christopher's 3 Day Cleansing Program, Mucusless Diet and Herbal Combinations.* Springville: Christopher Publications, Inc. 1998.

Christopher, Dr. John R. and Cathy Gileadi. *Every Womens Herbal.* Springville: Christopher Publications, Inc. 1987.

Christopher, John R., N.D., M.H. *Herbal Home Health Care.* Springville: Christopher Publications, Inc. 1976.

Christopher, John R., N.D., M.H. newsletter. *Echinacea* Springville: Christopher Publications, Inc.

Christopher, John R., N.D., M.H. newsletter. Vol. 1, No. 9 Springville: Christopher Publications, Inc.

Christopher, John R.,N.D.,M.H. *School of Natural Healing.* Springville: Christopher Publications, Inc. 1996.

Circumcision Resource Center. P.O. Box 232, Boston, MA 02133.

Doctors Prescription for Healthy Living. Newsletter. Progressive Health Publishing.

Dufty, William. *Sugar Blues*. New York: WARNER BOOKS EDITION, 1993.

Fairbanks, Bert L. *A Principle With Promise* S.L.C.: Publishers Press. 1978.

Frahm, Anne E. and David J. Frahm, *A Cancer Battle Plan: SIX STRATEGIES FOR BEATING CANCER, FROM A RECOVERED "HOPELESS CASE"*. New York: Penguin Putman Inc. 1997.

Frye, Anne. *Holistic Midwifery.* Portland: Labrys Press. 1995.

Gallo, Roe. Perfect *Body: The Raw Truth*. San Diego: ProMotion Publishing. 1997.

Goldman, Ronald, Ph.D. *CIRCUMCISION: The Hidden Trauma.* Boston: Vangurard Publications. 1997.

Greene, Bob and Oprah Winfrey, *Make the Connection: Ten Steps to a Better Body -- And a Better Life*. New York: Harpo, Inc. 1996.

Hitchcox, Lee, D.C. *Long Life Now: Strategies for Staying Alive*. Berkeley: Celestial Arts, 1996.

Holy Bible. Salt Lake City, Church of Jesus Christ of Latter-Day Saints. 1989.

King, Janie McCoy. *Back Labor No More!!! What Every Woman Should Know Before Labor.* Dallas: Plenary Systems, Inc. 1993.

Kloss, Jethro *Back to Eden.* Loma Linda: Back To Eden Books Publishing Company. 1992.

Kordich, Jay. *The Juiceman's Power of Juicing: Over 100 Delicious Juice Recipes For Energy, Health, Weight Loss, and Relief From Scores of Common Ailments.* New York: Warner Books. 1993.

Lust, John B. *RAW JUICE therapy.* London: Thorsons Publishers Limited. 1971.

Lyman, Howard F.and Glen Merzer. *Mad Cowboy: Plain Truth from the Cattle Rancher Who Won't Eat Meat.* New York: Scribner, 1998.

Mendelsohn, Robert S.,M.D. *Confessions of a Medical Heretic.* Chicago: Contemporary Books, 1979.

Mendelsohn, Robert S., M.D. *How to Raise a Healthy Child In Spite of Your Doctor.* N.Y.: Ballentine Books. 1984.

Miller, Neil Z. *Vaccines: Are They Really Safe and Effective?.* Santa Fe, N.M. 1998.

Nuzzi, Debra St. Claire. *Herbal Preparations and Natural Therapies.* Boulder: Morning Star Publications. 1989.

Oski, Frank A.,M.D. *Don't Drink Your Milk: New Frightening Medical Facts About the World's Most Overrated Nutrient.* Brushton: Teach Services, Inc., 1996.

Packer, Lester, Ph.D. and Carol Colman. *The Antioxidant Miracle.* New York: John Wiley & Sons, Inc. 1999.

Pearson, Carol Lynn. *Beginnings*. Provo: Trilogy Arts Publication 1969.

Perry, Janice Kapp and Joy Saunders Lundberg. <u>When It's Love.</u> Provo: Prime Recordings. 1991.

Phillips, Alan. "Vaccination Myths". 22 Jan 2002.
http:www.unc.edu/-aphillip/www/vaccine/dvm1.htm
    Dept. of Internal Medicine. "Failure to reach the goal of measles elimination".
        Mayo Vaccine Research Group, Mayo Clinic and Foundation, Archives of Internal Medicine 154(16). 22 Aug 1994.
    The Fresno Bee. Community Relations. "DPT Report". 1626 E. St., Fresno, CA 93786
    National Technical Information Service. Springfield, VA. 703-487-4650.
    Rabo, Trolifora B. "Whooping Cough in Adults". British Medical Journal. 1981. 696-97.
    Severyn, K.M. "Ohio Parents for Vaccine Safety". Dayton Daily News. 28 May 1993.
    Torch, W.C. "Diptheria-pertussis-tetanus (DPT) immunizations: A potential cause of the sudden infant death syndrome (SIDS)". American Academy of Neurology. 34th Annual Meeting. Apr 25-May 1, 1982.

Phillips, Bill. *Body For Life.* New York: HarperCollins Publishers. 1999.

Quinn, Dick. *Left for Dead.* Minneapolis: R.F. Quinn Publishing Co., 1994.

Schlosser, Eric *Fast Food Nation: The Dark Side of the All-*

American Meal. New York: Houghton Mifflin, 2002.

Schulze, Richard Dr. *Patient Handbook: Foundational Programs, Herbal Formulae, Therapeutic Benefits and Specific Dosages.* Santa Monica: Dr. Schulze's School of Natural Healing, 1995.

Shook, Dr. Edward E. *Elementary Treatise in Herbology.* Banning: Enos Publishing Co. 1993.

Shook, Edward, Dr. *Advanced Treatise in Herbology.* Banning: Enos Publishing Co. 1993.

Smith, Joseph (translator) *Book of Mormon.* Salt Lake City, Church of Jesus Christ of Latter-day Saints. 1981.

Smith, Joseph. *Doctrine & Covenants,* Salt Lake City, Church of Jesus Christ of Latter-day Saints. 1981.

Starfield, Barbara, M.D., MPH, "Deficiencies of U.S. Medical Care." *Journal of the American Medical Association* Vol. 284 No. 4 : July 26, 2000.

Stitt, Paul A. *Beating the Food Giants.* Manitowoc: Natural Press, 1993.

Szekely, Edmond Bordeauz. *The Essene Gospel of Peace.* United States of America: International Biogenic Society. 1981.

Tarr, Katherine. *Herbs, Pressure Points and Helps for Pregnancy And Childbirth.* Winona Lake: Wendell W. Whitman Co. 1994.

Truman, Karol K. *Feelings Buried Alive Never Die . . .* Las Vegas: Olympus Distributing. 2000.

Tisserand, Maggie *Aromatherapy for Women.* Rochester, VT.:
Healing Arts Press.

Weschler, Toni. *Taking Charge of Your Fertility.* N.Y.: Harper
Collins Publishers. 1995.

Wigmore, Ann. *The Wheatgrass Book.* USA: Avery, 1985.

Wigmore, Ann *Why Suffer* Boston: Rising Sun Christianity.

Willix, Dr. *Confessions of a Heart Surgeon.* Health & Longevity.

Wolfe, David. *Eating for Beauty.* San Diego: Maul Brothers
Publishing, 2002.

Wolfe, David. *SUNFOOD DIET SUCCESS SYSTEM.* San Diego:
Maul Brothers Publishing, 2002.

Wood, Memnler Cohen. *The Human Body in Health and Disease.*
Philadelphia: J. B. Lippincott Company. 1992.

Young, D. Gary, N.D. *Essential Oils Integrative Medical Guide:
Building Immunity, Increasing Longevity, and Enhancing
Mental Performance with Therapeutic-Grade Essential Oils.*
United States of America: Essential Science Publishing. 2003.

Young, Robert O., Ph.D., D.Sc., and Shelley Redford Young,
L.M.T. *Sick? And Tired: Reclaim Your Inner Terrain.* Pleasant
Grove: Woodland Publishing, 1999.

To order *Dr. Mom's Healthy Living,* Dr. Mom videos and DVDs, or to schedule a seminar in your area call:

1-800-403-2120

or visit our website at:

www.drmomshealthyliving.com

For any of the herbal products mentioned in this book, check with your local health food store, call us for a free catalog, or visit our website for a listing of products available.